THE
SOVIET CULTURAL
OFFENSIVE

THE
SOVIET CULTURAL
OFFENSIVE

THE ROLE OF CULTURAL DIPLOMACY
IN SOVIET FOREIGN POLICY

BY FREDERICK C. BARGHOORN

PRINCETON, NEW JERSEY
PRINCETON UNIVERSITY PRESS
1960

Frederick C. Barghoorn has been a member of the
Department of Political Science at Yale University
since 1947 and Professor since 1956. He has taught
at Chicago, Columbia, and Harvard universities and
lectured at the National and Army war colleges.
From 1943 to 1947 he was Press Attaché at the
United States Embassy in Moscow. He returned to
Russia for more information and further study in
1956, 1958, and again in 1959.

❖

Printed in the United States of America

Second Printing 1961

PREFACE

IMPORTANT techniques of Soviet foreign policy still remain almost unexamined. One of these is the complex amalgam of propaganda, deception, and sometimes mutually profitable transactions with non-Soviet states that is herein described as Cultural Diplomacy. Soviet Cultural Diplomacy represents what from a non-communist point of view usually seems to be a perversion of cultural exchange and intercultural communication.

This is an effort to project to all men an image of the Soviet way of life calculated to facilitate Soviet foreign policy objectives. It is accompanied by an equally massive effort to shield the Kremlin's subjects from harmful "alien" influences. It has almost nothing in common with democratic ideals of free intellectual communion. However, we live in an age when increased freedom of international communication, contacts, and travel is necessary for world welfare. Premier Khrushchev's cancellation of his invitation to President Eisenhower for a visit to Russia underscored Soviet determination to prevent even previously agreed upon contacts if they appeared to threaten, however indirectly, the Kremlin's absolute control over the thinking of the Soviet people. Nevertheless, there is every reason to believe that over the long run communists will make increasing use of the international propaganda procedures described in this study. While guarding against the perils inherent in communist duplicity, we should welcome the opportunities offered by exchanges of persons with Soviet Bloc countries to dissolve prejudices and facilitate whatever limited cooperation is possible between representatives of rival ways of life.

The encouragement, counsel, and assistance of many persons are reflected, however inadequately, in this book. Its defects belong only to the author. David C. Munford, while an official of the Ford Foundation, helped to arrange for a research grant to which Yale University also contributed. Yale also rendered indispensable aid through continued assistance from the Stimson Fund, and the author is grateful to all concerned with the administration of that Fund and to the Department of Political Science for granting him research leave.

Among those who generously offered advice, criticism, and in-

v

formation, reflected in various ways in what follows, special mention should be made of Professor Cyril E. Black of Princeton University, Dr. Philip E. Mosely, Director of Studies of the Council on Foreign Relations, and Professor Harold D. Lasswell of Yale University. Hadley Cantril, Senior Counselor of the Institute for International Social Research, included the author in a group of travelers to Russia in 1958; travel with this immensely congenial group provided a source of great knowledge and insight. Travel to the U.S.S.R. in 1956 and to Czechoslovakia and Poland in 1957 was financed by the Ford Foundation, Yale University, and the Inter-University Committee on Travel Grants.

The Inter-University Committee staff made available considerable valuable information, as did also Professor Ralph T. Fisher, Jr., of the University of Illinois, Mr. Denis Mickiewicz and other members of the Yale Russian Chorus, and numerous officials of the United States Government agencies and of such private organizations as the Institute of International Education. The author is deeply appreciative of the very useful assistance received from Dr. Paul W. Friedrich, Mr. Juris Padegs, and Mr. Allen Sinel in assembling some of the data on which this study is based. Mr. Sinel also compiled the index. Miss Veronica O'Neill, Secretary of the Yale Department of Political Science, Mrs. William H. Flanigan, and the other persons who helped in various ways to prepare or facilitate the preparation of the manuscript deserve a cordial word of thanks.

The staff of Princeton University Press, and in particular Mr. Gordon Hubel, have been most helpful and skillful in their guidance and assistance, and to them also gratitude is due.

FREDERICK C. BARGHOORN

New Haven
June 17, 1960

CONTENTS

CHAPTER I

CULTURAL DIPLOMACY AND EAST-WEST
RELATIONS

WITH the tactical flexibility and unity characteristic of tightly centralized organizations, the communist states have in recent years sought to turn to their own ends instruments of foreign policy which a few years ago even informed opinion in the democracies regarded as incompatible with the functioning of the closed society. Under the astute leadership of Nikita S. Khrushchev, the Kremlin partially succeeded in creating the impression that it had abandoned isolationism and chauvinism in favor of freedom of exchange and East-West contacts as a path toward the relaxation of international tensions and the fostering of peace between the communist and noncommunist worlds. Governments and political movements which accept Moscow leadership followed suit, so that even the Mongolian People's Republic, to mention one amazing example, invited foreign scholars, including Americans, to take part in a philological conference which was held in far-away Ulan-Bator in September 1959.

The Soviet "cultural offensive," unleashed shortly after Stalin's death, had assumed such proportions in the free world within a few years that the British and American governments set up new administrative machinery to deal with the problems which it posed. As of the summer of 1959, in several European countries and also in the United States a number of measures taken, both by governments and by private organizations, indicated that the quandary of coping with what in this book we shall call "Soviet cultural diplomacy" was perhaps beginning to be resolved. Two initiatives which seemed significant were the creation, by State Department Circular of June 15, 1959, of a Bureau of Intercultural Relations and the assignment to the U.S. Embassy in Moscow of a Counselor for Cultural Affairs, the first such appointment in a communist state.

Establishment of the above-mentioned bureau climaxed a series of steps by which the executive branch of the American government put itself in a better position to fulfill its responsibilities in the international cultural field. Unfortunately, these administrative moves were not accompanied by corresponding Congressional support in terms either of money or encouragement. Some members of Congress, to be sure, did do a great deal to arouse public awareness of the vital significance of the cultural contest, such as Senator Hubert H. Humphrey's speaking at the Third National Conference on Exchange of Persons at Washington, D.C., in January 1959 and his following with keen interest the background and events of the 1959 Vienna Youth Festival, the seventh of these vast Moscow-staged spectacles. Sometimes, however, even well-informed men like Senator Humphrey and other prominent figures, such as former Senator William Benton or the atomic scientist, Dr. Edward Teller, urged the adoption of ambitious projects for the political exploitation of cultural exchanges which, because they were impracticable in terms of available resources of money and personnel and were certain to impel the Kremlin further to intensify its obstructionism, seemed unlikely to be in the American national interest.

Private citizens interested in East-West exchanges have frequently displayed lack of sophistication about the problems inherent in transactions with totalitarian regimes.

As we had occasion to observe at the above-mentioned Third National Conference on Exchange of Persons, Americans sometimes pass public judgments—in this case in the presence of Soviet diplomats, who took copious notes—which may jeopardize the careers of Soviet exchangees or increase the difficulty of obtaining the Soviet cooperation necessary for the success of even a modest exchange program. It is more than naïve to talk at such gatherings about alleged possibilities for "integrating Soviet students into American life" or to complain if Soviet citizens who have been guests in American homes and have told their American hosts how favorably impressed they were with their American experiences subsequently report to Soviet officials, or in the Soviet press, that they were invited only to "rich" homes, carefully selected to prevent their meeting "ordinary people." Until the Kremlin's attitude mellows considerably, Soviet exchangees will have to be careful about their public statements.

As Diana Trilling observed in the *New Leader* for February 2, 1959, Englishmen, Frenchmen, and Americans only too often entertain "the wishful hope that culture has the same autonomy . . . in the Communist countries as it does in the free world." They refuse to see that the Soviet Union has "declared cultural war on us," says Mrs. Trilling, and forget that in the field of intercultural relations "one must proceed with caution and acuteness, with the knowledge, indeed, that our lives are at stake." One need not fully share Mrs. Trilling's pessimism, but her warning that one cannot expect reciprocity and mutuality in cultural relations with Moscow deserves to be pondered.

Before seeking to identify, in the bulk of this chapter, the motives of Soviet cultural diplomacy, it will be useful, by way of background, to describe briefly the policies of major Western nations in the field of international cultural exchange.

France was the first great nation to embark on an extensive program of officially organized cultural relations. Beginning on a large scale in the second half of the nineteenth century with extensive religious, educational, and philanthropic works in the Near and Far East, this program was directed by the Ministry of Foreign Affairs. Official efforts were supplemented by the activity of private agencies, still active in our day, such as the Alliance Francaise, which since 1883 has organized courses, schools, lectures, and gifts of books to encourage the teaching of the French language and to disseminate French culture beyond the frontiers of France.[1]

The flavor of the French effort—relatively modest in aims and yet at times ethnocentric and chauvinistic in tone—is suggested by an article on the Alliance Francaise which was published in 1886 in the *Grande Encyclopedie*. The article stated that the best way of "conquering" the natives of French colonies was by inculcating in them a love for the French language. It urged efforts to keep the language alive among Frenchmen living in foreign countries, as an offset to the excessively slow rate of increase of the French population at home. One is reminded of the significance attributed by patriotic Frenchmen to their country's foreign

[1] Ruth Emily McMurry and Muna Lee, *The Cultural Approach*, Chapel Hill, 1947, pp. 9-38.

3

cultural program by the satisfaction with its results which have been expressed, for example, in General Charles de Gaulle's *War Memoirs*.

After World War I, the French effort was intensified to cope with formidable German competition. Some Germans, especially during the Hitler period, regarded French cultural policy as a highly sinister weapon. A Nazi study of French academic exchange with Denmark, for example, referred to the "universalist and at the same time imperialist" character of French cultural pressure abroad.[2] Both before and after World War I, Germany carried on a vigorous program of exchange of students and professors and also, particularly under the Nazis, attempted to utilize persons of German background resident abroad as instruments of German foreign policy.

The United Kingdom entered the field of cultural diplomacy in 1934 with the creation of the British Council, which was incorporated by royal charter in 1940. As "an officially created and subsidized body," it began its activity with a grant from the Treasury of £5,000 in 1935; this had been increased to more than £100,000 by 1938. The official purpose of the Council was to "make British life and thought more widely known abroad, to encourage the study of the English language, and to render available abroad current British contributions to literature, science, or the fine arts."[3] As of 1939, it was estimated that the Germans, in seeking to counter the financially modest but extremely astute British effort, were spending some £4,000,000 to £6,000,000 annually on propaganda, while France was spending about £1,200,000 and Italy nearly £1,000,000.[4]

By 1957 the British Council had at its disposal for the conduct of cultural propaganda an annual budget of over £3,000,000—a small sum by Soviet standards, but one which reflected the growing significance attributed to this instrument of international politics even by governments which had traditionally looked with dis-

[2] Richard Carstensen, *Der Einfluss der Franzoesischen Kulturpropaganda auf das Geistesleben Daenemarks*, Berlin, 1941, p. 49.

[3] Harold Nicolson, *Diplomacy*, New York, 1939, p. 173.

[4] *Ibid.*, p, 172.

dain on such unconventional instruments of foreign policy as international broadcasting and large-scale cultural exchange.[5]

According to American officials interviewed, the Council apparently has at its disposal much larger funds than do the corresponding American governmental units, among which the International Educational Exchange Service of the Department of State and the same department's East-West Contacts Staff are the most important. The Council is able to enter vigorously into actual operations, particularly in the private and semiprivate fields, while the official United States cultural agencies have usually been forced to keep their functions largely advisory and facilitative, except for the official Soviet-American exchanges in which they are directly involved.

The British Council operates on a wide front, as indicated by its table of organization, which includes committees on books, drama, fine arts, movies, law, and many other fields. Its chairman in 1957 was Sir David Kelly, a former British ambassador to Russia. On behalf of the Colonial Office, it is responsible for the nonacademic welfare of colonial students in Britain. It sponsors and arranges visits from overseas of individuals and groups in various fields of cultural exchange. To it, rather than to the British foreign service, is entrusted the task of conducting British cultural diplomacy in all countries except Russia, where in 1959 a cultural attaché was appointed within the Moscow embassy, since the Council could not operate in the Soviet Union as it could in most parts of the world.

While it is outside the scope of this book to appraise the success of the British effort, it is not irrelevant to suggest that, particularly in India, but also in some other Commonwealth or colonial countries, not to mention the United States, the British have probably been the most successful practitioners of cultural diplomacy and have accomplished, considering the odds against them, more than the Russians. Certainly the prestige of the British in India—some ten years after that country's achievement of independence from Britain—not to mention the dominant role of the English lan-

[5] *The World of Learning*, 8th ed., London, 1957, pp. 361-362.

guage and English political ideas, has been little short of astonishing.

To deal with the Soviet cultural offensive the British Council in May 1955 created a Soviet Relations Committee, headed by Christopher Mayhew, a labor member of Parliament.[6] The council, although autonomous, works closely with British governmental departments and agencies, such as the Foreign Office, the Colonial Office, the Commonwealth Relations Office, the British Information Service, and the Educational Interchange Council.

If one were to survey the over-all British organization for cultural diplomacy, one would, of course, have to take into account a host of effective and closely coordinated semiofficial and private activities, such as the Rhodes scholarship program, and to keep in mind the British tradition of close cooperation between Foreign Office, press, radio, universities, and business, which makes many an Englishman abroad a kind of volunteer ambassador.

The United States was laggard in entering the international cultural competition, in so far as governmental action is concerned. In 1938 a Division of Cultural Relations was established in the Department of State. Until 1943 its work was limited by Congressional appropriations to the Western Hemisphere. With the passage of the Fulbright Act in 1946, public funds became available to supplement the large sums which had traditionally been provided by foundations and other private sources to such organizations as the Institute of International Education to enable American students, both graduate and undergraduate, to study abroad. Money provided by private sources and, under the terms of the Fulbright Act and the Smith-Mundt Act of 1948, from public funds has enabled the United States since World War II to maintain a program of exchange of students, professors, and experts, especially with the German Federal Republic and other European countries, which is far larger numerically than the comparable Soviet effort.

And, of course, if one compares the total American overseas involvement, public and private, with that of Russia, the latter seems almost negligible by comparison, at least in numbers. As the editorial in *Life* magazine for December 23, 1957, noted, "Outside

[6] *Christian Science Monitor*, June 2, 1955; *New York Times*, February 8, 1956.

the lands fully controlled by Communism, less than 5,000 Soviet citizens are at work." In contrast, there were at the same period 580,000 United States civilians resident abroad—many of them, incidentally, at a standard of life which elicited some local envy— and hundreds of thousands of members of the armed forces stationed overseas.[7] On the other hand, the Soviet Union had at its disposal the apparatus of foreign communist parties. Hence, it could focus and channel its efforts in ways not available to the democracies. Increasingly, many Americans, and Europeans too, were coming to feel that the information programs of noncommunist nations were not an adequate counter to the ideological pressures emanating from Moscow and Peking. There was a growing conviction that, while democratic societies could not and would not wish to tailor the truth to political ends, they should make a more vigorous effort to refute Soviet propaganda distortions and to achieve more effective communication with the people of communist-ruled lands.

In 1957 the East-West Contacts Staff was set up in the Department of State to develop and coordinate policies of the department applicable to exchanges between the United States and the countries of the Soviet bloc and to carry out arrangements for such exchanges.[8] In the same year the Soviet Union created, by setting up its State Committee for Cultural Relations with Foreign Countries, an agency with status and functions roughly corresponding to the new American unit. The East-West Staff, headed by Ambassador William B. Lacey, negotiated, under date of January 27, 1958, a Soviet-American Exchange Agreement. The agreement, as we shall see, paved the way for a significant expansion of the exchanges which had been under way since 1954 and 1955.

The summer of 1959 witnessed some interesting additions to American organizational equipment for the conduct of East-West exchanges, especially in the private sector. With the 1958 Lacey-Zarubin agreement under renegotiation, and with tourist travel to Russia on the way to becoming big business—according to various reports from 10,000 to 15,000 Americans visited the U.S.S.R. in

[7] *Life*, December 23, 1957, p. 21.
[8] *United States Government Organization Manual 1958-59*, Washington, D.C., 1958, p. 84.

1959 as against some 5,000 to 7,000 in 1958—the Governmental Affairs Institute of Washington, D.C., established an Information Center for American Travelers to Russia, "in response," as the Institute's announcement stated, "to a need expressed by many such visitors for essential background information on Soviet affairs and on the opportunities and limitations of tourist travel in Russia." One also heard of such enterprises as publication by the Freedom Fund of a Russian-language guidebook to New York, for the benefit, reported the *New York Times* of July 17, 1959, of Russians in the city for the Soviet exhibition, or of literature for American travelers published by the East European Student and Youth Service of New York.

At the same time, the State Department and other interested government and private agencies, although still somewhat hampered by lack of adequate funds, improved their facilities and expanded their personnel to provide hospitality for the increasing flow of Soviet visitors to America by, for instance, appointing competent persons to serve as tour directors.

By mid-1959 it was clear that, while mistakes had been made and effort wasted by both sides, East-West exchanges had been mutually beneficial in a variety of ways. Certainly they had contributed greatly to Western, particularly American, knowledge of conditions behind an Iron Curtain which, though it still existed, was no longer an impassable barrier. Very likely the opportunities to establish or renew contact with reality which was afforded by the reopening of Russia had, as one of my colleagues said, saved Russian studies in America from sterility.

Both France and the United States, among the Western nations, had already, despite all obstacles, derived enormous benefit from a carefully conducted program of graduate-student exchange with the U.S.S.R. This program, in the case of France, began in 1954-1955 and, in that of the United States, by the summer of 1959 had run its first full year, within the framework of the Soviet-American Exchange Agreement of January 28, 1958. Perhaps we should point out here that, particularly in the American case, it is only too easy to conclude from a superficial comparison of the massive, streamlined, centralized Soviet foreign cultural program with the sometimes fumbling official American response to its challenge, that we are doomed to defeat in the current contest of civilizations. Such a conclusion should certainly be carefully checked against the plentiful but scattered evidence which is available on the fruitful activity of private foundations, universities, business organizations, churches, and others, including hundreds—perhaps even thousands—of private citizens who have already made contributions to the dissipation of mutual ignorance between the Soviet and non-Soviet worlds, the clarification of issues, and, hopefully, the beginnings of mutual understanding. We shall have ample occasion to point with alarm to certain difficulties and dangers of the cultural encounter. It is all the more necessary, therefore, to make it clear at the outset that in our opinion cultural exchanges with communist countries—and, of course, also with noncommunist countries—offer rich opportunities for the facilitation of democratic, humanistic purposes. As Henry L. Roberts, director of the Russian Institute of Columbia University, pointed out in a thoughtful address at Harvard University in January 1958, the maximization of democratic values in a relationship which cannot be truly reciprocal is an immensely difficult task. It is, however, a task that should not be shirked; for it is evident that, as the communist world becomes richer and more powerful and achieves a gradually rising level of civilization, it will display, in a carefully controlled and increasingly ingratiating fashion, more and more of its achievements to growing numbers of foreigners. If proof of this assertion is needed, one has only to consider the boldness—perhaps some might say the brashness—of the emphasis in the Soviet exhibition in the New York Coliseum, in June and July 1959, on industry and even on consumers' goods. Perhaps Moscow could be accused of "carrying gadgets to gadgetland," but the effort bespeaks determination and official confidence, to say the least. It also expresses a pride of achievement on the part of Russian scientists, engineers, and workmen that we shall do well to appreciate if we wish to get on as friendly terms as possible with a people still suffering from the consequences of a centuries-old inferiority complex, and consequently inclined at times toward a touchy exaggeration of the significance of their achievements and quick to express indignation against those who display condescension regarding them or ignorance of the Russian cultural heritage of which they are increasingly proud.

In the address already mentioned, Henry Roberts summed up, as well as has anyone, the political significance of the subject of this book. He asked, "At a point in history when there seems to be a military stalemate of sorts, when diplomacy finds few serious negotiable issues, is it not quite possible . . . that the whole weight . . . of these two tremendous political and ideological systems will be brought to bear on one of the few areas of relative mobility and change—the realm of ideas and of cultural activities?" No believer in the values of the open society could find fault with Professor Roberts' conclusion that "we need to accept the challenge of educational exchanges not solely to avert the charges of presenting an Iron Curtain, but also because entering willingly such an arduous intellectual encounter is what, as free men trying to create a freer world, we should be doing anyway."[9]

Nor could men of good will reject, in principle, the idealism underlying the belief in the virtues of free cultural exchange expressed so optimistically by President Eisenhower in his address in 1956 accepting the Republican Party nomination for candidacy for a second term. Mr. Eisenhower stated then that as a result of interchange of ideas, books, magazines, students, tourists, artists, radio programs, technical experts, religious leaders, and government officials, "little by little, mistrust based on falsehoods" would "give way to international understanding based on truth."[10]

To cope with the challenge and to fulfill the promise of closer contact with the Soviet Union and its vast empire, we need full information about the motivations, methods, and dimensions of Soviet cultural diplomacy. Perhaps we should begin our exploration with an attempt at a definition of this key term.

"Cultural diplomacy" might be defined, briefly, as the manipulation of cultural materials and personnel for propaganda purposes. One might say of it, as Lindley Fraser has aptly said of propaganda in general, that it is an activity which induces "others to

---

[9] Professor Roberts' address was delivered at the celebration of the tenth anniversary of the Harvard Russian Research Center. The spring 1958 issue of the *Columbia University Forum* published the version from which the above parts are quoted. See especially p. 29 of that issue.

[10] *New York Times*, August 24, 1956.

behave in a way in which they would not behave in its absence."[11]

Cultural diplomacy is, then, a branch of intergovernmental propaganda, but it is a special and significant one. It is also one that has been much more highly developed by communist states than by noncommunist countries and is still so new to American foreign policy that it is doubtful if one could as yet very meaningfully speak of an American cultural diplomacy, or whether, in the sense in which we have been using the term, we shall ever be full-fledged practitioners of this art. At the same time, however, we would be unfair to ourselves if we were to forget that over a period of some ten years, after World War II, the American government and private American agencies appealed in vain to the Soviet authorities to assist interested and eager Americans in making arrangements for the free interchange of ideas, persons, and cultural products. Even in 1945, before the end of fighting in Europe, American manufacturers donated children's garments for a Moscow fashion show. On many occasions, especially in 1946, 1947, and 1948, before the cold-war "freeze" had congealed, U.S. Ambassador Walter Bedell Smith lent his good offices to proposals for the exchange of students, professors, symphony orchestras, tourists, et cetera. In July 1947, Professor Ernest J. Simmons of Columbia University journeyed to Moscow as the emissary of the American Council of Learned Societies with a list of proposals for cultural and educational exchanges which, if the U.S.S.R. had then felt free to accept them, would probably have resulted in an exchange program even more comprehensive and far-reaching than the one currently in progress.[12]

Central to communist cultural diplomacy is the systematic utilization of information, artistic, scientific, and other cultural materials, symbols and personnel, and ideas, as instruments of foreign policy. As Richard L. Walker has succinctly put it, "Activities which for democratic societies are basically uncontrolled are within the Soviet-style frame-work an essential ingredient of foreign relations and

[11] Lindley Fraser, *Propaganda*, London, 1957, p. 1.
[12] On these early efforts, see Ernest J. Simmons, "Negotiating on Cultural Exchange," in *Negotiating with the Russians*, Raymond Dennett and Joseph E. Johnson, eds., Boston, 1951; see also U.S. Department of State publication 3480, *Cultural Relations between the United States and the Soviet Union*, Washington, D.C., 1949.

the conduct of diplomacy."[13] It might be added that an important part of the pattern of Soviet cultural diplomacy consists in the use by the Kremlin of mass-communications media to create and maintain at home and abroad desired images, both of "Soviet culture" and also of "bourgeois culture," which is held to be in irreconcilable conflict with its communist counterpart. Furthermore—and this is an aspect of Soviet cultural policy which Americans find almost impossible to understand—Soviet citizens are expected, in all of their dealings with foreigners, perhaps particularly with noncommunist foreigners, to act as mouthpieces of official policy. Too often, in conversations with Soviet citizens, one gets the impression that one is talking not to a person but to a parrot.

One other characteristic of Soviet cultural diplomacy should perhaps be mentioned. Its mission is not merely the positive one of projecting the aspects of Soviet reality selected by the Soviet authorities for domestic and foreign disclosure and glorification. It has, in addition, a negative mission of considerable significance, which consists in vituperative criticism of aspects of foreign cultures deemed to be incompatible with Soviet values, as well as censorship, distortion, or denial of positive aspects of bourgeois cultures which, according to officially determined Soviet definitions of capitalism, are not supposed to exist. Soviet visitors to foreign countries are expected to do their part in preserving the official mythology. This fact helps to explain such experiences as the conversation of a scholar with a visiting Russian colleague who kept bombarding the American with propaganda clichés until the latter, in irritation, finally said, "You know that is not true, don't you?" Whereupon the Russian, less disciplined or more cynical than many of his fellow-countrymen, replied, "That is what they told us to say."

Somewhat akin to this tactic is the practice, as in the case of the American National Exhibition in Moscow in 1959, of seeking, by sniping in the press, to destroy in advance the credibility of the display. This seems particularly unfair, since the Soviet officials responsible for the Russian exhibition in New York had access to

---

[13] R. L. Walker, "The Developing Role of Cultural Diplomacy in Asia," in *Issues and Conflicts*, George L. Anderson, ed., University of Kansas Press, Lawrence, Kansas, 1959, p. 45.

all of the facilities of American public relations and advertising, and even hired a Madison Avenue firm to assist them in their publicity campaign. On the other hand, such behavior, in a way, represents the compliment which the controlled society feels constrained to pay to its democratic rival, with whom it dare not engage in free competition.

Soviet cultural diplomacy is often tinged by what noncommunists, at least, can only describe as deception. In large part, its task is to establish in the minds of its targets associations between, for example, classical Russian music and the Kremlin's alleged desire for peace. Or, to take another example, it seeks to plant the idea that communism generates technological progress. Again, it strives to prove that, since exhibitions of the art of India are displayed in Moscow, the Soviet Union values the culture, the human dignity, and the political freedom of Indians. In like manner, empty prison buildings or abandoned penal camps are shown to distinguished American visitors in the not-always-unfounded hope that they will draw from this limited evidence sweeping conclusions as to the scope of Soviet post-Stalin legal reform.

We must remember, of course, that Soviet communists, like all communists, use words in unusual ways. It is well known, for example, that the word "peace" in Soviet usage means, as Lindley Fraser observes, "the state of affairs inside a communist country." And yet it is a major objective of Soviet policy to persuade noncommunists that, when communists use the word peace, they give it the same meaning as do noncommunists.

A somewhat similar situation prevails with respect to Soviet usage of such terms as "cultural relations" or "cultural exchange." While professing reciprocity, the Kremlin practices, in so far as possible, a unilateral dissemination of Soviet influence; only too often, in the vital field of exchange of scientific and technical knowledge with noncommunist countries, Moscow seeks to obtain patents, blueprints, and processes and, in return, to offer flattery, vague promises, and, it must be admitted, an impressively cordial and often charming hospitality. The term "exchange" itself thus takes its place in the communist arsenal of double-talk.

The attitudes which shape Soviet policy in cultural contacts are firmly rooted in the dogmatism and provincialism of the Soviet

13

mentality. Their tenacity and persistence, and indeed their essential character, also owe a good deal to some of the more negative aspects of the political culture inherited by the bolsheviks from tsarist Russia. Tsarism, like Soviet communism, had a predilection for conspiracy and manipulation. The writings of Russian liberals such as Alexander Herzen were replete with denunciations of the Russian government's practice of "organizing a semi-official literature, with the task of praising, and lying in favor of the government."[14]

No one has better described the dissimulation which forms such a vital link between the diplomacy of old and of new Russia than that founding father of Marxism, Friedrich Engels, who wrote that "there was no . . . outrage . . . which was not carried out [by Russia] under the pretext of enlightenment, of liberalism, of the liberation of nations."[15]

There is much in common between tsarist and official Soviet fear of contact with what George F. Kennan described as "the more competent, more powerful, highly organized societies" which the Russian rulers encountered in the West.[16]

Soviet totalitarianism added new dimensions of ambition, of ruthlessness, of fanaticism, and of organizing genius to the legacy it took over from old Russian imperialism. It is only too obvious that in order to achieve their own purposes of truthful, objective reporting of facts, a two-way flow of influence, and mutual advantage in every aspect of exchanges, the democracies must know how to overcome the obstacles inherent in this firmly established Soviet approach. The benefits which free countries can derive from cultural exchanges will have to be worked for, planned for, even struggled for. They will not flow automatically from the signing of agreements, nor will they ever be achieved by the lazy, the un-

[14] Alexander Herzen, *Polnoe sobranie sochinenii i pisem*, Vol. v, Petrograd, 1919, p. 303. Herzen made this statement in 1849. Partly in defense against the impact of Western ideas, the tsarist regime had, in the eighteenth and nineteenth centuries, organized its well-known doctrine and practice of "official patriotism."

[15] Quoted by Robert Strausz-Hupe, et al., from Friedrich Engels, "The Foreign Policy of Russian Czarism," in *Protracted Conflict*, New York, 1959, p. 68, footnote 1.

[16] *Ibid.*, p. 173, quoting from a dispatch written by Mr. Kennan while he was chargé d'affaires of the American embassy in Moscow.

14

informed, or the naïve, or, one may add, by the self-righteous or the smug.

As we turn now to some of the major Soviet foreign-policy and propaganda objectives, the achievement of which cultural diplomacy is calculated to facilitate, there can be little doubt that one of the most important is exploitation of mankind's desire for peace in a world threatened by nuclear war. There is, to be sure, a measure of sincerity in Soviet peace propaganda. Like their bourgeois opponents, the communists prefer survival to mutual annihilation. In the element of mutuality which this fact brings to a troubled international situation lies a great potential of hope.

However, the Soviet communists also seek to exploit fear of war and hope for peace to expand the power of Russia. In the world ideological struggle the side that can most convincingly demonstrate its devotion to peace can win much support, especially in militarily weak or ideologically uncommitted countries. Soviet leaders have always insisted that their professed enthusiasm for international contacts was proof of their devotion to peace. This is an appealing thesis, for most people do tend to associate friendly personal contacts with hopeful prospects for peace. Soviet and other communist leaders often act as if they alone desired such contacts. In the period since the death of Stalin they have even tried to pin the onus for the Iron Curtain on the United States.

Soviet exploitation of cultural contacts has usually resolved around the strategy and propaganda of peaceful coexistence. Consequently, cultural relations play a more conspicuous role in Soviet foreign affairs during periods when coexistence is stressed than during periods of extreme international tension. However, the differences between these kinds of situations should not be exaggerated. In communist philosophy the struggle for survival goes on at all times, and there are only differences of degree, of intensity, of appearances, and of tactics. The coexistence line is intended, of course, to appeal mainly to noncommunists. As an editorial in the *Economist* for October 30, 1954, put it, "To the Russians peaceful coexistence is simply a temporary phase in which the free world is to be peacefully whittled away instead of aggressively beaten down." At no time has the Soviet Union followed a policy of complete isolation, but during periods such as the late Stalin years—roughly from 1948 to 1953—most of the contacts between Russia and the noncommunist world, especially Western Europe and America, were between Soviet delegations and foreign communists or fellow-traveler groups, or between visiting groups composed mainly or at least partly of such persons and Soviet communist party and government agencies. But when the "monolith" smiles, doors are opened to almost any kind of foreigner, regardless of ideology, though the visitor is kept under careful if usually unobtrusive surveillance, which, however, as contacts multiply, becomes more difficult to exercise.

An ingenious interpretation of the Soviet strategy of coexistence has been offered by Herbert Marcuse. According to Marcuse, Soviet doctrine, especially since Stalin, has held that the success of the Soviet policy of totalitarian industrialization and foreign political expansion had led to the political and economic consolidation of the West in a "permanent war economy," which was sustained by a "hard" Soviet policy. Such a policy also stood in the way of elevation of Soviet living standards to a point where they could compete with those of the West. Consequently, it would be useful to bring about a relaxation, which would serve a double purpose. It would help to soften up the Western "war economy," and it would facilitate "a transformation of Soviet society which is to establish the economic and cultural superiority of socialism over capitalism, to spread socialism 'by contagion,' and thus to provide the basis for unfreezing the class struggle in the capitalist world."[17] Perhaps some such calculation might, in a sense, be viewed as a Kremlin counterpart of the thesis, first propounded by Mr. George F. Kennan, that a mellowing of Soviet communism is inevitable with the progress of education, the gradual refinement of civilization, and the rise of standards of living in Russia. Each side in the ideological combat entertains hopes of changes in the enemy camp which will benefit it. But both sides, especially the Soviet side, have hesitated to go very far in relaxing tensions, each fearing that the other would take military or political advantage of its relaxation of vigilance.

[17] Herbert Marcuse, *Soviet Marxism*, New York, 1950, pp. 76-77, 99-100, and 172-173. The long quotation is on p. 100.

The back-stopping of coexistence propaganda by cultural diplomacy is a much older feature of Soviet foreign policy than is generally realized. Throughout its history VOKS—the All-Union Society for Cultural Relations with Foreign Countries, established in 1925 and replaced in 1958 by a new Union of Soviet Societies for Friendship and Cultural Relations with Foreign Countries—proclaimed as one of the motives for popularizing Soviet culture abroad the necessity for mobilizing foreign intellectuals against alleged plans for military attack on Soviet Russia. At the same time, however, Soviet intellectuals and their foreign collaborators were urged not to limit their activity to "disseminating neutral information which often hides a desire to efface our victories," but to engage in militant proselytism.[18] In 1925 Stalin told the Fourteenth Congress of the Soviet communist party that sojourns of "delegations of workers" from the West, or visits by Indian, Egyptian, and Chinese groups—in the case of the Easterners, Stalin said nothing about social origins—constituted "the best, most forceful and active propaganda for the Soviet system against the capitalist system." Orientals, he asserted, would be particularly impressed by Soviet nationality policy.[19] In 1926 he declared that visits by delegations of "foreign proletarians" to Soviet Russia could help to prevent "imperialistic intervention" against the U.S.S.R.[20]

During the period of the Soviet-Western united front against Fascism and of the Anglo-Soviet-American coalition against Nazi Germany and its allies, the role of cultural diplomacy was not so much one of disseminating anticapitalist or even "peace" propaganda, but of supporting Moscow's efforts to organize a Soviet-led front against Fascist and Japanese aggression.

During the late Stalin era, from 1948 to the dictator's death on March 5, 1953, the Soviet Union was preoccupied with consolidation of the power positions gained during the war and with recovery from the damage wrought by the war to the Soviet economy and to national morale. Foreign and domestic tensions dictated a limited and largely defensive policy in exchanges of persons and information. But even in the last two or three years of Stalin's

[18] McMurry and Lee, *op.cit.*, p. 117.
[19] J. V. Stalin, *Sochineniya*, Vol. 7, Moscow, 1947, pp. 291-292.
[20] *Ibid.*, Vol. 9, Moscow, 1948, p. 140.

life a slight relaxation of controls and some increase of foreign contacts occurred. Stalin's successors, almost immediately after assuming control of Soviet foreign relations, inaugurated a campaign designed to spread Soviet influence and to undo the harmful effects on the Soviet international position caused by the excesses of Stalinist rudeness, secrecy, bluster, and violence. Post-Stalin foreign policy was less defensive, in cultural and ideological terms, than Lenin's policy or than Stalin's policy of the 1920's and 1930's. The Soviet Union had enormously increased its absolute and relative power as a result of industrial development and the acquisition of super weapons and could afford to pursue a more confident policy than in the past. At the same time, the existence of nuclear weapons put a premium on the use of relatively subtle tactics, although it also offered unprecedented opportunities for exploitation of fear of war, and, in certain situations, for nuclear blackmail.

Second only to the peace theme, perhaps, in the context of Soviet cultural diplomacy is the dissemination of a positive image of Soviet socialist civilization. Moscow desires that Russia be regarded as the chief world center of progress, spiritual cultivation, enlightenment, and humanitarianism. This intention is revealed, often indirectly, in statements by Soviet politicians and intellectuals. It is powerfully reinforced by publication in the Soviet press of glowing and sometimes doctored testimonials by foreigners. For understanding of the political significance attributed by the Soviet leadership to the popularization of Soviet culture abroad it is useful to understand the Soviet doctrine of the "cultural revolution." According to the *Great Soviet Encyclopedia*, the cultural revolution is an integral part of the socialist revolution. It is directed by the communist party. The party effects the cultural revolution after it has seized political power. The Soviet conception of the cultural revolution was developed systematically in a book entitled *On Soviet Culture and the Cultural Revolution in the U.S.S.R.*,[21] published in 1954 by G. G. Karpov, head of the government agency which supervises the activities of the Russian Orthodox Church. Karpov's outlook is suggested by his statement that "our country is the country of the most advanced culture, the citadel of advanced scientific thought, of revolutionary humanism and of a new, Communist

---

[21] *O sovetskoi kulture i kulturnoi revolyutsii v sssr.*

morality." Karpov believes that bourgeois culture is "the chief obstacle to the progressive development of mankind." According to Karpov, Russian culture was always superior to that of the West, but only reached its full flowering after the adoption of Leninism, the summit of Russian national and world culture. After the destruction of bourgeois culture, the chief support of which is American imperialism, a "truly unified and universal human culture" will be established "under conditions of socialism."[22] One might regard Karpov's apocalyptic vision as a kind of cultural concomitant to Khrushchev's boast that the communists intended to "bury" what they call "capitalism."

A typical post-Stalin *Pravda* editorial on June 15, 1953, asserted that visits of foreigners to the Soviet Union counteracted falsehoods disseminated by the capitalist press, and helped to make known the truth about Soviet progress in industry and social welfare. *Uchitelskaya Gazeta* (*The Teacher's Newspaper*) for April 21, 1954, reported ecstatic comments by Swiss schoolteachers on the Soviet educational system and, in particular, on Soviet love of and care for small children. Perhaps particularly interesting is the effort made by Soviet leaders to cultivate cordial relations between Soviet and foreign motion-picture workers. This policy is pursued in many ways, such as holding festivals of foreign films in Russia and by arranging for joint Soviet-foreign film productions. An interesting detail on one aspect of this type of cultural diplomacy was contained in an article in *Pravda* for October 21, 1954, describing films shown in India by the Indo-Soviet Cultural Society, formed in 1951 by a group of Indian intellectuals who had just visited the Soviet Union. Commenting on "international ties of cinematography," *Sovetskaya Kultura* (*Soviet Culture*) for January 8, 1955, stated that "progressive cinematography serves to bring nations closer together."

Khrushchev, in a speech to coal miners in 1956, revealed one of the subjective, psychological motives for display of Soviet culture abroad. He said, "The country's growing authority abroad is reflected in the flood of foreign delegations coming here." It seems clear that if Soviet culture enjoyed, either at home or abroad, the prestige claimed for it, a less strident effort would be made to

[22] *Ibid.*, pp. 76-77.

demonstrate its superiority. That Kremlin chauvinism regarding Soviet culture has not necessarily inspired contempt or hostility toward foreign culture among ordinary Soviet citizens has often been revealed, as, for example, in the riotous welcome which hundreds of thousands of Leningraders gave to the British and Dutch fleet visits in 1955 and 1956. All of my visits to Russia, including one in July and August 1959, have confirmed my conviction of the vulnerability of Soviet culture to foreign penetration.

However, the Kremlin's expectation of gaining prestige among foreigners by skillful persuasion is certainly not entirely unfounded. During a trip to Russia in 1956 evidence was available of the impact of Soviet showmanship even on wealthy American businessmen. Partly because they carried in their minds a grotesque image of Russian backwardness, and partly because they saw only the best that Moscow had to offer, some of these men were favorably impressed by what they were shown and a few of them expressed approval of Soviet pleas for expansion of U.S.-Soviet trade, made frequently by their Soviet hosts. A British diplomat who remarked, "They've got their delegation technique working nicely," was convinced that a far more powerful impression was being made on more susceptible groups, carefully shielded from exposure to reality.

It seems likely, however, that the communists reap their richest rewards, particularly in terms of the good will of foreign intellectuals, artists, and scientists, not by display of their own achievements but by courteous and sympathetic appreciation of those of other countries. Soviet leaders, including the not-very-polished Khrushchev, have demonstrated considerable sensitivity to the self-image of almost every kind of national and cultural group. They seem to realize more clearly than Americans or even Western Europeans that one of the most effective ways of flattering an individual is to express appreciation of his national language, literature, and art. Probably the skills employed by Soviet leadership in cultural diplomacy represent to some extent an external application of experience acquired in governing the multinational Soviet state. The Soviet attitude toward foreign culture also draws on the eighteenth- and nineteenth-century Russian tradition of avid interest in things foreign, particularly things European. At its best, this was a tradition of civilized cosmopolitanism. At times, however, even in the nineteenth century and more often in the Soviet period, Russian interest in foreign cultures has been accompanied by the arrogant claim that Russians have a better understanding of foreign cultures than the natives of the countries concerned.

A succinct and appealing expression of Soviet appreciation of foreign cultures was made by Joseph Stalin in April 1948. At a dinner in honor of a Finnish governmental delegation Stalin said: "Soviet people consider that each nation, whether large or small, has its special characteristics which belong to it alone. These characteristics represent the contribution which each nation makes to the general treasure chest of world cultures, and adds to it and enriches it. In this sense all nations, both great and small, are on the same footing and each nation is as significant as any other nation."[23]

If skillfully applied, this is a formula certain to win friends, particularly among peoples and groups that feel threatened by American "cultural imperialism" or that have not overcome their resentment against colonialism. The underdeveloped countries, or, as Khrushchev called them in his speech in February 1956 at the Twentieth Congress of the communist party of the Soviet Union, the "poorly developed" countries, particularly those of Asia, Africa, and Latin America, offer rich opportunities for the exercise of Soviet cultural diplomacy. One of the major differences between post-Stalin strategy and that of the late Stalin era was the realization in the Kremlin that an appeal to nationalism and anti-Americanism might pay bigger political dividends, at least for a considerable time, than an attempt at early overthrow of "bourgeois" governments, such as those of Nehru, Nasser, or Sukarno.

The Soviet effort achieved a considerable impact in the economically less-developed countries, although events such as the judicial murder of Imre Nagy in 1958 and brutal communist suppression of the Tibetan revolt in 1959 detracted somewhat from its appeal. A Russian proverb says, "You can't hide a saw in a sack," and one of the West's advantages in the propaganda struggle is the disharmony between the realities and the idealization of communism. Yet, as the *Economist* for January 11, 1958, observed: "In Asia

[23] *Vneshnyaya politika sovetskogo soyuza*, Moscow, 1950, Part I, p. 24.

and Africa the personal gesture carries even more political weight than in the West. Messrs. Khrushchev and Chou En-lai have flatteringly . . . wooed South Asian opinion by making successive tours. . . ."

The narrowly political and indeed subversive aspects of Soviet cultural diplomacy, in so far as it is concerned with Asia and Africa, were revealed in an anonymous leading article in the journal of the Institute of Orientalogy of the U.S.S.R. Academy of Sciences in 1959. Entitled "Tasks of Orientalogy," the editorial urged the study, for example, of the ancient and modern history of Asian and African countries in order to dispel the "myth . . . of the civilizing mission" of the Western nations. It praised Soviet scholars for producing literary and linguistic studies which "strengthen the positions of the people of the East in the struggle against imperialism," and asserted that such studies had already struck a shattering blow against "reactionary theories of Europa-centrism."[24]

A similar utilitarian, partisan spirit, but with broader geographic applications, was displayed in an article on "The International Horizon of the Writer," by a leading literary critic, T. Motyleva, in *Literaturnaya Gazeta (Literary Gazette)* for April 28, 1959. Mrs. Motyleva asserted that not only the Soviet writers who spoke at international congresses or made long and frequent trips abroad, but, in fact, "all of Soviet literature" played a role in "the international political struggle." She added that at a time when the "international contacts of Soviet literature" were expanding, and would expand still farther, the way in which the selection and popularization of foreign literature in the U.S.S.R. was handled had taken on great political significance.

Perhaps the most obvious objective of Soviet cultural exchanges is to facilitate the acquisition of useful knowledge. After the death of Stalin, Soviet scientists and engineers were encouraged to alter their previous chauvinistic public view regarding foreign achievements to one which recognized the merits both of fatherland and of foreign science. Traces of scientific chauvinism remained, however, particularly in military circles. For example, the army news-

---

[24] Zadachi Vostokovedeniya," in *Problemy Vostokovedeniya*, No. 1, 1959, pp. 18-25.

paper *Red Star* for June 12, 1957, published an angry letter from distinguished air officers excoriating Soviet historians for sowing "seeds of doubt about our motherland's priority in building the world's first airplane."

However, these "Stalinist" notes, perhaps reflecting a resurgence of domestic and foreign tensions, were struck at a time when the post-Stalin program of scientific and technical exchanges was continuing to expand, particularly with the United States. Many top Soviet leaders, including Khrushchev and Bulganin, made public statements shedding light on Soviet motives for expanding scientific and technical exchanges. In a speech to the Supreme Soviet, a considerable part of which was devoted to urging Russian technical men to study Western methods, Bulganin said, "We cannot forget—and we do not have the right to—that technology in capitalist countries does not stand still, but, under the influence of the arms race and of the desire of capitalists for maximum profit, has, in a number of fields, moved ahead."[25] Bulganin called for more frequent exchanges of information with foreign scientists, increased purchases of foreign technical literature, and wider dissemination of such material in translations throughout the Soviet Union. He pointed out the inferiority of Soviet truck chassis to comparable American models and of Soviet tractors and portable generators to British and German models. *Sovetskaya Kultura* for September 8, 1955, declared that it was the "patriotic duty" of Soviet publishing houses and other institutions to make available to Soviet readers the achievements of "world science and technology."

These injunctions were followed by a vastly increased effort in the publication of review journals, translations of foreign treatises, and abstracts. An American expert has written that the Soviet scientific abstract program "may be the most ambitious and comprehensive scheme in existence of this kind," and that the Soviet leadership "is making a conscious, well-planned attempt to assume the scientific leadership of the world."[26] Apparently not satisfied that everything possible was being done to assimilate useful foreign

[25] *Pravda*, July 17, 1955.
[26] John Turkevich, "Soviet Science in the Post-Stalin Era," in the *Annals of the American Academy of Political and Social Science*, Vol. 303, January 1956, pp. 139-151. On this point see pp. 149-150.

information, the Central Committee of the communist party of the Soviet Union in February 1957 recommended the creation of a special commission to collect and spread technological information both from Russia itself and from foreign countries. These early exhortations and measures were followed by a scientific exchange program which has already taken on vast proportions and is still growing. In this connection it is interesting that, at the June 1959 plenum of the Soviet communist party central committee, the chairman of the state committee for the Soviet chemical industry urged the purchase of entire factories from Western industrial countries. There have been reports of transactions with Great Britain, for example, involving such purchases.

One possible consequence of cultural exchange which is feared both by Russia and the West is the opportunity it may afford for espionage and subversion. Soviet defectors such as former secret agents Yuri Rastvorov and Vladimir Petrov have testified regarding the use of Soviet cultural and athletic groups as a cover for such activities. Petrov, for example, wrote in the Sydney *Morning Herald* for October 10, 1955: "As well as consul, my open official duties included that of representative of VOKS, the Soviet cultural organization. In this way I had a chance to travel, meet people, and see the country, which my jealous colleagues greatly envied."

Even during the relatively relaxed period, from the 1955 summit conference to the Poznan riots in June 1956, the Soviet political press did not cease to publish occasional warnings that foreign tourists might, after all, be "imperialist spies." Since 1956 the frequency and intensity of these warnings have increased. The Kremlin is even more concerned about the danger of influence of "alien" attitudes on Soviet citizens than about possible espionage. Such concern was indicated, for example, in an article by V. Moskovsky, in *Kommunist*, Number twelve, August 1956, asserting that "the reactionary circles of the West" would utilize all available means to "influence the consciousness of backward people" in the Soviet Union. He demanded an irreconcilable struggle against every "manifestation of bourgeois ideology." Similar warnings were issued after the Sixth World Festival of Youth and Students in 1957, in an article in *Komsomolskaya Pravda* by A. N. Shelepin, head of the Communist Youth League, who in December 1958 became the head of the chief Soviet secret police agency. In his first major speech after assuming this post, in February 1959, Shelepin uttered Stalin-like warnings about the alleged dangers to the Soviet Union posed by "agents smuggled into our country by the imperialist states."

Anthony Quainton and George Abrams, two of the most observant among the American youths who were in Moscow during the 1957 festival, deplored, in published statements, the fact that the American contingent had been so small, and one of them criticized the United States government for applying a policy of "non-contamination."[27] In the light of these astute appraisals, the validity of which has been confirmed by other accounts obtained in interviews, it seems fortunate that the British Foreign Office did not discourage representative British youths, including graduate students of Soviet affairs, from attending the festival. On the whole, the festival, like many similar Soviet efforts in recent years, probably accomplished its purpose of convincing the majority of the participants of the Soviet desire for peace and in presenting an attractive view of Soviet culture and life to a crucially important audience. It is interesting to note that Mr. Quainton referred to an estimate of 150 million dollars as the cost of the festival to the Soviet government. This expenditure produced results, but the Kremlin's elaborate pageantry failed to impress the more sophisticated Western European and American youths who had the financial resources and the enterprise to go to see it for themselves.

Fortunately, the lesson of the 1957 Youth Festival—that one cannot deal with an energetic competitor simply by ostracism—was at least partially learned, as is indicated by the activities of well-organized private American youth groups which engaged in exchange with official Soviet groups in 1958 and 1959. It was a sign of growing political sophistication that in 1959 a dedicated group of private citizens, headed by Gloria Steinem, organized in Cambridge, Massachusetts, the Independent Service for Information on the Vienna Festival, and that, while discouraging participation in the gathering on an organization-to-organization

[27] *Washington Post*, September 4, 1957; *New York Herald Tribune*, September 12, 1957.

level, the Department of State adopted a more flexible strategy, better suited to the situation, than in 1957. This policy did not create unnecessary obstacles to participation by American youths who, as private individuals, felt that they could both learn and perhaps teach by observing the spectacle, the first of its kind to be held in a noncommunist country, and by seeking to break through communist stereotypes to real person-to-person communication with representatives of the communist youth movements sent out beyond the Iron Curtain to spread the Marxist-Leninist gospel. Although participants in this mission of freedom found the Soviet youth leaders much tougher opponents than they had expected, the knowledge they acquired about the formidable nature of the ideological enemy was in itself a useful, if sobering reward for their efforts.

We have, we hope, identified some of the main features of the strategy of Soviet cultural policy. The driving forces of this policy are complex, including as they do the surging vitality of a society overcoming the stigma of backwardness, as well as the distorting compulsions of communism. Perhaps we should point out that despite the curse of political exploitation from which Soviet cultural diplomacy suffers, it is not devoid of elements which, even from the democratic point of view, are thoroughly positive. To be sure, these more positive aspects are perhaps more accidental than essential, but their presence gives ground for hope of ultimate change for the better.

American and other free-world educators, scientists, and others who have participated with Soviet colleagues in exchanges have frequently reported that in Russian professional and expert circles, as distinguished from the political sphere, a desire for honest intellectual cooperation prevails. Reflecting this kind of experience, Eugene Rabinowitch, editor of the *Bulletin of the Atomic Scientists*, stated, in an article in the *New Leader* for September 23, 1957, that in a meeting of Soviet and Western atomic scientists at Pugwash, Nova Scotia, in the same year "with gratification one must record that, as scientists, they were all able—and willing—to set aside their emotional or political aims and settle down to factual, quantitative analysis of the radioactive contamination produced by test explosions."

Not all official Soviet statements regarding scientific exchanges, of course, reflect the selfish, utilitarian spirit which we have described. There are also, occasionally, perfectly unexceptionable statements such as the following, published in *Literaturnaya Gazeta* (*The Literary Gazette*) for August 4, 1955: "The threads of mutual cultural relations may be compared to the blood vessels of culture. The breaking of these contacts leads to stagnation; science for its development requires the exchange of information regarding its newest discoveries, and the successes achieved by art and science are better understood on a comparative basis."

If the time ever comes when these sentiments become the governing principle of Soviet-Western cultural exchange, and those elements of the Soviet intelligentsia who believe in them achieve predominancy in the formulation of their country's foreign policy, the cold war will be nothing but an unhappy memory. That a Western-oriented minority of Soviet citizens does genuinely aspire to a cultural relationship founded on mutual respect and appreciation of cultural diversity has long been one of my beliefs, and this belief was strengthened by my most recent observations, under the favorable circumstances created by the major American-Soviet cultural exchanges of the summer of 1959.

CHAPTER II

SOVIET CULTURAL DIPLOMACY UNDER LENIN AND STALIN

THE "two world" conception which shapes Soviet cultural diplomacy imparts to it attitudes alien both to the official tsarist Russian philosophy and to the mixture of nationalism and cosmopolitanism which has usually guided the cultural policy of Western nations. Despite the police state's dread of Western liberalism and radicalism, tsarist Russia desired, almost too anxiously, to be accepted as a "European" state, and the Russian imperial regime accepted as fully as did Western governments the norms and customs of the European "system of states," the destruction of which Lenin was to demand as essential to the survival and expansion of communism. Soviet Russia has, from 1917 to our day, claimed leadership of the "national liberation" movements in the non-European world and of the struggle of the Western proletariat—claims which tend to bring Soviet culture into conflict with the Europe-based and American-based mass culture of the modern industrial age. Soviet Russia has offered to the world, or even demanded that the world adopt, its version of mass culture. This messianic approach challenges and threatens the established cultures of East and West, though the effectiveness of the challenge is limited by the failure of the Soviet leaders to create a really new and appealing socialist culture.

The research on tsarist foreign cultural policy which would be necessary if one wished to compare it systematically with the Soviet pattern has not been done. It may, however, be useful to look at some high lights of the prerevolutionary picture, as we bear in mind that the crucial difference between the two eras consists in the absence from the earlier one of a unified policy.

In spite of Russia's progress toward modernization since Peter the Great, most Westerners, even in the last decades of the empire, found the country backward, but exotic—an adjective which was to become odious to Russian communists.

Russia and Turkey, it will be recalled, were the only European powers, as of 1914, which still controlled the movements of their citizens by internal passports. Control over entrance into and exit from these countries was correspondingly more severe than in Western countries, where, by 1900, travel without passports or visas had become the rule—a happy practice which lapsed after World War I and to which only a partial return has been achieved since 1945, notably among the countries which cooperated in the Marshall Plan. Writing in 1912, an American woman, Mrs. Ruth Kedzie Wood, called the "passport bogie" the worst obstacle to travel to Russia, but she praised the Russians for their exceptional kindness and hospitality to visitors. Much more surprising to a present-day reader than this finding, which, despite ideological changes, is confirmed daily by most Western travelers to Soviet Russia, was this early tourist's enthusiasm about the amenities of Russian travel. She observed that the service and cuisine of the Russian hotels could not be excelled, and she even expressed gratification at the low price of accommodations. Like other visitors, before and since, she admired the excellence of Russian music and theater, and was charmed by the exuberance and vitality of the Russian people.[1]

Mrs. Wood wrote at a time when barriers to communication between Russia and the West were crumbling and when it seemed likely that Russia might evolve into a parliamentary state of Western type. Western scholars, such as Samuel Harper, of the University of Chicago, and the British historian Sir Bernard Pares, who later founded the London University School of Slavonic Studies, were making almost annual visits to Russia. These men enjoyed the most intimate contacts with intellectuals and politicians of all points of view—and in those days every possible school of thought and taste flourished in Russia. Travel restrictions on Russians going abroad in those days seem severe now by liberal Western standards but incredibly lenient in contrast to those that Stalin was one day to impose.

In 1903 and 1904 the prominent liberal historian and politician Paul Milyukov made two separate visits to the United States, where he delivered, among others, the Crane Lectures at the University of Chicago and the Lowell Lectures in Boston. In 1905

[1] Ruth Kedzie Wood, *The Tourist's Russia*, New York, 1912, pp. 3, 9, 12-13, 34, 37.

Milyukov published in English a book entitled *Russia and Its Crisis*. Based on his American lectures, it attacked from many angles the "official Russia," to which he contrasted the "Russia of the future" that he was confident was soon to enjoy the blessings of liberty. As is well known, even revolutionaries like Lenin, who spent most of the period from 1900 to 1917 in Switzerland and other European countries, or Trotski, who was living in New York in 1917, succeeded without too much trouble in leaving and returning to Russia, although of course they could not, like Milyukov, carry on active legal political careers. Still, the fact that there was even a small bolshevik representation in the prerevolutionary Russian parliament helps to point up the contrast between the incipient pluralism of 1914 and the monolithism which has prevailed throughout most of the Soviet era. Unfortunately, as scholars such as Pares and the *émigré* Russian historian Michael Florinsky have noted, the old regime provided no positive program of action or beliefs, and the vast majority of educated Russians were probably in sympathy with opposition to the authorities. Despite censorship, the Russian press frequently criticized the government.[2]

In the years immediately before World War I, many outstanding Russian dancers, musicians, and writers made triumphal tours of Western Europe and the United States. In 1906 Maxim Gorki was warmly received in America, though the reception soured somewhat when it became known that the lady accompanying him was not his legal wife. Beginning in 1909, Russian ballet took Paris by storm. As Florinsky observes, ties with the West in many fields were intimate, and yet this fact was "not conclusive evidence that the traditional estrangement of Muscovy from the West was over."[3]

[2] See, for example, Sir Bernard Pares, *Russia and Reform*, London, 1907, especially Chapters II, V, and VII; Michael T. Florinsky, *Russia: A History and an Interpretation*, New York 1953, Vol. II, p. 1255; Sergei Pushkarev, *Rossiya v xix veke*, New York, 1956, p. 466.

[3] Florinsky, *loc.cit.* There is no comprehensive study of Russian-Western cultural relations under the tsarist regime, but much valuable material and insight is available in the great work of G. V. Plekhanov, *Istoriya russkoi obshchchestvennoi mysli*, three volumes, St. Petersburg and Moscow, 1914, 1915, 1917. See also, among others, E. J. Simmons, *English Literature and Culture in Russia*, Cambridge, Mass., 1935, D. S. von Mohrenschildt, *Russia in the Intellectual Life of Eighteenth Century France*, New York, 1936; Alexander von Schelting, *Russland und Europa*, Bern, 1948; and the very interesting article by Euphrosina Dvoichenko-Markov, "The American Philosophical Society and Early Russian-

In any case, the prestige acquired before 1917 by Russian literature and art in the West and in some Asian countries was later to prove very useful to the culture-conscious Soviet regime. Quite frequently in our own day foreigners entranced by Soviet performances of traditional Russian, Ukrainian, or Central Asian art forms have acclaimed as achievements of Soviet culture accomplishments that had their origins in "feudal" prerevolutionary cultures. For the preservation and mass dissemination of these, the Soviet regime has devoted great effort and expense.

Hating and fearing the corrupt and doomed—or so they perceived it—"capitalist environment" around them, to which, at least until they could remove it by gulps or by nibbles, they must make as advantageous an adjustment as possible, the Soviet leaders resorted increasingly to plausible but disingenuous persuasions in respect to the outside world.

At the same time they sought to protect the Soviet people against infection by "alien" ideas, which, they early began to assert, kept alive the "remnants of capitalism" in the consciousness of the masses. Unified, but in some cases nominally decentralized, administrative agencies were established to coordinate cultural diplomacy with over-all foreign policy. Under Kremlin direction this network of agencies has grown into a unique machinery for the guidance of culture contacts. The more positive functions required by this effort were assigned to organizations such as VOKS, which has already been mentioned, and Intourist, the official—and sole— Soviet tourist agency, which since 1929 has been responsible for what has facetiously been described as the "care and spoonfeeding" of foreign visitors. The State Committee for Cultural Relations with Foreign Countries, a powerful agency established in 1957, to which we have referred earlier, now exercises prime responsibility for exchanges at the governmental and semiofficial level. Representatives of this new agency travel with top-level American groups, such as the three-member delegation of United States observers of the elections to the Supreme Soviet in March 1958, which returned the visit of three Soviet citizens who came to this country in 1956

American Relations," in *Proceedings of the American Philosophical Society*, Vol. 94, 1950, pp. 549-610.

to watch the American presidential elections. Or, they direct Intourist to render special services to distinguished visitors, such as Mr. Averell Harriman, who made a very special tour in 1959. In the meantime, foreigners who traveled as ordinary tourists have usually remained solely within the jurisdiction of Intourist; while the Soviet cultural organizations, including, in the cases of very high-ranking persons, the Ministry of Culture itself, have assisted Intourist in arranging for meetings or supplying artistic materials or, in some cases, have acted as sponsors of important visits. Depending on the circumstances, other Soviet bodies, such as the Academy of Sciences of the U.S.S.R. or the Ministry of Health, have also continued in the past few years, as in the Stalin era, to play their parts in the exchange process.

The contemporary Soviet pattern, characterized by the existence of one or more organizations designed to deal with almost any conceivable type of exchange, took a while to take shape, and indeed is still evolving. But a peculiar sensitiveness about impressions made upon foreign visitors—and by Soviet representatives abroad —has characterized Soviet foreign policy from its inception. This is indicated by Lenin's statement that he would have liked to see John Reed's famous book, *Ten Days That Shook the World*, translated into all languages and distributed in millions of copies —a desire recalled in 1932 by the editor of an important collection of testimonials of foreign celebrities, entitled *Through Foreign Eyes*.[4]

Soviet foreign cultural policy has, of course, been affected by shifting currents of foreign and domestic politics, but it was shaped and achieved consistency under the pressure of Kremlin determination to exploit it for the survival and advancement of Soviet power. Consequently, formal aspects of international relations, such as the existence or nonexistence of diplomatic relations between Soviet Russia and other countries, have not usually played a decisive role in Soviet foreign cultural relations. As a matter of fact, such relations, at least between the United States and Russia, were, in significant respects, freer and more spontaneous during the 1920's,

---

[4] M. Zhivov, ed., *Glazami inostrantsev*, Moscow, 1932, p. 686. This is an extraordinarily interesting anthology of statements by distinguished foreign intellectuals who visited Soviet Russia in the 1920's and early 1930's.

when formal Soviet-United States diplomatic relations had not yet been established, than during any subsequent period.[5]

The typical Stalin pattern, which, of course, has become more flexible since the great dictator's death, was established during the tense, fear-ridden years of external threat from the Nazis and of internal deprivation necessitated by the first and second Five Year Plans in the late 1920's and early and mid-1930's. This pattern was marked by contradictions. While not repudiating world revolution and while continuing its proselytizing of foreign intellectuals—an effort facilitated, of course, by the 1929-1933 depression and the apparent success of the Soviet planned economy—Moscow also sought to normalize its diplomatic relations with the British, French, and American governments and to build a defensive coalition against Germany, Japan, and Italy. Stalinist policy, drawing on Marx, Machiavelli, and Peter the Great, was so full of paradoxes that foreign responses to it varied greatly. The Kremlin promised trade to profit-hungry industrialists, extolled old-fashioned humanitarianism to visiting clergymen, and talked socialism to "progressives." Naturally, a policy so warped by ulterior motives has not been easy for foreign governments to cope with or to understand, although in judging it we should not forget the Western attitudes of anti-Russian prejudice, smugness, and self-righteous moralizing which helped to exacerbate Soviet hostility toward the West.

Travel to and from the Soviet Union has normally been numerically restricted, highly selective, especially on the Soviet side, and politically significant. In comparison with the visits by two or three million Englishmen every year to France or by hundreds of thousands of Americans every year to Italy, France, or England, the few hundred or, at most, few thousand persons involved with any noncommunist foreign nation in Soviet exchanges of tourists or other categories of nonmilitary and nongovernmental travelers

[5] This statement can be confirmed by leafing through some of the volumes on Russia published by the Vanguard Press of New York in the 1920's, and comparing the fullness and richness of detail which their authors were able to achieve with the far more limited results of travel and observation, even by gifted writers such as Edmund Wilson, in the 1930's. Compare, for example, Karl Borders' *Village Life Under the Soviets*, 1927, or H. N. Brailsford's publication of the same year, *How the Soviets Work*, with the section on Russia in Wilson's *Red, Black, Blond and Olive*, New York, 1956.

seem like a thin trickle. However, travel to Russia has been unusually purposeful travel, performed in large part by opinion leaders from the upper strata of the professions, arts and sciences, and politics and business. Travel by Russians, of course, has been by military personnel or by officials or personnel ultimately under official guidance and supervision.

On both sides Soviet-non-Soviet exchanges have involved relatively few "workers and peasants" and a heavy proportion of executives and celebrities. Famous authors like H. G. Wells, press moguls like the head of the Associated Press, Roy Howard—both received by Stalin in the Kremlin—or engineers like Colonel Hugh L. Cooper played a more conspicuous and presumably a more influential role than did the few thousand European and American workingmen who, lured by promises of high wages during the depression of the early 1930's, worked in Soviet mines, mills, or factories—and either ended their lives in prisons or "corrective labor camps" or dropped into obscurity in Russia or at home. However, there were individuals who came to Russia as manual workers, returned home tempered and enlightened by their experience, and went on to achieve careers of distinction. Among them were John Scott, who, as a young American college graduate, learned welding in order to do useful work in Russia and recorded his experiences in a classic account, *Behind the Urals*, and Walter Reuther, who worked for more than a year in the first big Soviet automobile plant, at Gorki.[6]

Of course, much travel to Soviet Russia has been by communists on official business or for purposes of instruction. With this traffic, important though it is, we are only incidentally concerned. Its special character and clandestine nature make it difficult to study, and its significance, at least in terms of its influence on noncommunist opinion, has probably been far less than that of the more open and therefore apparently normal kinds of exchanges of persons described in this book.

A considerable number even of the bourgeois foreigners who have visited Russia have, in a sense, been ideological pilgrims. As

[6] For an account of the tribulations experienced by one American worker—in this case a communist—see Andrew Smith, *I Was a Soviet Worker*, New York, 1936.

far as the West is concerned, the element of ideological attraction or at least of sympathy—which in most cases probably did not involve conscious acceptance of Soviet doctrine, still less of communist discipline—was strongest in the late 1920's and early 1930's. It waned with the great purges of 1936-1938, the Nazi-Soviet Pact of 1939, and the outburst of Soviet imperialism after World War II. Many Asians, however, to whom the chief international evil has seemed to be Western foreign policy, rather than Soviet, tended in the 1940's and 1950's to cling to illusions about the new Soviet civilization which Western liberals had earlier discarded.

As Louis Fischer has pointed out, in the 1930's "for thousands of intellectuals and intelligent people a trip to Russia had become a compulsory summer course with credit."[7] Many of these visitors, as Fischer rightly notes, were idealists with "live hearts and a devotion to mankind."

In so far as the effects and impact of these exchanges can be gauged—and appraisal of their influence is usually difficult or even impossible—this can best be done as we proceed with their specific examination in time and space. However, a few preliminary observations may be ventured here. The exchanges prior to the death of Stalin, especially those of the 1920's and 1930's, helped to shape or to intensify some significant attitudes both on the Soviet and on the non-Soviet sides.

On the Soviet side, good will and even admiration for Western technical and scientific personnel were fostered by contacts and collaboration between Soviet and German, English, and American engineers and scientists. A very considerable reservoir of good will toward America, in particular, was built up by this type of relationship and by activities of Quaker, Y.M.C.A., Near East Relief, American Red Cross, Jewish Joint Distribution Committee, and other philanthropic agencies. As even an unfriendly critic of American policy toward Russia has noted, the relief work done in the U.S.S.R. by the American Relief Administration in 1921-1923 helped to create the "surprising degree of good will toward America" manifested in Russia all through the interwar years.[8]

[7] Louis Fischer, *Men and Politics*, New York, 1941, p. 196.
[8] William Appleman Williams, *American-Russian Relations 1781-1947*, New York and Toronto, 1952, p. 203.

Even if such influences did not change official Soviet attitudes, they may have mitigated official hostility and they certainly left a very positive impression on the Soviet "man in the street."

Because of the heterogeneity of views and personnel involved on the non-Soviet side, it is even more difficult than in the U.S.S.R. to generalize about the impact of these early exchanges there. It is certain, however, that in many cases adroit Soviet stage management succeeded in creating in the minds of Western and Oriental visitors an impression that Russian life and culture were distinguished by a higher level of progress and a greater degree of social welfare and social justice than would have been discovered by free and unmanipulated field study. (Most visitors would not have been technically competent to engage in such study.) In some cases, particularly where fellow-travelers were concerned, the use of psychological or even of partly veiled financial bribery played its part in the creation and dissemination of impressions deemed desirable by Moscow.[9]

Certainly Kremlin exploitation of the ideological predispositions and personal foibles of many distinguished guests had its effect, as did outright deception and concealment of reality, combined very often with colossal ignorance on the part of the visitor. However, it would be a mistake to attribute the favorable impressions made on some foreign intellectuals entirely to Soviet public relations techniques. At least in the period before the full unleashing of police terror in the late 1930's, there were features of Soviet life to which many Western intellectuals were likely to respond with sincere approval, regardless of official hospitality, which in any case was usually less elaborate in the earlier period than it has been since the mid 1930's. The Soviet atmosphere of apparent optimism, idealism, and dedication to the community interest made an enormously favorable impression upon early visitors such as William C. Bullitt, Lincoln Steffens, who accompanied Bullitt on an official mission in 1919, H. N. Brailsford, John Dewey, and many others. Lincoln Steffens reported on his return from Russia,

[9] A particularly subtle form of this technique and relationship is obliquely suggested in Nathan Leites and Elsa Bernaut, *Ritual of Liquidation*, Glencoe, Illinois, 1954. See pp. 110 and 405 in connection with the alleged Kremlin "selection" of André Gide and another prominent Western writer as "Western highbrow" sympathizers.

"I have been over into the future, and it works." As Theodore Draper has observed, Steffens' remark, made casually to Bernard Baruch, became one of the most seductive of communist slogans in a streamlined version: "I have seen the Future, and it works."[10]

After his Russian trip in 1928 John Dewey reported that he had found among the Russians "a vitality and a kind of confidence in life" that afforded one of the most stimulating experiences of his own life. Dewey, like many other representatives of a West long since grown skeptical, was impressed by the communists' depth of conviction, which he described as "religious." It should be noted that Dewey was careful to state that he did not wish to see the Russian experiment tried in his own country. He advocated American recognition of the Soviet government, asserting, "I came away with the feeling that the maintenance of barriers that prevent intercourse, knowledge and understanding is close to a crime against humanity."[11] Like H. N. Brailsford in 1927, Dewey sensed dangers in bolshevik intolerance and dogmatism; in particular he feared a future when Soviet idealism and enthusiasm would be replaced by careerism and bureaucracy.

Even H. G. Wells on his first Russian trip in 1920 and Bertrand Russell, in the same year, had been impressed by Soviet energy and sense of purpose, although both rejected bolshevism. Russell, in particular, took a position of utter condemnation which was long to put him in a very small minority among Western liberals.

The views of men like John Dewey regarding the Soviet Union were probably fairly representative of Western enlightened opinion during most of the first two decades of communist power. Western liberals were repelled by Soviet dictatorship—Dewey later took a prominent part in discrediting the accusations made against Leon Trotski in the notorious Moscow "show" trials— but in a world recovering from war and threatened by a new war, and a world whose economy alternated between mad inflation and dismal depression, they were inclined to listen with a certain sympathy to Soviet protestations of peaceful intent and claims of steady social progress. Perhaps the findings of Western liberals in this

[10] Theodore Draper, *The Roots of American Communism*, New York, 1957, p. 115.
[11] John Dewey, *Impressions of Soviet Russia*, New York, 1929, pp. 93, 114, 131.

period lent to Soviet propaganda claims a greater degree of credence than they deserved, but they were not so inappropriate to their day as they seem to later observers.

The partly favorable, partly negative images resulting from the contacts which occurred in the 1920's were reinforced by the much more numerous encounters of the 1930's, when a veritable flood of professors, theologians, musicians, writers, artists, and critics swelled the coffers and taxed the facilities of Intourist. Among the visitors one might mention Will Rogers, George Bernard Shaw, Harold Laski, Jawaharlal Nehru, John Gunther, Sherwood Eddy, and the peripatetic American journalist Maurice Hindus, whose long summer visits resulted in almost annual books. Some of the "commuters" of the 1930's, of course, had already made trips in the 1920's. Such travelers as Hindus or Samuel Harper or the German scholar Klaus Mehnert who, in 1957, made his twelfth trip, enjoyed, even as late as the early 1930's, a degree of freedom not duplicated until the brief "thaw" of 1954-1955—and probably not even then. Klaus Mehnert was allowed, in the late 1920's, to live like a Russian student while he gathered material for his book *Youth in Soviet Russia*.[12] He lived, not in hotels, but in student hostels and dormitories. Karl Borders spent more than a year as a member of the staff of an American organization supervising a group of government agricultural enterprises in the North Caucasus and traveled in scores of villages.

As late as 1934 Samuel Harper was urged by a local secretary of the Soviet communist party to go "without a chaperone" on his visit to a village.[13] And as late as 1934-1937 William H. E. Johnson "was enabled to pursue his graduate studies in one of the finest Soviet institutions of learning."[14]

Independent thinkers like Brailsford or Dewey, who were capable of picking and choosing from an alien system elements they thought worthy of application to or at least of study in their own society, were of course not the only type of foreign intellectuals who came to Russia in the 1920's and 1930's. To many

[12] Klaus Mehnert, *Youth in Soviet Russia*, trans. by Michael Davidson, New York, 1933.

[13] Paul Harper, ed., *The Russia I Believe In*, Chicago, 1945, p. 213.

[14] W. H. E. Johnson, *Russia's Educational Heritage*, New Brunswick, 1950, p. ix.

visitors a statement contained in the Soviet anthology to which we have referred was at least partly applicable. By 1932, according to its editor, the more than one hundred foreign writers who had visited Russia had recognized that the U.S.S.R. was "the only country where there is life, and where a new man is being born, who is hammering out a new future."[15]

Among the writers represented in this collection was the Dane, Martin Andersen-Nexe, who after his visit in 1922 became one of Soviet Russia's most ardent admirers and frequent visitors. John Dos Passos, who arrived in 1928, was also favorably impressed, though he never became a communist and was later to turn violently anti-Soviet—an evolution similar to that experienced by many of his fellow writers, such as Upton Sinclair, who was represented in this early anthology, or André Malraux, who was not. It is, incidentally, interesting that many of the names represented in this collection, such as those of Johannes Becher and Anna Seghers, Michael Gold, Jean Richard Block, and Romain Rolland, were destined for prominence in communist and "progressive" literary circles in later years.

In the 1930's VOKS and other Soviet organizations perfected the sometimes seductive practice of sending favored guests on free tours of selected parts of Russia—a practice which in various forms has persisted to our own day. For lesser lights the VOKS Bureau for the Reception of Foreigners often held literary teas or dispensed other forms of hospitality. Much of this activity was on a superficial level and had little effect, although it helped to nurture the illusions of visitors about Soviet conditions and played its part in concealing ugly realities.

Edmund Wilson, in the diary of his 1935 Soviet trip, gives us glimpses of some of the more innocuous kinds of guided-tour techniques. He refers, for example, to a "meeting especially held for the enlightenment of a delegation of American schoolteachers," at which Prince Dmitri Mirski, a gifted Russian aristocrat who, having been converted to Marxism in London and permitted to return to Russia through the aid of Maxim Gorki in 1932, presented the official Kremlin line on bourgeois literature. Some hint of the grim reality undreamed of by the foreign innocents is con-

[15] Zhivov, *op.cit.*, p. 685.

39

veyed, incidentally, by Wilson's account of Mirski's fate. He disappeared almost without trace in 1937.[16] Although Wilson was not at the time fully aware of the terroristic aspects of Soviet communism, he recorded many interesting bits of evidence of the all-pervading police surveillance.

Arthur Koestler had joined the German communist party shortly before he spent his year in the U.S.S.R., in 1932-1933, but his experiences were representative of Soviet political exploitation of susceptible intellectuals, regardless of party affiliation. Koestler went to Russia on invitation of the International Organization of Revolutionary Writers, arranged by his then friend, the German communist writer Johannes Becher, with the purpose of producing a laudatory account of the benefits of the first Five Year Plan. Despite the prevailing famine conditions, Intourist, VOKS, and other agencies saw to it that he was surprisingly well provided with the amenities of life.

Koestler records with sourish humor the experiences, for example, of a noncommunist Negro American writer who had come to Russia together with forty other Negroes, upon invitation of the Soviet film trust, to make a film concerning persecution of Negroes in America. When this project was cancelled, apparently to avoid offense to the United States government in the negotiations looking toward establishment of diplomatic relations which were then proceeding, a new one, for the production of a book comparing Soviet Central Asia with the American South, was substituted. Ample funds, of course, were provided.[17] For a while Koestler was pressed into service, together with a motley crew of other writers who bore the odd designation of "international proletarian writers' brigade," and sent on a propaganda tour of Uzbekistan. In Koestler's case, although several Soviet publishing houses contracted to publish his *Red Days*—on the strength, he states, of the Comintern letter that he carried—only one small edition appeared. Many writers—including both communists and noncommunists—who were considered by the Soviet authorities to be more reliable than the volatile Koestler, fared better. As Koestler notes,

[16] Wilson, *op.cit.* See especially pp. 281-299.
[17] Arthur Koestler, *The Invisible Writing*, Boston, 1954, pp. 45, 50, 61, 69, 112-120, 152-153.

"Such writers were delighted at the news that the Uzbeks, Tadz-hiks, and Eskimos were all eager to read their books, and they would have been very indignant at the suggestion that the advance payments from the various State publishing firms amounted to bribes."[18]

In some instances, of course, even the most lavish literary hos-pitality did not achieve its political objective. The case of the French writer André Gide furnishes an example. In 1936 Gide, who had already been lauded in that year in an article in *The Small Soviet Encyclopedia* as a "partisan of the U.S.S.R. and the proletarian revolution," made a triumphal tour of Russia. And yet, somehow, fulsome adulation and an endless succession of monotonously similar ceremonies in his honor disgusted Gide, who, after his return to France, wrote his jeering *Retour de l'URSS* in which he lashed out at Soviet cultural sterility and growing social inequality.

Perhaps, in part, the prestige lost by the Kremlin cultural strate-gists as a result of this fiasco was regained in 1937 with publication of the late Lion Feuchtwanger's *Moscow 1937*. Feuchtwanger ridiculed Gide's report. He found in Russia only radiant happiness and firm ideological conviction. Like many other Western intel-lectuals of that era—even including the incipiently skeptical Ed-mund Wilson—Feuchtwanger waxed ecstatic over the "pampered" position of "savants, artists and writers" in Russia. Presumably he had not read, or taken seriously, the exposure of the sycophantic role to which Russian men of letters had been reduced, published a few years earlier by Max Eastman.[19]

Like many another foreign celebrity before and since whom the regime considered worth cultivating, Feuchtwanger was received in the Kremlin. A few years earlier his fellow German writer Emil Ludwig had also seen Stalin. The latter took pains to assure Ludwig that Russians had at least as high an opinion of Germans as of other peoples. Warmed perhaps by hospitality, Feuchtwanger assured the world that all was well in a country in which visiting writers were received by the supreme leader himself and in which,

[18] *Ibid.*, p. 153.
[19] *Artists in Uniform*, New York, 1934.

he purred, "interpreters of amazing understanding are at one's disposal."[20]

In the thirties, as in the forties and fifties, Moscow probed ceaselessly for areas susceptible to ideological penetration. After the rise of Hitler, Poland, wracked by nationality conflicts and fearful of its mighty Teutonic neighbor, became one of the most vulnerable. Yuli Margolin, a Polish Jew and the author of one of the best accounts of life in Soviet forced-labor camps, writes that ten to fifteen per cent of the Jewish youth of Poland in the 1930's were "communized," although most of those attracted by dialectical materialism had only the foggiest notion of Soviet reality.[21]

As Margolin points out, many Polish tourists spent a week in the U.S.S.R. and returned "with a box of Soviet chocolates and with pleasant memories," but with no knowledge of the secret world of Soviet concentration camps. Many of the "illegal tourists" who crossed the border into Russia to escape Polish poverty and anti-Semitism dropped completely from sight, although Margolin, who was arrested by the Russians when they seized Eastern Poland in 1939, did meet one of these unfortunate escapees in a camp in North Russia.

The Polish radical intelligentsia was cultivated in the Hitler period by the dispatching of prominent Soviet intellectuals to such international congresses in Poland as the Warsaw Historical Congress of 1933. Helen Lerner, then vice chairman of VOKS, expressed keen satisfaction in an article in *Soviet Culture Review*, Number one, 1934, regarding the progress of Soviet-Polish "cultural *rapprochement*." Among other things, Mrs. Lerner noted that a special number of a leading Polish literary journal had for the first time been devoted to Soviet literature, with stress on its "cheerfulness" and "confidence."

One Pole who experienced Soviet hospitality in two rather different capacities and who consequently spoke with unusual authority on certain aspects of Soviet culture was the former Warsaw socialist lawyer, Jerzy Gliksman. His brother, Victor Alter, together with Henryk Erlich, who like Alter was a renowned socialist leader, was put to death by Stalin in 1941, although this

---

[20] Lion Feuchtwanger, *Moscow 1937*, New York, 1937, p. 55.
[21] Yuli Margolin, *Puteshestvie v stranu ze-ka*, New York, 1952, p. 5.

fact was not officially admitted by the Soviet authorities until February 1943, in reply to an inquiry from William Green, president of the American Federation of Labor. In 1935 Gliksman was a guest of Intourist. In 1939 he became a prisoner of the Soviet secret police. During Gliksman's 1935 visit VOKS extended every courtesy to him and his colleagues. As he notes: "VOKS representatives always accompanied us to all places we visited. A young girl, a pretty brunette, was assigned to me as my guide."[22] As a lawyer of humanitarian leanings Gliksman was interested in Soviet penal practice. He requested permission to visit a prison, and to his surprise the request was granted. VOKS took him, together with a "distinguished group of people, which included correspondents of great foreign newspapers, several writers, artists, labor leaders, et cetera," to the model prison camp at Bolshevo, near Moscow. Life at Bolshevo, it appeared, was idyllic. "How beautiful the world could be!" a French movie director in Gliksman's party exclaimed.[23] One must read Jerzy Gliksman's moving book from cover to cover for the answer to the question he put to himself after visiting Bolshevo—was all that he had seen "artful propaganda, make-believe, mere fiction"?

Mention has already been made of a peculiarly Soviet type of cultural exchange, namely the entertainment and instruction of foreign labor delegations. A few early, influential delegations of this character should be mentioned, for travel by, and slanted reporting of the experiences of, important groups has probably been an even more seductive Soviet propaganda weapon than the exploitation of distinguished individual visitors. Groups, especially if they represent organizations with millions of members, usually command more prestige and influence in their home countries than even the most distinguished individual travelers. Moreover, it is, on the whole, easier to keep members of groups, with full schedules of formal activities, away from sights and sounds and smells not intended for foreigners. It is of course more economical to assign top-flight interpreters and skilled guides to groups than to individuals. Both before and since World War II, very few persons who have traveled in Russia, whether alone or in delega-

---

[22] Jerzy Gliksman, *Tell the West*, New York, 1948, p. 164.
[23] *Ibid.*, p. 175.

tions, have had either the background knowledge or the linguistic equipment necessary to look behind the curtain in the tourist's Soviet Union. The Soviet regime has been rather successful, particularly in the handling of delegations, in combining the appearance of spontaneity with a maximum of surveillance. Moreover, especially in the period when it was still plausible for Western liberals to credit the U.S.S.R. with having, if not political, at least economic democracy, both ideological preconceptions and the natural desire of decent people to refrain from saying harsh things about gracious hosts—and no one who has been in Russia, whatever his ideological position, can deny that Russians can be warmly hospitable—have helped to shape an outcome of many delegation visits that has been very satisfactory from the Kremlin's point of view. On the other hand, many delegations—particularly trade-union delegations—published excellent, objective reports that contributed greatly to Western knowledge of Soviet conditions and helped to combat the tendency to hysteria evident in extremist circles, both of the left and of the right.

One such report was that entitled *Russia Today*, published in 1925 by a British labor delegation that was in the Soviet Union in November and December 1924. The British group criticized the dictatorial aspects of the Soviet regime, which of course at that time had not reached the monstrous proportions they were to attain later, but it found much to praise in Soviet social welfare and nationality policies. In 1927 an American labor delegation was received by Stalin himself. Stalin's remarks to this group were published in every edition of his *Problems of Leninism* until 1946 when, perhaps in anticipation of a deterioration of Soviet-American relations, they were omitted. According to one scholar, the reports of the British and American trade-union delegations constituted "milestones in the change of opinion" in the West toward a more balanced attitude regarding Russia.[24]

Some of the persons who traveled to Soviet Russia in the 1920's

[24] Meno J. Lovenstein, *American Opinion of Soviet Russia*, Washington, 1941, p. 162. Among the many informative works which resulted from delegation travel in the 1930's, mention should be made of the book *Twelve Studies in Soviet Russia*, published in London in 1933. This was edited for the New Fabian Research Bureau by Margaret I. Cole and had introductions by G. D. H. Cole and Clement Attlee.

and 1930's went as ordinary tourists, if indeed one may so describe the relatively small number of intellectually venturesome individuals who undertook to visit the "land of socialism." Soviet tourism prior to World War II was on a smaller scale than after the death of Stalin, but it was on a fairly substantial scale in comparison to the late Stalin freeze, at least as far as travel by noncommunists, especially Americans, is concerned. Normal tourist traffic faded out in 1940 and only began to be resumed on a substantial scale in 1952. Travel by noncommunists spurted suddenly in 1955. On August 14 of that year Clifton Daniel reported in the *New York Times* that by August 1, 30,000 foreigners had been accommodated by Intourist and that this figure was, according to Intourist, larger than the total of any full year before the war. This figure, of course, was greatly exceeded in 1958, 1959 and 1960.

Interesting material on tourists and other travelers in Russia both before and after the establishment of Intourist is contained in the *Soviet Union Review*, a relatively objective magazine published in the 1920's and 1930's by Amtorg, a Soviet trading organization which has operated in the United States since 1923. The issue of this publication for October 1, 1923, reported that in that year 411 foreigners had attended the All-Russian Agricultural Exhibition in Moscow in August and September.[25] More than 1,200 foreigners visited the Soviet Union during the last two months of 1927, mostly to attend the celebration of the tenth anniversary of the bolshevik revolution. The largest groups came from Germany, England, and France. Egypt, Syria, Palestine, Brazil, Cuba, Java, and India sent delegations for the first time. Presumably most of these visitors were communists.

In 1928 about 1,600 tourists visited the Soviet Union during the summer months. Ninety-five per cent of these were Americans. Soviet-regulated tourism as we know it even today began with

[25] One hundred and seven of these were from Germany, 57 from Estonia, 53 from Latvia, 44 from Japan, 11 from the United States, 10 from England, 3 from Palestine, 9 from France, 2 from Persia, and small numbers from other countries of Europe and Asia. According to the same source for February 15, 1926, the Bureau for the Reception of Foreigners registered 1,664 visits by foreigners during 1925. One hundred and twenty-two were from Germany, and 113 from the United States, these being the two largest groups. Among the visitors were 109 scientists, 79 artists, 36 official representatives, 61 persons "in public and political life," 109 journalists, 17 teachers, 53 industrialists, 33 students, and 40 workers and clerks.

the establishment in 1929 of Intourist, set up by joint action of the Commissariats for Foreign and Domestic Trade, and Ways of Communications, and by the Soviet mercantile fleet. Intourist was authorized to provide for all the needs of foreign tourists. Tourists booked for trips were entitled to all necessary transportation, the services of guides and interpreters and, of course, escorted visits to museums and other places of interest. Intourist even arranged for hunting trips for foreigners. Intourist organized an extensive advertising campaign throughout Europe and the United States in 1929. Rather extravagant plans apparently were made for a future that was slow in coming. The first Five Year Plan included a program for building new hotels; according to one official American publication, Intourist hoped to have accommodations by 1933 for 150,000 tourists. This source also reported that Intourist had booked a special train with shower baths and electric fans on the occasion of the visit of a group of Americans in 1929.[26] While efforts—not always successful—were made to assure the comfort and pleasure of tourists and in some cases to exert propaganda pressures on them, elaborate regulations concerning passports, visas, photography, free association with Soviet citizens, and related matters were also introduced as fear of alleged foreign espionage developed and Soviet Russia reverted increasingly to traditional despotic practices.[27] Even as late as the early 1930's the Soviet authorities were far more candid in admitting the existence of strict regulations than they became in the later Stalin era.

The favorable image of the Soviet Union implanted in the minds of some Western intellectuals in the late 1920's and early 1930's tended to resist change. It grew faded and tarnished, perhaps, but its value to the Kremlin lay in its blurring of the abhorrent record, by democratic standards, made in those years by Soviet totalitarianism. Many factors contributed to the Kremlin's success in disseminating and preserving illusions. The well-known American novelist James T. Farrell has recently pointed to some of these. What he says about the attractions of communism is, in many ways, even more applicable to the vaguer, more diffuse appeal of "pro-

[26] *The Promotion of Tourist Travel by Foreign Countries*, Washington, D. C., 1931, pp. 57-58.
[27] *A Pocket Guide to the Soviet Union*, Moscow, 1932, p. 594.

gressivism" and "economic democracy": "A cult of hardboiledness and a profound political innocence on the part of many people in the 1920's were two of the main causes determining the influx of many intellectuals into the Communist Party. A further factor was the lack of sufficient critical evidence about the course of events in the Soviet Union. Not only were American visitors self-deceived, but others distorted the evidence in the late 1920's and the early 1930's."[28]

The *Soviet Union Review* reported in December 1929 that more than 3,000 tourists had visited the U.S.S.R. in the summer of that year.[29] The *Review* reported in November 1931 that tourist travel that year was double that of two years before. By 1934 it was able to state that "travel has grown steadily as an organized institution since 1928." In 1934, it reported, six ships were scheduled to come to the U.S.S.R. in connection with European tours, and thirty organized tour parties had already made arrangements to visit the country. A 5,000-mile tour, headed by the distinguished journalist H. V. Kaltenborn, enabled American businessmen, in 1934, to investigate trade possibilities. It was sponsored by the Russian-American Chamber of Commerce, an organization that flourished with the spurt of Soviet-American trade in the early 1930's but became moribund about 1940.

No figures seem to be available for the middle and late thirties. With increasing hostility between Nazi Germany and Russia many of the bright, if grandiose, hopes of Intourist had to be deferred, to be revived only after the death of Stalin.

By the summer of 1939, although travel to Russia was continuing on a considerable scale, grim tension was in the air. When I made my first Soviet trip in June and July of that year, I had a number of grotesque experiences which, even if of a superficial nature, reflected the existence of an almost paranoid suspicion. Like other travelers of that year—and of many other years—I was

---

[28] James T. Farrell, "Communism in the U.S.A.," in *Problems of Communism*, No. 4, Vol. VII, July-August 1958, pp. 47-49. Quotation on p. 48.

[29] Sixty-six per cent of these tourists were Americans, 15 per cent were British, and 8 per cent were Germans. By profession, 25 per cent were businessmen; 24 per cent were teachers, students, scientists, doctors, engineers, artists, or writers; 3 per cent were artisans and farmers; and 17 per cent were industrial or clerical workers.

astounded and irritated by the maniacal thoroughness of frontier formalities and baggage examination, to which my experience in post-Stalin travel in Russia has, it should be recorded, contrasted very pleasantly. Tough, unsmiling border guards actually tapped an orange that I carried as if it might have been a bomb. The lining of a suitcase was torn out in the course of a fantastically detailed examination, and the contents of wallets had to be fully exposed to examination. The border crossing set a pattern of regulation which, combined with the obstructionism practiced by Intourist and VOKS officials and the evasiveness of scholars whom I attempted to contact, left a sour taste. The contrast between such treatment in Russia and the courtesy and helpfulness encountered in Finland immediately thereafter, or even the relative normality of behavior of Germans during the same summer, left a deep and permanent impression. After all, other countries were also in danger, but it was only in Russia that one was actually taken to an unfinished building in response to a request for permission to work in a library, or that after a week of persistent asking for interviews with scholars one was finally invited to a stiff and formal VOKS tea.

During World War II, Soviet cultural organizations supported the Kremlin's efforts to obtain maximum American and British help with Soviet war aims. At this time VOKS, for example, acted as consignee for relief supplies collected in America by Russian War Relief and other private philanthropic organizations. Naturally enough, VOKS devoted much effort during World War II to assisting such organizations as the National Council of American-Soviet Friendship and the Society for Cultural Relations between the Peoples of the British Commonwealth and the U.S.S.R. in sponsoring Soviet films and exhibitions, celebrating Soviet holidays, showing posters, selling pro-Soviet literature, and the like. VOKS furnished assistance to Walter Graebner, an editor of *Life* magazine, who spent three months in Russia in 1942 gathering material for a special Russian issue published on March 29, 1943. A *Life* publicity release dated March 23, 1943, stated, among other things, that "VOKS got together ten thousand photographs covering every phase of the U.S.S.R. that *Life* was interested in."

During and shortly after World War II, VOKS arranged for

concerts of English and American music and joined with the American embassy in sponsoring an exhibition of American prefabricated housing. VOKS played a major role in welcoming foreign scientists and other scholars who attended the celebration of the 220th anniversary of the Academy of Sciences of the U.S.S.R. in June 1945. Some of the scientists were disappointed, however, in the superficial nature of the formal program of entertainment and after a few days began to arrange conferences on their own. They were able to do so, probably, because the Soviet government at this period was anxious to make the best possible impression upon them. In this connection it is interesting that the Australian botanist Eric Ashby, who, as scientific attaché of the Australian legation, attended the 1945 celebration, wrote later that VOKS was quite expert in conducting brief, standardized tours, escorting visitors to museums and the ballet, and setting up formal meetings with representatives of the Soviet intelligentsia, but "for the serious student who comes to Russia for more than a month, and who wants more information than is contained in the official 'handouts,' VOKS is a major obstacle to cultural and scientific relations."[30]

The correctness of Ashby's judgment is indicated by an incident that came to my attention while I was on the staff of the American embassy in Moscow. An American scientist who had attended the Academy anniversary was sent back a few months later as a United States government official charged with effecting cooperation between Soviet and American weather services. The scientist had been treated with hearty cordiality as a guest. He had had many pleasant conversations and had been presented with valuable publications. But when he returned as an official, to transact practical government business, he ran into a stone wall of obstructiveness. He could not even make contact on the telephone with his former friends. Disheartened and disgusted, he soon returned to the United States. Even in 1959, when in connection with the American-Soviet exchange of exhibitions and the propaganda build-up for the Eisenhower-Khrushchev exchange of visits there was a new wave of official Soviet cordiality, the "run-around" was administered to many travelers who sought in Russia to achieve goals more substantial than sight-seeing.

[30] Eric Ashby, *Scientist in Russia*, New York, 1947, p. 13.

According to one expert, in the first eight months after the surrender of Nazi Germany "nearly 3,000 Soviet artists and other citizens were sent abroad in small companies, usually led by a VOKS official. They gave thousands of performances and speeches in most countries of Europe and Eastern Asia. . . ."[31] Perhaps partly as a result of these activities, a Soviet journalist was able to state in 1947 that "whereas formerly the U.S.S.R. Friendship Societies included mostly representatives of the progressive intelligentsia, chiefly from the capitals of the world, today these organizations have acquired a broad base among the masses."[32] Within a relatively short time after the end of the war, however, the prestige of VOKS and its affiliates in the noncommunist countries began to decline. Many noncommunist intellectuals who had joined Soviet friendship societies resigned in indignation or embarrassment. During the most intense period of the cold war, and especially during the Korean conflict, the tone of the VOKS *Bulletin* did not differ very much from that of *Pravda*. Screaming war propaganda crowded out cultural material from the pages even of this magazine, intended for foreign consumption.

The attitude which dominated Soviet cultural diplomacy in Stalin's last years was well represented in a statement made by Alexander Gerasimov, then president of the Academy of Arts of the Soviet Union, who wrote in the party weekly, *Kultura i Zhizn (Culture and Life)* for July 21, 1950, that, although not everyone was able to come to the U.S.S.R., paintings by Soviet artists were available for all to see and that they would help the people of Europe and Asia to study the building of socialism. Soviet artists, he went on, must continually remember their duty to the working people of the whole world.

Soviet travel to noncommunist countries has, at least until recent years, always been on a much smaller scale than travel by bourgeois foreigners to Russia. However, the sending of cultural, scientific, and athletic groups abroad did play an important part in Soviet foreign relations even before World War II. For example, in April 1928 the Moscow Art Theater presented in London a num-

[31] Louis Nemzer, "The Soviet Friendship Societies," in *Public Opinion Quarterly*, Vol. XIII, No. 2, Summer 1949, pp. 265-284. Quotation on p. 272.
[32] *Ibid.*, p. 281.

ber of classical Russian plays, including Ostrovski's *Poverty Is No Crime* and Chekhov's *Cherry Orchard*. In July 1929 a Soviet ballet company performed at Covent Garden. The great Russian physiologist Pavlov visited the United States in 1923 and again in 1929. During the second visit he attended the thirteenth International Physiological Congress in Boston and was a guest of Professor Walter Cannon of Harvard University. He also attended an international psychological conference at Yale University. Professor Cannon was Pavlov's guest at the International Physiological Congress in the Soviet Union in 1935. Scientific congresses held in Moscow, such as this International Physiological Congress, or the 1937 International Geological Congress, helped to establish friendly collaboration between Soviet and foreign scientists.

Unfortunately, some Soviet scientists fell under Kremlin suspicion partly as a result of ties with foreign colleagues and a number, such as the famous geneticist Sergei Vavilov, perished in exile. In connection with several international scientific congresses in the late 1930's, permission to attend, which had been granted to Soviet savants, was withdrawn without explanation by the Soviet authorities—a phenomenon not unknown, incidentally, even in the post-Stalin era.

Very favorable publicity for Soviet culture was gained by impressive Soviet pavilions and exhibits at the Paris International Exposition in 1937 and the New York World's Fair in 1938 and 1939. The latter, however, stirred up considerable controversy in the United States. There was indignation because the Soviet pavilion towered above all others. There were even the inevitable demands for a Congressional investigation.

By 1940 a Soviet political handbook made bold to say, with what was then still considerable exaggeration, that "in international sports contests the representatives of the Soviet Union gain the first places."[33] Although Soviet teams had played abroad in soccer and other matches, athletics did not become a major instrument of Soviet propaganda until after World War II. In 1945 a Soviet soccer team went to England, where it scored impressive victories. As of the end of 1946 the Soviet Union was represented in only two athletic organizations, but between 1946 and 1955 it joined

[33] *Politicheski slovar*, Moscow, 1940, p. 602.

twenty-five more. Russia was able to participate in the 1952 Olympic Games as a result of official recognition of the Soviet Olympic Committee in May 1951.[34]

In chess, which has been considered a "mass sport" in the Soviet Union for several decades and in which, of course, tsarist Russia also held a position of leadership, the Soviet master Botvinnik gained prestige for his country in 1936 by sharing first place in the International Chess Tournament at Nottingham. *Pravda* went so far as to devote its lead article for August 29, 1936, to Botvinnik's showing. As is well known, Soviet chess masters have dominated the world chess arena since the early 1940's.[35]

In the 1920's and 1930's Soviet films won much acclaim abroad and received many prizes at international festivals.[36] As early as 1923 a Soviet film was awarded a prize in an American festival and by 1937, when the historical film *Peter I* won a special certificate at the Paris Exposition, Soviet films, like the Soviet theater, had achieved a brilliant reputation for originality of theme and technique. Soviet films did not take part in international contests between 1937 and 1945, however—a fact which reflected not only international tensions but the deterioration of Soviet artistic life under the impact of purges and intimidation of artists. Great artists like Sergei Eisenstein emerged from this experience mere shadows of their former vibrant selves.

Soviet studios did, however, continue to turn out outstanding productions in certain categories, such as documentaries and science films, and the Soviet cinema played an important role in early postwar propaganda successes, with victories, for example, at the Rome and Venice film festivals in 1945 and 1946.

It is clear from the foregoing that display of the achievements of Soviet culture had, by the end of the 1930's, become an important instrument of Soviet foreign policy. An elaborate, expensive, and effective machinery had been built up to facilitate cultural advertisement.

[34] John N. Washburn, "Sport as a Soviet Tool," in *Foreign Affairs*, Vol. 34, No. 3, April 1956, pp. 488-499.

[35] On this subject see *Soviet Chess*, Philadelphia, 1949.

[36] Considerable interesting data on the international impact of Soviet films is available in *The Soviet Cinematography*, Bombay, 1950. This is apparently a communist publication.

Let us turn now to the other major aspect of cultural exchange—the Soviet importation of foreign "know-how." The history of this process is full of irony. If it found dupes in the West, they were, in the main, the supposedly hardheaded businessmen and engineers who powerfully assisted the Soviet leaders in the industrialization of Russia. Stalin himself acknowledged the contribution made by Western help to Soviet economic growth when he told Eric Johnston in 1944 that about two thirds of all the large industrial enterprises in the U.S.S.R. had been built with United States material aid or technical assistance.[37]

Stalin's statement—which was only one of many—highlights the paradox of a situation in which Western intellectuals were proclaiming the superiority of Soviet socialism to the economic system of their own countries, without whose technical assistance Russia would have developed far more slowly than it did. Of course, as we have suggested, the technical assistance furnished by foreigners, at least by Americans, appears to have paid at least some psychological dividends in terms of Russian good will toward the persons involved. It certainly was financially profitable. Foreign corporations and their personnel employed in Russia were well paid and well treated. Moreover, there were slack years when Soviet orders were important to certain branches of the German, British, or American national economies. For example, in 1930 the U.S.S.R. purchased thirty-six per cent of all American exports of agricultural machinery. In 1931 Russia apparently bought sixty-five per cent of the exports of the United States machine-tool industry.[38] These figures help to explain why, during and shortly after World War II, when there was fear in the United States of a postwar depression, many Americans hoped for large-scale trade with Russia. For a while optimism appeared to be justified. For example, the General Electric Company played a major role in rebuilding the famous Dnepr Dam in the immediate postwar years.

Despite the blows dealt to prospects for large-scale Soviet-American trade by the Soviet return to autarchy after World War II, hopes for such trade died hard in American business circles and

[37] *Cultural Relations Between the United States and the Soviet Union*, Department of State Publication 3480, Washington, D. C., 1949, p. 3.
[38] Williams, *op.cit.*, p. 218.

of course they played a much bigger part in the thinking of British and West German industrialists, particularly in periods of recession. They are periodically revived by official Soviet statements designed to arouse optimism about the advantages of commerce with Russia.

Obviously none of these tactics were or are uniquely Soviet and objectivity requires that they be viewed in perspective. All countries have sought, with varying degrees of success, to benefit by the scientific and industrial experience of neighbors and competitors. The role of European science in the industrial growth of America is often discussed. And in recent years it has become increasingly clear that the West has much to learn from the Soviet Union. A striking expression of this realization was contained in a statement in the *Economist* for April 27, 1957, which observed that "four or five years ago, the fashion was for British industry to send productivity teams to the U.S.; in the last two years technical teams have been going to Russia." This trend is a very recent one, of course. For many years the flow of knowledge was overwhelmingly in the other direction. Foreign scientists, beginning in the 1920's, contributed mightily to the progress of Soviet agriculture and industry.

The American geneticist, H. J. Muller, helped to found Soviet research in his field by importing the Drosophila fly in 1921. Another American brought the first grapefruit trees to Russia in the late 1920's. Frank E. Dickie helped the Russians to establish their aluminum industry and John D. Littlepage helped to introduce modern mining techniques. Colonel Hugh L. Cooper, perhaps the most famous of all of the American engineers who worked in Russia, designed the Dnepr Dam, after having received the contract award in competition with German engineers. About 1,500 Americans "contributed their highly varied industrial talents to assist in the Soviet industrialization carried out under the first Five Year Plan, from 1928 to 1932."[39] As early as 1922 the Russian-American Industrial Corporation was founded by the Amalgamated Clothing Workers of America to help the Russians revive their textile industries.[40] According to the January-February 1930 issue

[39] Andrew J. Steiger, *American Engineers in the Soviet Union*, New York, 1944, p. 4.
[40] *Soviet Union Review*, November 15, 1923, p. 122.

of *VOKS*, a Soviet publication, in the period 1923-1929 Soviet Russia signed fifty-eight technical-assistance agreements with firms of seven capitalist countries, twenty-seven of these being with German firms and fifteen with United States firms. The same source also stated that a contract with Henry Ford had enabled the Soviet Union to create in a short time a completely new industry. According to the *New York Times* for May 17, 1935, at the opening of the famous Moscow subway toasts were proposed to the foreign engineers who had helped the Russians to design it and build it. Fascinating books were written by participants in foreign—particularly American—technical assistance to the Soviet Union. Among them outstanding ones are John Scott's *Behind the Urals*, already mentioned, and John W. Littlepage's *In Search of Soviet Gold*, written in collaboration with Demaree Bess.

American engineers in the Soviet Union numbered more than a thousand around 1930, but they had dwindled to "tens" by about 1940.[41] During the last two years of World War II and for about a year or two after the war, a considerable number of American engineers and other experts worked in the Soviet Union. In 1944 a number of American engineers who had worked in Russia publicly expressed their optimism regarding future Russian-American economic collaboration.[42] However, rapid Soviet technical progress and control of the advanced industrial areas of East Germany and Czechoslovakia by Moscow enabled the Soviets to limit to relatively few the technical-assistance contracts made with American firms after 1945. Perhaps several years were required anyway to digest and apply the knowledge of American industrial methods gained by Russia as a result of the gigantic program of American assistance during World War II. Although personal contacts were reduced to a bare minimum and the Soviet press proclaimed in the years 1948-1952 that Russia no longer had anything to learn from the West, the Soviet Union continued to purchase, through foreign affiliates of its International Book Company (Mezhkniga), such as the Four Continent Book Corporation in New York or the Maison du Livre Etranger in Paris, huge quantities of European and

[41] Steiger, *op.cit.*, p. 7.
[42] *Ibid.*, pp. 5-8.

American scientific publications, even during the xenophobic late-Stalin years.[43]

After the death of Stalin the program for translation and abstracting of foreign technical literature was vastly expanded. Apparently its effectiveness had been hampered before Stalin's death because of fear among scientists and scholars that if they displayed too much interest in Western findings they might fall victim to accusations of "cosmopolitanism." Stalin's successors, particularly the boldly experimental Khrushchev, were determined to correct the damage done to Russian technical development by Stalin's cultural isolationism, although they of course continued to warn Soviet intellectuals not to be seduced by Western ideas.

In the 1920's and 1930's a surprisingly large number of highly trained and often very highly placed Russians were sent on missions to the West in search of information or for training. These travelers even included some top-ranking party leaders or future leaders. Among them was V. V. Kuznetsov, an engineer by training, who spent three years in the United States as a student in the 1930's, one at Columbia University and the other two at Carnegie Institute of Technology. During the 1940's Kuznetsov became the head of the All-Union Central Council of Trade Unions and after the death of Stalin he became a full member of the Central Committee of the communist party of the Soviet Union and a first deputy minister of foreign affairs. It seems highly probable that the experience in America of a man of Kuznetsov's caliber helped to increase respect in high Soviet circles for American technical capabilities and power, and, one can hope, served to counterbalance somewhat the ill will engendered by international tensions.

The most influential Soviet visitor to the United States in the 1930's, of course, was Anastas I. Mikoyan. He came here in 1936 to study canning and bottling processes.[44] He brought with him his wife and nine engineers. Mikoyan, who became a member of the politburo of the Soviet communist party in 1935, probably made the greatest single contribution among Soviet leaders to the development of both domestic and foreign trade and to the pro-

---

[43] Nicholas De Witt, *Soviet Professional Manpower*, U.S. Government Printing Office, Washington, D.C., 1955, pp. 129, 149.

[44] *New York Times*, August 12, 18, and 21, 1936.

vision of at least some rudiments of modern service industries and amenities of life. During my service in the American embassy in Russia, from 1942 to 1947, I was often told by Soviet citizens that Mikoyan had been responsible for introducing canned juices, corn flakes, and the first Moscow automat, located about a block away from the Metropole Hotel, near the headquarters of the political police. Mikoyan's party also visited France and Germany to study perfume and soap manufacturing.

During Mikoyan's 1936 visit the Soviet group was received in New York by the leaders of the New York Stock Exchange. The brokers listened to the playing of the Soviet national anthem. Mikoyan's trip set the pattern for others made by important Soviet leaders. Post-Stalin visits by men such as Vladimir Matskevich, and his party of Soviet agricultural experts in 1955, resembled that of Mikoyan in many ways, including the almost invariable trip to the Stock Exchange. On his 1959 American journey, Mikoyan brought not his wife but his son Sergi, who wrote poisonous accounts of the trip after returning home. Perhaps the high point of Soviet appreciation of Western, and especially American, technical progress, reflecting the opinion of men like Mikoyan, was registered in the famous travel book by Ilya Ilf and Eugene Petrov, *Little Golden America*, published in both Russian and English in 1937.

Probably hundreds, perhaps thousands, of Soviet engineers, scientists, and other specialists studied or were trained in Europe and America in the 1920's, 1930's, and even in the 1940's. Occasionally vacation trips in foreign countries were awarded to competent and faithful workers. For example, the *New York Times* for August 23, 1931, reported that 340 Russian agricultural and industrial workers had been granted a trip to Italy as a prize for good work. However, even in this relatively free period, the general rule was to permit only exceptionally trusted technical students and commercial agents to go abroad.[45]

During the years 1943-1946 scores of Soviet students took special eight-month intensive courses in the English language and American history and government at Columbia University and were

[45] William Henry Chamberlin, *Soviet Russia*, New York, 1930, pp. 40-43; Sherwood Eddy, *Russia Today*, New York, 1934, p. 19.

subsequently employed in the Soviet diplomatic and consular service.[46]

As late as October 1947 a party of Russian engineers, one of six groups which had come to America after the war on technical-assistance contracts, was studying the technology of axle-housing construction in the plant of the Clark Manufacturing Company in Buchanan, Michigan.[47] A CIO-led strike put an end to this contract.

Perhaps we have presented enough evidence to show that the impact of Western technology and production methods has been very great in Soviet Russia. But, of course, Soviet borrowing of Western culture, even in this field, is selective and controlled. There has been a feeling in Moscow that if Western influence, even in the sphere of technology, is not strictly controlled, the Soviet social system may be undermined. This defensive attitude is reflected in many facts, including cancellations, with the inauguration of the first Five Year Plan, of the small number of foreign business concessions which had been allowed to operate up to that time. Rigid currency controls and, above all, the operation of the state monopoly of foreign trade were among the defenses employed by the Soviet Union from 1917 on in its struggle to establish and maintain economic independence from the great Western industrial countries.

An official Soviet publication in 1928 set forth candidly an attitude toward foreign economic and cultural influences which remains dominant, apparently, even in the post-Stalin period. According to this study, before the bolshevik revolution foreign capitalists with interests in Russia "controlled the entire economy." After the revolution they attempted to convert the Soviet Union "into a colonial country." In the struggle of the Soviet Union to become an industrial country, rigid state control and planning of foreign economic relations had been necessary, since, in view of the enormous difference of power between rich and poor countries, free foreign trade would amount to a weapon of "speculators" against the industrial proletariat.[48] So vast is the gulf between Soviet and West-

---

[46] *New York Times*, September 15, 1943; additional information on these Soviet students was obtained from Columbia University faculty members concerned with this program.

[47] *Newsweek*, October 6, 1947.

[48] *Vneshnyaya torgovlya soyuza SSSR za 10 let*, Moscow, 1928, p. 7.

ern standards of living, even in 1960, and so great is the craving among at least a venturesome minority of Soviet youth for a more "modern," less regimented way of life—this quoted adjective was used by several Russian youths in conversations in Moscow in July and August 1959—that the Kremlin's defensiveness regarding the subversive potential even of imported technology is understandable. For years Soviet engineers have been familiar with American technical magazines, and one wonders whether the advertisements, for example, in such magazines have not done much to build an alluring image of America. For many years great American industrial firms have enjoyed a prestige among Soviet readers that has probably done much to offset the ill will engendered by hostile communist propaganda.

CHAPTER III

CHANGE AND CONTINUITY IN
POST-STALIN POLICY

STALIN, until 1951 or 1952 at least, adhered rigidly to the "two camp" approach to international relations bluntly announced in his election speech of February 9, 1946, and later elaborated in a series of speeches by his lieutenant, Andrei A. Zhdanov. Stalin's address, together with Winston Churchill's reply a month later at Fulton, Missouri, clarified the issues of the East-West cold war. Stalin's policy required establishment and maintenance of monolithic controls throughout Moscow's domain and restriction to the barest minimum of contacts with all governments and political groups over which police control could not be established. His policy represented, in its way, an isolationist's dream, but, of course, isolationism as practiced by a regime with world revolutionary pretensions did not involve complete withdrawal from contacts with the noncommunist world. Rather, it constituted an effort to force the pluralistic non-Soviet world to deal on the Kremlin's terms with Soviet monolithism. This policy shielded a war-weakened Russia against penetration by noncommunist ideas, but had the corresponding disadvantage of arousing antagonism even in quarters potentially susceptible to Soviet influence. Its ineptness was typified by Soviet denunciation of the new, anti-Western governments of some Asian and African countries as "lackeys" of Wall Street.

The West should have expected that an ambitious communist empire, once it recovered from the effects of World War II, would move decisively to exploit the opportunities for "peaceful" penetration inherent in the new international constellation. Even Stalin showed signs, during the Korean War stalemate, of realizing his mistakes and by the time of the Nineteenth Party Congress in October 1952 he had, after a year or two of cautious feelers, come out clearly for a strategy of coexistence, relying heavily on the internal "contradictions" in the non-Soviet world. The new phase, which began with the opening in 1951 of armistice negotiations, was accompanied by such gestures as the Moscow International

Economic Conference of April 1952, attended by, among others, the thoroughly capitalistic California businessman Oliver Vickery, who described his bizarre experiences in an article in *Life* for June 2, 1952, entitled "Capitalist on the Loose in Moscow."

One might almost say that Stalin's successors, especially Khrushchev, have attempted a "three world" strategy in place of the "two world" strategy to which Stalin clung, in spite of minor modifications, during the last year or two of his life. This new strategy, which promised big dividends but involved ideological risks, looked toward "the transformation of Eurasia into a great neutralized buffer zone ('peace zone') of the Soviet Empire, a *cordon sanitaire* in reverse."[1] Its implementation required, so the Kremlin felt, a public-relations effort which would dwarf anything ever attempted by Madison Avenue. The campaign could count on the "orchestration" of communications which the Soviet regime commands. As a distinguished Western diplomat told me in Moscow in 1956, the Russians suddenly became "ruthlessly friendly." However, the increased role of cultural diplomacy never fully concealed the Kremlin's undiminished hostility and increasing contempt for the free world. Moreover, even the ebullient Khrushchev, after the disturbing events in Poznan, Warsaw, and Budapest in 1956, occasionally acted as if he realized that Stalin had not been wrong in insisting that a little freedom was a luxury that communist countries would not soon be able to afford. The cultural-exchange program, stepped up almost immediately after Stalin's death, continued in many ways to expand, particularly in terms of quantity, but there were striking indications, from early 1957 on, of determination to guard against the dangers inherent in showing too much of Russia to the world, and especially in showing very much of the non-Soviet world to Russians. Soviet delegations in bourgeois countries—and, so far as we know, in socialist countries also—continued to display considerable fear of informality, not to mention intimacy, in social relations. Youth leaders, for example, appeared anxious to deal with youth in the mass, to address big meetings and the like, but almost never to engage in unchaperoned, person-to-person encounters.

[1] Robert C. Tucker, in *New Leader*, July 15, 1957, p. 5.

An amusing but instructive example, in 1958, of the Soviet "non-contamination" policy in action was furnished by the apparent fear of the leader of one of the two subgroups, into which the Soviet youth and student delegation in America in July and August was divided, to allow his charges to sleep in the same room with American students attending the Middlebury College Summer Russian School. After some argument the issue was compromised by putting most of the Soviet group of about ten into a larger group, which stayed by itself in a basement room not originally intended for this use. In addition, a pair of Soviet youths were permitted to spend this one night in a dormitory with Americans. To some Americans who met the Soviet delegation it almost seemed as though its leaders were afraid that some member of the delegation might, if not guarded, defect or be kidnapped.

One result of this extreme caution on the Soviet side was that the American delegation, in this first exchange, was twice as large as the Soviet one, although it seems probable that the American group, with the exception of its leaders and a few of its members, was on a lower level of training, linguistic ability, and general competence than their Soviet counterparts. Certainly the Americans were a less-disciplined lot than their Soviet peers.

There were many indications, even in the post-Stalin era, of Kremlin fears that the "new Soviet man," if allowed to see or hear too much, might arrive at nonpermissible conclusions. Some of these have been mentioned and we shall deal with others in due course. The fear of freedom reflected in Soviet opposition to reciprocity in exchanges was certainly one factor in the post-Hungary revival of violent forms of anti-Western propaganda and actions, including, in July 1958, the barbarity of the stoning of the American and other noncommunist embassies in Moscow. While ostensibly spontaneous, this spectacle bore marks of official sponsorship, as indicated by the role of professional agitators and by the fact that some of the factory workers who took part actually complained, facetiously, to Americans watching it that it went on after working hours at their plant, from which they had apparently been sent en masse to "demonstrate." On the day when the stoning occurred, there were cheers for the American Olympic team at a Moscow sports stadium.

On the credit side of the Soviet ledger, the post-Stalin era saw the resumption by Moscow of long-suspended practices, such as the exchange of students between the Soviet Union and Western countries, as well as the inauguration of a number of types of exchanges, and the granting of increasing numbers of three-month, six-month, or even full-year visas, the latter for students and, in a handful of cases, for professors. Particularly in the first three years after Stalin's death, almost every month saw some new "first" in Soviet international communications and exchange practices, including in 1956, for example, the first visits since the communist revolution of groups of American and European rabbis and clergymen. Certainly the reopening of Russia, while not so considerable as it seemed to superficial observers, was on a sufficient scale to surprise even experts on Soviet affairs, who had underestimated Soviet flexibility and confidence.

Many Western experts, moreover, had seriously underestimated the pace of Russian economic growth, which enabled the U.S.S.R. to make a recovery from the effects of World War II comparable, at least in terms of industrial development, to that of West Germany. By 1953 or 1954 the Kremlin felt that it could afford to begin displaying selected aspects of Soviet life to an increasing number of visitors, particularly Western natural scientists, engineers, and businessmen, many of whom brought back such startling impressions of Soviet progress that for a time few in the West gave much credence to them. A few discerning foreign students of Soviet affairs began to warn that cultural competition would bulk larger in future Soviet calculations as Soviet economic, scientific, and cultural development was accelerated. After 1955 it became increasingly clear that the euphoria associated with rapid economic growth—a phenomenon familiar to Americans, Canadians, and Australians—was beginning to influence the Kremlin's mood, although many a goods-starved Soviet citizen had reservations about the benefits of a growth heavily concentrated in cyclotrons, tractors, and sputniks. This was suggested to us in 1956 in Kiev when a Soviet citizen asserted that such improvements as increased pensions had been introduced in order to make a favorable impression on foreign tourists, and again in 1959 by Soviet citizens who said that display of Soviet atomic devices in New York did not put clothing on the backs of ordinary Russians.

The new, more civilized treatment of foreign visitors attracted much attention and was heartily welcomed abroad. Another conspicuous characteristic of the "new look" was the eagerness of Stalin's successors to promote well-advertised contacts between Soviet citizens and noncommunist and anticommunist foreigners. This trend was accompanied by a modest increase in the availability of Western art, movies, and literature, particularly if produced by pro-Soviet artists, to the Soviet upper classes. Finally, and most obviously, there was an impressive, although in some ways deceptive, quantitative growth of many kinds of contacts.

Medieval practices, such as the assigning of detectives to trail foreign ambassadors, were modified but by no means abandoned. An elaborate system of regulations of movements of foreign diplomatic personnel remained on the books, but it was usually not strictly enforced. It was, for a year or so after Stalin's death, easier for an American to enter the Soviet Union, as far as the formalities were concerned, than for Soviet citizens to come to the United States. However, of course Americans could freely choose to travel to Russia, while Russians, in effect, could come to America only with the encouragement of their government. It is even possible that Western diplomats in Russia during the first few post-Stalin years had easier access to Soviet officials and in certain respects more freedom of observation than their Soviet counterparts in Western countries. Unfortunately, by 1958, when we were again in the U.S.S.R., conditions, as far as the American embassy staff, at least, was concerned, had deteriorated somewhat in comparison with those we observed in 1956. Even relatively junior members of the staff of the American embassy were again subjected, although only intermittently, to annoying forms of surveillance, such as "tailing" of their automobiles by official Soviet cars. Needless to say, such practices rendered especially difficult the work of members of foreign missions concerned with informational and cultural activities. It is particularly unfortunate that an elaborate system of surveillance is imposed on foreign students in Russia— a surveillance disguised at times by provocations calculated to play upon the natural desire of young men away from home for female companionship.

If objectivity requires recognition of a new finesse and even a measure of cordiality in Soviet cultural diplomacy, it also demands acquaintance with the calculations behind them. The editorial in *Pravda* for June 15, 1953, entitled "The Word of Truth," commented on the growth of foreign travel to the Soviet Union. Thousands of friends of the Soviet Union from the capitalist countries, *Pravda* asserted, had visited the U.S.S.R. over the years. Visitors from the "people's democracies" came to acquire experience to help them in building a new life. In the future all visitors who came to the Soviet Union "with honorable intentions" would be hospitably received.

The editorial painted a bright picture of the reception of foreign visitors in Russia. It quoted statements by Chinese, English, French, and United States visitors. Foreigners who had visited Russia, it said, agreed "unanimously" on the desire of the Soviet people for peace. Reactionaries henceforth would find it impossible to conceal from their people the truth about the Soviet Union. In the future Soviet people would seek still broader cultural relations with the peoples of other states. Cultural exchange, continued the editorial, fostered mutual understanding. Its growth would contribute to the strengthening of peace in the whole world and to the spiritual development of mankind.

Two days later the expanding Soviet cultural-relations drive was reflected in what amounted to an instruction to Moscow's network of world communist-front organizations. The Soviet delegate at the World Peace Council's meeting in Budapest, Wanda Wasilewska, devoted her speech to "Problems of Cultural and Scientific Relations Among the Peoples." These "links of friendship on a mass scale" were as necessary to the cause of peace as air was to life, according to Wasilewska, as reported in *Pravda* for June 18. The Soviet delegation was empowered to state that the "broadest circles of the Soviet public" were prepared to expand scientific and cultural links with other countries considerably.

In November 1953 the Soviet censors released for publication a three-hundred-page book, with an introduction by Professor A. I. Denisov, then president of VOKS, entitled *Foreign Delega-*

tions Report on the Soviet Union. This volume, designed no doubt for instruction of Soviet personnel authorized to deal with foreigners, as well as to exploit, in the interests of Soviet propaganda abroad, the testimonials of foreign visitors on the greatness of "Soviet culture," the advantages of "Soviet democracy," and the "happiest youth in the world," quoted Indians, Chileans, Africans, "an American trade unionist," a "representative of a French catholic organization," and others on the "new civilization" of Russia, the absence of visible evidence of an Iron Curtain, et cetera.[2]

Soon Moscow became less finicky than before about the "intentions" of foreign visitors. In 1953 New York attorney Marshall MacDuffie sent a telegram to Khrushchev, whom he had known seven years before as head of an UNRRA mission in the Ukraine, expressing the desire to see for himself what changes had taken place in Russia during the years since he had served in the U.S.S.R. After tedious months of waiting MacDuffie received a visa. He was able to make an interesting ten-thousand-mile trip, in the fall of 1953, during which he saw much evidence of progress, that, together with some less positive findings, he described in his book *The Red Carpet.*

During the month that Mr. MacDuffie returned from Russia eight students and graduates of the Russian Institute of Columbia University applied for permission to make a two-month trip. Contrary to previous practice, they were not required to state on the visa application forms where they had studied or whether or not they could speak Russian. In August 1954 four of these students were granted visas, but only for one month. Thus a pattern was set from which, subsequently, there were departures in an increasing number of cases. Francis B. Randall, a member of this pioneer quartet, contributed a delightful account of the expedition to the *Amherst Alumni News* for January 1955. Mr. Randall reported that the Iron Curtain was still intact and that, despite great progress, Russia was still a very poor country and a police state, since various members of his party had been arrested a total of sixteen times. Like most subsequent noncommunist visitors, he was staggered by the ignorance of the Soviet people about the outside world and shocked by Soviet slums. On the other hand, he found

[2] *Inostrannye delegatsii o sovetskom soyuze*, Moscow, 1953.

that there was no "popular feeling against eggheads"; that, though poor by Western standards, students were comparatively well off; and that many Soviet students had read books by American authors, such as Theodore Dreiser, Howard Fast, John Steinbeck, and Jack London. They had also read a few American books he had never heard of, including *Live with Lightning*, by Mitchell Wilson, a specialist in science fiction whose already-great prestige in Russia was climaxed during a triumphal trip to the Soviet Union in 1958.

The faucet of friendliness was opened wide in the weeks just before and after the 1955 summit conference. In many ways 1955 was the gayest of years, but it was, unfortunately, also the year when the firmest foundations were laid for Soviet penetration of the Middle East and for the resulting revival in 1956-1959 of severe international tensions.

The climax of cordiality came at a picnic for the diplomatic corps given by the then Soviet premier, Nikolai Bulganin, on a pleasant Sunday in August 1955. Reporting this event in the *New York Times* for August 9, Clifton Daniel observed, a trifle prematurely, that if things went much farther along these lines *Pravda* would soon need a society editor.

The picnic followed hard on another spectacular gesture of amiability which occurred when almost the full—then still "collective" —leadership of the party presidium attended the Fourth of July reception at the American embassy. Nothing like this had happened since 1945, and even then Stalin had not come. Presidium representation on July 4, 1956, was almost as good. On that date I, together with hundreds of other foreigners, had the opportunity of chatting with Khrushchev. But in 1957 and 1958 it fell off to two, of whom one each time was the colorless N. M. Shvernik, a man of vast experience in routine ceremonial roles. In 1959 presidium member Mikoyan was apparently the only member of the highest party body at the reception, although total Soviet representation hit a new high in numbers.

This might be as convenient a point as any for discussion of some distinctive features and conditions of Soviet exchange policy, including bottlenecks to its expansion, which help to explain why even in the 1953-1960 period Russia has remained a relatively inaccessible country. The most obvious, perhaps, was the continued shortage of hotel space, aggravated by lavish Soviet hospitality to foreign guests, at least to those traveling first class or, in Soviet terminology, "de luxe." Since, if one travels alone or in a group numbering less than four, one is automatically placed in this category, persons who at home would stay in modest hotels are likely to find themselves, while in Russia, rattling around in huge suites of rooms palatial in dimensions even if archaic in *décor* and "rheumatic" in plumbing. My suite, for example, at the Metropole Hotel in Moscow in 1956 had a huge rug, eight chairs, a long glass-topped table, several chests of drawers, a big mirror, and a large bathroom. At the Moskva in the same city there was a small television set in the room. Contrary to the situation which prevailed when I left Russia in 1947, the hotels generally provide soap and toilet paper. Dial telephones, made in Hungary, are in use in some Intourist hotels. Another welcome change, in the best hotels, is an abundance of hot water. Such amenities as, for example, impressive new motorbusses mean much in a country where the majority of the population still live in log huts—although rural electrification has progressed far—and when not far from the center of big cities one can still find householders going out to public hydrants to fill buckets with water.

During my 1956 trip there were so few Moscow hotels reserved wholly or partly for ordinary, mainly noncommunist foreigners that most of them may as well be named here. The National, the Metropole, and the Savoy were the old tourist haunts, as they had been also during my 1939 trip. The New Moscow was no longer in use, but some of the rooms in the Moskva, formerly open only to Soviet "big wheels," were being used to accommodate tourists. A large group of midwestern American businessmen spent a week there in June 1956. The new 26-story Leningradskaya and the posh Sovetskaya which, under the tsars, had housed the luxurious Yar Restaurant were used mainly for high-ranking visiting delegations, with the former specializing on hospitality for groups from communist countries. The American election-observation group in 1958 were put up in the Sovetskaya. The 30-story Ukraina, which according to Soviet sources has a thousand rooms and is thus by far the largest hotel in Europe, was opened in 1957. Among other features this enormous edifice has the only taproom in Moscow open after one P.M. It achieved a certain fame during British Prime Minister Macmillan's Soviet visit in 1959, when the British journalist Randolph Churchill rudely proclaimed that it might be good enough for Ukrainians but was not good enough for him. All told, counting small hotels used mainly for Chinese and other Oriental communist groups, there are, even today, probably not more than a dozen hotels in Moscow which by American standards would be considered to be even second-rate.

As for Leningrad, I was told by an Intourist official in July 1956 that that city of three million inhabitants had only five hotels, of which only the two that were officially rated as first-class were open to Western Europeans and Americans. These were, of course, the well-known antique but quite charming Astoria and Europa. It is only fair to note that according to the most recent available Soviet travel literature Leningrad now has at least seven hotels. In most Soviet cities, especially in the areas in which industrialization has been recent, the hotel situation is much more difficult than it is in Moscow and Leningrad. For this reason, and partly for strategic and political reasons, only about twenty Soviet cities have normally been open to foreign tourists. Exceptions have, however, often been made for diplomats and for favored private personages, particularly for Asians.

Tashkent and a few other big Central Asian cities, as well as Siberian cities like Irkutsk, which before the war were seldom visited by foreigners are now included in the regular tourist circuit. Perhaps it should be noted here that United States official regulations on travel by Soviet visitors in America have at times seemed fully as bizarre as the corresponding—and prior—Soviet restrictions, against which they have constituted countermeasures, imposed in hopes of causing Moscow to open up more of Russia to travel. In connection with all this, it is of interest to record that far fewer consulates, at least of noncommunist countries, were operating in Russia in 1945-1953 or in 1953-1960 than before 1939. Closed were the American and Japanese consulates in Vladivostok, and those of Germany, Britain, and the then-independent Baltic states in Leningrad, as well, of course, as the Soviet consulates in San Francisco and New York.

The holding of the World Youth Festival in the Soviet Union in 1957 involved, for the Soviet authorities, difficult housekeeping problems, which were apparently handled quite successfully by construction of special hostels and other needed buildings. About thirty thousand delegates and guests from abroad attended this great propaganda festival. It was impossible to ascertain whether or not crowding resulting from this event was the principal reason for Intourist's "closing the books" on American tourist business in May 1957. Those whose applications already were in, as well as a few other lucky individuals, received their visas.

Those who had applied sufficiently far in advance were given permission to go to Moscow, Leningrad, and other main centers during July and August, while less fortunate latecomers were told that they must plan their trips for earlier or later dates. These details were coupled with a visa procedure that was still cumbersome, although less bothersome than other peculiarities of travel to the U.S.S.R. By 1958-1959 visas could be obtained in a week or two after their receipt by a Soviet embassy or consulate. The discouragement to casual travel inherent in this situation had certain advantages. Thus far relations between the Soviet Union and the West have at least been spared many of the irritations that can be caused by ignorant and irresponsible tourists. One shudders to think of the harm that could be done to Soviet-American relations if both sides had full freedom for the promiscuous exchange of prejudices, although, of course, one must also hope for a gradual growth of freer contacts between responsible representatives of the two cultures. One cannot become unreservedly enthusiastic about recent efforts of American tourist agencies to "sell" Russia as a glamorous travel attraction.

Travel to the U.S.S.R. even six years after the death of Stalin was still, at least for many who had not made a serious study of Soviet affairs, a minor adventure in which new chapters were constantly being written. Depending on background, luck, and personality, individuals reacted to it quite variously.

One obvious reason why so few workingmen have traveled to the "proletarian fatherland" either after or before Stalin's death has been the high cost of such travel. For Americans, for example, as recently as the summer and fall of 1959 the "de luxe" rate, payable in advance in dollars, remained at thirty dollars a day for · food, hotel room, and other services, such as guide service. Other costs, such as those of souvenirs, theater tickets, and travel, were reduced considerably from 1957 on by introduction of a "tourist ruble," exchangeable at ten to the dollar instead of the usual official rate of four to the dollar. Corresponding rates prevail for citizens of other nations.

In some ways, despite these relatively high prices, tourism in Russia offers one of the great travel bargains of the world, in terms of service rendered per dollar, pound, or franc. However, such rates as we have described would be prohibitive for persons of moderate means, unless they were subsidized, either by private or official agencies of their own country or of the Soviet Union.

It is easier for the Soviet Union than for our own government to assist foreign travelers whose missions are deemed worthy of support. Among the methods used in Russia for this purpose are the furnishing of hotel accommodations free of charge or at a nominal cost, the payment of fees for lectures, radio broadcasts, musical performances, and so on, and greatly reduced rates of travel, especially while such travelers are in the U.S.S.R. but also on the growing system of air lines with foreign links which Aeroflot, the Soviet air-line monopoly, has established in recent years with, for example, Air India, the Belgian Sabena, the Dutch K.L.M., Air France, the Scandinavian S.A.S., the British B.O.A.C., and other lines. Naturally, a state such as the U.S.S.R., which exercises control over the national economy, enjoys certain advantages in the employment of such methods. Still, a rich private-enterprise economy like that of the United States could compete much more effectively with the Russians in this field than it usually has if Congress and the public were better-informed regarding the problems involved.

In a good many cases, particularly in student exchanges—including the Soviet-United States exchange which began in 1958-1959, in which persons of Soviet and of foreign nationality reside simultaneously in one another's countries—the practice has been adopted of having the appropriate Soviet agency, such as the foreign department of a university, pay the foreign students or technicians money for living costs while the corresponding agency in the foreign country concerned pays the expenses of their Soviet guests.

For Americans, at least, travel to Russia since Stalin was facilitated by the enterprise of a number of travel agents, particularly by Mr. Gabriel Reiner and his Cosmos Travel Bureau of New York, but also by competing agencies such as Union Tours, also of New York, or Tom Maupin Associates, of Lawrence, Kansas, which in 1959 began running tourist busses to Moscow and Leningrad from Helsinki, and, more recently, by the American Express Company. By 1959 eight American travel agencies, as well as Intourist's own office in New York, were channeling American tourists to Russia. Mr. Reiner had pioneered by going to Moscow in 1955 and, at the American embassy Fourth of July party, catching the attention of such Kremlin notables as Bulganin and Marshal Zhukov, who introduced him to Khrushchev himself. His energetic sales talk to this sympathetic audience on the benefits of tourist travel led to fruitful negotiations, which he later described in a diverting piece in the *New Yorker* for November 19, 1955, entitled, appropriately enough, "Party Going." In 1958 an International Youth Travel Bureau was set up in Moscow to facilitate youth travel to and from the Soviet Union, and Soviet authorities estimated that 3,000 youths from foreign countries visited the U.S.S.R. in that year.

Prior to the beginning of full-scale operations by commercial tourist agencies, Americans who desired to travel to Russia had to deal directly with the Soviet embassy in Washington. Some, like the author, paid visits to the embassy, where they were received by startled Soviet officials who were likely to be poorly informed about travel arrangements and conditions. For example, I was definitely assured by an embassy staff member that I could go to Russia without arranging in advance for a tour itinerary, and, if I wished, stay my full 30 days in Moscow. It soon became clear, in Moscow, that such a protracted residence in the capital was regarded as undesirable. An Intourist official even went so far as to threaten me, although he relented eventually and somewhat apologetically explained that he had to account to the local police authorities for the residence plans of guests in the hotel where his office was located. As of 1959, perhaps partly because of the influx of visitors to Moscow occasioned by the American Exhibition, tourists' stays in that city were limited, as a rule, to a maximum of eight days.

From early 1956 on, foreign travel agencies took over most of the detail involved in obtaining visas and arranging for transportation and accommodations in the U.S.S.R. At the same time the old complicated process of application was greatly simplified and most of the objectionable police-state procedures, such as the submission of an autobiography, were eliminated from it. Nevertheless, it still remained necessary to stipulate, for example, the exact date and point of entry and departure from the U.S.S.R. contemplated by the visa applicant. Despite the recent increase in the efficiency of Soviet travel authorities, irksome inflexibility characterizes their operations, and changes in a previously accepted program can lead to unpleasant complications. In 1959, because of the exceptional volume of tourist traffic, near chaos often prevailed at Soviet airports and in the Intourist service bureaus of hotels.

Concurrently with the facilitation of travel described in the foregoing paragraphs came another step in the normalization of cultural relations—part of the broader pattern, after Stalin, of a Soviet desire to achieve greater respectability in noncommunist eyes. Normalization was furthered by the conclusion of a number of agreements on cultural exchanges and in some cases on cultural collaboration between the U.S.S.R. and a dozen or more noncommunist governments. Most of the agreements were bilateral in form, but one of the first was a multilateral convention of May 1954 regarding the protection of cultural treasures in case of armed conflicts. Some cultural agreements were limited in scope, such as the Argentine-Soviet arrangement concluded in 1954 on the exchange of motion pictures, or a Burmese-Soviet agreement of January 1957 concerning the construction by the Soviet Union of public buildings in Burma. Others, including those with Egypt, Syria, Ceylon, France, and the United States, for example, covered a broad range of activities.[3]

As we shall have occasion to note in various connections, fulfill-

[3] These five agreements were reported in the following publications: *Izvestiya*, October 20, 1957; *New York Times*, same date; *Vedomosti verkhovnogo soveta*, 1957, No. 13, art. 231; *New York Times*, February 26, 1958; *Le Monde*, October 11, 1957; *Treaties and Other International Acts Series*, Washington, 1958, No. 3975, and also *New York Times*, January 28, 1958.

ment of these agreements was dependent on the vicissitudes of world politics. Some of them, such as those with Syria and Egypt, had significant propaganda implications, since they not only flattered peoples smarting under an inferiority complex reflected from a former colonial status, but also facilitated access to these areas by Soviet propagandists. In some cases, as in those of Belgium or Norway, agreements were suspended or failed of ratification because of public indignation against Soviet suppression of the Hungarian revolution. British-Soviet negotiations for a formal agreement were broken off in June 1958, after the Soviets rejected a British offer for an agreement listing specific steps toward a fully free exchange of information, such as the free sale of books and periodicals in each other's country, unrestricted travel by British diplomats and journalists in Russia, and an end to Soviet jamming of B.B.C. radio broadcasts. Nevertheless, Prime Minister Macmillan concluded a cultural-exchange agreement with the U.S.S.R. during his 1959 visit to that country. As one might expect, the Soviet Union, in its cultural agreements with other countries including the United States, as well as in the discussion of such matters at the 1955 Geneva Conference of Foreign Ministers and elsewhere, consistently refused to make substantial concessions to persistent Western demands of the kind put forward by the British Council in the June 1958 negotiation. The Soviet tactic, on many basic issues, has been one of apparent constructiveness, often vitiated, unfortunately, by the "fly-paper stickiness" of subsequent bureaucratic obstruction and delay in implementation of promises smilingly made.

There has been marked quantitative growth in some major categories of exchanges. In 1953 only forty-two private travelers enjoyed Soviet hospitality. No figures, apparently, were released for 1954. A rough estimate of group travel in delegations yields a figure for 1954 of between six thousand and eight thousand foreigners and between three thousand and four thousand Soviet citizens as participants in cultural or related missions.[4]

1955 and 1956 saw the first startling expansion of the Soviet cultural-exchange program, although even as late as 1959 this pro-

[4] F. Bowen Evans, ed., *Worldwide Communist Propaganda Activities*, New York, 1955, pp. 89-91.

gram remained puny by comparison with travel and exchange among Western countries and continued to be dominated by a "guided tour" pattern. Apparently some three to four hundred American officials, businessmen, and leading citizens in other categories traveled to Russia in 1955.[5] In 1955 and 1956 there were negotiations between American and Soviet educational institutions regarding the possibility of exchanges of students and scholars, but these did not bear fruit until 1958, when such exchanges were included in the Soviet-American agreement of January 28 and actually began with the preliminary summer exchange of youth delegations already mentioned. Throughout the period from the death of Stalin through the summer of 1958 most Soviet visas for foreign travel were limited to thirty days, but extensions of two weeks or a month were fairly common. A number of visas were granted for much longer periods, as in the case of Professor Martin Malia, then of Harvard, who spent five months in Russia on a book-exchange mission in 1955. However, Professor Malia's trip was one of a small number of important semiofficial missions by private citizens and he was granted an official visa and a status which opened to him some doors usually closed to tourists. In 1958 and 1959 a few foreign scientists were given permission to spend periods of three months or more doing scientific research in Soviet institutions. Even longer stays are now possible.

In each of the years 1956 and 1957, it appears, between 2,500 and 3,000 Americans visited the Soviet Union either as individual tourists or as members of organized groups. The number may have reached 7,000 in 1958, according to a statement attributed to Gabriel Reiner. Marquis W. Childs, in the same year, predicted —it now appears correctly—that the 1959 figure was likely to be at least twice as large as that for 1958 if the Soviets continued to encourage visitors by granting visas with a minimum of red tape. By the summer of 1958 American tourists had to wait only about two weeks for Soviet visas, a considerable improvement over the situation prevailing in 1956. Childs also observed—it seems to me with some exaggeration—that Americans arrived in Russia "with varying emotions of fear, suspicion and wide-eyed wonder."[6]

[5] *New York Times,* August 4, 1955.
[6] *Washington Post and Times Herald,* July 7, 1958. The above figure of 7,000 was in an Associated Press Budapest dispatch for August 19, 1958.

Only approximate indications of the dimensions of travel and exchange between Russia and the rest of the world are available, of course, since none of the governments involved have furnished comprehensive or definitive statistics. Most of the statistical information available on the Soviet exchange program is ultimately derived from Soviet sources, which do not present a fully consistent or complete record.

However, there is no doubt that the following numerical data, obtained from unclassified United States government reports, from the Institute of International Education, and from Soviet publications, are substantially accurate and useful as indicators of trends.

In 1954 1,046 delegations were exchanged between the Soviet Union and other countries. Three hundred and ninety of these came from noncommunist countries; 204 traveled to noncommunist countries. In 1955 the corresponding total delegations-exchange figure was 1,415. In 1956 it reached 1,500. The 1957 Soviet exchange figure, according to American official sources, was fifty per cent larger than that of 1956, with the free-world portion up by twenty per cent over the previous year. This increase in contacts between the U.S.S.R. and noncommunist countries took place mostly in the second half of 1957, after a sharp contraction in the first half because of reactions to the Hungarian situation. Compilations made by American government sources show that in 1958 over 3,000 delegations were exchanged, over half of them with free-world countries. As in all previous years, the largest single group of exchanges continued to be in the technical, professional, and scientific fields, and, also consistent with past years, over sixty per cent of Soviet-free world exchanges were with Western Europe and the United States. Asia and Africa accounted, in 1958, for about twenty-five per cent of the total.

It would be useful perhaps to some readers if I should list here such more or less reliable figures as are available on numbers and kinds of travelers over the post-Stalin years between the Soviet Union and individual foreign countries.[7] *Pravda* for February 18, 1958 stated that, not counting 34,000 visitors to the Youth Festi-

---

[7] A wealth of data of this kind is available in Evans, *op.cit.*, and in the successor volumes to his study, Evron M. Kirkpatrick's *Target: The World*, New York, 1956, and *Year of Crisis*, New York, 1957.

val in 1957, 25,000 foreigners had visited the U.S.S.R. in 1956-1957 as members of cultural and other official delegations. By April 4, 1958, *Pravda* was claiming that, all told, more than half a million foreigners had been in the Soviet Union in the previous year. United States official sources estimate that in 1958 over 50,000 foreign tourists from the free world, including 5,000 Americans, visited the Soviet Union, as compared with 30,000 in 1957. According to *Sovietskaya Kultura* for September 24, 1959, the Ministry of Culture alone, in the previous twelve months had sent 7,000 Soviet "masters of culture" to 61 foreign countries and acted as host to more than 3,000 artists from 45 foreign countries.

The growth of contacts between Russia and the outside world was accompanied by increasing attention to cultural and other visits in the Soviet press. Although in numbers of exchanges Soviet contacts with Western Europe and the United States have bulked much larger than those with other parts of the world, the Soviet press has devoted a disproportionate amount of its space to exchanges with Asia and Africa. To mention one example taken from my files, during the four years 1954-1957, 196 Indian delegations visited Russia, compared with 348 from France and 368 from England; however, *Pravda* reporting of these Indian exchanges got twice as much space as those with France and considerably more than those with Britain.

Perhaps it should be pointed out that, especially in 1958 and 1959, new kinds of travel were constantly becoming available, usually, to be sure, on a very small scale. Thus, for example, motor trips into the U.S.S.R., available in 1956 for Western Europeans, were opened to Americans in 1957. Four American parties took advantage of this travel opportunity in 1957. A participant in one of these trips, Mr. Harry Walton, described, in *Popular Science* for February 1958, his and a friend's rambling in a Nash Rambler, never off Intourist's carefully chosen path. In 1959 an American tourist agency pioneered in arranging Finland-U.S.S.R. coach trips, and a number of European agencies also ran bus-loads of tourists in and out for whirlwind sight-seeing.

With sensational Russian progress in the development of civilian jet aviation—behind Britain, but two years or more ahead of the United States—foreign tourists had the opportunity of flying into, inside, and out of the Soviet Union on big, comfortable, but noisy six-hundred-mile-an-hour jet air liners. When I was in Prague in 1957 I read in *Pravda* a boast that citizens of that city had gotten into the habit of setting their watches by the Soviet jets' arrival. My last memory of the airport was an argument between an obdurate Czech air-line official and a distinguished American correspondent who had just been refused passage to Moscow on the jet in spite of his pointing out that nothing like this had ever happened to him. All of this was in sharp contrast to my experience in the summer of 1956, when Aeroflot was still flying mostly old Soviet versions of American DC-3 and Convair planes, and not a civilian jet or even a four-engined propeller-driven passenger aircraft was to be seen on any Soviet airfield. Such lightning changes, even if only in a few sectors of life, lent credence to the Soviet claim that Russia had become the chief world center of technology. A telling bit of evidence of Soviet aeronautical progress was furnished by the arrival of First Deputy Premier Frol R. Kozlov at New York International Airport in June 1959 in an enormous Soviet jet-prop plane, which, however, unknown to most Soviet citizens, made a much slower trip than did the Boeing 707 in which Vice President Nixon flew to Russia.

Somewhat to my amazement, I, who had never heard of the use of seat belts on Soviet commercial planes, began in 1957 and 1958 to hear of their introduction, together with limited-scale adoption of other Western practices, such as the serving of regular meals on planes. Increasing use of such amenities and conveniences is indication of Russian determination to catch up in every way with the West.

A feature of the post-Stalin pattern was a growing tendency for the number, though not usually the size, of Soviet delegations sent abroad to equal that of foreign groups entering Russia, although, as American Ambassador Thompson took occasion to emphasize in 1959, very few Russians came to America, even in connection with the Soviet exhibition in New York, in that year. This balance contrasted with the nearly four-to-one ratio by which, during the period 1950-1953, those entering the U.S.S.R. outnumbered those leaving. Willingness to permit selected Soviet citizens to engage in group travel abroad reflected the decrease in anxiety about the dangers of foreign contacts which followed the death of Stalin and the intense desire of the post-Stalin regime to acquire useful information from abroad. It did not, of course, lead to any substantial relaxation of government controls over the activities of Soviet citizens allowed to go abroad. With regard to the United States, in particular, Moscow remained skittish about sending "ordinary Russians" on tours or as students.

It should be emphasized that Soviet citizens rarely have been permitted to travel abroad alone, and when they have, unlike some of the citizens of other communist-ruled countries, such as Poland, they have seldom been accompanied by spouses. A handful of top-ranking individuals, such as the writer Boris Polevoi, who in 1955-1957 seemed to have become a kind of cultural plenipotentiary, constituted exceptions that proved the rule. However, by 1959 such "exceptions" were beginning to become numerous enough to cast some doubt upon the validity of the above generalizations.

Soviet citizens abroad, even more than at home, are subject to strict discipline, partly self-administered but often with assistance from Soviet embassy officials. They act as eyes, ears, and mouthpieces of the Soviet government. They take care, as a rule, not to become separated from one another or to violate state discipline in any way. Foreign groups in Russia, by way of contrast, are less carefully selected than their Soviet counterparts, and their members usually represent a variety of points of view. Often such groups include one or more communists or fellow-travelers. For these and other reasons foreigners traveling in Russia sometimes actually serve as propaganda instruments of the Soviet government, rather than as cultural or ideological missionaries for their own countries.

A novel feature of the post-Stalin period was the appearance in Western Europe, for the first time in many years, of Soviet tourists. According to the *New York Times* for September 12, 1955, thirty-six Soviet tourists arrived in Stockholm on a Scandinavian Airlines plane on September 11. They were led by an Intourist employee from Leningrad who acted as their spokesman. In this connection it is interesting that one of the five languages taught at the Leningrad Foreign Language Institute is Swedish. With the arrival of

Soviet tourists in Europe in 1955 and 1956 a significant new chapter of the intercultural experience may have begun.

Before 1956 hardly any Soviet citizens had, at least since the early 1930's, traveled as tourists to countries not under communist rule. The appearance, then, of Russian tourists in considerable numbers in Germany, France, Britain, Italy, Holland, Sweden, and other countries in 1956 created something of a sensation. About 2,000 distinguished, highly placed, and highly paid Soviet citizens in that year enjoyed a privilege which aroused the envy of many of their fellow-countrymen. That this was the case was indicated by remarks made to me in Leningrad by a teacher of English. The teacher expressed doubt that he would ever be among the fortunate few with the rank and means to travel abroad and referred nostalgically to the "good old days" before the war when many foreign cruise ships had put in at Leningrad. In 1959, not at Leningrad but at Odessa, foreign cruise ships again began to visit the Soviet Union.

The Soviet motor vessel *Pobeda*, formerly a German luxury liner, made two complete cruises from Odessa to Leningrad and return in 1956. Each group of about 400 passengers made only half of the round-trip voyage. Stops were made in Greek ports and at Naples, Paris, Rotterdam, and Stockholm. Two groups of Soviet citizens visited England in the same year. A party of experts on German literature, together with scientists and engineers, twenty-five in all, made a two-week bus tour of West Germany. Most of them spoke excellent German.[8]

Twenty-five Russian tourists, the first to visit Norway since World War II, arrived in Oslo in May 1956 for an eleven-day vacation. Some Soviet tourists also attended the Winter Olympic Games in Italy in 1956 and there were reports of other small groups in such countries as Afghanistan, West Germany, India, and Egypt. By far the largest and most interesting of these first ventures in tourism for Russians was the series of cruises made by the *Pobeda*. This highly coveted trip cost the well-heeled Russians who made it from 3,000 to 6,000 rubles, depending on the class of accommodations that they or their sponsoring organizations could afford.

[8] *Frankfurter Allgemeine Zeitung*, June 25, 1956.

Despite the dampening effects of the Hungarian situation, Soviet foreign tourism continued to expand in 1957. Cruises by the *Pobeda* and a sister ship around Europe continued and many kinds and routes of travel were added. Then in 1958 came new surprises, when approximately 10,000 Soviet tourists visited the Brussels World's Fair, and the first Soviet private citizens journeyed to the United States. With these ventures contact between the U.S.S.R. and the world took on new dimensions, even though it still retained characteristics which did not permit one to equate it with a pattern that would be considered normal by the people of non-totalitarian societies. For example, Soviet visitors to the Brussels Fair were reportedly housed on Soviet ships at Antwerp. In spite of elaborate precautions, however, contacts were made with some of them by anticommunist Russian political *émigrés* and, according to a Reuters dispatch published in the *New York Times* for August 28, 1958, a number of Soviet citizens were among 300 World's Fair visitors from communist countries who took advantage of the opportunity afforded by the visit to defect from communist rule and seek political asylum abroad. Some of the Soviet visitors to the Fair availed themselves of the opportunity, made available by refugee organizations, to read Boris Pasternak's novel *Dr. Zhivago*.

On August 20, 1958, the first of four parties of Soviet tourists, totaling some seventy persons, who visited the United States in 1958 arrived in New York for a two-week jaunt.

The first group of fourteen consisted mostly of engineers. It was led by Vladimir Babkin, an Intourist official, who was apparently the only English-speaking member of the party. Like other Soviet tourist groups, and unlike all nontourist Soviet travelers, the members of this expedition paid at least part of their travel expenses. The remainder was paid by their trade-union organizations, who played a major role in selecting these well-screened travelers. One of the friendliest stories about this first group appeared, interestingly enough, in the *Wall Street Journal* for August 22. The financial paper's interest, typical of its objectivity toward the U.S.S.R.—and a refreshing contrast to *Pravda's* attitude toward Wall Street—was perhaps stimulated by the Soviet visitors' choice, as the first main sight to see, of that favorite haunt of most previous Soviet travelers in America, the New York Stock Exchange.

Leon Volkov, himself a refugee from Soviet rule and a shrewd interpreter of the attitudes of his former fellow-countrymen, argued in *Newsweek* for September 1 that Wall Street had been selected because the Russian tourists "wanted to see the worst of America first," but that the visitors were "disappointed," because they met pleasant-looking men and women who, as one of the Russians remarked of an American financier, didn't look as if they would "drop atom bombs on the Soviet Union." According to Volkov, who regarded the Soviet trip as a success both from the point of view of the tourists and that of their American hosts, the Soviet visitors, like the official Soviet government visitors who preceded them, found most of what they saw "majestic," "breath-taking," "impressive," and "stupendous." Volkov's observations, based on personal contact with the Russian tourists, were informative and encouraging. Volkov guessed that in the future Wall Street would not be included in Soviet tourists' itineraries, since it proved to be "not so horrible" as the visitors expected. But the best-known of Soviet "tourists," Anastas Mikoyan, revived memories of his 1936 visit to the financial center by trekking there to talk trade with leading financiers in January, 1959.

Of the four 1958 Soviet tourist parties to visit America, only the last, composed of eighteen motion-picture personalities, was not accompanied by guides brought from Russia.

A curious aspect of Russian tourism in that same year was an expedition by twelve Soviet citizens, including several Jews, to Israel. Promptly upon its return home the delegation published extremely negative eyewitness accounts of life in Israel.

The revival of Soviet foreign tourism after some twenty-five years was one of many signs of increased, but still limited Kremlin confidence in the *savoir-faire* of Soviet citizens and in their ability, under proper supervision, to see the world without being conquered by it. Still, in order to keep this policy in perspective, it is important to remember that in the Soviet Union tourism, like sport, is an instrument of state policy. According to the *Great Soviet Encyclopedia*, tourism is "one of the means of the communist education of the masses." The encyclopedia's article indicates that the Kremlin regards tourism as an important political and military activity.[9]

Post-Stalin Soviet tourists have probably been reasonably effective in their role as exponents of Soviet culture. Their good manners, discipline, and knowledge of foreign languages and cultures made a positive impression on many Westerners, who found themselves favorably revising their previous negative image of the Russians. A German journalist, for example, reported that the first party of Soviet tourists in his country conversed affably with all who approached them, though he added in wonderment that not a single word was said about politics during the entire tour.[10]

Neither European culture nor European consumers' goods could impress the prosperous Soviet citizens permitted to travel as tourists as much as they might impress Soviet workers or peasants. Perhaps the successful Soviet men of today, assured as they constantly are in their press that the future belongs to socialism, regard Europe as a museum of antiquities. And yet the precautions taken to limit spontaneous communication between Soviet tourists and foreigners suggest that the Kremlin still fears that the chic and charm and diversity of Europe could cast a spell on many a Russian if he were fully exposed to them. These observations probably apply with even more force, though in somewhat different ways, to the potential effects on Soviet citizens of tourist trips to America.

A particularly important kind of cultural exchange is that involving students, especially if it is for periods of a full academic year or longer. Perhaps most of all in Asia and Latin America, but to a substantial degree throughout the world, university students furnish a disproportionate share of the potential future cultural, scientific, and political leaders. In countries where social change is rapid and political life is disturbed, students are likely at an early age to play a significant role in radical political movements. For this reason the Soviet Union has always sought to win the sympathy of foreign students. The governments of some of the weaker noncommunist countries, particularly those where fear

---

[9] *Bolshaya sovetskaya entsiklopediya*, second edition, Volume 43, Moscow, 1956, pp. 436-438.
[10] Wilhelm Martin, in *Christ und Welt*, July 5, 1956.

of social unrest has been acute, have tended to interpose obstacles to student travel to Soviet Russia. On the Soviet side morbid fear of alien ideas, particularly among members of the younger generation, has made the Kremlin cautious as a rule about going far beyond effusive verbal support for educational exchange with bourgeois countries.

The sensitive nature of this type of exchange makes it exceptionally difficult to obtain precise data on it. Soviet skittishness on this score was reflected, for example, in the fact that it was not until 1955 that the U.S.S.R. proved willing to respond at all, and then only to a very limited degree, to UNESCO's annual request for information on scholarships and other matters connected with foreign study.[11]

For some of the data that follows we are indebted to official sources or to private individuals in foreign countries, who did not authorize the use of their names. Where possible, however, published sources have been used. Detail, except for countries not subsequently discussed, has been held to a minimum since data regarding student exchanges with some important countries are presented in Chapters vii, viii, and ix.

As of 1955 it appeared that around 8,000 to 9,000 students from the Eastern European Soviet-orbit countries had studied in the U.S.S.R. A Tass communiqué from Peiping on August 29, 1955, announced that 1,810 Chinese students had just left for study in Russia. Subsequently, Soviet-Chinese exchanges were stepped up.

The number of Eastern European and Chinese students in the Soviet Union apparently increased considerably during the academic year 1955-1956. According to an article in *Pravda* for July 3, 1956, more than 12,000 undergraduate students and about 1,500 graduate students from the countries of "people's democracy" were studying in Soviet higher educational institutions. Six thousand of these students were in Moscow. The *Pravda* article quoted enthusiastic statements made by Hungarian, Chinese, and Korean students at a farewell reception in the Kremlin which was attended

---

[11] *Study Abroad*, No. viii, 1956-1957, p. 435. Subsequent annual issues contained increasingly full reports from the Soviet side, but never anything like the fullness of detail furnished by all Western countries.

by such high dignitaries as V. P. Elyutin, the U.S.S.R. Minister of Higher Education.

These relatively modest figures do not support fears expressed in the United States shortly after World War II that America might lose its leadership in the field of student exchange to Russia.[12] On the basis of the Fulbright and Smith-Mundt Acts and many other, mostly private, programs, a tremendous expansion of the American international educational and professional exchange effort occurred in the first postwar decade. For example, during the 1954-1955 academic year 40,000 foreign students studied in the United States. They represented 129 nations, dependent areas, and military-government-administered areas.[13] By 1958-1959, 43,000 students were studying here and 12,000 Americans were enrolled in foreign educational institutions.[14] In the same year the whole Soviet bloc was host to only 17,000 foreign students. Of these apparently about 700 came from the U.A.R.

The course of Soviet and Soviet-orbit educational exchange has not run smoothly, even with communist countries, especially since the stormy events of late 1956. Sydney Gruson reported in the *New York Times* for February 4, 1957, that many of the two thousand or so Poles studying in the U.S.S.R. were being recalled to Poland, following their exclusion from meetings and lectures that they previously attended freely. Even communist Poles, or at any rate many of them, like Yugoslavs some years earlier, but to an even more dangerous degree perhaps, had come to be regarded as bearers of alien ideas. Large Polish and Yugoslav delegations attended the 1957 Youth Festival and, according to Americans whom I interviewed, they exerted a somewhat disturbing influence on Soviet youths. In spite of all this, however, large numbers of Polish, Hungarian, and other Eastern European students remained on the rosters of Soviet higher educational institutions in 1957-1958 and 1958-1959. It may be of interest to mention here that a Soviet student of Polish extraction told me in 1959 that Polish students were regarded with some suspicion by the authorities at Moscow University.

[12] See, for example, *New York Times*, October 9, 1947.
[13] *Ibid.*, May 14, 1957.
[14] *Ibid.*, June 15, 1958.

As of the spring of 1957, Egyptian, Sudanese, French, Icelandic, Italian, Indian, and Burmese students, all in relatively small numbers, were studying in the Soviet Union. At that time there were apparently forty Egyptian students, mostly studying engineering; fifty Italians, all having left their country illegally to go to the Soviet Union, according to reliable sources, and probably selected by the Italian communist party; and fourteen Indian students. The number of Italians had grown to seventy by 1958-1959, and all but ten were thought to be communists. In the fall of 1957 seven Indian students, three Indonesians, three Ceylonese, twenty-one Egyptians, and about fifty other Arab-speaking students were enrolled at Moscow University, according to an American official source. Also, according to United States sources, the Syrians were planning, early in 1958, to send twenty-nine students to Russia. Later in 1958 reports by American newsmen in Damascus indicated that more Syrians were studying in Russia than in all Western countries combined. American official sources indicated that during the 1958-1959 academic year 160 Syrians were studying in that country, while Egyptian students in Russia numbered 335.

As far as could be determined, the most important Asian country, India, was pursuing a cautious policy with respect to study in Russia. Indian students in the U.S.S.R. were on an officially sponsored government exchange, primarily to study the Russian language. They were selected by the Indian Ministry of Education. As of the academic year 1958-1959 they numbered only seventeen, so far as was known to United States sources. At the end of 1956 the Soviet Union was planning to begin a fairly large-scale program to train Indian metallurgists, some of whom would, it was planned, work at the steel mill being built by the Soviet government in Bhilai, in India. The United States, incidentally, was planning in 1957 to train from 900 to 1,000 Indian engineers during the next five years.[15] During the 1958-1959 school year fifteen students from Nepal, ten from Indonesia, and one from Nigeria were enrolled in Soviet institutions.

Figures compiled by American government agencies showed that

[15] *Kazakhstanskaya Pravda*, December 11, 1956; *New York Times*, March 15, 1957.

even the 1957-1958 and 1958-1959 Soviet student exchange programs were still very small compared to corresponding free-world programs. An indication thereof was the fact that the entire Sino-Soviet bloc, with its population of close to a billion, received less than half as many foreign students as the United States. More than ninety-eight per cent of the foreign students in the U.S.S.R. in 1957 came from other communist-ruled countries, although exchange with some of these, such as Poland and Hungary, had apparently grown little or perhaps had fallen slightly.

Confirmation of the relatively modest size, by Western standards, of the Soviet program came in a polemic article by Georgi Zhukov, chairman of the State Committee for Cultural Relations with Foreigners, in *Pravda* for June 9, 1958. Among numerous figures he cited to prove that there was no longer a Soviet Iron Curtain—Zhukov in this connection blasted, among others, John Foster Dulles and "the American capitalist Conrad Hilton"!—Zhukov included one of 14,500 "foreign students and graduate students" and asserted that "hundreds" of Soviet students were studying abroad. This article, written in a style that strikes an American as more military than cultural, contained other figures, but they were presented in a fashion which made them much less useful for purposes of comparison with foreign cultural exchange programs than one might wish.

A significant episode in the cultural competition was the Brussels World's Fair of 1958, the first international exposition of such magnitude since the one held in New York in 1939. Soviet strategy for the fair was foreshadowed in a *Pravda* article for February 6, 1958, listing eighteen fields in which the Soviets intended to exhibit and stressing Soviet earth satellites, the cultural achievements of the Soviet peoples since 1917, and the value of the fair in relaxing international tensions and in acquainting the peoples of the world with Soviet science and culture. Among the exhibits mentioned was one on "tourism in the U.S.S.R." Clearly the Kremlin regarded the fair as an opportunity to display to fifty or sixty million visitors Soviet achievements which had already acquired unprecedented prestige as a result of the sputniks. Ironically, one American Congressman reported after a visit that the model sputniks displayed in the Soviet pavilion were marked "made in Switzerland," and it was also reliably reported that this pavilion had British sound equipment, American air conditioning, and West German escalators.

While, judging from numerous European and American reports, the main theme of the Soviet exhibition was Soviet pretensions to leadership in technology and heavy industry—designed, no doubt, to prove that Russia had "overtaken and surpassed" the West in its own special fields of modern technology and mass production—music critics like Howard Taubman of the *New York Times* warned American readers that such Russian artistic attractions as the Academic Choir and the Bolshoi Ballet, with its dazzling Galina Ulanova and its "personality kid," Olga Lepeshinskaya, were making the Russians the "dominant force in the artistic phase" of the fair.[16]

Wisely, at least in terms of impact on sophisticated Europeans, the persons responsible for the United States performance exercised more restraint and sensitivity in telling the American story than did the eager Russians in telling theirs. Stress on modern art and architecture, an effective though small public-health display, and a candid exhibition sponsored by *Time-Life* Incorporated dealing with some "unfinished business" in areas such as race relations, while also describing progress achieved therein, seems to have produced a desired—and desirable—impression of intellectual integrity and sophistication. Unfortunately, this candid display was withdrawn after a time, reportedly at the request of certain Americans. One of my colleagues, a discriminating observer of European background and wide European acquaintance, reported after his trip to the fair that the American pavilion had made a hit with European intellectuals, while the big and brassy Soviet pavilion had impressed middle-class and worker visitors by its sheer size and implication of power and vitality.

The Soviets went out of their way, also, to create an image of culture and of abundance, but apparently they were unable to make much of a dent on European and American viewers with a display so lavish that it may even, in some cases, have served only to reinforce negative stereotypes of Russian poverty and backwardness. However, expert American visitors gave the Soviets credit for a

[16] See, for example, dispatches for May 15 and June 24.

more systematic organization of their exhibits than that achieved by the United States and were sharply critical of the American exhibition for conspicuous weakness in its book display—a defect from which the American Exhibition in Moscow in 1959 did not suffer, fortunately. At Brussels the Russians scored heavily with some Europeans with their excellent book displays, featuring foreign-language works, especially those of Shakespeare, Victor Hugo, and the like. Unfortunately, the overall American showing, despite the brilliant success, for example, of Circarama and, oddly enough, of some American food items such as hot dogs, was probably not so strong as it might have been, primarily because of lack of fully adequate financial support. The Soviet government spent from fifty to sixty million dollars on their pavilion, while about fourteen million was voted by Congress for ours and even this figure was reached only after a hard struggle by champions of a strong American exhibit, including many leaders of art and music and political figures such as Senator John F. Kennedy of Massachusetts. While lack of funds did not prevent the United States having a splendid building, it did limit the scope of exhibitions shown in it. Worst of all, it made it impossible—despite numerous laudable private efforts, such as the Westinghouse Broadcasting Company's sponsorship of a Jack Benny week which for a few days "chased the blues" from the U.S. pavilion or the excellent children's art classes organized by the Museum of Modern Art—to match the stream of successes scored week after week by the Soviets, who spared no effort or expense in sending most of their best talent to Brussels. However, the balance, in terms of weight of representation in the arts, was probably redressed for at least the later fall weeks of the fair with arrival of many leading American theatrical performers, such as Susan Strasberg, Franchot Tone, and the members of the San Francisco Actors Workshop.

The Soviets went out of their way to indicate their interest in the fair by such political gestures as the sending of presidium members Mikoyan and Voroshilov on highly publicized visits. They had, a few weeks before the fair opened, underscored good will toward Belgium by inviting the Belgian Dowager Queen Elizabeth to attend the Chaikovski music festival in Moscow as the guest of President Voroshilov. Elizabeth was reportedly the first European royal visitor to Russia since the bolshevik revolution. Her lavishly reported visit and the hearty good will shown by the Soviet authorities and the Soviet musical public in connection with the concurrent success in the Chaikovski festival of the American pianist Van Cliburn added to Moscow's already great status as a music center and won much good will for the Russians abroad.

While the Soviet exhibition was, in the opinion of many observers, blatant but effective, particularly in its impact on unsophisticated viewers, the relatively favorable effect produced by that of the United States was to some extent marred by fiascos such as that experienced by a troupe of Indians whose Wild West show was rained out so often that the performers had to be bailed out with American embassy funds and sent home. Sensational reporting of petty criticisms of the American artistic exhibition, culminating in President Eisenhower's hasty and undignified sending of United States Information Service Director George V. Allen to Brussels to investigate charges by an irate midwestern businessman that our exhibit included reproductions of nudes—fantastic as this must have seemed to Europeans—detracted somewhat from the impression made by this country.

As an antidote against too facile a conclusion regarding Soviet success or American failure at Brussels, it might be worth-while to mention the report that I received from a former student. This tough-minded young man reported that it was not necessary to come to see the Soviet pavilion. One would find in it, he said, "poster art and odes to tractors." He considered, however, that the Czechoslovak pavilion was the best of all at the fair.

Perhaps it should be noted here that the United States mounted a particularly impressive effort in preparation for the second United Nations Atomic Energy Conference, which opened in Geneva on September 1, 1958. According to a dispatch to the *Wall Street Journal* for August 29, 1958, the U.S. exhibit was four times the size of the Russian one. Western scientists were reported as speculating that the unexpectedly modest Soviet showing reflected, perhaps, an at least temporary bogging down of the Soviet atomic power production program and consequent loss of political support in the Kremlin.

A more cogent explanation for the modesty of the Soviet effort was a certain cooling in the Kremlin, apparently reversed in 1959, toward sending too many Soviet scientists abroad to mingle with their foreign colleagues. Some Soviet scientists withdrew from a genetics conference in Montreal, for example, despite, as the *Wall Street Journal* put it, "the obvious attraction of a chance for propaganda on A-bomb fall-out." A much smaller number of Soviet scientists than had been expected took part in the International Radiation Congress at the University of Vermont.

In the meantime, friends of the United States in Europe were pointing to lessons in the Brussels Fair and other similar experiences that they hoped this country would take to heart. It may have seemed odd to some that the relatively poor Russians could afford—of course, their government decided they could—to spend three or four times as much as the rich Americans on such an exercise in public relations. And, of course, this was by no means the first big success for the Russians and their satellites in the international exhibition field. Some Soviet triumphs in this form of advertising may actually have exerted a not-inconsiderable influence on the course of world politics.

One such, perhaps, was the brilliant Soviet—and Soviet bloc—showing at the Damascus Fair of 1954, when the United States was represented only by Cinerama, which was popular but no match for a full panoply of Soviet scientific and technological displays. Britain and France did not have even a single exhibit at this important exposition, and Soviet success by Western default marked the 1955 Damascus Fair also. Fortunately, America and Britain made what appears to have been a successful showing at the 1959 Damascus Fair, after years of absence. One among many additional indications that could be cited here to prove how seriously and with what determination Moscow has exploited international fairs for political effect appeared in the Tashkent newspaper, *Pravda Vostoka*, for November 27, 1957. *Pravda Vostoka* noted that displays of wares from Soviet Uzbekistan alone—certainly an infinitesimal part of the total Soviet effort—had been made in recent years in Argentina, Holland, Spain, Pakistan, Iran, Sweden, India, Japan, Austria, and other nations and that Uzbek items had already been sent to Brussels in preparation for the fair scheduled to open the following April. Reading such items in the Soviet press, one finds it easy to understand why American correspondents reporting on the crisis which flared up in the Middle East in July 1958 agreed that in the economic and cultural competition in that vital area the Russians were getting a pretty good "run for the ruble."

Of particular interest to Americans and perhaps second in significance to the Soviet show at Brussels as a device for telling the world about Soviet achievements was the 1959 Soviet Exhibition of Science, Technology, and Culture at the New York Coliseum. Opened by Vice President Nixon and Soviet First Deputy Premier Kozlov on June 29, the exhibition ran for six weeks. Hundreds of thousands of Americans saw the bevatrons, synchrotrons, earth satellite models, computers, huge agricultural machines, TV sets, cameras, microscopes, and innumerable other evidences of what the official Soviet brochure describing the exhibition called the "unprecedented scope of scientific activities" in the U.S.S.R.

Although the portions of the exhibition devoted to culture were overshadowed by its overwhelming emphasis on scientific achievement and industrial development, they also offered a generous sampling of the best contemporary Soviet art, books, fashions, canned goods, cosmetics, as well as icons, lacquer boxes, and a few other reminders of the pre-Soviet era. Very large sections were devoted to education and public health. Dr. Howard Rusk gave qualified praise to the latter in a long article in the *New York Times* for July 11, 1959. Experts in various fields, such as photography and even fashion, were favorably impressed by a few of the items which they examined at the exhibition.

Over all, this was an impressive show, calculated, as the *New Yorker's* "Talk of the Town" column put it, to "make you stand and gawk"—and not, mainly, at picturesque scenes of old Russia, but at the latest advances of twentieth-century technology. It dotted the i's and crossed the t's of the Russian success story— at least as far as material development is concerned. It struck yet another salutary blow at what remained of American complacency regarding Soviet scientific-technological progress.

The show at the Coliseum and the American National Exhibition at the Moscow Sokolniki Park were prime examples of cultural diplomacy. Each sought to create a favorable image of the social system that it purported to exemplify. The impact of each probably depended more on the predispositions of those who saw it than on the quality of what it displayed, although the millions of rubles and dollars expended bespoke the significance attached on both sides to effective presentation. The context of crisis and rivalry in which this exchange occurred was, of course, discouraging, but the fact of its occurrence despite all difficulties was heartening. It represented a certain intermingling of cultures, with many subtle indirect effects, the full influence of which might be slow to appear.

Perhaps the impact of the Soviet exhibition was heightened by the grass-roots approach taken by Frol R. Kozlov in his whirlwind tour of America in late June and early July. Retired State Department Soviet specialist Francis B. Stevens, in *U.S. News and World Report* for July 13, expressed the opinion that Kozlov's mission was to "soften up the average American's suspicion of the Soviet Union." Although Kozlov committed some egregious gaucheries, he did a skillful-enough job to lend credence to Mr. Stevens' view that Khrushchev was confident that in the exchange of visits featuring Kozlov and Vice President Nixon the advantage lay on the Soviet side. Kozlov told American reporters in a final press conference that he still agreed with Khrushchev that the grandchildren of the present generation of Americans would live under a socialist system. Whether or not such experiences as Mr. Nixon's correction of his false charge that the Soviet people had been made to "pay in gold" for American famine relief in the 1920's, or Admiral Hyman Rickover's reminder that it would be more useful to "do something" about peace than to talk about it, reduced·the level of Kozlov's ignorance or were even reported to Khrushchev, would probably never be known, either to the Soviet people or to Americans. What the *New York Times* described editorially as Kozlov's "amazing performance" in refusing invitations to American workers' homes and declining to admit that what he had seen constituted refutation of Soviet propaganda about the poverty of the American proletariat indicated, at least outwardly, an indifference to empirical data which cast some doubt on the value to this country of junkets to America by Soviet rulers. One wondered whether the Soviet leaders came to learn or merely to see what they hoped some day to conquer, and in the meantime to disarm Americans by masquerading as quiet family men.

However, the price Khrushchev and his colleagues paid for the Soviet show at the Coliseum and for Mikoyan's, Kozlov's, and his own baby-kissing was the surprising success scored by Mr. Nixon in Russia, which, in turn, strengthened the impact on Russians of the dazzling American National Exhibition. Two weeks of on-the-spot investigation in July and August, 1959, left little doubt in my mind that the "Russian in the street" liked Mr. Nixon and was fascinated by the exhibition. Three out of four Russians with whom the Nixon visit was discussed expressed admiration for the Vice-President personally or for his skill in debate. Twenty out of twenty-eight interviewed apparently liked the exhibition. Only two of the twenty-eight seemed at all hostile. At least six expressed unqualified approval and two of the six, young Moscow artists, even singled out for enthusiastic praise the "abstract art" which was a target of vitriolically hostile criticism in the Soviet press.

On the whole the strategy of emphasizing American everyday life rather than machinery and technology paid off. An informal poll of about twenty Soviet citizens taken in November 1958 indicated that this might be the case, although it is likely that a somewhat bigger display of heavy machinery might have taken some of the wind out of the sails of the provincial and captious official Soviet criticism to which the exhibition was subjected. The technomania of some segments of the Soviet engineering and administrative elite must be experienced to be believed, and the success of the American exhibition would have been even greater than it was had that rabid interest been more fully satisfied. It should, incidentally, be emphasized that America owes a debt of gratitude to the dedicated men and women who worked to make the U.S. exhibition a success. This statement applies particularly to the 75-odd Russian-speaking guides. The guides, many of them students or graduates of Russian area programs of American universities, probably answered millions of questions, not only on the exhibition itself but also on all aspects of American life. Despite the fact that many of these questions were malicious ones put by communist agitators and that others reflected abysmal ignorance, they were

94

answered courteously and patiently and often with a sense of humor that elicited a favorable response. Attendance at the American exhibition was more than double that at the Soviet one, in spite of elaborately organized obstacles to attendance on the part of ordinary Soviet citizens, a torrent of hostile propaganda, and the staging of several obviously competitive attractions. Tickets were made available, as a Moscow taxi driver who could not get one because he was not a communist explained, by invitation, first of all, to high-ranking party members and then to other persons, in accordance with officially determined priorities. Even the American embassy had only a handful of tickets and passes at its disposal.

Soviet hostility toward the American exhibition may help explain Khrushchev's cancellation of the Eisenhower visit, which some naïve people thought might lead to a dramatic "breakthrough" in American-Soviet communications. At least some Soviet citizens, in 1959, seemed doubtful whether, as one bright young man put it, "friendship" would, in the foreseeable future, amount to more than "something in the newspapers." The skepticism of this young man must have been deep, for he said that if he were to visit an American in his hotel room he would be sent to Siberia!

One's feeling that not merely the amazing "stickiness" of Soviet bureaucracy but deep fears and suspicions still remained to be overcome, on the Soviet side, was heightened, for example, by information about the difficulties encountered by Ed Sullivan in connection with the variety show he put on in Moscow and Leningrad and more particularly in connection with his plans for filming several acts against Moscow settings for later TV broadcasting in America. Some of the tribulations, shortcomings, and triumphs of the Sullivan tour in Russia were, incidentally, skillfully described by Mrs. Anne W. Langman in an article in *McCall's* magazine for November 1959. Like some features of the American exhibition, Mr. Sullivan's show probably had a greater appeal for a relatively sophisticated minority of Soviet people, especially young people, than for the many to whom some of its numbers seemed strange and even incomprehensible. It would have been more successful than it was had the Soviet Ministry of Culture provided scenery— totally lacking—and a more appropriate theater than they did.

A final cheery note, so far as these most recent observations are concerned, was struck in a conversation in Leningrad on August 11 with a cultivated, English-speaking young engineer. The engineer, at 10:30 that morning, said that he held position number 14 in the queue for tickets for the first of a series of concerts to be given later in August by the New York Philharmonic Orchestra. Tickets were scheduled to go on sale at 11 A.M., and he had been waiting in line, without sleep, since 8 P.M. the previous evening. Subsequent press reports indicated that the performances of the New York Philharmonic, sixth American performing organization to appear in Russia since the death of Stalin, were received enthusiastically. There is no doubt that a top-flight American jazz orchestra would arouse even greater enthusiasm, but as of late 1959 the Soviet authorities had refused American offers to send one.

Prospects for the development of cultural relations during the next few years were evaluated toward the end of 1959 in an important article by Georgi Zhukov entitled "Two Approaches to the Development of Cultural Relations." The article, which appeared in the November issue of *Mezhdunarodnaya Zhizn* (*International Affairs*), an organ of the All-Union Society for the Dissemination of Political and Scientific Knowledge, expressed satisfaction with the degree to which the development of cultural exchange was contributing to an improvement of the "international climate," but it warned that there was an increasing tendency on the part of Western governments to attempt to utilize cultural exchanges and tourist travel "to carry on propaganda in favor of capitalism." Quoting Khrushchev on the necessity of protecting the Soviet people against the influence of harmful ideas, disseminated in the guise of "free cultural exchange," Zhukov made it clear that as far as the Soviet government was concerned the only satisfactory type of cultural exchange was that which proceeded through channels designated or approved by the Kremlin. At the same time, he asserted that those in the West who thought that they could score a political victory over the Soviet Union by provoking it into closing its doors to any kind of exchange would not be successful. The Soviet people, asserted Zhukov, have "strong nerves and sharp eyes."

Some of the allegations in Zhukov's article reflected the vigilance with which Soviet personnel, in the United States, for example, appeared to be following the activities both of government agencies and of private organizations concerned with international cultural exchanges. For example, Zhukov criticized sharply and in considerable detail the activities of the Institute of International Education, the Governmental Affairs Institute, and others. His article at the same time presented some useful albeit fragmentary numerical data, of which the following were perhaps among the most worthy of note. In 1958, 11,504 undergraduate and graduate students from twenty countries had studied in Soviet higher educational institutions. Two hundred and sixteen foreigners had received technical instruction in the Soviet Union. Four hundred and fifteen Soviet students had studied in foreign countries. In 1954-1958, 1,066 Soviet "sports delegations" had traveled to thirty-eight foreign countries, while more than 1,037 foreign athletic groups from forty-six countries had visited the U.S.S.R. The Soviet Union, according to Zhukov, was participating in 240 international "governmental and non-governmental organizations." In 1958, Soviet representatives had taken part in more than 500 "international measures," including congresses, conferences, competitions, and so on. More than thirty Soviet cities had established cultural relations with seventy foreign cities.

During the first eight months of 1959 alone, 3,198 Soviet artists and "other cultural leaders" had traveled to foreign countries, 1,543 of them to the "socialist" countries. During the same period, 1,488 foreigners in these categories, 1,050 of them from Soviet orbit countries, had been in the Soviet Union.

Despite the caution indicated in Zhukov's—and Khrushchev's—statements regarding the future of Soviet exchange policy, events so far in 1959 and 1960 have indicated that further quantitative growth and even some slight liberalization of the pattern of Soviet-Western communication are likely. Symptomatic, perhaps, are continued reductions in the cost of travel in Russia, the establishment of a new category of first-class travel at substantially reduced rates for foreigners whose Russian is good enough for them to dispense with the services of guides, and such measures as special trips for foreigners wishing to visit relatives in the U.S.S.R. While these moves probably do not involve serious security risks, they enable Soviet spokesmen to make an increasingly plausible case for the argument that barriers to free cultural exchange no longer exist on the Soviet side. In the meantime, in 1959-60 the U.S.S.R. has negotiated several new agreements and treaties on cultural exchange, with Iraq, Afghanistan, Indonesia and other countries.

CHAPTER IV

BARRIERS AND CONTROLS

THE Kremlin in its foreign cultural relations strives to eat its cake and have it too. Moscow's impulse toward unilateral rather than reciprocal communication imparts a baffling tortuousness to Soviet cultural policy. Concealment, as well as display, figures in the implementation of this ambivalent policy.

Despite appearances and protestations to the contrary, a restrictionist pattern is fundamental to Soviet communications behavior. Adjustments and relaxations which occur from time to time must be evaluated against a background of totalitarian controls if their significance is not to be optimistically exaggerated. But, of course, we must also remember that all modern states exercise controls over international communication by means of frontier guards, passports, visas, and the like. In recent years there has been much discussion in the United States, for instance, of problems connected with restrictions on the entry of foreign visitors into the country and also of refusals, allegedly based, in some cases, on ideological considerations, of passports for foreign travel to a number of American citizens. In both of these fields 1957 and 1958 saw a significant and salutary liberalization of United States policy—a relaxation which, in the matter of State Department control over granting of passports to American citizens, we carried so far that the President, in a request to Congress for new legislation to deal with the situation created by the Supreme Court decision, described it as dangerous to United States security.

As for United States restrictions on the entry of tourists and other nonofficial visitors and travelers, the August 1957 revision of the fingerprinting provisions of the Immigration and Nationality Act removed one important source of irritation and leveled an important barrier to communication between Russia and America. The revision authorized the Secretary of State and the Attorney General to waive the fingerprinting requirement not only for officials or individuals so classified, which had formerly been the practice, but for all visitors. Foreign critics of American policy were deprived of one of their favorite propaganda weapons and, what was more important, contemporary American practice was brought more closely into line with traditional United States policies. Together with other recent American measures, such as the removal in 1955 of restrictions on travel to the U.S.S.R. and some other communist countries, United States reaffirmation in 1957 and 1958 of belief in such basic principles of the open society as freedom to travel contrasted favorably with Soviet refusal to move toward uncontrolled contact and communication. Some important difficulties remained, of course, on the American side—for example, obstacles posed by nonrecognition of communist China and difficulties connected with the holding in the United States of some kinds of international gatherings. But even these were at least partially cleared up by administrative action, and State Department officials pressed for legislation to facilitate East-West contacts further. Unfortunately, the continued opposition of powerful elements in Congress impeded further liberalization and even, perhaps, constituted a threat to the improvements which had been effected.

Such actions as were taken on our side toward eliminating interference with normal international contacts elicited a very modest response from Moscow. The Soviet press took only perfunctory notice of the revision of U.S. fingerprinting provisions, in contrast to the voluminous criticism directed against the provisions while they were still in force, when they had been cited as evidence that the Iron Curtain had been moved to America. A Soviet master of ceremonies at a concert by Paul Robeson in Moscow in August 1958 did not express satisfaction at the American liberalism which permitted an outspoken critic of United States policy to travel in Russia, but, instead, attributed the American policy change which made Robeson's visit possible to communist pressures on the United States government.

In contrast, in September 1958, the world watched the odd spectacle of Soviet radio jamming of the UN General Assembly debate on the Middle East, which even sought to prevent Soviet citizens from listening to a major speech by Soviet Foreign Minister Andrei Gromyko, despite the fact that the address was subsequently published in Soviet newspapers. Was the Kremlin afraid that Gromyko spoke, for reasons of external propaganda, in too moderate a tone? Of course, the jamming of Gromyko's speech was a minor matter in comparison with other paradoxical Kremlin behavior, such as, to recall one of the best known, failure to publish Nikita Khrushchev's eloquent "secret" denunciation of Stalin's "mistakes" at the Twentieth Party Congress, despite the fact that in the whole noncommunist world the contents of the speech, or most of them, were fully known and exhaustively discussed within weeks after the delivery of the speech in Moscow. Similarly, in 1959 Moscow, in its world-wide foreign broadcasts, angrily denied the authenticity of the tape recording released by the American government to prove that Soviet planes in September 1958 had shot down an unarmed American air force transport plane, but did not at the same time inform the Soviet public of its own or the United States position regarding this incident. Moreover, even during Khrushchev's American journey in September 1959 Soviet jamming of American-Russian-language radio broadcasts to the Soviet Union was only partially relaxed. Selective jamming continued after Khrushchev's departure.

Normal relations between Soviet citizens and foreigners are made difficult, of course, by fundamental features of the Soviet system. The Kremlin's determination to prevent dissemination of "counterrevolutionary" ideas among Soviet citizens receives legislative expression in a number of loosely drafted, far-reaching laws and regulations. Perhaps the most important of these, until 1959, was the notorious Article 58 of the Special Section of the R.S.F.S.R. Criminal Code, applicable throughout the entire Soviet Union. Section I of this code defined as counterrevolutionary "any activity directed toward the overthrowing, subversion or weakening of the authority of the workers and peasants Soviet," and any "weakening of the external security of the Soviet Union in its basic economic, political and national achievements."[1] Recent changes in the Soviet Criminal Code do not appear to indicate fundamental modification of the threats to freedom of communication posed by Kremlin obsession with "security." In fact, six years after Stalin's death the U.S.S.R. had retrogressed, in some ways, from the modest liberali-

---

[1] R.S.F.S.R., *Ugolovny kodeks*, Moscow, 1943, p. 25.

zation in control over freedom of speech, association, and movement achieved during the "thaw" of 1954-1956.

Soviet administrative law contains both "political" and "sanitary" provisions for the safeguarding of frontiers. The political protection of frontiers is achieved by "the struggle against all attempts at illegal importation into the Soviet Union of subversive publications, and of weapons, as well as crossing the frontier for the purpose of committing counterrevolutionary crimes."[2]

The impact of legislation against "counterrevolutionary crimes" was intensified by the June 1947 law prohibiting the disclosure by Soviet citizens of "state secrets." This was followed by a propaganda campaign, involving, among other matters, the production of plays and films designed to demonstrate the dangers to Russia caused by discussing even apparently innocuous matters with foreigners. As Bertram D. Wolfe pointed out in the *New Leader* for November 30, 1953, under the "state secrets" decree a Soviet economist, statistician, or official could be imprisoned for eight to twelve years for disclosing information published "as a matter of simple obligation by every government which has the slightest claim to being regarded as democratic."

Knowledge of such legislation helps us to understand why, in spite of considerable relaxation in its enforcement and application since 1953, many foreign scientists and scholars have continued to find Soviet colleagues, both at home and abroad, less communicative and candid than they hoped they would be. In connection with exchange of scientific information, it is of some interest that a law of May 9, 1927, apparently still in force, requires that no trips may be made by Soviet citizens to international congresses or conferences without the consent of the Ministry of Foreign Affairs. Another pertinent provision of Soviet law, particularly in the fields of jurisprudence and penology, is that of August 22, 1924, providing punishment for any Soviet citizen who publishes a law without securing permission to do so. It is also of interest that formal Soviet legislation concerning frontier controls, freedom of movement, and disclosure of information—to mention a few matters decisive for the nature and even the very possibility of the exchange of ideas—is supplemented by a host of mostly unpublished ad-

[2] *Sovetskoe administrativnoe pravo*, Moscow, 1950, pp. 277-278.

ministrative regulations and practices which tend in the same oppressive direction. Added to these, of course, is a formidable combination of illusions and ignorance among foreigners who regard the U.S.S.R. as the home of peace, democracy, and socialism and of techniques designed to achieve total control of the perception of reality of those whose thinking the Kremlin wishes to mold. In such a situation only the alert and enterprising foreign visitor can hope to see far below the carefully presented surfaces. And yet at least some post-Stalin visitors have caught glimpses of the police-state structure behind the hospitality curtain. For example, Russian-speaking travelers have returned with at least oral evidence, furnished by Soviet citizens, that a record is kept, for transmission to the proper authorities, of conversations in hotel rooms, or by telephone thereto, between foreign visitors and Soviet citizens. They have found that while Soviet officials, usually in twos or threes, now often invite foreigners to dinner, the meals are usually eaten in public restaurants rather than at home, partly, no doubt, because of space shortages in Soviet apartments, but perhaps also to facilitate surveillance. It has also been noted that warnings, and sometimes arrests, have befallen Soviet citizens who, without instructions, enter into more than casual, accidental contacts with foreign visitors. Even Soviet scientists, though far freer than under Stalin, cannot with impunity conduct professional correspondence with foreign colleagues without clearance from their superiors.

We should, perhaps, say a few words here about conditions of work of foreign newspaper correspondents in Moscow and about Soviet policy regarding jamming of foreign radio broadcasts, since these are indications of Soviet attitudes toward cultural contacts and at the same time play a large part in shaping the Soviet image of the outside world and that world's picture of Russia.

In the Soviet political tradition journalists are perceived as "agents" of the "ruling classes" of their native land. This view, which conforms both to the Lenin-Khrushchev image of capitalism and to internal Soviet practice, requires that bourgeois foreign journalists be controlled and curtailed in their contacts with Soviet citizens but also that if possible they be used to confirm and disseminate Soviet propaganda. It is no easy task for a journalist to function in the atmosphere of suspicion and restriction fostered by such conceptions. Most foreign newsmen in Soviet Russia have, nevertheless, struggled against odds to preserve their journalistic integrity, although a few have allowed themselves to become Kremlin tools. The Soviet authorities have from time to time applied to foreign journalists varying mixtures of pressures and blandishments, which are described in books by such correspondents as Eugene Lyons, Eddy Gilmore, Harrison E. Salisbury, John Gunther, Irving R. Levine, and many others. In addition to capricious censorship practices, controls over foreign correspondents have included veiled threats of expulsion or of refusal to grant return visas to authors of dispatches displeasing to the authorities. Favored correspondents have been rewarded on occasion by permission to visit usually forbidden areas. Similar rewards and punishments have, of course, been employed to influence foreign scholars and intellectuals—a fact which helps to explain the behavior of some fellow-travelers both before and after World War II.

Outright refusal to grant visas to journalists, tourists, or others occurred infinitely less often after the death of Stalin than before. One notable instance was the refusal in January 1956 of a visa to *New York Times* correspondent Harrison E. Salisbury. He was, however, permitted to return to the U.S.S.R. in June 1959, perhaps as part of an attempt to sweeten the atmosphere for the American visit of First Deputy Premier Frol R. Kozlov, to heighten the effect of the Soviet exhibition in New York, and perhaps to help pave the way for Khrushchev's visit to America. In 1958 C.B.S. radio correspondent Daniel Schorr was refused a return visa. The number of visa refusals to foreign scientists, experts, and technicians, which had been negligible up to 1958, increased considerably in that year. In October 1958, following presentation on the C.B.S. television network of an "anti-Soviet" play, the Soviet authorities ordered the indefinite closure of the C.B.S. Moscow bureau. Correspondent Paul Niven, expelled from Moscow with the closing of the bureau, reported that in the months before his departure farewell parties for expelled correspondents had become a routine affair. However, Niven also was granted a visa to return with Vice President Nixon in July 1959.

Reflecting heightened international tension in 1958 and also, perhaps, unrest inside Russia, Soviet censorship, reported Daniel

Schorr in an article in the *New York Times Magazine* for August 17, "reached a point of severity described by American correspondents as the most oppressive in recent years." As Mr. Schorr remarked, the comments of American correspondents on Soviet Ambassador Menshikov's bland remark, on American television, that there was no censorship in Russia would themselves have been censorable—and picturesque.

Radio jamming, in the official Soviet view, serves the same prophylactic purposes as censorship. Requests for its abolition, like requests for elimination of restrictions on travel to and from Russia, have been rejected and the governments making them have frequently been subjected to streams of abuse. Perhaps the fullest East-West discussion of the issues involved took place in October and November 1955 at the Geneva Conference of Foreign Ministers. Consequently, it may be worth while to recall the proposals put forth at that conference by England, France, and the United States. The three Western governments submitted seventeen concrete, fundamental proposals looking toward the reduction of barriers to Soviet-Western communication. These included discontinuance of Soviet jamming of foreign radio broadcasts, the opening of information centers by each country in the capitals of the others, exchange of uncensored radio broadcasts, abolition of censorship on outgoing press dispatches, the establishment of direct air transport service between the Western countries and the Soviet Union, and the encouragement of tourism and many other kinds of travel and exchanges of persons. Molotov, representing the Soviet Union, countered by demanding the abolition of Western strategic controls over trade with Russia, Eastern Europe, and Communist China. Molotov took the position that such questions as censorship and radio jamming were purely internal problems of the Soviet Union and outside the scope of the conference. Much haggling, of the type so familiar in such conferences, did not narrow the gulf between the Western and the Soviet positions. In general, the Soviets displayed interest primarily in the obtaining of technological information from the West and in the removal of trade controls—a line, incidentally, pursued by Premier Khrushchev while he was in the United States in 1959.

During the Geneva Conference of Foreign Ministers Molotov

vigorously defended Soviet thought-control measures. Rejecting the Western proposals, he made it clear that the Soviet Union did not grant and would never grant such "freedom of exchange of ideas" as would mean freedom of "propaganda for war" or would lead to the unleashing of subversive activities by the "scum of society" working on the staffs of foreign radio stations.[3] In contrast, Harold Macmillan, then British Foreign Secretary, summed up the Western position very well when he said on November 17: "There was genuine longing on both sides of the Iron Curtain to break down the wretched thing. The terrible fact is that the Soviet Union fears our friendship more than our enmity. Yet this isolation cannot last forever."

And, despite many setbacks, substantial progress was made in reducing some barriers to communication in the three years after the Foreign Ministers Conference. Among those we have not discussed was the renewal by Russia and America of publication of official magazines in one another's countries. The United States resumed publication of the very attractive Russian-language magazine *Amerika*, which had been suspended long before Stalin's death because, despite written agreements regarding its distribution, sly and calculated Soviet obstructions had tied up most copies in warehouses. According to the new arrangement the Soviets began publishing *USSR*, a magazine in English. The Soviet embassy in Washington also briskly stepped up its propaganda activities. Its press department bulletin of July 21, 1958, even took the unfriendly step of reprinting and mailing to a wide list an anti-United States "appeal" of Soviet trade unions entitled "Peaceloving peoples will thwart the criminal plans of the aggressors." The new Soviet ambassador, "Smiling Mike" Menshikov, was, in the meantime, taking good advantage of frequent invitations to address luncheon clubs, speak on radio, and appear on television. Several members of his staff participated frequently, by invitation, in meetings of World Affairs Councils, university conferences on international affairs, and the like. American Ambassador Thompson, of course, had no comparable opportunities to mingle with private Soviet citizens in their clubs and homes, even in Moscow, and was only

[3] The text of Molotov's statement was published in the *New York Times*, November 15, 1955.

finally allowed to make his first short TV appearance on July 4, 1958, more than a year after Khrushchev had been interviewed on C.B.S. television and after much junketing and many TV appearances in America by Menshikov.

Exactly one year after his 1958 Independence Day TV appearance, Mr. Thompson was given another ten minutes before the Soviet TV cameras. On this occasion he did not learn that he was to have the opportunity until the morning of his address, and, according to a *New York Times* account thereof, it was not known whether it would be heard outside of Moscow. Perhaps mention should also be made here of such encouraging events as British Prime Minister Macmillan's TV address in Moscow in March 1959, in which Mr. Macmillan was enabled to broadcast facts about the British standard of living in sharp contrast to the archaic image of capitalism consistently disseminated by Soviet propaganda, and Vice President Nixon's TV speech in July, limited in its impact because it was carried only to Moscow listeners and on the least popular of Moscow's three TV networks. Also, while on a trip to the Soviet Union in September 1959, the two top leaders of the British labor party, Hugh Gaitskell and Aneurin Bevan, made a joint appearance on Soviet television.

Although the January 1958 U.S.-Soviet agreement envisaged exchanges of radio and television programs in scientific and other nonpolitical fields and even provided for further negotiation "to organize from time to time an exchange of broadcasts devoted to discussion of such international political problems as may be agreed upon between the two parties,"[4] no such exchange, so far as television was concerned, had yet occurred more than a year and a half after the signing of the agreement. There had, however, been radio exchanges between American and Soviet scientists, educators, and students.

The efforts made by Washington and London to secure from Moscow some concessions to reciprocity were not entirely unsuccessful and even gave rise to hope of further gradual progress. On the debit side was the fact that Soviet leaders felt constrained, even after Stalin's death, to cling to the self-righteous doctrine that they alone had the best interests of mankind at heart. Most

[4] Department of State Press Release, No. 33, January 27, 1958, p. 4.

Soviet statements regarding exchanges of persons and ideas continued to maintain, or at least to imply, that while instruments of mass communication brought benefit to mankind if employed by socialists, they constituted, in the hands of "imperialists," weapons of "propaganda for a new war."

In the last chapter we discussed the post-Stalin expansion of the Soviet system of official tourism. We need not here describe how it limits and channels the observations and experiences of travelers. Since Intourist's Russia is but a tiny part of the whole, the necessary dependence of most travelers on its services and personnel effectively curtains off most of the U.S.S.R. from foreign eyes, while at the same time the apparent freedom to roam within this tourist corral sends many satisfied customers home to sing the praises of Soviet hospitality. Gradual expansion of Intourist services in recent years, in such matters as numbers of hotels and numbers and scope of tourist itineraries, as well as removal of a few Soviet cities and even areas from the list of those to which foreigners are not permitted to travel, partially altered an essentially restrictive pattern, but there were frequent returns to the old tight controls—for example, the American youth delegation in July 1958 was not permitted to visit the Caucasus, despite previous official consent to such a visit. Even after the partial reopening of Russia the foreign guest was not encouraged, as Khrushchev put it in one of his off-the-cuff remarks, to "wander into the bedroom." For this reason much interest and perhaps some hope attached to signs of Soviet willingness, expressed in negotiations which began in 1958, to agree on principles for controlling a suspension of nuclear weapons testing which would involve stationing of foreign inspectors in the U.S.S.R.

Intourist-affiliated travel agencies abroad, which arranged itineraries for most foreign visitors to the U.S.S.R., sold tours to Moscow, Leningrad, Riga, Tallin, Kiev, Odessa, Yalta, Tbilisi, Sochi, Minsk, Kharkov, Stalingrad, Rostov, Sukhumi, Irkutsk, and a few other major cities, including Tashkent and Alma-Ata. It remained very difficult to change an itinerary, or, in Intourist jargon, a "program," once one arrived in the Soviet Union, although occasionally a traveler's insistence or the appeal of his argument brought an alteration. One competent American social scientist who traveled in Russia in 1956 reported, incidentally, that there were two lists of cities available to foreigners, one for Americans and a more extensive one for people from other countries. Elaborate regulations on sale of gasoline, as well as the requirement that motorist-tourists be accompanied by guides, served to limit severely the mobility of such travelers, and careful surveillance was exercised over official personnel stationed in the U.S.S.R. when they traveled by automobile.

Even the Soviet press, which offers a very favorable image of communist reality, continued to find it difficult to present a very impressive picture of travel possibilities in Russia. For example, in one of its rare specific statements on this subject, *Pravda* for March 3, 1955, was able to list only twenty-five cities to which Americans had been allowed to travel in 1953 and 1954. A number of these, such as Yakutsk, Khabarovsk, and other eastern points, were accounted for by a trip made by Harrison E. Salisbury. By occasionally relaxing restrictions, of course, the Kremlin conceals the fact that the restrictions are in force most of the time. It is, however, a mistake to make sweeping generalizations about travel restrictions or other Soviet practices. One unfortunate result of careless statements in the foreign press regarding Soviet travel restrictions is that naïve or poorly informed visitors who find conditions not so bad or restrictions not so severe as they had been led to expect may lose confidence in their own sources of information.

While restrictions on photography, for example, were relaxed after Stalin's death, they remained strict and their enforcement continued to be capricious. Soviet reluctance to admit the existence of or to specify the nature of rules governing photography was somewhat lessened, however, and in a circular note to all foreign embassies and missions in Moscow, dated February 11, 1954, five major categories of objects and situations in which taking of photographs and sketching is forbidden were briefly described. They included "the 25 kilometer frontier zone," "all types of military technology and armaments," railroad junctions, tunnels, bridges, et cetera, industrial establishments and scientific research institutions, radio and telegraph stations, et cetera. No photography is permitted on airplane flights, and, in fact, passengers are usually asked to check their cameras in the baggage compartments of Soviet planes. In the case of some normally forbidden objects, such as "industrial enterprises engaged in the manufacture of civilian products," photographs and sketches may, "in individual cases, be made with the permission of the administration of these institutions and organizations." Intourist personnel and other Soviet officials are likely to become very angry if their pictures are taken without permission. They are also touchy about foreigners' photographing scenes or objects which might reflect unfavorably on Soviet life if they were displayed or published abroad.

Again and again in the post-Stalin period visitors of all kinds, ranging from United States Senators through writers, artists, and other professionals, and even including military personnel, reported satisfactory visits to the Soviet Union. In many instances such visitors have stated that they met with no difficulties, no restrictions, and no chaperonage. On the other hand, when, as was the case in the visit of the American child specialists Herschel and Edith Alt in 1956, an attempt was made to investigate such touchy matters as juvenile delinquency, frustrations can multiply.[5] In the technical field, of course, security restrictions can be of compelling force, and it is also possible that Soviet technical institutions do not wish to admit foreign visitors until they have produced equipment equal to or superior in quality to that of other countries. This consideration may, perhaps, explain the fact that up to mid-1959 no American computer expert had been granted access to the laboratory of the Institute of Scientific and Technical Information, although the director of this institute, in 1958, visited American laboratories working in his field.

Prior to the post-Stalin reforms, restrictions on travel by foreign diplomats and newspaper correspondents, particularly Americans, had been steadily tightened since May 16, 1941, when a circular note from the Soviet Commissariat for Foreign Affairs declared travel to certain points and localities prohibited. A procedure, which is still in force, was established under which travel on the territory

---

[5] See, for example, statement by American archeologist reported in *New York Times*, January 14, 1956. The Alts recorded their experiences in their book *Russia's Children*, New York, 1959. See especially Chapter IV, "Our Struggle with Intourist." No data was available on another trip they made in 1959.

of the U.S.S.R. by members of foreign embassies, legations, and consulates could take place "only on condition that such persons previously inform appropriate organs of the People's Commissariat for Foreign Affairs, People's Commissariat for Defense, and People's Commissariat for Navy with regard to trips planned, indicating itinerary, points of stop-over and length of travel so that such trips may be registered by above-mentioned organs."[6] In 1952 the Soviet authorities further restricted the areas of the Soviet Union to which foreign officials could travel. As a result of the January 1952 restrictions, visits by foreigners, both diplomatic and nondiplomatic, were prohibited in about eighty per cent of Soviet territory, containing more than sixty-five per cent of the population. In notes of June and November 1953 the Soviet government indicated that travel restrictions would be relaxed. However, the United States government protested in January 1955 that approximately thirty per cent of the land area of the U.S.S.R. still remained closed to travel by American citizens or other foreigners. The United States proposed that Soviet travel regulations, as well as American regulations imposed in retaliation, be mutually relaxed. Mr. Khrushchev, in a statement during his now-famous appearance before an American television audience on June 2, 1957, declared that the Soviet government would agree to abolish travel restrictions on a reciprocal basis. Despite this promise, Soviet authorities imposed new travel restrictions in the spring of 1957, frequently involving the closure of officially open areas as well as police interference calculated to make travel by American diplomats in open areas most difficult.

In a note of June 15, 1957, the Soviet Ministry of Foreign Affairs rejected American proposals for reciprocal liberalization of travel controls and stated that interference with travel by American officials had been dictated by "circumstances of a temporary character."[7] Exchanges of notes regarding this matter continued throughout 1958, but as of October 1959 Moscow had given no indication of a basic change of attitude. Even in 1958-1959, vast areas of the Soviet Union, including the entire Pacific coast, much

---

[6] Quoted in Department of State Press Release, No. 181, March 10, 1952.
[7] See Department of State Press Releases, No. 1, January 3, 1955, and No. 382, January 22, 1957.

of Central Asia, a broad belt around Moscow, and large parts of the city of Moscow itself, were closed to all foreign travel. Among other things, foreigners were prohibited from visiting the city of Vladivostok. This prohibition is of interest to me, since I was fortunate enough to spend two weeks in that city in 1946. Although travel from the port of Nakhodka, near Vladivostok, via the Trans-Siberian Railroad to Moscow is occasionally permitted, I have not heard of any Americans or Western Europeans who have made this trip in recent years. As this sentence is written, Vice President Nixon had been denied permission by the Soviet authorities to pass through Vladivostok as his point of exit from the Soviet Union. The opening of a few border cities, such as Riga and Lvov, to widely publicized trips by foreign correspondents in September 1957 obscured, perhaps, the simultaneous shutting off of new large areas in Soviet Asia. In 1959, perhaps to help strengthen the "spirit of Gettysburg," *New York Times* correspondent Osgood Caruthers was allowed to visit the Baltic area.

On the whole, restrictions on official travel apply also to non-official travel. Because of pressure by foreign governments, the Soviet government usually feels constrained to be more explicit in disclosing the nature and extent of restrictions on official than on nonofficial travel. At the same time, the Kremlin achieves important propaganda gains by according to occasional nonofficial visitors, communist or not as circumstances dictate, preferential treatment which contrasts sharply with the harsh restrictions often imposed on foreign officials and newspaper correspondents on long-term assignments in Moscow. By allowing a few selected guests to travel, sometimes free of charge, to areas usually closed to foreign officials, the Kremlin sometimes even succeeds in discrediting reports regarding Soviet travel restrictions made by foreign officials or by prominent but anticommunist foreigners. The highly developed techniques of differential treatment applied in Russia to different kinds of visitors have many effects, among which one of the most important, perhaps, is the engendering in some Western officials and newspapermen stationed in Moscow, particularly British and American, of an attitude resembling persecution mania.

Stalin's "guided tour" techniques, as should have been expected, were not abandoned by his successors, although at times they were so modified as to stimulate optimism in the West regarding an early lifting of the Iron Curtain. Foreigners who have traveled in the Soviet Union since Stalin's death have experienced and reported perhaps a greater variety of surveillance, or the absence thereof, by guides, interpreters, and chauffeurs, than has been the case with regard to border and internal travel controls. This is obviously a very complex subject, and one in connection with which the traveler's previous experience and predispositions play a great role. It would, of course, be foolish to condemn the Soviet system of guides and interpreters as solely a means of surveillance. Since the majority of foreign visitors to Russia either know no Russian, or have a very inadequate knowledge of the language, they need the services of interpreters if they are to enjoy or profit by their visit. Even visitors with a good knowledge of Russian may sometimes need the services of a guide. Some of us who were in Moscow during the relatively relaxed spring and summer of 1956, when Intourist was still struggling with a shortage of guides and floundering somewhat in dealing with the first big influx of noncommunist tourists since 1939, sometimes wished that guides were more, rather than less, available.

However, a citizen of a free country wants guides and interpreters only when he needs them. The all-too-often-normal Soviet practice is to make them available and even to require their use whether the traveler requests them or not. This, at least, is the conclusion to which one is led by most of the available accounts of post-Stalin visitors.

In 1956 during almost three weeks in Moscow I was never asked to take a guide to any of my appointments or on any sight-seeing trips. In Leningrad, Kiev, and Odessa, on the other hand, I was asked upon arrival what my "program" was, and guides accompanied me during the day, although I was left to my own devices in the evening. Other travelers reported that after they had taken one or two sight-seeing trips in a town it was easy to dispense with the services of Intourist. Some of the travelers that I interviewed felt that the guides were used more to take travelers to places that would make a desirable impression than for purposes of surveillance. Many observed that the Intourist personnel were so busy that they made little effort to keep track of the activities or where-abouts of travelers.

Even in 1955 and 1956, however, a number of European or American visitors reported that they were occasionally shadowed, or subjected to other forms of surveillance or interference. One leading American scholar reported: "Contacts of Soviet citizens with foreign visitors are not unrestricted or unsupervised. A foreign visitor is informed politely but firmly that he is not permitted to consult a Moscow telephone directory, although any numbers required are furnished to him at his request. When a visitor approaches the building of the United States Embassy, for example, to collect mail, he is greeted by the piercing stares of one, two, or three security officers; when they are addressed in English, their gaze softens and turns away."[8]

My experiences in 1956 confirm the correctness of some of the above observations. I was asked several times to show my passport to police guarding the American Embassy. This probably happened because I approached the embassy on foot and was dressed plainly enough to look like a Soviet citizen. Even Soviet officials and policemen seem to entertain the myth that only wealthy foreigners can afford to visit Russia, and they are surprised when a foreigner does not travel by automobile.

In 1957 surveillance over foreign visitors was tightened somewhat. The new system was so elaborate that it is safe to say that it is unprecedented in history. Almost all returning Americans whom I interviewed in 1957, 1958, and 1959 reported that they had been accompanied, throughout their journey in the Soviet Union, usually beginning in Moscow, by a guide who traveled with them on trains, boats, and planes, often took meals with them, and was usually, though not always, difficult to shake. Apparently in some cases these guides stuck to travelers like burrs. Sometimes in provincial cities such as Kiev or Kharkov travelers in the summer of 1957 were accompanied by their Moscow guide and a local guide. In one instance described to me, two American tourists in Samarkand in 1958 were chaperoned by five guides, representing Moscow and local Intourist offices. While there was general agree-

---

[8] Philip E. Mosely, "Russia Revisited: Moscow Dialogues, 1956," in *Foreign Affairs*, Vol. 39, No. 1, October, 1956, pp. 72-84. Quotation on p. 75.

ment among travelers interviewed that this system imposed a considerable nervous strain both upon traveler and guide, and certainly interfered seriously with efforts to engage in casual conversations with ordinary people on the streets, in trains, or in restaurants, it was also noted that in some instances guides agreed to leave their charges to their own devices.

Some travelers also reported that guides were embarrassed by many of the questions put to them by foreign travelers. In particular they seemed to be embarrassed by the fact that foreigners had access to more information about the Soviet Union than they themselves did. It is possible that the price paid by the Soviet authorities for imposing this kind of surveillance on foreign tourists is the exposure of some of the best-educated Soviet young people to disturbing experiences, which may in some cases even lead to the ideological corruption of some of the guides, who are usually graduates of the Moscow or Leningrad Foreign Language Institutes, or of the Moscow Institute of Foreign Trade. Despite training in Intourist schools and special indoctrination in the Intourist party cells, guides are sometimes shaken by contact with citizens of freer, happier societies.

However, a security-minded Kremlin is willing to pay this price. A few not-very-subtle guides have virtually admitted this to Americans traveling in Russia in the last few years. One American professor was told by an Intourist guide: "We don't know what kind of people you are. Some foreigners are bad people." It is possible that the tightening up which occurred in 1957 reflected irritation in the Kremlin over the success of foreign visitors in 1956 in establishing a number of relatively free contacts with Soviet people and in reporting to the outside world facts about Soviet life previously concealed by censorship. Perhaps even more important was the concern felt by the Kremlin over the post-Hungary state of mind of some Soviet students. In spite of precautionary measures to which this concern gave rise, a considerable number of American and European students succeeded in establishing fruitful contacts with Soviet comrades.

Americans, unfortunately, were not in a very strong position to complain about some of the Kremlin's restrictive practices. American official restrictions on Soviet visits to the United States in 1957 and 1958 were, formally at least, more severe than corresponding Soviet regulations regarding Americans. Despite relaxation of fingerprinting, American visa policy was such as to furnish Moscow with propaganda ammunition. Even in the United States, tourist agencies such as the Cosmos Travel Bureau pleaded with the State Department to make it easier for Soviet tourists to visit America. The United States, of course, exercised a mild surveillance over Soviet delegations in America. In all probability most of the Soviet visitors did not resent the system of travel arrangements and guides provided for them, partly by the Department of State and other governmental agencies, partly by private organizations such as the Governmental Affairs Institute of Washington, D.C. or the Council on Student Travel in New York. However, members or leaders of some of the more politically oriented delegations, such as the group of seven Soviet journalists who visited the United States in October and November 1955 or the leaders of the 1958 Soviet youth group, made considerable adverse propaganda out of alleged restrictions imposed upon them in America. They also had more legitimate grievances, arising from insults and occasional rowdyism on the part of participants in anti-Soviet demonstrations near hotels and other places which they visited.

This matter of anti-Soviet demonstrations against Soviet visitors highlights some of the problems connected with East-West contacts. Accustomed as they are to complete state control of political opinion, Soviet travelers abroad probably find it difficult to believe that demonstrations against them, or even press criticisms of them, are not officially inspired or instigated. With the possibility of increased contacts, American officials, educators, and others concerned were worried, in the post-Stalin years, about the possible damage that the actions of some aggressive minorities in this country might do to cultural relations.

Another source of concern was the difficulty faced by a free society in providing funds and personnel necessary for proper accommodations and hospitality for Soviet visitors. In some cases this problem is well handled, particularly by some private hosts such as the American steel executives who in 1958 entertained Soviet colleagues in homes and country clubs. In a few which came to my attention inefficiency, lack of competent guides and interpreters, and clumsy security measures have detracted unnecessarily from the beneficial results of American-Soviet contacts in the United States.

The increased access by foreign visitors to the Soviet Union discussed in the last chapter and in this one was not matched by a comparable availability to the Soviet people of bourgeois foreign books, periodicals, films, plays, or radio broadcasts. A tiny but growing elite of trusted and competent specialists in each field of science and learning continued to receive access to all of the foreign materials necessary for maximum efficiency in performing their tasks. Certain institutions, such as the Library of Foreign Literature, located on a rather obscure alley off Razin Street in Moscow, not far from the Kremlin, have excellent collections of foreign newspapers, magazines, and journals. Great libraries, such as the Saltykov-Shchedrin Library in Leningrad or the Lenin Library in Moscow, have fine collections of foreign materials. On the other hand, the Odessa Public Library, one of the ten largest libraries in the Soviet Union, was not, in 1956, receiving any English-language newspapers except the British *Daily Worker*. The director told us this, adding that he hoped in the future to have more funds for foreign newspapers. Although before World War II the London *Daily Worker* and its New York counterpart were sold at a few newsstands in Moscow, even these newspapers were not available to ordinary Soviet readers in 1956, 1957, or 1958. The Soviet public continued to form its impressions of American literature from a few selected classics of Mark Twain, Walt Whitman, Longfellow, et cetera, and from the relatively unknown Russophile writer, Mitchell Wilson.[9] The brightest, best-informed Intourist guide whom I met during my trip in 1956 had never seen a copy of the *New York Times* and had never heard of the *New Yorker*. A few American travelers, however, reported in 1956 that Soviet graduate students did have free access to the *New York Times* in one or two of the biggest Soviet libraries. Even this limited access to publications containing uncensored information about the outside world was curtailed, according to some observant travelers, after

[9] See article by Max Frankel in *New York Times*, August 19, 1957. See also the interesting piece by Deming Brown, "American Best-Sellers in Soviet Bookstores," in *Reporter*, November 29, 1956.

1956, although trusted specialists have, in the last three or four years, been receiving increasing access to foreign sources.

The American ideal of the free, and freely accessible, library could scarcely be expected to flourish under Soviet conditions, of course; but probably few Americans, or Western Europeans, can imagine the degree of control exercised over books and readers alike in Russia. A number of foreign travelers in recent years have verified on the spot the existence in Soviet libraries of special "secret collections," access to which can be obtained only with permission of party, police, and appropriate administrative or educational authorities. Apparently most of the contents of these collections consist of items, including ordinary American and European mass-circulation magazines and newspapers, that would not be regarded as at all secret in a nontotalitarian society. I have never, of course, doubted the existence of police controls in Soviet libraries. I was, therefore, less surprised than amused to find myself in 1956 in the Saltykov-Shchedrin Public Library face to face with a stern-looking, gun-toting policewoman, standing near a door marked "special section," from whom permission had to be obtained for me and for an official of the library to proceed into the parts of the library which were shown to me and to another American scholar. Incidentally, we were told at this library that Ernest Hemingway's novels were popular in the U.S.S.R., and one of the librarians expressed pride in the fact that the library had five copies, in English, of *For Whom the Bell Tolls*.

While access to foreign technical literature has always been freer than that to overtly political or ideological material, it is by no means unrestricted. An episode of my 1956 stay in Moscow may illustrate this point. One day while I was waiting to gain admission to the Library of Foreign Literature, the librarian at the desk was filling out a card for a young engineer. She asked him many searching questions about his professional "profile," as well as such questions, certainly amazing to an American, as whether or not he was a party member. The elaborate machinery of reader classification, the notices regarding criminal prosecution for failure to return library books, and the other procedures of police controls in Soviet libraries remind the foreigner that access to information of all kinds, particularly that which is concerned with foreign countries, is fraught with political significance.

In spite of all this, and partly because of it, many Soviet people are interested in Western novels, plays, and poems, and even in bourgeois political or philosophical works. Increased contacts since the death of Stalin have quickened this interest and provided at least limited channels for satisfying it.

Many Europeans and Americans have in recent years been asked by Intourist guides and other Soviet citizens to send them both popular novels, such as *Gone with the Wind*, and scholarly books and periodicals. When books are mailed to individual Soviet citizens in response to such requests, they do not always reach their destination. Even foreign students in Russia complain that their mail is often held up for weeks, and, of course, they are in a favored position as compared with Soviet citizens. Some doubt as to the future of even a limited, informal dissemination of foreign books to Soviet citizens was suggested, late in 1958, by a New York broadcast in which N.B.C. correspondent Irving R. Levine reported that inspection of tourist luggage, abandoned after the death of Stalin, had been temporarily resumed.

One may infer from Mr. Levine's report that reimposition of tourist baggage inspection may have been, in some degree, a temporary retaliation against such actions by foreigners as the bringing in to the Nobel Prize-winning author, Boris Pasternak, of an English-language copy of his novel *Doctor Zhivago*. While Western liberals can only deplore the negation of intellectual freedom symbolized by Kremlin treatment of Pasternak, including refusal to permit publication of *Doctor Zhivago* in Russia, it is doubtful if any useful purpose is served by actions which aggravate Soviet fears regarding the possible consequences of relaxing controls over interpersonal and intercultural exchanges and can lead to flare-ups of vigilance.

Reports in the fall of 1958 indicated sudden imposition of severe requirements governing the taking of photographs and the development and exportation of films. Although the tactless and insensitive proclivity of some foreigners for photographing the worst aspects of Soviet life did not justify such controls, it might have furnished a pretext for them.

We must remember that in the Russian, and not merely in the Soviet, tradition government has rights of custody and tutelage which far exceed those to which Englishmen, Frenchmen, or Americans are accustomed. Not only militant communists, but ordinary Soviet citizens, are likely to regard as breaches of hospitality, or worse, actions which Americans would be inclined to attribute to intellectual curiosity or, perhaps, to youthful exuberance. Some Soviet actions, at least, which seemed to be in contradiction to the over-all post-Stalin pattern of a modest increase in freedom probably represented, in Soviet eyes, a legitimate drawing of the line beyond which, for the present, freedom would degenerate into license.

It will take time for Soviet leaders to learn that suppression and concealment serve to stimulate curiosity and suspicion. An American who was in Russia recently gave good advice, in our opinion, to some Soviet communists when they complained about the alleged tendency of Americans to stress the negative features of Soviet life in reporting on their travel experiences to their fellow-countrymen. The American replied that if visitors were allowed to take pictures, for example, of some of the less-developed residential areas of big cities and were then shown such sources of Soviet pride as the Moscow Agricultural Exposition, they would gradually acquire a better-balanced approach and would be less likely to stress the sensational.

It will, of course, be difficult for the Soviet communists to moderate their system of controls as long as they insist upon making exaggerated claims of progress toward the ideal goals suggested by the assertion that a socialist society has been established in the Soviet Union and that the country is now engaged in the "transition to communism." For some time to come, we can be sure, such claims will scarcely stand the test of comparison, either with the full texts of Marx's writings or with the image of life under capitalism that might flow from fuller access to uncensored information about the non-Soviet world.

Some observations made to me by one of the leaders of a recent major American delegation to the U.S.S.R. remind us how touchy the Soviet authorities still are about contacts between Soviet citizens and visitors who might provide myth-disturbing information or points of view. The American reported that, although he was not always accompanied by guides, he was asked questions by Soviet officials apparently designed to draw him out regarding the political implications of conversations he had had in casual encounters with Soviet citizens at which the officials making the inquiries had not been present. Various Soviet officials, in different parts of the Soviet Union, put such questions and there was, perhaps, in all this an implication of the desire on the part of the Kremlin to utilize what could be gleaned in this fashion to assist the authorities in ascertaining the existence of opinions in disharmony with the official line, or perhaps even to ferret out individuals who might have expressed such opinions.

American films were still, even in 1958, almost completely unavailable to Soviet Russians, but an increasing number of French, Italian, Austrian, and other European films, mostly light comedies, were made available in the years after the death of Stalin. I can testify, on the basis of observation inside Russia, that these foreign films not only were popular but whetted the appetite of the Soviet cinema-going public for more of the same. Despite radio jamming, some Russians continued, in the years under study, to listen to foreign radio broadcasts, particularly those of the B.B.C. Since, as a rule, broadcasts in English have not been jammed, Russians with a good knowledge of that language have had readier access than their fellow-countrymen to at least some uncensored information about events in the outside world, as they are perceived by that world's opinion leaders.

More accessible to Soviet readers with the necessary linguistic competence than Western bourgeois publications have been the communist but, by Moscow standards, sometimes-unorthodox newspapers and magazines of Poland and Yugoslavia. Both in Leningrad and Moscow there are large, fine bookstores devoted exclusively to sale of publications of the "people's democracies." With the exception of Polish and Yugoslav publications, these, of course, present the same ideological line as *Pravda*. In 1958, according to some reports, the Soviet authorities instituted restrictive and prohibitory measures against Yugoslav publications.

Polish publications were probably, at times, particularly interesting to some of the more alert, daring, and inquisitive Soviet readers. This may be true for two reasons. Heretical ideas, of a "revisionist" character, began to be reflected in the Polish press as early as 1955. Secondly, a Soviet reader of the Polish or Yugoslav press could learn a good deal about Western European and American art and culture which is not reported in the Soviet press. Moreover, he could learn from the Polish and Yugoslav newspapers that in those countries people were allowed to see, hear, and do many things not permitted in the Soviet Union. There was probably some truth in the statement often made to foreign visitors in Poland and Yugoslavia that cultural contacts between these countries and the Soviet Union exerted a certain liberalizing influence on Russians. One Pole told me in Warsaw in 1957 that Russians regarded the Polish capital as a "little Paris." Another told me that, while Poland desired a great expansion of contacts with the United States, these had to be managed carefully, as the Kremlin, fearful of contagion, was "watching us."

It is only fair to report in conclusion of this chapter that the post-Stalin era saw a welcome increase in Soviet willingness to open up libraries and even to provide, to a very limited extent, access to archival material to foreign scholars and experts. A handful of foreigners were, in fact, granted permission to work for brief periods in historical archives. Sometimes, unfortunately, this permission came so close to departure date as to be of very limited value. Even after a full year of American-Soviet graduate-student exchange, access to historical archives remained the exception rather than the rule, future possibilities were still obscure, and attempts to use interview methods in gathering the kinds of economic, sociological, and political data, the availability of which is taken for granted in the West, particularly in the United States, had run up against a maze of obstructionism and taboos. A few scholars, to be sure, were given access to unpublished masters- or doctoral-level dissertations, some of which contained excerpts from semiconfidential sources, as Professor John A. Armstrong of the University of Wisconsin reported in an informative article in the April 1957 issue of the *Russian Review*. Professor Armstrong made further fruitful use of such sources on another Soviet journey in 1958.

Access to dissertations was part of a pattern of modest relaxation of communications controls, other features of which included exchanges of photographs, microfilms, photostats of manuscripts, mainly in the field of literature, and, of course, a resumption of controlled but useful contacts and correspondence between Soviet and foreign scholars, scientists, and artists. These trends did much to break the nearly hermetical isolation of the 1947-1953 era. An interesting indication of the attitude disseminated in party circles toward the relative freedom of communication after Stalin's death was contained in a dissertation presented in 1955 to the Institute for Improvement of Preparation of Teachers of Marxism-Leninism, of Leningrad University, by V. A. Bondarenko, under the title "The Struggle of the Communist Party of the Soviet Union for the Elevation of the Political Vigilance of the Soviet People in the Post-War Period."

Mr. Bondarenko took occasion, among other things, to assert that Britain and America had tried to use Russian-language publications such as *Amerika* and *Britanski Soyuznik* (*British Ally*), distributed in the Soviet Union by official government agreement, to propagandize the superiority of the British and American way of life. He accused these "imperialist states" of attempting to utilize the Anglo-Soviet-American alliance to create an espionage network in Russia. Also, he stated that, while Soviet membership in the United Nations, exchanges of delegations, and the like were desirable, they had disadvantages too, for the "imperialists" sought to use their relations with the U.S.S.R. to the detriment of the latter.[10]

Persistence of the suspicions reflected in such writings, as well as in public statements by Soviet leaders, warns us not to expect an early disappearance of the Iron Curtain. Recent and striking reminders of the continued Soviet fear of freedom were contained in some of Mr. Khrushchev's angry replies to queries addressed to him during his trip to America regarding the possibility of removal of the restrictions still in existence on access by Soviet citizens to uncensored information from abroad. At the same time, Khrushchev displayed resourcefulness in concealing this major

---

[10] V. A. Bondarenko, "Borba kommunisticheskoi partii sovetskogo soyuza za povyshenie politicheskoi bditelnosti sovetskogo naroda v poslevoennyi period," Leningrad, 1955, unpublished typescript, pp. 62, 63, 66. I am indebted to Professor Armstrong for bringing to my attention this dissertation and the material contained in the above pages.

Soviet vulnerability. Indeed, he sought to create the false impression that Washington, rather than Moscow, was blocking expansion of exchanges of persons. This line is taken, of course, by Soviet Embassy staff-members on their now frequent speaking tours to universities and clubs. It will deceive no one who takes the trouble to check Soviet assurances of a belief in the free competition of ideas against the draconian provisions of the Law on Criminal Liability for State Crimes published on December 26, 1958, and amended on January 13, 1960. According to this law even such vague concepts as dissemination of "fabrications defaming the Soviet state and social system" can be punished by exile or "deprivation of freedom" for periods up to ten years, while flight from the U.S.S.R. or refusal to return can carry the death penalty. The January 1960 amendment, providing that a Soviet citizen "recruited by a foreign intelligence service" is not subject to prosecution if he voluntarily reports his "assignment" may indicate realization of the difficulty of continuing to exercise minute surveillance over increasingly frequent communications between Soviet citizens and foreigners.

CHAPTER V

PATTERNS OF COMMUNICATION, GUIDED
AND MISGUIDED

IN SPITE of the obstacles discussed in the preceding chapter, an encouraging, and perhaps surprising, feature of the cultural encounter is the amount of communication in which it results. Since a Westerner can most easily study the East-West or, more correctly, the Soviet-Western, sector of this complex pattern, it is that aspect with which this chapter deals. We are concerned here with the setting and tone of East-West communication more than with its content.

The term "communication" is, of course, used here in a broad sense. Some readers may feel that "manipulation" would better describe the intent, at least, of the Soviet effort. Moscow's incessant attacks on "alien" foreign influences indicate the persistence of Soviet cultural unilateralism. Most participants in exchanges may remain "of the same opinion still," particularly when there is a determined and usually sensible effort on both sides to avoid controversial subjects. In spite of all this, however, there is evidence that learning, thinking, and feeling, as well as furious and exhausting activity, occur in these contacts of rival systems.

This chapter is based upon personal experience in Russia in 1956, 1958, and 1959 and in Poland and Czechoslovakia in 1957, four years of earlier experience in the Soviet Union, more than one hundred unpublished travel reports, and extensive correspondence and hundreds of interviews. Despite all precautions, the results of such a study must inevitably remain somewhat impressionistic. In the present state of knowledge, this would probably be true even in relations between, let us say, England and America, where complete freedom of research and the application of statistical methods would be possible. As for Soviet Russia, it is impossible even to estimate how many Soviet citizens see, come in contact with, or talk to the average foreign visitor. However, if one assumes that each of the 15,000 to 20,000 Americans, for example, who were in Russia during the four years 1956-1959, "interacted" in some way with perhaps 200 Soviet citizens, one can derive a rather impressive figure.

One explanation for the spectacular variety of reports brought back by foreign travelers from Russia is that most of them do not understand the difference between the Soviet and the Western conceptions of personal opinion. Even in a country as anticommunist as the United States there is no general or obligatory official doctrine regarding the Soviet Union. In Soviet Russia, on the other hand, there is not only a dogmatic official philosophy but also an official opinion, or even an instruction, on every problem of life. These directives are constantly brought up to date in public statements by political leaders and are incessantly repeated by the official press and radio. The loyal, or prudent, Soviet citizen usually echoes the official line in his conversations with a foreigner, although of course he does not always do so, particularly if for some reason he trusts him or is pretty certain he will never see him again. One of the delightful surprises of travel in Russia consists of conversations in which Soviet citizens express personal, unorthodox opinions.

Still, it remains true that candid exchanges of opinions between Soviet citizens and noncommunist foreigners are likely to be either covert and clandestine or the result of ignorance or irresponsibility upon one side or the other. In so far as the rulers of a closed society are successful, manipulation replaces discussion. As one returned traveler put it, when one talks to Soviet officials, at least on formal occasions, with the inevitable witnesses present, one usually receives stock answers to stock questions.

Some of the minor but time-consuming administrative aspects of Soviet travel, of course, take up much of the time that under more normal conditions would be devoted to exchange of opinions. While the extension of hospitality to foreigners is obviously regarded as politically important, the ablest Soviet citizens are not, as a rule, assigned to this type of work. This is, however, much more true with respect to chauffeurs, waiters, and other service personnel than with respect to the sometimes very highly educated guides and interpreters. There are many pleasant exceptions, of course, but inefficiency and even obstructionism are all too common. In general, the traveler is likely to find himself spending so much time trying to find almost-but-not-quite nonexistent telephone books, making appointments, getting service in restaurants, et cetera, that much of the time and energy that he hoped to devote to observation is lost. It is indeed amazing how chaotic the "planned" society can often be. Perhaps this is one reason why so many travelers, including young and vigorous ones, report fatigue and even exhaustion after travel in Russia. A succession of irritations helps to jangle the nerves. Europeans and Americans unaccustomed to Soviet regulations can find it disconcerting to be without their passports, which are normally taken up upon arrival in each Soviet city, and are often held for several days by the Intourist authorities. As in the case of Soviet citizens in transit, the documents of foreign travelers have to be registered in each city with the police. It is also very wearing to be rushed without rest from one sight-seeing tour to another, to the accompaniment of shouts of *"programma, programma!"* ("program, program!"). To some degree the frustrations inherent in this pattern can be avoided by careful advance preparation. If one knows exactly what and whom one wishes to see, and is armed with names and addresses and telephone numbers, one naturally is treated with greater respect and courtesy than if one asks aimless and superfluous questions.

Perhaps the decisive factor determining the atmosphere of communication between a visiting foreigner and his Soviet hosts is the foreigner's political perspective. It is not a question of whether or not the foreigner is a communist or a fellow-traveler. If for any reason a foreigner during the period while he is in the Soviet Union is in a mood to listen sympathetically to the Soviet case, he is, of course, likely to receive much more friendly treatment than if he is hostile or indifferent. In part, this is only the pattern that one should expect in any society. However, because of the political element in Soviet hospitality, the range in Soviet Russia between "red carpet" treatment and the relative indifference displayed toward ordinary visitors is wider than in most other countries. Soviet hospitality is likely to be particularly seductive when applied to individuals with above-average susceptibility to flattery. Impecunious intellectuals, ignored or slighted in their home countries, are extraordinarily amenable to calculated flattery. However, experienced politicians also have sometimes responded, at least temporarily, to this treatment.[1] So also, on occasion, have Western businessmen, both in Russia and abroad, as perhaps was the case when some Americans were exposed, in January 1959, to the blandishments of Anastas Ivanovich Mikoyan. Official hospitality, plus the spontaneous friendliness and charm of the Russian people, create an atmosphere of cordiality. Klaus Mehnert, one of the most perceptive German observers of Russian affairs, has expressed the opinion that the warm and open-hearted reception accorded by Soviet citizens to Prime Minister Nehru of India during his visit in 1955 favorably influenced Nehru's attitude not only toward the Russian people but toward the Soviet regime as well.[2]

Even the most cordial hospitality could not, probably, make a lasting impression on a person basically hostile to the Soviet regime. On the other hand, persons who come to Russia with favorable predispositions tend to overlook or explain away discrepancies between myth and reality. There are still a few Western intellectuals who attribute magic properties to socialism. Persons imbued with this semireligious attitude toward the U.S.S.R. view the most trivial details of daily life through enchanted eyes. I once pointed out to an American university professor, in Finland, the superiority of the Finnish standard of living to that of Soviet Russia. We had both recently been in Russia. Our friend swept the comparison aside with the remark, "But Finland is a bourgeois country." This kind of self-deception was brilliantly analyzed in Arthur Koestler's *The Yogi and the Commissar*. It may well be an important element in the psychology of many Asian and African intellectuals today. Persons in this blissful condition, of course, make life easier for Intourist than do those who ask embarrassing questions.

Wide-eyed, gaping curiosity of Soviet crowds, subway riders stealing furtive glances at foreigners' shoes, or young black marketeers approaching tourists on Leningrad streets with the question, "Do you want to sell your suit?" have for years been familiar features of the tourist's U.S.S.R. After the death of Stalin, a number of articles by European visitors asserted that the Russians had become so chauvinistic that they no longer displayed gawking

[1] Some of the statements made by some members of the United States Congress during visits to Russia in the summer of 1955 tend to bear out this hypothesis.

[2] *Christ und Welt*, July 26, 1956, p. 3.

curiosity about foreigners. In fact, it was often asserted that the average Soviet citizen was likely to lecture a visiting foreigner on the superiority of Soviet culture to the "decadent" Western culture. The change perhaps reflected a growth of self-confidence among the upper strata of Soviet citizens, who are gradually overcoming the traditional Russian inferiority complex toward the West. If this is happening, it is not necessarily cause for concern. Confidence in one's own culture is an indispensable basis for sympathetic understanding of foreign cultures. It is, in fact, the best antidote to chauvinism and provincialism.

Professor Philip E. Mosely, a leading American authority on Russia, reported in 1956: "Today there is almost no trace left of the former Russian deference for the science and culture of the West; it has given way to self-confidence, boasting and arrogance."[3] While this observation may appear to be borne out by the behavior of party and administrative bigwigs, especially in the self-conscious atmosphere of formal conversations with visiting notables, during my 1956, 1958, and 1959 trips to Russia, I found that American technological achievements and the American standard of living still enjoyed tremendous prestige among Soviet people; the events of the post-Stalin years have not caused me to alter my opinion on this score, nor to shake my confidence in the appeal of freedom of choice to Soviet citizens, if and when they become aware of its nature, scope, and allure. Again and again, in recent years, I have been told by American literary scholars, historians, and other sensitive observers how impressed, embarrassed, or envious Soviet colleagues appeared to be when it was pointed out to them that in America we feel that a scholar simply must have access to all of the facts and sources about, for example, Dudintsev or Pasternak, in order properly to perform his functions of analysis and interpretation. Similarly, while it is probably true that the majority of Soviet citizens cannot understand the give and take of American democratic politics, some of the more thoughtful among them are impressed favorably by the freedom of Americans, even while traveling in the U.S.S.R., for example, to criticize particular aspects of American domestic and foreign policy with which they are in disagreement. The existence of varied trends of thought among

---

[3] Mosely, *Foreign Affairs*, October 1956, p. 81.

Soviet people becomes apparent to the foreign observer, not only from on-the-spot experience and interviews with those who have had such experience, but by inference from Kremlin behavior, as, for example, in the effort made by Soviet authorities to force Soviet writers to eliminate, even from already published novels and plays, passages which may exert a disturbing influence on Soviet citizens who feel, as one young man put it to a visiting American, "in disharmony" with the prevalent intellectual atmosphere. We should add here that, when asked if the conditions of life in Russia had improved in recent years, this young man said, "Yes." About one point almost all post-Stalin visitors in the U.S.S.R. are in agreement. This is the enormous, unquenchable curiosity of Soviet people, especially the young people, about foreign visitors. This has, to be sure, diminished somewhat in Moscow, but is still intense in provincial cities.

The opposite of chauvinism was indicated by the statement of a young man to me in a hotel dining room. When I told the youth that I found conditions improved in comparison with those I had earlier observed in the Soviet Union, the latter smiled indulgently and replied: "This is Moscow. You ought to see the countryside." A Soviet science student spent about three hours one evening telling two Americans that everything in Russia, from technology to beer and night life, was inferior to what was available in the West. Many travelers, even in 1958 and 1959, reported the almost-abnormal popularity of Western jazz and other symbols of "decadent" Western culture among Soviet young people. Some wishful thinkers even regard these attitudes as indications of a process of decomposition in the Soviet system. While this seems a naïve conclusion, it is, at any rate, pretty certain that foreign visitors who get away from their Intourist guides will find themselves subjects of an intense curiosity, which may reflect boredom with Soviet drabness and regimentation.

This is particularly true if the foreigners are young and conspicuously Western in dress. A typical American college boy is likely to find himself the center of friendly, autograph-seeking crowds. A middle-aged man in a dark blue suit and sport shirt will perhaps be ignored, partly because his national identity is difficult to establish. On the other hand, the group of well-heeled Oklahoma farmers and small-town bankers that visited Russia in May 1956 made a hit with their ten-gallon hats, good-luck chains, and other paraphernalia which doubtless made them as exotic to Russians as Russians seemed to Oklahomans. Roy Steward gave a breezy account of the trip in his "Country Boy" column in the *Daily Oklahoman.*

The Russian, Ukrainian, Uzbek, and Georgian "country boys" and girls of the Soviet folk-dance groups that made a tremendous impression in America in 1958 and 1959 received at least as cordial a reception from concert-hall audiences and radio and television viewers as did visiting Oklahomans from Soviet farmers in 1956 or the skaters of the Holiday on Ice company whose performances were watched by nearly a million Muscovites in 1959. Such events were typical of the hundreds that demonstrated the inability of propaganda stereotypes to destroy the feeling of common humanity, so easily rekindled by direct contact under favorable circumstances. Sensing this, ordinary people in most countries favor relaxing barriers to communication. Despite its element of naïvete, the desire is a sound one.

Soviet Russians, by and large, seem to be less mistrustful of foreigners than of one another. This fact, combined with curiosity and with the highly developed Russian sense of hospitality, makes them set an astonishing premium on association with foreigners, at least so long as party and police do not interfere. For example, a group of Turkish airmen on their way home from the Moscow Air Parade in 1956 were almost mobbed by an amazingly friendly crowd in Odessa. Even when one or two of the Russian-speaking Turks explained who they were, the crowd displayed no hostility, but continued to gape at the proud, handsome, and smartly uniformed aviators. Incidentally, one of the Turks took the opportunity to point out to an American that Soviet personnel in Turkey had done a much better job of learning the Turkish language than had their American counterparts.

The occupation, specific professional interests, and status of a traveler, of course, have a good deal to do with determining his access to Soviet citizens and the degree of rapport he can establish with his hosts. Students and teachers, for example, are relatively favored groups in Soviet society, at least in terms of financial support and prestige. Visiting foreigners sometimes fail to realize that Soviet scholars pay a price for their privileges in conformity to official political and ideological objectives. Foreign students and professors are often gratified by the deference displayed toward them by Soviet colleagues and political authorities, especially if they are in the U.S.S.R. on short trips. If they stay more than the tourist's thirty days, they become better acquainted with surveillance and controls, although during the "thaw" of 1955-1956 the few Western students in Soviet universities enjoyed a surprising degree of personal freedom.

According to information in my possession the French, Norwegian, and other foreign students at Moscow University were able, before the Hungarian revolution, to mingle freely with Soviet students, although this report must be tempered by our knowledge of Soviet ability to veil the exercise of oversight. At least one American traveler in 1955-1956 attributed much of the success of his very rewarding visit to Russia to his contacts with French students, who put him in touch with Soviet students. Toward the end of his stay, to be sure, he was shadowed, perhaps because of his contacts with suspect Soviet intellectuals.

Two Norwegian students, selected by the National Union of Norwegian Students and the Norwegian Student Society under an official exchange program with the Anti-Fascist Committee of the Soviet Youth, not only were permitted to live in the students' dormitory on the new university campus of the University of Moscow, as have other foreign students, but were allowed to travel widely in the Soviet Union without guides or interpreters. One of the students reported in a letter to me that he and his friend preferred "to make personal observations of the life in the Soviet Union, rather than concentrating on books." The two students were furnished with teachers of Russian and apparently were given every assistance, and at the same time allowed considerable freedom.

As we have noted earlier, there were reports that relations between some of the French students and the university authorities cooled somewhat after the Hungarian uprising. Perhaps the relations of Soviet students with students of those communist countries with which the Soviet Union still has close and cordial relations remained unaffected by the trouble in Hungary and other disturbing events. Information on this subject is extremely scarce. According to an issue of the Moscow University newspaper, a Czech woman student in her history examination in the spring of 1956 described "how Czechoslovakia in 1938 was handed over by the Anglo-American imperialists to the tortures of Hitler."[4] One surmises that publication of such items in Soviet periodicals is a defensive reaction against "alien" ideas, likely to have a certain fascination for students.

It seems probable that the Soviet authorities are less wary about permitting students, professors, and intellectuals of "underdeveloped" countries to come in close and intimate contact with Soviet citizens than they are about Western Europeans and Americans, particularly the latter. However, some of the most outspokenly anticommunist American students who attended the Sixth World Festival of Youth and Students in 1957 reported keen interest among Soviet students in such controversial subjects as the United Nations Report on Hungary. It is difficult to disagree with the conclusions of several of these young men that it was a mistake for the United States government to discourage attendance at the festival. As Harvard Law School graduate George S. Abrams said, "Other countries sent delegations of 2,000 to 2,500 people. We should have sent 2,500."[5]

The kinds of situations in which foreigners in the U.S.S.R. can communicate with Soviet citizens may be divided into three main categories. There is formal, organized communication with officials or professionals, usually arranged in advance. This pattern prevails, usually, in the experience of foreign delegations. Many travelers, including perhaps most ordinary tourists, come in contact mainly with workers of Intourist or occasionally with members of the staff of the Union of Soviet Friendship Societies, the Foreign Commission of the Union of Soviet Writers, or other organizations whose duty it is to play host to foreigners. The highest-ranking foreign groups are likely to be taken in hand, as was noted earlier, by the State Committee on Cultural Relations. Finally, depending

[4] *Moskovski Universitet*, No. 37, June 1956. One copy of this newspaper was obtained in the Soviet Union and later the editors, in response to a letter, sent me three other copies, but it proved to be impossible to obtain additional ones.
[5] *New York Herald Tribune*, August 26, 1957.

upon the luck, resourcefulness, and energy of the foreign traveler, he may have all manner of casual encounters with ordinary Soviet citizens. Usually in such encounters a Soviet citizen finds himself talking to a foreigner for the first time in his life.

Because of the highly political nature of Soviet tourism and other foreign travel, contacts between Soviet travelers in capitalist countries and natives of those countries are likely to be mainly on a formal, official basis, and Soviet travelers abroad, except for glad-handing politicos like Mikoyan, Kozlov, or Khrushchev, maintain a stance of collective aloofness. There are some exceptions to this rule. For example, the N.T.S., an organization of Russian anticommunists, claims that it establishes contact with Soviet sailors and diplomats abroad and with most of the Soviet scientific, cultural, and sporting delegations traveling in the free world.[6] A number of Soviet refugees have communicated effectively, even intimately, with members of Soviet delegations. Also, we have been informed by persons who have traveled with Soviet delegations in America that some of their members, after the ice has been broken, become almost embarrassingly communicative. This seems to apply especially to rugged Soviet engineers and industrial executives, whose behavior, like that of some American counterparts, is a good deal less circumspect than is the conduct of either politicians or academics.

Particularly well coached in the Soviet arts of one-way communication, apparently, were the more than five hundred guides, experts, and officials who represented communism at the Soviet exhibition in New York in 1959. Both from on-the-spot observation and from an informative special section of *Newsweek* for July 14, 1959, one gained the impression that these people were acting under the most precise instructions. According to *Newsweek*, the Soviet staff were not permitted, while off duty, to engage in such dangerous activities as "fraternizing" with Americans, drinking in bars, et cetera. Accounts of conversations with some of the Soviet guides indicated that their answers to questions were laconic and impersonal and that they were usually careful not to be drawn into extended talk and themselves refrained from asking questions of visitors to the exhibition.

[6] Circular letter from editor of N.T.S. magazine *Possev*, dated July 18, 1956.

In the first five years following the death of Stalin about three hundred Western scholars, including most of the leading American experts on the Soviet Union, traveled on an individual basis in Russia. There seems to be a rather high degree of consensus among travelers of this type regarding the nature of communication between them and Soviet citizens. This does not, however, preclude striking differences of opinion about details. The impression that one gets from reading the reports of these scholars, and from talking with them, is that they found their trips extremely useful and interesting, but that on the whole neither Soviet officials nor ordinary citizens opened up very much in conversation with them. However, even the relatively cautious type of conversations that were the norm were a pleasant surprise to many Western students and professors. Fairly typical is the remark, "I found the people much more friendly than I had dared to hope." Expectations, in the case of these well-prepared travelers, seem to have been modest, with the result that they were relatively easy to please. In part, this response probably represents something of a reaction against the tendentious tone of much Western press reporting on the Soviet Union.

There seems to be overwhelming agreement among most of the Americans, at least, who have visited Russia as tourists that it is extremely difficult to talk politics with Soviet citizens. There are, however, exceptions even to this generalization. For example, one American professor told us that he felt that questions put by Soviet law students reflected genuine concern over the problem of concentration of political authority in Russia. However, feigned incomprehension, ingeniously tangential replies, or indignant parroting of the official policy are among the common responses to political questions. Some foreigners have reported that Soviet people are equipped with a wealth of slogans but with a minimum of facts about either domestic or foreign politics.

In such a situation real discussion is difficult. Each side states its case and it is doubtful if either understands the position of the other. After our 1956 summer trip to the Soviet Union and to several countries of Western Europe we returned more than ever convinced that real discussion is possible only among citizens of free countries. Among countries under communist rule, however,

Poland seems to be an anomaly. In six days in Warsaw in 1957 we learned more and had more good discussions than in our thirty-two days in Russia in 1956. There is overwhelming evidence from the accounts of dozens of other travelers that, in this respect at least, Poland after October 1956 became a more normal country, by Western standards, than any other Soviet-orbit state.

Almost any Russian-speaking traveler could give examples of the ludicrous lengths to which Soviet people, particularly officials, can carry tactics of evasion. I accompanied a delegation of American rabbis on a visit to the chief of the Leningrad Administration of Culture in July 1956. The rabbis asked difficult, even provocative questions regarding various aspects of Jewish cultural life in the Soviet Union. Someone asked the official why the famous Moscow Jewish Theater had been closed. He, and the Intourist guide who was also present, attempted to ignore this question. When pressed hard, the official said that it had been closed "because of the war." This was a peculiarly unsatisfactory answer. Many of us on the American embassy staff had witnessed performances of this theater several times in 1944 and 1945. Moreover, the war had been over for more than ten years.

A participant in a delegation of French members of the Russian Orthodox Church reported that the only frank conversations they had with Soviet clergymen and other citizens took place by accident when the Russians were alone with members of the French group. While visiting a Kiev church I recognized an American who had once been one of my students. The Intourist guides almost resorted to physical violence in their effort to prevent conversation between us.

It is well to realize that official and individual fears are not the only factors involved in the pattern described here. A touchy chauvinism, which is associated with remnants of the old Russian inferiority complex toward the West, undoubtedly plays an important part. Moreover, the Soviet government, and patriotic Soviet citizens, find it almost impossible to admit that Russians are not morally superior to citizens of the "decadent" capitalist countries. For some years now they have even been loath to admit that Russia was not superior to the West in terms of material culture, although, as we have noted earlier, many Soviet citizens, particularly in the lower-income brackets, still make no attempt to conceal their admiration for Western wares. For example, in 1958 a Soviet store clerk obligingly demonstrated to us the uses of the abacus, and then said that foreigners who come from countries where more advanced methods of calculation are in use consider the abacus primitive.

Some foreigners have found that tact and a sense of humor can break down the smug, self-righteous façade with which Soviet people often begin a conversation with a traveler. Professor Harold J. Berman reported that during his visit in 1955 in almost every casual conversation he was asked questions "which expressed in unmistakable terms a passionate belief in Soviet superiority, coupled with an eagerness for foreign confirmation of that superiority." But when this self-satisfaction was challenged, the reply was usually a sober statement to the effect that Soviet material conditions, though still not easy, had been improving steadily.[7]

In Leningrad I had a long and friendly argument with a political worker about international relations. When we told him that we were willing to credit the Soviet people and government with a desire for peace but that it seemed to us that Soviet ideology made it impossible for Soviet people to entertain the same attitude toward the United States, he replied, "Ideology is ideology, but bombs are bombs." Evasive and even fatuous though it was, this remark seemed to indicate the possibility of a certain amount of what might be described as unacknowledged communication. A similar impression is derived from reading some of the accounts by Americans of conversations with the highly sophisticated delegation of Soviet journalists in the United States in 1955. Well-educated Soviet citizens seem to be saying, at times, that, while they cannot openly admit the correctness of a foreigner's argument, they are impressed by its merit. The obvious sincerity with which Soviet intellectuals, even those in semiofficial posts, express their delight that since the death of Stalin it has at least become possible once again to meet foreign colleagues confirms the impression that such contacts are more useful than a tape recording might indicate.

It would be grossly inaccurate to assert that no real arguments

[7] "Impressions of Moscow," in *Harvard Law School Bulletin*, December 1955, pp. 7-8.

take place between Soviet citizens and foreigners. It would be still more inaccurate to report that a foreign traveler in Russia never hears an unorthodox opinion. If one challenges any major proposition of the official ideology, particularly in the office of a *Pravda* editor, for example, one is likely to be subjected to a vehement counterattack. When I objected to an assertion in an article in *New Times* by Eugene Varga, noted Soviet economist, that in America the workers were "slaves of capital," a *Pravda* editor told me, "Just because we believe in coexistence does not mean that we are going to stop criticizing you." My statement that at least American workers had the right to strike was met with the indignant question, "Do you recommend that Soviet workers should strike against the state?" Both sides soon realized the fruitlessness of this kind of argument and the conversation turned to relatively innocuous subjects such as education. Throughout the discussion it was difficult to know whether the two Soviet editors were sincere in their indignation or whether they were putting on an act.

Every kind of authoritarianism breeds an appropriate heresy. The attempt to create the "new Soviet man" leads, at least in some cases, not only to heresy but also to apathy, cynicism, crude materialism, "hooliganism," and even to a kind of amoralism which rejects all forms of social control. People imbued with attitudes of criticism and protest sometimes seek out visiting foreigners and pour out their troubles to them. Many youths who have studied foreign languages, particularly English, lurk at dusk near the entrances of Intourist hotels. Conversations with this type of Soviet citizen have often been reported in the Western press. Individuals of this type are likely to converge in unusually large numbers on such groups of foreign visitors as the British naval personnel who visited Leningrad in October 1955 or the Dutch naval visitors of July 1956. It is impossible to know how significant or representative are the complaints about Soviet life sometimes voiced by such people, but conversations with citizens who seek out foreign visitors are one of the most conspicuous new features of the Soviet scene.

There is a fairly high degree of consensus among competent observers that only a very small minority even of this category of Soviet people are fundamentally opposed to the Soviet political system. One of the most perceptive accounts of recent travel contains the statement, "Certainly it may exist, but I did not encounter any of that desperate desire to escape political persecution or cultural backwardness which has characterized so many *émigré* intellectuals in the past."[8] On the basis of many such reports, one tends to conclude that Soviet intellectuals, and probably even student youths, accept the basic values and premises of the system. Their grievances are either individual or are directed against what they consider to be misapplication or perversion of socialist principles. There seems to be an almost total lack of ability to conceive of an alternative to the planned economy and the one-party state. If this is true, it is easy to understand why foreign travelers report that Soviet citizens cannot conceive that there could be more than "one truth." Such a pattern of thought obviously interposes formidable barriers to communication. It does, however, pose challenges to communications and is, perhaps, one of the main reasons why believers in the open society will want to continue their efforts to provide alternative concepts to people in whom there may be a latent desire for cultural and eventually political freedom.

A few travelers have reported conversations with Soviet citizens whose denunciations of the regime were so bitter that they could not help thinking that the surface conformity of the majority concealed a desire for drastic change. Continual defection from Soviet rule of even privileged elements of communist society, including army officers and diplomats, lends some credence to such a surmise. Some foreign visitors felt that among the reactions to denunciation of Stalin at the Twentieth Party Congress was anger that the truth about Stalin had been so long concealed from the people. An American college student reported that his Intourist guide had somewhat cynically commented on the exposure of Stalin's "mistakes." The young guide said that previously all good had been attributed to Stalin; now all evil was blamed on him. On the whole, however, depressing though the conclusion may be to believers in constitutional democracy, the results of post-Stalin travel indicate that for some time to come there will be little possibility of communicating political ideas to the essentially unpolitical Soviet people.

There is widespread but by no means universal agreement among

[8] Kathryn Feuer, "Russia's Young Intellectuals," in *Encounter*, February 1957, pp. 10-25. Quotation on p. 14.

Western experts that it is difficult to achieve spontaneity in communicating with Russians, even when they are alone and safe from the prying eyes of officials. Most travel accounts, both published and unpublished, contain few and usually brief references to visits to Soviet homes. Concern for the welfare of Soviet citizens may cause many foreign travelers to fail to report such visits. When visits to Soviet homes can be arranged, it is often because official permission has been requested and granted. Some members of the two groups of American rabbis that visited the Soviet Union in 1956 and of the group of French socialists in that year made this type of chaperoned visit. There is wide agreement that, just as during the days of Stalin, Soviet people feel more at ease with foreigners on trains, in theaters, in parks, and in non-Intourist restaurants than in most other places. Some visitors, however, have found that the people's courts, which are freely open to the public, offer excellent opportunities to observe Soviet life and to engage in conversations with Soviet people. Ingenious individuals have devised various ways of attracting attention, which have sometimes led to rewarding conversations. For example, interesting and sometimes harrowing conversations between Soviet and foreign Jews have resulted from display by the latter of Yiddish newspapers.

Probably the majority even of the rather special category of travelers who go to the Soviet Union are not very much interested in politics or in ideology. The exchange of professional or technical information is less difficult than the communication of ideas. This statement probably applies equally to individuals and to group interaction. Of course, much depends upon the emotional atmosphere of even an informational or technical conversation. Since one of the major objectives of the post-Stalin Soviet leadership has been to obtain useful information from the capitalist countries, persons who are considered to possess such information are likely to receive cordial hospitality. Scientists and scholars in all countries are usually men of good will. Many Western intellectuals, particularly natural scientists, are not inclined to make an energetic demand for reciprocity in exchanges with their colleagues in communist countries.

At any rate, most American scientists queried regarding scientific exchanges with the Russians have expressed enthusiasm regarding the results of exchanges in which they or their colleagues have participated. Most of the Americans and Western Europeans interviewed regarding other kinds of exchanges, including those in the field of history and social science, have also taken a favorable view of their results. This generally favorable attitude seems to be shared also by many businessmen, at least by American businessmen, who have been in Russia.

Soviet officials and professional men, even if somewhat tense, are usually smooth and tactful in dealing with foreign visiting groups. A considerable effort is made to avoid overt propaganda. This policy involves not only self-censorship, tact, and restraint but also a certain amount of dissimulation. In 1956 I had the good fortune to accompany a large party of wealthy American businessmen on some of their sight-seeing trips in Moscow. An exceptionally fine tour, conducted by some of the ablest and most experienced Intourist guides, was arranged for this select group.

In factories, at the famous Moscow GUM Department Store, in the Lenin Library, and elsewhere the group was cordially received by top-ranking executives. Refreshments, including cognac and several kinds of wine, were served on several occasions. A very impressive program of entertainment was provided in the Palace of Culture of the Moscow automobile factory.

Every effort was made to convey the impression to this important group that there was no real ideological or political difference between the Soviet Union and the United States. When a member of the group asked an executive of the Moscow automobile factory what kinds of personnel were employed there, he replied, "As in America, management and labor." No mention was made of the communist party. During a tour of the impressive thirty-three-story skyscraper of Moscow University, the Intourist guide mentioned philosophy as one of the subjects taught, but said nothing about instruction in Marxism-Leninism.

During our postwar trips we gained the impression that soft-pedaling of ideological differences was Intourist's order of the day. Guides in Odessa and Leningrad made no mention of the communist party, but, in referring to what was obviously the headquarters building of the party, used the euphemism of "political center." When a guide in one Soviet city was asked where the children were during the summer, the reply was that they were away for the entire summer in camps. Only by accident was it learned that children who were sent to camps at all normally went for periods of three weeks. Guides were eager to take individuals or groups to see palaces of culture, museums, libraries, nurseries, and other institutions by which visiting scholars, scientists, and professional men, as well as many of the businessmen of the type who visit the Soviet Union, are most likely to be impressed.

Careful preparation and presentation cannot deceive real experts. In some fields, of course, it is not necessary for the Soviet authorities to resort to "window-dressing." In others, military security rules an object completely out of bounds. Sometimes part of an industrial plant, for example, is shown, while some of the shops, presumably making military goods, are not displayed. A similar selectivity seems to apply in deciding whether or not foreigners should be allowed to take photographs. The only shop of the Moscow automobile plant in which the American businessmen referred to above were allowed to take pictures was the bicycle shop.

It may be interesting briefly to report the impressions of some American experts. A ballet critic reported that in 1956 he had no trouble in seeing anything he wanted to see, even to getting into school examinations and ballet classes and rehearsals which are not usually open to the public in any other country. He and his wife were allowed to take all the pictures that they desired. Similar friendly helpfulness was accorded to a student of the Soviet children's theater in 1959. On the other hand, a political scientist reported a conversation with two engineering students who "were disappointed to find that I was not an engineer," and one of whom "parted abruptly from me when I told him I was a professor of government."[9] Members of several American medical groups informed me in letters that they were well satisfied with their visits to Russia, during which they had been permitted to see everything that they wished to see. However, visiting physicians have failed to get some of the statistics, for example, that they requested on mortality and morbidity rates.

[9] Merle Fainsod, "What Russian Students Think," in *Atlantic Monthly*, Vol. 199, February, 1957, pp. 31-36.

Three outstanding American engineers, selected by the American Society of Chemical Engineers, made a sixteen-day trip to study Soviet industrial plants and technical institutions in December 1955. A member of the group wrote a thirty-nine-page pamphlet describing the trip. While the report was soberly factual, it indicated that the Soviet authorities were willing to make a good deal of information available to competent foreigners, in return for equal access to similar information in the latter's countries. Members of the American group were asked to detail faults and shortcomings that they had noticed. The author stated that the Russians seemed pleased that the criticism was offered in good faith and without intention to belittle and added, "Their eagerness to improve industrial conditions and industrial techniques is matched only by their aggressiveness in attacking problems involved in bringing their industry abreast with manufacturing conditions in other countries."[10] The president of the National Cash Register Company, S. C. Allyn, stated in a report on his trip in June and July 1956 that he and his party had freedom of movement, talked to scores of Russians in all levels of society, and engaged in dozens of spontaneous conversations. Mr. Allyn presented these and other findings in a very attractive illustrated special issue of the *NCR Factory News* for September 1956.

One of the high lights of 1955 was travel by twenty-seven American Congressmen—nine Senators and eighteen Representatives—in the Soviet Union. While little information is available on the degree to which the Congressmen were able to exchange ideas with Soviet people, it is clear from American press reports published shortly after their return that travel in Russia made at least a short-term impression on many of them. Senator Ellender of Louisiana, for example, reportedly said after a conversation with Khrushchev that he believed the Russians wanted peace just as Americans did.[11] Most of the Congressmen came away with the impression that the Soviet leaders had a sincere desire for peace, although most also warned that "the West should not drop its guard." Most also seemed to feel that there should be "more

[10] Nevil Bean, "The New Soviet Machine Age—A Look at Automation in Russia," Ford Motor Co., Dearborn, Michigan, p. 39.

[11] *New York Times*, September 4, 1955.

trade" between East and West.[12] When Senator Russell B. Long of Louisiana visited the Soviet Union in August 1956, he had to travel as an ordinary tourist and experienced some of the frustrations inherent in this status. Senator Long reported after his trip that "Americans will make a bad mistake to underrate the effectiveness of the Soviet Intourist program. Their guides are extremely courteous and polite. With finesse and adroitness they conduct visitors to see the Soviet best, carefully and effectively steering them around and away from the worst or even the average. They succeed in making a favorable impression, even on an American of considerable means."[13]

A number of American artists have performed in the Soviet Union since the death of Stalin. In addition, many executives, producers, and other notables of stage and screen have gone to Russia for the purpose of selling or exchanging films or other productions. Despite a great deal of lavish hospitality on the Soviet side, and the exercise of energetic salesmanship on the American side, the results of these activities have not, on the whole, been impressive, at least from the point of view of securing access to the Soviet market for American films and the like.

One of the most interesting American cultural ventures in Russia was the four-week tour of the Everyman Opera, which presented *Porgy and Bess* in January 1956. This probably was the first tour of an American theatrical group to the Soviet Union. *Porgy and Bess* received excellent reviews in the Soviet press. The American ambassador attended the opening performance in Leningrad. In the summer of 1956 a Leningrad official spoke with obvious pleasure of having met the ambassador and other Americans after the performance. A Leningrad Intourist guide said that he had "loved" *Porgy and Bess*. There seems to be no doubt that the *Porgy and Bess* tour was a success.

Among other things, the tour brought American Negro artists to the Soviet stage. It also provided the occasion for a number of bizarre, semifurtive meetings between Soviet people and foreigners, the exotic flavor of which can be caught only by a professional

[12] Neal Stanford, in *Christian Science Monitor*, November 2, 1955.
[13] *Report on the Soviet Union, Poland and Czechoslovakia—August 1956*, U.S. Government Printing Office, Washington, 1957, p. 2.

writer. Fortunately Truman Capote was in the *Porgy and Bess* entourage. His two articles in the *New Yorker* for October 20 and 27, 1956, replete with odd incidents, some of them horrifying, suggest a mixed pattern of awkwardness, amusement, and self-conscious good will on both sides.

The appearances in Russia of, for example, Blanche Thebom, Jan Peerce, Van Cliburn, Isaac Stern, Leonard Warren, Leonard Bernstein and the tours of the Boston and Philadelphia Symphony Orchestras all received enthusiastic reviews in the Soviet press. Like the individual tours made here by the Soviet artists David Oistrakh, Emil Gilels, or Leonid Kogan, not to mention the sensational success of the Moiseiv or Beryozka troupes, these visits furnished a great deal of pleasure to many music lovers. On both sides the Soviet-American musical exchange was both a professional and a personal success.

Intourist guides spoke with special enthusiasm about Jan Peerce. Soviet critic Kabalevski wrote that the three concerts of the Boston Symphony Orchestra had been an outstanding success and that the public, including most of the outstanding Soviet musicians, had expressed its "sincere gratitude" for the genuine pleasure furnished by the orchestra's artistry.[14]

The strengths and weaknesses of Soviet cultural diplomacy are especially apparent in the behavior of Soviet travelers abroad. Whether they be tourists, artists and scientists, or officials, Soviet travelers are more carefully selected and work harder and more purposefully than their bourgeois counterparts. On the whole, they are effective in their assigned roles. They know what to say and when to say nothing. They also know what to publish when they return home.

Soviet artists and scientists have made an excellent impression in foreign countries since the death of Stalin. They make even less effort to conduct overt propaganda than do Soviet journalists or officials. Soviet artists and scientists, like Soviet chess players and athletes, do not have to engage in propaganda. The excellence of their performances is the best possible advertisement of Soviet culture.

Before 1952 the presence of a Soviet delegation at an inter-

14 *Pravda*, September 14, 1956.

145

national scientific conference was a rare event. Since the death of Stalin there has been a dramatic reversal of the old policy of scientific isolationism. Almost every issue of any leading European or United States newspaper, magazine, or scientific journal contains one or more items reporting participation by Soviet scientists in international gatherings. In science, as in every other kind of international activity, the Soviets today are ubiquitous. Fourteen Soviet delegations attended scientific meetings in 1952, thirty in 1953, and sixty-five in 1954. In August 1955 the Soviet Union sent to the Conference on Peaceful Uses of Atomic Energy at Geneva a delegation of over one hundred scientists, engineers, and technicians. The Soviet representatives, who displayed a high level of technical ability, presented seventy-four papers on various phases of atomic energy—the United States presented 166, the United Kingdom sixty-four, and France twenty-seven papers—and participated freely in scientific discussions.[15]

Like the summit conference which it followed, the Geneva Atomic Conference soothed the nerves of a troubled world. Socially and scientifically the Soviet delegation occupied the center of the stage. In her sympathetic account of the conference Laura Fermi states: "Russian scientists made, in general, an excellent impression on their Western colleagues. There is no doubt that scientists on both sides of the Iron Curtain enjoyed their new friendship immensely. Most of our American delegates found the Soviets quite free and willing to answer questions, although this was not always true."[16] Mrs. Fermi notes, although in passing, that a certain Soviet interpreter, who spoke technical English fluently, "was seen wherever any Russians went."[17] Interesting is her observation that "at our exhibit, in our technical library, and in discussions of all kinds, the Russians were the most eager of all the foreign delegates to obtain detailed information."[18]

One well-known American political philosopher presented a sharply negative point of view regarding Soviet behavior at Geneva. He wrote: "There is certainly a willingness to listen to

[15] Turkevich, *Annals*, January 1956, p. 146.
[16] *Atoms for the World*, Chicago, 1957, p. 128. Chapter VIII is entitled "Russian Scientists in Geneva."
[17] *Ibid.*, p. 122.
[18] *Ibid.*, p. 129.

what scientists of other lands are prepared to disclose about novel discoveries and processes, but—as some American members (Dr. Wigner, for example) of the Geneva Conference on Atomic Affairs have reported—the Soviet scientists feel no reciprocal need to tell much in return."[19]

The Soviet public relations policy in the field of scientific exchanges displayed at Geneva in 1955 was, on the whole, continued in subsequent years. Soviet scientists and scholars began to behave almost normally in their conversations with foreign colleagues. The change is illustrated by the experience of an American geologist who met Soviet geologists in India in 1954 and then in Mexico in 1956. In 1954 when the American tried to talk to his Soviet colleagues a Soviet interpreter cut off the conversation. In 1956 Soviet scientists approached him, were willing to engage in long and friendly conversations and to ride alone with him in busses. They eagerly presented reprints of their work and pointed out to him places in which they had cited his scientific publications. Soviet scientists, as well as scholars in other fields, began to engage in correspondence with foreign colleagues, usually regarding bibliographical and other nonpolitical matters. Summaries of scientific publications in foreign languages were resumed, and Soviet representatives at international gatherings no longer insisted that the Russian language be spoken at conferences, although they were pleased to meet Russian-speaking foreign scientists.

On the whole, however, Soviet intellectuals of all kinds have continued to behave with extreme caution while abroad. Nevertheless, their words or manner offer occasional hints of unorthodox thinking. Members of scientific, artistic, and medical groups have occasionally admitted that they had been "confused" by travel in America, and had found that life in this country was quite different from the official Soviet image. Sometimes questions asked by members of Soviet delegations are quite revealing. For examples, one is likely to hear, from American guides attached to Soviet visiting groups, of questions regarding prices of houses, automobiles, and clothing, which indicate keen interest in the material aspects of American life. Perhaps more significant are questions addressed to

[19] James Burnham, "Why Secrets?" in *Confluence*, Vol. 5, No. 2, July, 1956, pp. 166-176. Quotation on p. 173.

Americans—and Canadians—by, for example, members of the dance troupes that toured North America in 1959, regarding health insurance, educational opportunities for ordinary citizens, personal freedoms, et cetera.

Members of Soviet delegations abroad have on occasion expressed cryptic amusement at the sight of anti-Soviet historical and political books in libraries or in the offices of their hosts. One happy result of renewed Soviet travel abroad was the rediscovery of the Russian sense of humor. Members of Soviet delegations freely poke fun at one another and sometimes engage in banter regarding minor political questions. For example, a member of one Soviet delegation remarked that in arranging an elaborate guided tour the Americans were "treating us as we treat you in the Soviet Union."

In recent years a few trusted Russians have been permitted to travel alone to and in foreign countries. It has become a fairly common occurrence for small groups of Soviet travelers—as in the case of some of the women dancers, for example—to accept chaperoned dinner invitations. I have also heard of visits, even by staid Soviet university professors, to Negro night clubs and to Third Avenue bars in New York. There is fairly widespread agreement among those who have had the most intimate contact with Soviet travelers that after a few weeks abroad they seem gayer and more relaxed, but nevertheless remain careful to avoid ticklish topics and usually shun political ones.

The more "ideological" a Soviet delegation is, the less relaxed and intimate are its relations likely to be with its hosts. A number of East-West cultural get-togethers were held in Switzerland in the summer of 1956. Apparently the initiative for most of these came from West European intellectuals. Michael Hoffman reported that the two sides found it much more difficult to find common ground in the social sciences than in atomic energy problems.[20] One of the 1956 Geneva conferences, called by UNESCO, discussed such topics as "differences in the theory and concept of peaceful coexistence from the communist and the Western points of view." A participant reported that the discussions "developed in a generally conciliatory atmosphere, and there was a good deal of easy give-and-take between the two ideological groups."[21]

[20] *New York Times*, July 10, 1956.
[21] Walter R. Sharp, in *Yale Alumni Magazine*, December 1956, p. 19.

The UNESCO conference, the first of its kind in some ten years, was a preliminary conference called to seek to reach agreement on general principles. This is the type of meeting at which Soviet representatives behave most amiably. As in diplomatic negotiations, Soviet representatives at cultural conferences profess to subscribe enthusiastically to universally accepted values, such as peace and international cooperation.

Numerous published and unpublished reports by noncommunist Western social scientists, writers, and journalists indicate that communication with Soviet colleagues at working conferences has been awkward and sometimes acrimonious. An American historian, describing the behavior of the Soviet representative at an international conference in Yugoslavia, reported: "Only the Russian was an outsider. A dignified man of 60, he had never before ventured out of the Soviet Union. The marks of the provincial showed in his reticence, in his inability to adjust to the men about him, and in his wary expectation of rebuffs that never came."[22]

Dwight MacDonald has observed: "Now that the Russians are beginning again to attend international scholarly meetings, special problems arise because the Soviet delegations have an official status, and so tend to stick to a dogged repetition of the orthodox Marxist platitudes. Also as representatives of the state, they must react with official virulence and verbosity to criticism of their country's institutions."[23]

At a number of recent East-West conferences the freedom displayed by the Poles has been in refreshing contrast to that of other Iron Curtain delegations. MacDonald quotes the French sociologist Raymond Aron, to the effect that the Poles, at a Warsaw international social-science gathering, didn't seem to know which side of the Iron Curtain they were on.

A number of German and American historians interviewed in 1956 reported that the behavior of the thirty-odd Soviet representatives at the Tenth International Congress of Historical Science in Rome, in September 1955, despite the ostensible sweetness and tolerance

[22] Oscar Handlin, "Worlds Apart," in *Atlantic Monthly*, Vol. 199, May 1957, pp. 53-56. Quotation on p. 53.
[23] "Reflections," in *Encounter*, December 1956, p. 58. MacDonald presents interesting material on the self-censorship imposed by Western sociologists in an effort to get along with the Soviets at an international conference in Amsterdam in 1956.

displayed by the Soviet historians, made a very bad impression on noncommunists. As S. V. Utechin noted in the *Russian Review* for October 1956, the public statements of the Soviet historians were "dull, doctrinaire and lifeless," and the Soviet representatives at this and at subsequent international meetings of scholars displayed astounding ignorance about all points of view which differed in any way from the current Kremlin line, including non-Soviet interpretations of Marxism. However, a considerable amount of useful communication has taken place even at such meetings. They provide for at least limited social contact. The Russians who attend them are usually for the first time in their lives, or at least for many years, exposed to the give-and-take of free discussion, even if they cannot fully participate therein. In quite a few instances contacts made at such congresses have resulted in invitations to foreign scholars to visit Russia and have contributed much to the success of the visits. They have also led frequently to subsequent correspondence and to both individual and institutional exchanges of publications, et cetera.

Two extraordinarily interesting intellectual encounters took place at Venice and Zurich, respectively, in 1956. At the Venice conference, in March, Ignazio Silone, Stephen Spender, Jean-Paul Sartre, and several other leading Western writers engaged in discussions with writers from the Soviet Union, Poland, and Yugoslavia. Among the Soviet writers present were Boris Polevoi and Konstantin Fedin. The Zurich meeting in September brought together editors of leading Western European, Soviet, and Polish literary journals. At both of these meetings blunt questions were put by some of the Western writers. It seems certain that the Soviet participants underwent a severe ordeal. These dialogues probably played a part in the largely covert, but intense, re-evaluation of fundamental concepts stimulated on both sides of the ideological frontier by Khrushchev's exposure of Stalin's crimes.[24]

Perhaps the extreme manifestations of what one expert calls the Soviet "caution reflex" was displayed by the three Soviet election observers in the United States in October and November 1956. Members of most Soviet delegations while in the United States

---

[24] See, for example, Maurice Nadeau, "La Rencontre de Zurich," in *Preuves*, November 1956, pp. 628-640.

have avoided discussion of politics like the plague, but have made no secret of their eagerness to take back to the Soviet Union every scrap of useful information. It has also been reliably reported that special conferences have been held in Moscow by the members of Soviet technical delegations to discuss and evaluate the findings made during trips to foreign countries—a not uncommon practice, it is only candid to note, in this country also.

Sources close to the election observers noted that they not only refrained from controversy but hardly even asked questions. To be sure, the Soviet election observers were here at a ticklish time. They left the United States on November 10. According to one source, when they were asked some questions about Hungary, their only comment was, "We don't know anything about it."

Partly because, for the moment, international tensions were at relatively low ebb, but mainly because it is easier for Americans to be objective about Russia than vice versa, the American election observers who in March 1958 returned the visit of their Soviet predecessors of 1956 to study the 1958 Supreme Soviet elections enjoyed a more normal visit than did their Russian colleagues in this country. They had many friendly conversations, as well as some hot arguments. They found that provincial Soviet officials were much more willing to discuss their work and their problems than were their superiors in Moscow. While they received "prefabricated" answers to political questions, they found that straightforward replies were often given to less sensitive questions. Professor Cyril E. Black, a member of the three-man group—the others were Dr. Richard Scammon of the Governmental Affairs Institute and Mr. Hedley Donovan of *Fortune* magazine—recorded his findings in an article in *Foreign Affairs* for July 1958. I agree heartily with Professor Black's observation that "perhaps the one way in which we can seriously influence Soviet politics is by seeing to it that Soviet leadership gets a better idea of what our world is like." One can surely add that it is equally useful for Americans in positions of influence to make on-the-spot comparisons between Soviet reality and the image of the U.S.S.R. conveyed by Soviet propaganda or by American mass media.

In November 1958 we had the good fortune to accompany three distinguished American psychologists and an expert on advanced data-processing techniques on a tour, organized by Dr. Hadley Cantril, of psychological and educational institutions and laboratories in Russia. The Russian—and Georgian and Ukrainian— "man on the street" seemed to be even more relaxed and easy to talk to than in June and July 1956. The caution with which Soviet psychologists and educators handled all questions verging on politics, ideology, or even on some areas of social-science method, indicated that intellectuals were in a somewhat more anxious mood than they had been a year or two earlier; but we lacked a firm basis for comparison, since during my 1956 trip even I did not have quite the same pattern of contacts as in 1958, and none of the other members of our group had been in the U.S.S.R. since the death of Stalin. Well-informed members of the Moscow diplomatic colony told us that in subtle ways, such as availability of early communist writings to foreign book buyers, or reluctance of Soviet scientists and artists to attend social gatherings in the residences of diplomats without prior clearance, the situation had deteriorated slightly, beginning in early 1957.

The most interesting and hopeful aspect of the tour in terms of Soviet-Western communication was the fact that all three of our psychologists lectured to enthusiastic audiences of Soviet psychologists, educators, and students. The Americans chose the topics and content of their lectures and no preliminary conditions of any kind were attached to these performances. We all felt that, whatever may have been the motives of our Soviet hosts and of the higher authorities with whom our visit had been cleared in encouraging this semipublic display of American behavioral-science techniques, the effects had been stimulating and salutary—as was also the opportunity we had to observe the excellent work being done by Soviet psychologists within the framework set by Marxist and Pavlovian concepts. While there were still some very important "vacant lots" in Soviet psychology, particularly in the areas of psychometric tests, "depth" psychology, and social psychology— the area covered in the West by social psychology and sociology was, we were told, left to the historians—we found, particularly outside of Moscow, that Soviet psychologists were eager to learn more about these subjects and to begin to work in some of them when and if conditions permitted. One friendly young scholar reminded us that social psychology had been developing in the U.S.S.R. in the 1920's but that Stalin had decided that it "was not necessary."

While the Americans realized that it would have been tactless and rude to embarrass our generous hosts by departing from the framework, tacitly accepted by both sides, of a purely professional, even technical exchange, we occasionally felt it necessary to ask questions designed to clarify the political context in which, after all, we were operating. The replies of the Soviet scholars, educators, and educational officials to political questions proved as a rule evasive, noncommittal, or even ludicrous. On one occasion, for example, one of the Americans asked a Soviet colleague, "What is the role of the communist party in psychology?" The latter, who spoke excellent English, replied, "I do not understand your question." Then he had the car stopped in which he and the American were riding and, immediately upon getting out, said, "I want to show you this building"!

The overwhelming cordiality of Soviet hosts, the excellent rapport which usually prevailed between them and their guests, and their very evident desire to see a vast expansion of all kinds of Soviet-American scholarly contacts gave rise to the feeling that the trip had not only been valuable from an individual professional point of view but that it had given grounds for hope that in the long future a more normal pattern of communication might develop. In this connection perhaps we should mention the fact that the interviews with our group, published in both Leningrad and Moscow, were, while cautiously conducted and written, scrupulously accurate and truthful. Unfortunately, the Soviet satirical magazine *Krokodil* for April 10, 1959, falsely accused the group of eavesdropping with tape recorders on private conversations of Soviet citizens. While not unamusing, the take-off on American social science in this article could be regarded as a warning to Soviet scholars and ordinary citizens also that communication must be constrained within the bounds of official prescription if dire consequences were to be avoided.

Also on the darker side of the picture, it was noted that jamming of all foreign radio broadcasts in the Russian language still continued unabated. Once or twice during our stay even English-language Voice of America broadcasts were jammed. One night, for example, we heard the jamming of most of the portion of a V.O.A. broadcast which touched on the Kremlin's attitude toward the award of a Nobel Prize to the writer Boris Pasternak. However, we found that the English-language broadcasts of the V.O.A. and the B.B.C. are immensely popular and we even learned that the head of the English Department of the University of Moscow had recently told a foreign ambassador that Soviet students were learning the American pronunciation of English by listening to the V.O.A.

Fantastic misrepresentations of American foreign policy and American institutions continued to dominate the content of the Soviet press and radio. The impact of this propaganda was reflected in statements by Soviet citizens about the international situation. However, the few evidences of unfriendliness encountered were a minor note in a chorus of friendliness. Occasional notes of anxiety or arrogance seemed to represent surface attitudes under which there was a desire for friendly relations. However, there was evidence that Soviet people think of American capitalism in terms of archaic stereotypes, and this fact furnishes a basis for acceptance of anti-American propaganda.

In professional and social meetings with Soviet psychologists and educators and also in several extremely relaxed gatherings with ordinary citizens in airplanes and restaurants, the usual toasts to peace and friendship were pronounced. Future American travelers to Russia should develop a technique to deal with "peace" toasts, for by implication such toasts place the visitor at a psychological disadvantage. The implication is that Moscow wants peace and that it is up to the West to prove that it does too. One reply that we sometimes used was to ask our Soviet hosts what they thought they, and we, could do specifically to insure peace. As a rule they limited themselves to the cautious answer that "contacts"—particularly friendly gatherings around the banquet table—could do a great deal for the cause of peace. The cautious reply usually given to such a question suggested that our hosts, while certainly sincere in their desire for peace, did not feel that they as individuals or as scholars could take upon themselves the responsibility of recommendations about policy matters. In effect, they were acting as Kremlin mouthpieces when they proposed such toasts.

Closely related to the Soviet attitude toward matters of war and peace is the pride and satisfaction expressed by many Soviet citizens about such achievements as the Soviet artificial earth satellites. Earth satellites were a main theme of the very attractive and colorful floats displayed in downtown Moscow during the November 7th parade. Laika, the dog carried into space by one of the Soviet sputniks, is displayed on cigarette packages, one of which was presented to me by a Soviet citizen. Perhaps the most dramatic illustration of the way in which some Soviet people conceive of the sputniks as assurances of national security came to light at the end of a very warm and friendly airplane conversation with a young Soviet movie director. For several hours there was talk on many subjects, ranging from international cultural exchanges through modern art and Ukrainian and Georgian national customs and languages, with never a jarring note. But suddenly as the plane was about to land, the Soviet motion picture executive asked his American traveling companion, "Do your diplomats understand the significance of the Soviet sputniks?"

It is interesting to compare Soviet attitudes toward communist China with attitudes toward the United States. One formed the distinct impression that, in terms of personal relations, Russians feel much more at home with Americans than with the Chinese communists. As one fairly high-ranking communist party official put it, "We don't know anything about China." Since the same man said that he listened to the Voice of America, although he professed to dislike the broadcasts intensely, it was clear that his interest in and probably his respect for the United States were greater than his corresponding sympathies for communist China. Several Russians smiled, perhaps in embarrassment, at the remark that "communist China is a powerful force."

Our experiences confirmed the observation of other travelers that it is extremely difficult for tourists to discuss political and ideological matters with Soviet citizens. Nevertheless, it seemed that one could learn a good deal about political institutions and attitudes by taking a tactful, indirect approach. In general, one can learn more about such matters as a by-product of conversations concerned primarily with nonpolitical affairs than if one makes a direct attack, which is likely to result either in the Soviet citizen's changing the subject or resorting to evasive double-talk, or, occasionally, in his delivering a *Pravda*-style harangue. The latter type of response is, of course, more likely if communist party officials or official Soviet youth leaders are participating in the conversation than if one is dealing with persons who, regardless of institutional affiliation, think of themselves primarily as scholars or experts.

During the visit of the American psychologists the Pasternak affair was at the center of international interest. Apparently among Soviet students and intellectuals there were considerable differences of opinion about Pasternak. There was a good deal of sympathy with him and, in connection with Pasternak and his novel *Doctor Zhivago*, some people pointed out that because of the pressure of political controls over literature, most of the best writers had stopped writing at all. Much less was known about Pasternak among Soviet people in their twenties and thirties than one might have expected. However, people who knew him only as a translator of Shakespeare were, in some cases, discovering his poetry and fiction. There was apparently a great demand for the few copies of *Doctor Zhivago* which had somehow been brought into the Soviet Union. Rather dramatic evidence came indirectly to my attention, indicating that some Soviet young people regarded Pasternak as a hero. On the other hand, there was also substantial evidence that many, perhaps the majority, of students in the literary, historical, and philosophical faculties of Moscow and Leningrad higher-educational institutions accepted the official line condemning Pasternak as a traitor to Russia. Acceptance of the official point of view seems to have been based, in part, upon resentment of what was felt to have been exploitation in the West of the Pasternak matter in the interests of anti-Russian propaganda.

The most interesting political conversation that I enjoyed on the 1958 tour was with a communist official whom we met in a restaurant. He seemed to feel quite free to talk about the communist party and about his own work. When he was asked what the function of the communist organization in a factory, for example, was, he said that it was mainly to sign up the workers for greater production. This man was obviously a loyal communist and he vigorously but calmly supported the official Kremlin line on domestic and international questions. When he was asked whether or not the Soviet communist party desired the extension of communism throughout the world, he replied immediately in the affirmative. He said that communism was a "necessity" and that the desirability of its extension did not depend upon the wishes of the peoples among whom it was to be established. However, when I pointed out to him that the American people did not want communism, he said that as far as he was concerned they could have any system they liked. As is so often the case with Soviet people, including even heavily indoctrinated individuals, this particular party worker gave the impression of being far less doctrinaire than one might think such a person might be if one's information were based solely on reading official Soviet sources. If this is true, perhaps there is hope that the remaining shell of ideological orthodoxy may wear thinner as contacts increase and if they become more cordial. However, this will not happen soon and not at all if communist zealots can prevent it. An important resolution on propaganda published by the Central Committee of the Communist Party of the Soviet Union in January 1960 made the surprising admission that whole strata of the population were still not influenced by official ideology but it also furnished evidence of a determination to put an end to this situation. It is within the framework of ideological pressures of this sort that one must appraise future possibilities for intercultural communication.

CHAPTER VI

ORGANIZATION AND TRAINING

ULTURAL diplomacy as practised by the Soviet regime requires massive financial and organizational support. It also presupposes scholarly research, a large-scale training program, for example, in the field of foreign languages, and the supplying and processing of foreign cultural materials for the information and instruction of Soviet personnel employed in propaganda, diplomacy, and cultural relations. This logistic support, as it might be called, is impressive in its dimensions, although it must be remembered, in attempting to compare the Soviet effort with that of the United States, for example, that many programs conducted by party and government agencies in Russia are carried on in noncommunist countries by private foundations, religious organizations, and educational institutions.

The Soviet cultural-relations program is, of course, only a part of an over-all communications effort which apparently cost the equivalent of about a billion dollars as early as 1950, and by 1953, was estimated to have required an expenditure equivalent to more than $1,167,000,000.[1] The largest single item in the over-all Soviet propaganda budget is that for paying about 375,000 full-time propagandists, and an additional two million-odd part-time propagandists.[2] This immense effort is carried on at the party level by the section for propaganda and agitation of the Central Committee and on the government level by the Ministry of Culture of the Soviet Union. These agencies are, of course, instruments of the party high

[1] See Subcommittee on Overseas Information Program of the United States Senate Committee on Foreign Relations, Staff Study No. 3, *The Soviet Propaganda Program*, 82nd Congress, Second Session, Washington, 1952, pp. 18-20, and F. Bowen Evans, *Worldwide Communist Propaganda Activities*, p. 41. See also *New York Times*, December 12, 1950.

[2] The above figures are contained in Evans, *loc.cit.* The Senate Subcommittee Report cited above stated on p. 2 that more than 325,000 persons were normally enrolled in schools for training propagandists, that 6,900 students were reported to have been enrolled in the three highest-level schools—the Academy of Social Sciences, the Higher Party School, and the correspondence department—and that altogether some 1,400,000 full-time professional propagandists were, as of 1952, engaged in the Soviet propaganda effort.

command.[3] Many other agencies and organizations, some of which have already been mentioned in this book, administer parts of the over-all program.

Since May 1957 the most powerful Soviet agency in the cultural-exchange field has been the already-mentioned State Committee for Cultural Relations with Foreign Countries, a body with ministerial status, directly attached to the U.S.S.R. Council of Ministers, which works in close coordination with the Ministry of Foreign Affairs. Georgi Zhukov, former deputy editor of *Pravda*, was named chairman of this committee, and one of his deputies, A. N. Kuznetsov, helped to negotiate the 1958 Soviet-American exchange agreement. In 1959 Zhukov became a Deputy Minister of Culture, but continued to serve as head of the State Committee. B. N. Krylov, a former Tass correspondent in the United States, was made head of the committee's American section. It may be of incidental interest that we were told, while on a visit to that section in November 1958, that one of the committee's employees, whom we met, was a son of Soviet Foreign Minister A. A. Gromyko.

The State Committee took over some functions formerly handled directly by the Ministry of Foreign Affairs and by VOKS. Reports in the Soviet press and by Americans, such as the three-man team of observers of Soviet elections in March 1958, whose trips under the exchange agreement brought them into contact with members of the State Committee, disclosed that it organized and financed major exchanges, especially at the intergovernmental level, and saw to it that politically important guests were catered to. Formation of this body reflected the increasing importance of cultural relations in Soviet foreign policy and the accompanying shift of emphasis in world-wide communist propaganda from overtly revolutionary appeals to a coexistence policy requiring some measure of intergovernmental cooperation. It fitted well into the pattern indicated by negotiation of cultural treaties and agreements, discussed in Chapter III. Establishment of the committee meant that the U.S.S.R. also had a governmental agency which could appro-

[3] The "Theses" issued in connection with the fortieth anniversary of the "Great October Socialist Revolution" were, according to *Pravda* for September 15, 1957, a joint production of the section for propaganda and agitation and the Central Committee's Institute of Marxism-Leninism.

priately deal with such bodies as the British Council or the American State Department's East-West Contacts Staff.

A front-page *Pravda* account of the arrival in Russia of President Nasser of the United Arab Republic, on April 30, 1958, revealed that among the Soviet notables who greeted the U.A.R. leader was the chairman of the State Committee. This story also mentioned the presence of S. V. Kaftanov, a former minister of higher education, and now Deputy Minister of Culture, but it identified Kaftanov for purposes of this occasion as president of the new Soviet Society for Friendship and Cultural Relations with the Countries of the Arab East. The presence of these two executives symbolizes the new significance and, perhaps at the same time, the continued organizational duality of Soviet foreign cultural policy. The society headed by Kaftanov is only one of the many under the over-all coordination of the Union of Soviet Societies for Friendship and Cultural Relations with Foreign Countries, established in February 1958. By January 1959 twenty-five national friendship societies had been founded, and these in turn were setting up branches in the constituent republics. The establishment in the U.S.S.R. of counterpart national friendship societies, such as the U.S.S.R.-Italy, U.S.S.R.-Sweden, and similar groups, represented a new departure in the structure of the system of friendship societies. Formation of the new grouping was regarded in Western diplomatic circles as part of an effort to bring into existence new foreign branches with a broadly representative membership. There was speculation in Washington, for example, that Moscow might encourage creation of an American-Soviet society to seek to influence cultural exchanges between the two countries. Apparently, however, the results of the first year and a half of the new policy had not achieved success in divesting the activity of VOKS' successor organization of a conspicuously partisan flavor.

For all practical purposes the new alliance represented a continuation of VOKS under a new name, but it was made clear at its founding that VOKS had pursued what were now condemned as "outmoded" policies. VOKS' conspicuous association with foreign communist parties and the crudity and obstructionism of its past policies, one inferred, were to be modified and its activities brought into better coordination with the foreign policy of coexistence. We can better understand the significance of this change if we briefly survey the activities of VOKS as a major agency of Soviet policy in earlier years. But first it should be noted that the functions of such agencies as VOKS and the State Committee for Cultural Relations intermesh with those of a whole system of propaganda organizations, only a few of which need be named here.

Foreign communist parties, the Soviet diplomatic service, sometimes serving as a cover for secret-police operations, the Soviet friendship societies in foreign countries, and the Telegraphic Agency of the Soviet Union (Tass) are among the other important Soviet foreign-propaganda and, on occasion, cultural-exchange instrumentalities. With the growth in the last few years of scientific and trade contacts and student exchanges, other Soviet government and semi-official bodies such as the Ministry of Higher Education, the Academy of Sciences of the U.S.S.R., the R.S.F.S.R. Academy of Pedagogical Sciences, the All-Union Chamber of Commerce, and others have entered the exchange picture. Foreigners with wide experience in the negotiation of exchanges have gained a strong impression that the scholars, professors, and experts, and even, to a degree, some of the bureaucratic personnel with whom they deal on the Soviet side are far more enthusiastic regarding exchanges than are the party—and perhaps police—officials who play an invisible but sometimes-decisive part in shaping the character of the exchanges.

In addition to the agencies named, a host of communist fronts, of which the most important is probably the World Peace Council, play an important if sometimes-obscure role. The World Federation of Trade Unions (W.F.T.U.), the World Federation of Democratic Youth, and the International Union of Students—the latter two jointly sponsor international youth festivals—are among the other Soviet-dominated bodies with a hand in foreign cultural activity. An important role has been played in recent years in organization of contacts between Soviet and foreign youth movements by the Committee of Youth Organizations which acts as a front for the Komsomol, the official Soviet youth league. A new body, the Bureau on International Youth Travel, began to operate in 1959. The Russian Orthodox Church and other religious groups, such as the Soviet Moslems and Soviet Armenian Christians, have been exploited in recent years as instruments of Soviet foreign policy. Despite Soviet anti-Zionism and anti-Semitism, periodic efforts are made to press Soviet Jews into service as intermediaries between the Soviet Union and world Jewry. Moscow also attempts to utilize the traditional Russian instrument of pan-Slavism, for example in wooing the large Ukrainian population of Canada. The All-Slav Committee, founded in 1941, still publishes a monthly magazine, *Slavyane* (*The Slavs*). When, in 1956, I talked to Mr. Luka Kizya, head of the Ukrainian branch of VOKS, I gained the impression that one of the main tasks of Kizya's organization was to maintain cultural relations with Ukrainians and other Slavs in Canada. Among the constituent republics of the U.S.S.R. the Ukraine plays an exceptionally important role in cultural relations with foreign states, in which its republic cultural society—now no longer a part of VOKS but of the Union of Societies for Friendship and Cultural Relations—is prominent. In such activities an active part is played also by the rather shadowy ministries of foreign affairs of the union republics, the apparatus of which can be useful in giving Asian and African dignitaries a somewhat-exaggerated impression of the sovereignty as well as the cultural autonomy of the non-Russian republics.

According to a Soviet encyclopedia article published in 1951, VOKS in that year already had more than one million members. It was described as a "voluntary" organization of scholars and artists with an elected leadership. According to the article, VOKS carried on its activities abroad through "plenipotentiaries" and through foreign societies for friendship with the Soviet Union, as well as through "progressive individuals" in foreign countries. It enabled foreign intellectuals and workers to learn about the "heroism" of the Soviet Union through a variety of means "among which the most important" was the exchange of delegations and artistic troupes.

Until the adoption of the "popular front" foreign policy of the Soviet Union in 1934, VOKS and its foreign affiliates acted openly as auxiliary agencies of the world communist movement. Symbolically, the first president of VOKS was Anna Kameneva, a sister of Leon Trotski; while subsequent presidents such as F. N. Petrov, Vladimir Kemenov, and A. I. Denisov, who became president in

1947, were scholars who could appropriately perform liaison functions between the Soviet leadership and foreign intellectuals and scientists.

However, VOKS' last president, Mrs. Nina Popova, who became president also of the successor organization, is a prominent Soviet politician who formerly headed the Women's Anti-Fascist Committee. This fact, together with the circumstances that among the five vice-presidents of the new organization two at least, Messrs. Kalishyan and Vyzhilin, were formerly vice-presidents of VOKS, made it appear that the new Union was, in fact, VOKS under another name. After the formation of the new body, as before, the types of exchanges most likely to win favor with non-communists abroad continued to be carried on mainly under the auspices of the powerful State Committee for Cultural Relations with Foreign Countries. Presumably the new friendship societies, however, would carry on, perhaps in a more subdued or tactful fashion, the traditional work of VOKS in cultivating good will among pro-Soviet intellectuals abroad and turning to Kremlin advantage the influence, including sometimes a full-scale commitment to communism, which could thus be generated.

Of course, differences between the old and new patterns of organization should not be exaggerated. An effort had been made for many years to conceal the dependence of VOKS on Kremlin control by classifying it as a "voluntary, public organization."[4] Mr. Kizya, in the interview already referred to, took pains to stress that VOKS was not a state organization and that its Ukrainian branch was an independent body.

When, in 1946, I visited Mr. Mikhava, then head of the Georgian branch, the Georgian made the same point. Undoubtedly, emphasis upon the "autonomous" character of VOKS and its branches was intended to facilitate its work with noncommunist foreign intellectuals, by making it appear to resemble the types of nongovernmental organizations with which they were familiar at home. VOKS had sections for law, literature, natural science, agriculture, theater, music, and other fields. It also had geographic sections, specializing in individual countries and areas. Scattered references in the Soviet press enable one to learn of the existence

---

[4] *Bolshaya sovetskaya entsiklopediya*, Vol. 9, pp. 327-328.

of various sections of VOKS, but, as in the case of other Soviet organizations, no comprehensive description was ever given. We learned of the existence of a "section for Soviet culture" during the first of two visits to VOKS in June 1956. An officer of this section was present at both of the meetings which VOKS arranged with Soviet professors.

In my first 1956 visit to the Moscow headquarters of VOKS, perhaps because I was not an invited guest and in fact had appeared one day, unannounced, in the office of a Soviet law-institute graduate who was at the time in charge of the American section, I was treated as something of a "hot potato." The first question put by the officer in charge of the American section was, "How did you find us?" His perplexity may have been increased by my reply that I would like to meet Soviet intellectuals who could explain what the Soviets meant by "coexistence." However, after a rather long wait, two interviews, one with historians and the other with economists, were arranged. On both occasions visitor and hosts drank tea and ate cookies and candies.

Although the atmosphere was somewhat "sticky," both conversations were interesting. The Soviet professors made a rather half-hearted attempt to push the propaganda line that while their country was doing everything possible to encourage cultural exchange, Americans, especially workers, were "afraid" to come to Russia because of the reactionary attitude of the United States government. Like many a foreign visitor's conversations with Soviet intellectuals, these were devoted mostly to interesting but not-very-controversial questions of fact. However, at one point, in self-defense I pointed out that in the United States fingerprinting might be required of foreign visitors, but that we did not have the Soviet system of internal passports. A long moment of apparently nervous silence followed this remark.

According to Soviet sources, VOKS maintained "plenipotentiaries" in foreign countries, who established contacts with foreign friendship societies, and with "individual progressive leaders of culture in foreign countries." It invited foreign cultural delegations to the Soviet Union. It also carried on a broad program of exchange of publications and other cultural materials. In addition, from its founding in 1925, it carried on a considerable publications program of its own. Until October 1956 VOKS published an attractively printed monthly *Bulletin* in French, German, English, and other languages. In January 1956 VOKS took over publication of the newspaper *Moscow News*, to provide English-reading foreign tourists with an "unbiased picture of the development of the Soviet Union."[5] In October 1956 the VOKS *Bulletin* was replaced by *Culture and Life*, a magazine published monthly in English, Russian, French, Spanish, and German.[6]

A few Soviet press reports on VOKS activities may illustrate its role in Soviet cultural diplomacy. When a delegation of the Mongolian People's Republic left Moscow in February 1943, after presenting gifts to the Red Army, it was seen off by the then-chairman of the Administrative Board of VOKS, V. S. Kemenov, together with Deputy Commissar for Internal Affairs Merkulov and other high officials.[7] In November 1947 Mr. Kemenov held a reception for delegates of Czechoslovak-, Finnish-, and Norwegian-Soviet Friendship Societies, which was attended by G. G. Karpov, chairman of the Council for the Affairs of the Orthodox Church; I. V. Polyanski, chairman of the Council for the Affairs of Religious Cults; N. N. Romanov, chairman of the Committee for Physical Culture and Sports; and a number of leading Soviet artists and scientists.[8] *Pravda* for January 4, 1955, reported a reception given by the governing board of VOKS in honor of visiting Afghan physicians and cultural leaders, which was attended by the then-new president of VOKS, Professor A. I. Denisov, by three VOKS deputy chairmen, by a deputy minister of culture, and by members of the medical-, theatrical-, musical-, and Oriental-studies sections. VOKS, together with the Soviet Committee for the Defense of Peace—the Soviet section of the World Peace Council—and other Soviet-controlled international organizations, held a celebration, attended by more than two thousand persons, in honor of the tenth anniversary of the Franco-Soviet Treaty in 1954.[9] On this occasion,

[5] VOKS *Bulletin*, No. 1 (96), January 1956, p. 10.
[6] The announcement of this new publication in the October 1956 issue of the VOKS *Bulletin* listed some sixty firms, in India, Indonesia, Syria, Japan, Mexico, Uruguay, Australia, the United States, Ethiopia, Egypt, and most Western European countries through which subscriptions might be placed.
[7] *Krasnaya Zvezda*, February 7, 1943.
[8] *Pravda*, November 11, 1947.
[9] *Ibid.*, December 11, 1954.

Messrs. Bulganin, Malenkov, Molotov, and Khrushchev were among those present. A list of the top officials of the Ministry of Culture published in *Pravda* for February 6, 1955, included the name of Kemenov, who had by this date become Deputy Minister of Culture.

An illustration of the role of VOKS in action as exporter of Soviet culture was furnished by the mission of a seven-member VOKS delegation to India in 1957. Headed by E. I. Afanasenko, Minister of Education of the R.S.F.S.R., this delegation also included a leading Soviet Indologist, the deputy chairman of the Uzbekistan branch of VOKS, and other appropriate personnel. The group spent three weeks in India. Its activities were reported in detail in the *Times of India*, though, interestingly enough, neither *Pravda* nor *Izvestiya* published a line about them.[10]

Speaking in Bombay, Afanasenko assured Indians of the "warm and friendly feelings" of Russians toward India, and in Mysore he declared that new Indian industrial construction was as impressive as the magnificent classical art and culture of India. Personal contact, he said, was an even more important link between peoples than exchange of art and literature.

The functions of Intourist were described in earlier chapters. However, it is of interest to note that Vladimir Ankudinov, president of Intourist, in an article published in the Soviet English-language magazine *U.S.S.R.* in 1957, stated that the staff of his organization numbered five thousand. Intourist, according to Mr. Ankudinov, was affiliated with the International Union of Travel Organizations and had business relations with sixty-eight travel agencies on four continents, including, in the United States, Union Tours, the American Express, the Cosmos Travel Bureau, and three other firms.[11] By 1958 Intourist apparently had agreements with eighty foreign tourist bureaus. Perhaps in part as a result of its contacts with businesslike Western tourist agencies, Intourist in 1958 and 1959 developed increased efficiency in expediting travel to the U.S.S.R.

An important part in the Soviet foreign cultural program is played by the International Book Company, a little-known organ-

---

[10] *Times of India*, January 4 and January 10, 1957.
[11] *USSR*, No. 12, 1957, p. 1.

ization usually referred to by the Russian abbreviation, Mezhkniga. According to the *Great Soviet Encyclopedia*, this organization was founded in 1923. It exports books, periodicals, music, and records. An outstanding place, said the encyclopedia, was occupied in its operations by the "countries of the democratic camp."[12] Mezhkniga does not, of course, confine its activities to the Soviet orbit. A report by United States Attorney General Herbert S. Brownell in 1953 stated that its American branch, the Four Continent Book Corporation, had done a business of almost two and a half million dollars in the period 1948-1952. Mr. Brownell listed Mezhkniga as one of "four principal outlets for communist political propaganda within the United States." The other three listed were Artkino Pictures, Inc., a distributor of Soviet films; Edwin S. Smith, a literary and photographic agent; and Imported Publications and Products, a distributing agency for Eastern European Publications.[13] In October 1958, according to U.S. official sources, Mezhkniga, dealing in artistic and scientific literature, phonograph records, and postage stamps, had business contacts with over eight hundred firms in fifty-eight countries. Probably most American specialists on Russia are familiar with the huge bookstore operated by Four Continent in New York. Similarly well-known outlets for the sale of Soviet publications are the fine Collett Stores in London. In France, West Germany, Italy, and other Western European countries, and particularly in India, where there are six or seven big stores which specialize in Soviet publications, the Soviets actively merchandise the printed word. However, especially in Western Europe and the United States, Mezhkniga's most important function, perhaps, is procurement of foreign publications rather than sale of Soviet publications. According to an article by Harry Schwartz in the *New York Times* for April 9, 1955, the American branch of Mezhkniga bought $150,000 worth of American publications in that year. About three fourths of this sum was apparently spent on scientific materials. Because of differences in organization between totalitarian and democratic systems, noncommunist countries are at a disadvantage as compared with the Soviet Union both in procurement of Soviet publications and sale of their own publications in the Soviet Union.

[12] *Bolshaya sovetskaya entsiklopediya*, 2nd ed., Vol. 27, pp. 10-11.
[13] *New York Times*, June 6, 1953.

A phase of Mezhkniga's activities which has aroused concern in American publishing circles in recent years is its growing exports of books in English and other languages of noncommunist countries, amounting, according to a statement by Curtis G. Benjamin on behalf of the American Book Publishers Council in the *New York Times* for May 10, 1959, to thirty million books, published exclusively for export, in 1957. Apparently these books are sold abroad at prices below the cost of publication. The McGraw-Hill Publishing Company, in a full-page statement in the same newspaper three days later, pointed out that the United States exported only about two thirds as many books as Russia.

Other revelations in the statement included reference to a section of the Soviet-Indian technical-assistance agreement of December 1958 providing that Soviet textbooks on engineering are to be published in English in India, and the fact that in the languages of the Near East alone the Russians printed and distributed 413,-600 books in 1957, as compared with 166,415 in 1956.

Since 1953, through the Informational Media Guaranty Program, which enables American publishers to sell their books for local currency in many countries which would otherwise be unable to buy them because of a shortage of U.S. dollar exchange, the United States has made good progress in the book-export race with the U.S.S.R. Unfortunately, Congress in August 1958 reduced a requested appropriation for the revolving fund necessary for continuation of the IMG program, and in mid-1959 the possibility of the program's continued functioning on an adequate scale was apparently in doubt.

Soviet professional organizations, including the Union of Soviet Writers, the Union of Soviet Composers, the Union of Soviet Journalists, and the Academy of Sciences of the U.S.S.R., play an important part in the conduct of Soviet cultural-exchange policy. Major libraries, such as the Lenin Library in Moscow or the Saltykov-Shchedrin Library of Leningrad, are also among the numerous agencies whose activities are, at least to some degree, coordinated for maximum success in this effort. During World War II, I received cordial cooperation from Michael Apletin, chairman of the Foreign Commission of the Union of Soviet Writers, and from several top officials of the Lenin Library in my efforts to expand publications exchange between Soviet and American libraries. In a conversation in June 1956 Mr. Apletin referred to our previous acquaintance. This affable man probably did all that was possible to put foreign writers and literary scholars in touch with Soviet colleagues. During our 1956 conversation Apletin stated, among other things, that sixty persons were employed in his organization's section for Polish literature. This bit of data gives some idea of the contribution which the Writers' Union makes to the large-scale international effort about which we are reading.

Apletin, like many other Soviet cultural functionaries, is a charming and gracious person. It was, therefore, disconcerting to find, in the Moscow Library of Foreign Literature, a conventionally chauvinistic work by him on *The World Role of Soviet Literature*. The contrast between what Soviet intellectuals, officials, and party leaders are likely to say in conversation with noncommunist foreigners and what they say and write for domestic consumption is one of the most discouraging aspects of their behavior, although, in view of the political controls exercised over them by their party bosses, we should not find it surprising. In December 1955, on the occasion of his seventieth birthday, Mr. Apletin was awarded the Red Banner of Labor for "many years of social and literary activity."

Material support alone cannot explain the vigor, flexibility, and sometimes the sensitivity of Soviet cultural policy. Its greatest strength, probably, consists in a training program designed to provide educated Soviet citizens with a politically guided but appreciative view of foreign culture. Although the benefits of this policy are limited by ideological orthodoxy, they are still considerable. As Isaac Deutscher somewhat indulgently observed a few years ago: "It should be remarked that, although Stalin has kept Russia isolated from the contemporary influences of the West, he has encouraged and fostered every interest in what he calls the 'cultural heritage' of the West. Perhaps in no country have the young been imbued with so great a respect and love for the classical literature and art of other nations as in Russia."[14]

By 1941 three million copies of works by Victor Hugo had been published in the Soviet Union, as well as two million by Dickens,

[14] Isaac Deutscher, *Stalin*, New York and London, 1949, p. 568.

half a million by Goethe, one million two hundred thousand by Shakespeare, and so on.[15] After the death of Stalin the Soviet attitude toward contemporary Western literature and the arts, as contrasted with classical Western culture, became more liberal, although pugnacious orthodoxy continued to dominate Moscow's appraisal of bourgeois philosophy, history, and social science. *Inostrannaya Literatura (Foreign Literature)*, an expensive and handsomely printed new magazine, began in July 1955 to make available to sophisticated Soviet readers such works as Hemingway's *The Old Man and the Sea*, as well as selected writings by Jean-Paul Sartre and other noncommunists. The main criterion used in deciding whether or not to add a noncommunist play or novel to the previously approved list of "progressive" works seemed to be that the work in question was neutral in respect to ideological issues, or that its author had not been consistently hostile to the Soviet Union.[16]

In 1957-1960 a somewhat harsher attitude, perhaps temporary, was taken toward bourgeois literature than in 1953-1956. At the Fourth International Congress of Slavicists in September 1958, this was reflected, for example, in acid comments by Soviet literary scholars on Western authors and critics and on some of the Western guests present.

Critics like Motyleva have busied themselves in recent years with reports on such matters as "the reflection of reality in its revolutionary development"—the title, according to *Literaturnaya Gazeta* for April 16, 1959, of her contribution to a "scientific conference, devoted to problems of critical and socialist realism in contemporary Western literature," which was held at the Department of Foreign Literature of the Gorki Institute of Literature in Moscow. On April 14, 1959, the first of a series of academic lectures on contemporary foreign literature was delivered at the Moscow House of Friendship with the Peoples of Foreign Countries, formerly the headquarters of VOKS.

During all of my trips to Russia I have been impressed by the immensity of the effort made by the Soviet authorities to disseminate among all age groups appreciation of approved works

[15] *Ibid.*
[16] Walter Z. Laqueur, in *Soviet Culture*, London, No. 1, January, 1956, p. 1.

of classical Russian and foreign music, literature, and art, as well as to arouse interest from the earliest possible age in science, technology, handicrafts, and hobbies. One of the major agencies of this program is the system of Pioneer "palaces" in which children receive instruction in singing, art, music, horticulture, railroad and aircraft modelling, dramatics, and other skills. The Odessa Pioneer Palace, for example, had forty-four such circles in 1956. The successors of Stalin continue Lenin's and Stalin's policy of not merely appropriating the material wealth of the aristocracy and bourgeoisie but of attempting also to make available to the masses the best in the cultural heritage of the past. Post-Stalin comment on this program did not, of course, cease to present it as proof of the cultural superiority of Soviet socialism to American capitalism.

According to a dispatch to the *New York Times* for February 24, 1957, sixty-seven books by American authors were scheduled for publication in Russia that year. An interesting, fact-crammed survey in *Sovetskaya Kultura* for September 5, 1957, asserted, among other things, that 15,971 titles by 1,872 foreign authors, in numbers amounting to almost half a billion copies, had been translated "during the years of Soviet power" into the Russian language and other languages of the peoples of the Soviet Union. The Soviet Union, the newspaper boasted, held first place in the world in the translation of foreign literature, while the United States occupied only the eleventh place. According to this article, translations of French authors were most numerous, followed in order by American, English, and German authors. In recent years the bibliographical weekly *Novye Knigi* has included a section listing translations into Russian from foreign languages.

Significant illustrations of the curious Soviet compound of doctrinal intolerance and cultural internationalism can be found, for instance, in the field of education. In a sense the heavy emphasis in Soviet primary and secondary education on the study of mathematics, biology, physics, chemistry, and astronomy represents a form of cultural internationalism, for the principles of natural science are identical in all lands. At times, of course, implications of this fact, as in the field of genetics or in the relativity theory in physics, have led to suppression of theories and persecution of scientists. The teaching of the humanities in Soviet schools is guided by a combination of Soviet patriotism and Leninism. Despite all ideological distortions, the requirements of three years of world literature in the eighth, ninth, and tenth grades of secondary school, together with the study of four years of ancient, medieval, and modern history, also obligatory for all pupils, provides a useful background for future cultural intercourse with foreigners.[17] It is interesting, and impressive, that a thorough knowledge, tested by written examination, of Shakespeare's *Hamlet* and the first part of Goethe's *Faust* is listed among the requirements for admission to all Soviet higher educational institutions.[18] At the same time, requirements in the field of literature still include a mastery of the theses of Lenin's article "Party Organization and Party Literature" and of the ideological decrees promulgated in 1946 by the Party Central Committee.[19]

The mass study of foreign languages, with emphasis on their practical application, occupies a central position in Soviet training for intercultural communication. Mass training is accompanied by scholarly specialization of high quality for advanced students. There is little doubt that in this field, even more than in natural science, Soviet primary and secondary schools, as well, probably, as higher educational institutions, are doing a better job than their American competitors. This is especially true in terms of numbers of students involved. From the liberal Western point of view, of course, the Soviet approach to language study has peculiar overtones. According to one Soviet textbook for English, "a Soviet officer must be . . . stronger in technique than his enemy. He must know . . . especially mathematics, physics and languages."[20]

Apparently until 1953 the study of one foreign language, usually English, French, or German, began for all Soviet school pupils in the third grade. Beginning in 1954 all graduates of Soviet secondary, or ten-year, schools were required to have studied a foreign language for six years.[21] Before World War II German

[17] Details of Soviet primary and secondary school curricula in De Witt, *Soviet Professional Manpower*, pp. 276-277.

[18] *Spravochnik dlya postupayushchikh v vysshie uchebnye zavedeniya soyuza ssr v 1956 g.*, Moscow, 1956, p. 23.

[19] *Ibid.*, p. 24.

[20] William R. Parker, *The National Interest and Foreign Languages*, U.S. National Commission for UNESCO, Washington, D.C., 1954, p. 71.

[21] *Ibid.*, p. 9. *Uchitelskaya Gazeta*, December 11, 1954, p. 2.

was the most commonly studied foreign language in the U.S.S.R. Since the war first rank has been accorded to English. It has been estimated that about ten million Soviet students were studying English in 1957.[22] In contrast, only about four thousand Americans were studying Russian, in 155 of America's nearly 1,800 colleges.[23] In addition, there are in 1959, perhaps, a few hundred high school students of Russian in the United States, although this situation is changing rapidly as preparatory schools, colleges, and giant corporations awaken to the significance of Russian.

It may be interesting to record here that when in 1956 I remarked to an apparently friendly Soviet teacher of English that far more Soviet people were studying English than Americans were studying Russian she replied, "But of course you Americans regard Russian as some sort of Asiatic language."

Millions of Soviet school children study German and French. Since 1949 Spanish has been offered in a number of Soviet elementary schools as the required foreign language, at least for some pupils.[24] *Pravda* for April 2, 1957, published a story entitled "Children Are Studying Eastern Languages." Beginning in the second half of the 1956-1957 school year, instruction in Chinese, Hindi, and Arabic was begun in some of the Uzbek secondary schools of Tashkent. "Specialist-teachers" were assigned to these tasks and the Ministry of Education of Uzbekistan began preparation of textbooks. This report indicated that, in spite of the curtailment of foreign-language instruction to which we have referred, some special schools still began it at a very early age. Apparently Tashkent was not the only Soviet center in which Oriental languages were being taught in 1957 at the secondary level, for the *Times of India* for January 10, 1957, reported that Hindi and Urdu were being taught in some Moscow secondary schools. Significantly enough, the source of the Indian newspaper's informa-

---

[22] Jacob Ornstein, in *New York Times Magazine*, September 15, 1957, p. 49.

[23] *Ibid.* An excellent article in the *Wall Street Journal* for June 2, 1959, gave many details of the spurt in study of Russian in the United States in the years since the first Soviet artificial earth satellite called public attention to the value of a knowledge of Russian for scientific, technical, and cultural purposes, and a letter to the same newspaper for June 11 called attention to Choate School's ambitious Russian and Chinese programs.

[24] *Inostrannye yazyki v shkole*, No. 1, 1953, pp. 104-108, reviewing school textbook in Spanish for the third and fourth grades.

tion was Mr. E. I. Afanasenko, the Minister of Education of the Russian Soviet Republic, who was then visiting India.

Evidence continued to accumulate in 1958 of growing Soviet interest in the languages of India. For example, according to *Uchitelskaya Gazeta* for October 4, 1958, in order to satisfy the growing demand for study aids in Bengali, Hindi, Urdu, Marati, and other Indian languages, conversation manuals, grammars, and texts were being published by the State Publishing House for Foreign Literature. The same item reported lively interest, in India, in a Russian grammar published by a former member of the Indian embassy staff in Moscow.

As of August 5, 1958, according to a State Department report of that date on "Soviet Language and Area Programs for Asia and Africa," more than a dozen Soviet schools were taking part in a program of teaching Near Eastern and Asian languages to pupils beginning at the age of eight. The report cited Soviet sources indicating that the program had been successful and would be expanded. It also expressed the view that, if it continued to grow, the U.S.S.R. in a decade would have hundreds of individuals who could combine exotic language proficiency with a variety of trades and professions. Many of these would be Uzbeks, Tatars, Azerbaidzhanis, and other Soviet Asians.

According to several reliable sources, a number of elite schools, in which instruction is conducted in English, French, or German, were founded in 1949. A Reuters dispatch in the *Christian Science Monitor* for March 12, 1956, reported that children in School Number One in Moscow began the study of the English language at age eight. It stated that the objective of this English-language school was to turn out groups of almost bilingual youngsters who might afterward take jobs as translators or in posts where a good knowledge of English is an asset. The school library had a wide range of classics of English literature, published in the Soviet Union, but the children had no access to contemporary British or American magazines or newspapers.

Recent confirmation of the existence and probable growth of a network of such special English-language schools as the one above mentioned was furnished by a Yale undergraduate who in September 1958 visited a school in Kiev where, he reports, instruction in all subjects was conducted exclusively in English, beginning in the second grade, and by a Soviet visitor to Yale in 1960.

With a few exceptions, such as in the case of centers for training in veterinary science, agriculture, and elementary school teaching, applicants for admission to Soviet higher educational institutions must pass examinations in one foreign language. English, French, German, or Spanish are listed in the official guide to entrance requirements.[25] Work in one or more foreign languages is continued at the university and graduate school level.[26] Eric Ashby, who has probably done more than any other single writer to alert the English-speaking world to Soviet progress in science, recently wrote, "Now every qualified research worker in Russia has had to pass a severe test in the reading of two foreign languages; so it can be assumed that all we publish is not only available in Russia but is in fact being carefully read."[27]

For several decades the Soviet Union has possessed an excellent system of specialized higher educational institutions, known as "institutes," which train foreign-language teachers, translators, and interpreters. Without this network of foreign-language institutes, the work of Intourist and, indeed, the entire Soviet cultural relations program discussed in this book would probably be impossible, or at any rate would not function with nearly its present effectiveness. As of 1956 there were seventeen "pedagogical institutes" of foreign languages in the Soviet Union.[28] Of these the best known is the First Moscow State Pedagogical Institute of Foreign Languages. Minister of Higher Education Elyutin told us in 1956 that approximately ten thousand persons were studying English in specialized Soviet higher educational institutions. About the same number was studying German, and perhaps half as many were specializing in French. From the minister, and from members of the faculty of the Moscow Foreign Language Institute and Intourist guides in Moscow and Leningrad, I learned that some of the students at the Moscow Institute were specializing in Spanish or Italian, and, at the Leningrad Institute, some were specializing in Swedish.

[25] *Spravochnik, 1956*, pp. 5-7.
[26] DeWitt, *Soviet Professional Manpower*, pp. 110-112, 134.
[27] *The Red Army*, New York, 1956, p. 460.
[28] *Spravochnik, 1956*, pp. 212-214.

Soviet foreign-language institutes offer a five-year course. In addition to intensive language study, culminating in two years of study conducted exclusively in the language of specialization, there are general subjects, such as geography, history, and Marxism-Leninism, and there is a great deal of instruction designed to make the student an over-all expert on the country, the language of which he is studying. The work in advanced foreign-language schools represents a Soviet equivalent of American "area studies."[29] The emphasis in such studies in the U.S.S.R. is on history and literature. There is no Soviet equivalent to the "behavioral" studies so prominent in America. In addition to this type of training there is, of course, a great deal of advanced work in philology and linguistics in Soviet universities, which includes some of the best work in the world on both Western and Oriental languages. I was told by a member of the staff of Intourist that the Oriental Faculty of the University of Leningrad was the main center for the study of Eastern languages in the Soviet Union. This source stated that classes in these languages were small, averaging about ten students to a class. Subsequently, an American graduate student studied in this faculty, apparently with considerable benefit both to him and to its students and staff.

There have been many indications in the last three or four years that Soviet practical and theoretical training in foreign languages and cultures, especially those of Asia and Africa, has been rapidly expanding. The chairman of the Department of the English Language at Moscow University published an article in June 1956 on the importance of intensifying study of foreign languages in preparation for the 1957 Youth Festival. She expressed the opinion that there were too few Soviet university graduates who could fluently speak a foreign language, despite the fact that the Ministry of Higher Education had recently issued instructions to higher educational institutions to extend the study of foreign languages into the third and fourth years of university work. Logically enough, she pointed out that knowledge of foreign languages was an elementary prerequisite for the development of cultural relations

[29] A good brief description of Soviet advanced foreign-language study is contained in an article by William J. Jorden in the *New York Times* of October 4, 1956.

and personal contacts with foreigners.[30] Like many of the numerous other criticisms published by Soviet sources regarding the quality of foreign-language instruction in contemporary Russia, the above article indirectly also indicated the great scope and power of the Soviet language-training program. For example, one of its criticisms was that language instruction in the secondary schools was not yet good enough to permit Soviet university students "knowing one language" to proceed boldly to the study of a second foreign language.

While, by German or French university standards, this may seem a modest goal, it must be remembered that the number of persons receiving a higher education in the Soviet Union is many times as large, both absolutely and in proportion to the population, as it is in Germany or France, Switzerland or Holland. *Komsomolskaya Pravda* for August 8, 1957, reported that one of the Indian delegates at the World Youth Festival said that he felt very much at home because he had learned that many Soviet youths spoke languages such as Hindi, Urdu, or Bengali.

One keen observer, who attended the festival, wrote: "It might be worthwhile to note that the Russians were able to find top rate interpreters for each language spoken by the Festival delegates. Not one, but several. I asked some of the Russians whether it was difficult to find interpreters for some of the dialects and lesser-known languages. The answer was, 'We make sure that we have enough people studying all the different languages to provide for our language needs whenever such things as the Youth Festival come up.' "[31]

By contrast, according to a competent survey, "all but a few Americans—working in all but a very few countries—find themselves entirely dependent on interpreters and translators."[32] Some of the Intourist guides that I encountered in 1956 certainly did not have a mastery of spoken English. In one or two cases guides actually expressed a desire to switch to Russian. On the whole, however, it would be fair to say that most Western specialists on

[30] *Moskovski universitet,* June 19, 1956, p. 3.

[31] George Abrams, "Talking with Russians," in *New Republic,* October 14, 1957, p. 14.

[32] Shirley Duncan Hudson, "Asian Languages—a U. S. Weakness and What Can Be Done About It," in *ACLS Newsletter,* Vol. VI, No. 2, Summer 1955, pp. 12-29.

the Russian area who have been in the Soviet Union in recent years would agree that the Intourist guides whom they met knew English considerably better than most of the Westerners knew Russian. It must be remembered also that even in 1957 the post-Stalin tourist and exchange-of-persons program was still quite new. One could expect that with practice there would come improvement. Almost every day prominent Americans report some new evidence of Soviet success in producing and sending to key areas persons with competence in foreign languages. Chester Bowles, for example, told the Ninth Student Conference on United States Affairs at West Point in 1957 that as American ambassador in India he had never seen a Russian who was not learning Hindi or had not already learned to speak it with reasonable fluency.

Students of the specialized Soviet foreign-language schools must decide, at the end of the second year, whether they wish to become teachers, translators, or interpreters. Those who are accepted for the coveted and difficult translator and interpreter programs often find employment with Intourist, the Ministry of Foreign Trade, the Soviet UN staff, et cetera.

In addition to the foreign-language institutes, and the Soviet area-studies programs, which will be discussed presently, there are at least two important graduate training and research institutions at which advanced study of international relations and specialized training for foreign-service work and related occupations may be obtained. These are the Institute of World Economy and International Relations of the U.S.S.R. Academy of Sciences and the highly specialized Diplomatic School. The Diplomatic School is operated by the Ministry of Foreign Affairs. In 1956 an Intourist guide told me that competition for entry to the Diplomatic School was exceptionally keen, partly because so many young people sought an opportunity to travel abroad, especially to the United States. He thought that only party members were admitted. Although he himself belonged to the party he seemed dubious about his chances of obtaining admission. No information on the Diplomatic School is available, to our knowledge, in Soviet publications. Not all Soviet diplomats attend it.

The only reference to the Institute that could be located in any Soviet publication was one in the 1958 edition of a handbook for

Soviet graduate students. The handbook announced that entrance examinations for the Institute were required in the following subjects: political economy, history of the communist party of the Soviet Union, foreign language, and "economics of the capitalist countries." The Institute offered graduate instruction in the following "specialties": "general economic problems of imperialism; the situation and the struggle of the working class of the capitalist countries; economics and politics of the capitalist countries; agrarian problems of imperialism; contemporary international relations; problems of militarization of the economy of capitalist countries." No doubt degree-holders of this Institute are well prepared for the practice of "peaceful coexistence," or at any rate for the production of monographs thereon.[33]

There is also an undergraduate six-year program in international relations, with Western and Eastern departments, and Soviet and Soviet bloc students, at the Moscow State Institute of International Relations. An American scholar who visited this undergraduate Institute reported that its program was heavily linguistic but with strong political-economic and "area" components. Several American scholars have succeeded in establishing contact in recent years with this faculty and with the above Institute, but none, to our knowledge, has obtained any sort of access to the highly sensitive Diplomatic School, admission to which is apparently restricted to personnel of the Ministry of Foreign Affairs. Its graduates continue their careers in the ministry, which also draws on other institutes and on Soviet universities for its personnel. Also, if present Soviet practice continues past traditions, the ministry presumably recruits many of its officials from the academic and engineering professions and from the ranks of the communist party apparatus. Graduates of the above institutions who do not enter foreign service are employed by Soviet foreign-language publications, translating and propaganda agencies, and the like.

Perhaps it should be noted here that graduates, and indeed admittees, of the higher educational institutions mentioned in this chapter, and of Soviet higher educational institutions in general, automatically receive a privileged status in Soviet society. In this respect, as in many others, Soviet society carries on tsarist traditions. Students receive stipends which vary with grades and with family

---

[33] *Spravochnik dlya postupayushchikh v aspiranturu*, Moscow, 1958, p. 158.

income but do not in any case cover all expenses, although full tuition is, of course, covered. Soviet Minister of Higher Education Elyutin told me in 1956 that "rich" fathers, such as professors, sometimes paid the full expenses of their children's education. University and institute students are exempt from the obligations of military service, except for officer reserve training, which takes relatively little time.

Even before the death of Stalin, and on a rapidly expanding scale thereafter, Soviet academic institutions embarked on a large-scale foreign-area research and training program. A notable feature of this program was the revival of Oriental and African studies, which had flourished in tsarist and early Soviet times but had languished since the purges and repressions of Soviet Orientalists in the 1930's.[34] Orientalists were directed to shift emphasis from antiquarian-philological interests to more urgent, contemporary political problems. The Oriental Institute of the Academy of Sciences was reorganized in 1950. After sharp, prodding criticism—including presidium member Anastas Mikoyan's derisive remark at the Twentieth Party Congress that "although in our day the whole East has awakened, the Institute is still dozing"—a second, more important reorganization was effected in 1956.

Perhaps as a demonstrative gesture, this second reorganization brought a Soviet Asian to leadership of Soviet Asian studies. The prominent Tadzhik politician and former first secretary of the communist party of Tadzhikistan, B. G. Gafurov, became director of the Institute. As Moscow, while cultivating the "Geneva spirit" in the West, also exploited the "Bandung spirit" in the East, academic activity burgeoned all along the Asian-African front. After almost twenty years without a scholarly magazine, Soviet Orientalists in 1955 resumed publication of the *Sovetskoe Vostokovedenie (Soviet Orientalogy)*. As of 1958, four periodicals were being published in the U.S.S.R. in the field of Oriental studies,

[34] Those portions of the material on Soviet Oriental and African studies not obtained directly from Soviet sources were derived in considerable measure from W. Z. Laqueur, "The Shifting Line in Soviet Orientalogy," in *Problems of Communism*, Vol. v, No. 2, March-April 1956, pp. 20-26, and Rodger Swearingen, "Asian Studies in the Soviet Union," in *Journal of Asian Studies*, Vol. XVII, No. 3, May 1958, pp. 515-537

and the State Publishing House for Eastern Literature had scheduled 109 titles for early publication.

Pravda for March 29, 1955, reported a conference, called by the Academy of Science of the U.S.S.R., which was attended by more than five hundred specialists in Oriental languages, history, literature, and economics. The new significance attributed to Eastern affairs was reflected in the fact that the conference was opened by K. V. Ostrovityanov, vice-president of the Academy, and the most influential of Soviet economists. A "Congress of the Intelligentsia of Uzbekistan," held in 1956, was attended by prominent Soviet officials and intellectuals, as well as by Indian and Egyptian guests. Mr. Mukhitdinov, first secretary of the communist party of Uzbekistan, and the first Uzbek ever to achieve alternate membership of the party presidium, was the principal speaker.

Sovetskaya Kultura for July 12, 1957, reported plans to establish a new Oriental Institute in Tashkent, to specialize in the history, ethnography, and economics of the "Soviet and foreign East."

In conjunction with these organizational-political initiatives, serious undergraduate and graduate study of Eastern and African cultures, economics and politics, mostly concentrated in the Oriental Faculty of the University of Leningrad, the Institute of Oriental Languages of the University of Moscow, and the Central Asian State University in Tashkent, got under way in 1955 and 1956. Despite new emphasis on the nonlinguistic aspects of area studies, especially at Moscow, these intensive six-year programs also featured intensive and very practical work in the spoken languages of India, China, Japan, the Middle Eastern countries and others. Native informants from these countries, and in some cases professors, were employed in these programs. The Moscow Institute, at least, had already, in 1957, dispatched a number of students for training abroad. The comparative scope of Soviet Asian studies may be illustrated by the example of Iran, in the language and history of which Russia has scores of specialists in at least four major centers, and dozens of graduate students, while America has only two or three individual scholars and a handful of students doing serious work in this vital area.

In an appraisal of Soviet Asian studies published in 1958, based in part on data gathered on a trip to the U.S.S.R. in 1957, Professor Rodger Swearingen of the University of Southern California wrote that Soviet language and area programs "compared favorably" with similar efforts in the United States. Considering their relative newness, such a result represented an achievement testifying to Soviet determination and efficiency. Professor Swearingen also reported a rapid build-up of Soviet library holdings of Western publications on the Orient. Many studies, such as his—with Paul Langer—*Red Flag in Japan*, were still outwardly unavailable, but a Soviet colleague confessed he had read it and liked it in most ways but disliked its conclusions!

By no means all Soviet advanced study of Oriental countries takes place in area institutes, as is indicated, for example, by the fact that as early as the academic year 1954-1955 *Pravda Ukrainy* reported that twenty-five students in the Moscow Institute of Foreign Trade were engaged in studies of the economy, foreign trade, and finances of India. Graduate students in the Department of Eastern History of Moscow University were at the same time writing dissertations on such topics as "The Agrarian Pattern in Southern India Before the English Conquest." Students in these fields were required to study Hindi, Urdu, Bengali, Sanskrit, or other appropriate languages.

In 1957 and 1958 the Academy of Sciences held coordinating meetings to stimulate research and teaching in the field of African studies. The February 1958 meeting endorsed a proposal to establish an All-Union Society of Africanists and suggested introduction of special courses on African history, economics, and languages in universities, et cetera. Indications of the political flavor of Soviet African studies may be gleaned from lists of projects in a research plan published in *Sovetskaya Etnografiya*, Number three, 1957, which included such titles as "Liberia Under the Yoke of American Monopoly" and "The Economic Development and Struggle of the Peoples of Nigeria Against Imperialist Enslavement After World War II." In May 1958 the Ministry of Higher Education issued a directive calling for invitations to foreign African specialists to visit Leningrad, where Swahili, Amharic, and Hawsa were already being offered, and courses in other languages were planned, and called for the sending of a small number of Soviet teachers and students of African languages abroad to increase their proficiency.

The ministry announced that students specializing in African languages at Leningrad, the major university for such instruction, would acquire conversational knowledge of no less than two related African languages, according to the State Department report already cited.

In addition to providing cadres of specialists for the processing of material relating to Asia and Africa, and facilitating the Kremlin's dissemination to the Soviet public of attitudes toward these areas which it deems appropriate, the growing Soviet program of language and area training and research—probably modeled, in part, on American programs—would assist Moscow in implementing its foreign economic and cultural policy in these areas.

In the meantime, as one part of an over-all effort in the publication of foreign-language dictionaries which apparently far surpasses the corresponding American effort, Soviet scholars stepped up their work on rare Asian and African languages. Soviet linguists as well as social scientists and historians asserted in connection with these efforts that the attention they paid to "the peoples of the East" contrasted sharply with the practice of bourgeois scholars who, they claimed, neglected and even despised Oriental as well as Slavic cultures.[35]

Post-Stalin development of Oriental and African studies has not implied any lack of attention to Western societies, particularly in the crucial field of economics, as has already been suggested previously in this chapter. Presidium member Anastas Mikoyan, in his address to the Twentieth Party Congress, indicated that Soviet scholars in the future would be expected to study deeply all aspects of the economic and social development of the advanced Western countries. He taxed Soviet scholars with having displayed less energy in studying the American economy than Americans had expended in research on the U.S.S.R. His line appeared to be that Russia could still learn much, even from a dying, but by no means yet dead, capitalist society. His audience applauded when he promised that more statistical and archival information would be made available to scholars than in Stalinist times.[36]

[35] *Pravda*, April 11, 1954; *Current Digest of the Soviet Press*, May 12, 1954; *Sovetskaya Kultura*, June 9, 1955; *Kommunist*, No. 8, May 1955, pp. 74-83.

[36] *XX Sezd kommunisticheskoi partii sovetskogo soyuza*, Moscow, 1956, Vol. I, pp. 323-327.

Even before Mikoyan's somewhat demagogic speech, the Soviet Academy of Sciences had opened an Institute of Contemporary Capitalist Economy.[37] A leading Soviet authority on American history Professor Leo Zubok, told me in 1956 that he was teaching a special course on American history at Moscow University and that similar courses were about to be started at a few other major institutions, such as the University of Kiev and Gorki State University. Zubok has a friendly manner, but Americans should remember that he has recently written a history of the United States in the standard Soviet pattern, stressing "aggression," "imperialism," et cetera. However, a few years ago he was severely criticized by Soviet authorities for allegedly glossing over the sins of the United States, and one can surmise that, like many of his colleagues, he is really more objective than his publications might suggest. Zubok, according to one well-informed American source, is the "American expert" at the already-mentioned Institute of International Relations, a function he performs concurrently with his other duties.

The Soviet economists with whom we spoke in 1956 were well informed regarding American economic journals, though they somewhat surprisingly asked if the pamphlets and information bulletins compiled by American banks and corporations were available to the public and could be obtained by Soviet scholars. They stated that their main source of supply of American economic journals was the Social Science Library of the Academy of Sciences. In 1959 Professor Vasili Leontiev of the Harvard economics department publicly reported, upon returning from the U.S.S.R., where he was a member of the Harvard exchange delegation, that he had seen on the desk of some Soviet economists copies of Standard and Poor's investment reports. Professor Leontiev found Soviet economists less doctrinaire than he had expected, though they continued to pay lip service to Marxist dogmas. Perhaps the indications of increasing rationality in Soviet thinking reported to Dr. Leontiev can be attributed, to some degree, to renewal of scholarly contact with the West.

In addition to language and area studies, the Soviet leadership is alert to the importance of other significant techniques for the

[37] *New York Times*, September 15, 1955.

information and guidance of its cultural cadres. For example, conspicuous observances of anniversaries of great foreign writers, artists, and scientists are a regular feature of the Soviet cultural scene. On April 28, 1955, the Soviet Academy of Arts held a special memorial meeting in honor of the fiftieth anniversary of the death of the Belgian sculptor Constantine Mene. The Belgian ambassador spoke at the ceremony, which was attended also by the president of the section of VOKS for "representational art."[38] In the same year the World Peace Council called upon "progressive mankind" to mark the 200th anniversary of the death of Montesquieu, who was described in *Sovetskaya Kultura* for March 15 as "a noble thinker, champion of freedom, and of peaceful life and prosperity of the peoples." Interestingly, a considerable portion of *Sovetskaya Kultura's* long article was devoted to the alleged friendship between notable Russians, such as the poet Kantemir, and Montesquieu, and to the fact that other outstanding Russian writers such as Radishchev had thought highly of the French "enlightener."

In 1956 extensive ceremonies were held in Russia in honor of the 2500th death anniversary of Gautama Buddha. In 1959 the 200th anniversary of the death of Handel was commemorated, and Handel was hailed as a creator of music for the "broad masses," a somewhat strange emphasis, considering his aristocratic connections. Like other Soviet techniques, commemoration is adapted to time and circumstances. And so, with the shift to a somewhat softer line toward the United States after Stalin's death, the Soviet press once again began to publish favorable articles about Walt Whitman, Benjamin Franklin, Abraham Lincoln, and other "progressive" figures of the American past.

On appropriate occasions, such as visits to the Soviet Union of important foreign personages and cultural groups, artistic, literary, or historical exhibitions are arranged. These exhibitions serve to supplement Soviet propaganda regarding some matter of current interest, but they also fit into a larger perspective. They have the dual purpose of acquainting the interested Soviet public with appropriate aspects of foreign cultures and of demonstrating to foreigners Soviet appreciation of non-Soviet culture. As a representative example of the educational and political function of such

[38] *Sovetskaya Kultura*, May 1, 1955.

exhibitions, one might mention the display in the Central Park of Culture and Rest in Moscow, in November 1955, of Indian arts and crafts.

A leading Soviet art authority described the exhibition in a two-column article in *Sovetskaya Kultura* for November 10. The author combined ecstasy of mood with rich factual detail. His approach was suggested by the statement that "entering the exposition the viewer literally enters India, the country of miracles."

While I was in the Soviet Union in 1956, I visited an exhibition of Indian art sponsored by the Union of Soviet Artists in Moscow, an exhibition of Iranian publications and of Soviet and foreign works on Iran at the Moscow Library of Foreign Literature, and exhibitions of French books and manuscripts in the Moscow and Odessa public libraries.

The Iranian exhibition included books on that country by such bourgeois scholars as Professor Richard C. Frye of Harvard. There were no Indians, Iranians, or Frenchmen at any of these exhibitions during my visits and to questions as to whether or not natives of these countries had visited them I received only vague replies.

All of these exhibitions seemed to be, from a technical point of view, of excellent quality. Perhaps we should mention here that the impressive Museum of Fine Arts in Odessa had, a few months previous to our 1956 visit, added an Eastern Hall. While I was unsuccessful in my effort to learn what, if any, impact these exhibitions had on natives of the countries that they were designed to honor, I did observe many interested Soviet citizens intently studying them. If one considers that dozens, and perhaps hundreds, of these exhibitions are held in the Soviet Union every year and that they are usually on a high level, one cannot fail to admire the magnitude, if not the purpose, of this effort.

In the conditioning of Soviet cadres for cultural combat, the role of other media, such as school and university textbooks, motion pictures, and television might be discussed at length. On July 9 and 10, 1956, to mention an example, the Leningrad television studio presented a film regarding a Rumanian official delegation, as well as a Polish comedy film, a Yugoslav ballet, and a documentary on Pakistan. The latter, according to the official Leningrad TV program for that week, which was on public sale, dealt with "the ancient culture of Pakistan, its splendid architectural monuments and the landscape, economy and way of life of its peoples." The total effort surveyed in this chapter is so vast as almost to defy description. A full study of Soviet planning for cultural penetration would require years of effort by a large research staff. This program may exert greater influence abroad than Soviet research and development in atomic energy or artificial earth satellites, which, indeed, it helps to translate into propaganda.

CHAPTER VII

CULTURAL STRATEGY IN ASIA, AFRICA, AND LATIN AMERICA

THUS far we have described Soviet cultural policy without much regard to geography. In this and the next two chapters we examine Soviet strategy as it is applied in specific areas, starting with the "poorly developed" countries, as Khrushchev in his public speech at the Twentieth Party Congress referred to the less-industrialized lands. It is in the underdeveloped countries that post-Stalin policy has secured its greatest successes. In terms of numbers of exchanges, Soviet contacts with Asia, Africa, and Latin America have not bulked as large as those with Western Europe and the United States, but the Soviet press has usually devoted more space to exchanges with the less-developed countries than to Europe or America. For example, during the years 1954-1957, 196 Indian delegations visited the Soviet Union, compared to 348 from France and 368 from Great Britain; *Pravda's* reporting on exchanges with India, however, gave them twice as much space as those with France and considerably more than to those with Great Britain.[1]

The prominence with which Soviet-Indian, or Soviet-Arab, cultural exchanges have been reported reflects the significance attributed to these areas in the Kremlin's calculations. It also, probably, reflects the fact that it is easier for the Soviet Union to make a favorable impression in the unindustrialized world than in the West. The Soviet leaders feel less constrained about expressing admiration for the cultures and folk of India, Iraq, or Indonesia than for Western cultures. Perhaps they reason that there is not much reason to fear that Burmese, Syrians, Egyptians, Indians, or even Brazilians could subvert Soviet intellectuals or students. It seems safe, as well as profitable, therefore, to display enthusiasm for the national culture and national character of such peoples; this can be a potent instrument for winning the affection of nations still smarting under a sense of inferiority to, or burdened by resentments against, "Western imperialism."

[1] These ratios are my own calculations, based on available data on exchanges and a careful culling of *Pravda*.

The Soviet wooing of Asia and Africa is as old as Leninism. Despite the subtler methods employed since the death of Stalin, the long-run objective of Soviet policy in the underdeveloped countries remains that of smoothing the path for the eventual accession of communists to power. The short-run objectives are several. Highest priority, perhaps, is assigned to the undermining of Western influence. Another major purpose is to present to the peoples, and particularly to the intellectuals, of these countries an appealing picture of Soviet life and of Soviet domestic and foreign policy. A related purpose is the establishment of personal and organizational links between Soviet artistic, scientific, and academic institutions and counterparts in target areas. An attempt is also made to use cultural exchanges to influence the policies and attitudes of local noncommunist political leaders.

To informed noncommunists Soviet behavior toward the developing countries seems to be corroded by deception. While it outwardly professes respect for values to which all thinking men must subscribe, such as the need for increasing understanding among peoples, and pays lip service to patriotism and religious freedom, Soviet policy reassures communist "insiders" that the Kremlin remains faithful to the Leninist tradition of ceaseless pressure for the extension of communist power. In this connection it is instructive, for example, to compare the speeches of Bulganin and Khrushchev in India with those made by them and other leaders at such gatherings as the Twentieth Congress of the Soviet communist party. While in India, Soviet leaders assured Prime Minister Nehru and the Indian people that differences in ideologies or economic systems constituted no obstacle to the settlement of international problems. All that was necessary, according to B and K, was good will and honorable intentions. They took particular pains to avow that Moscow had neither the intention nor the desire to export communism to India or to other countries.[2] In contrast, Khrushchev, in his speech to the Twentieth Congress a few months later, proclaimed anew the need for "social revolution" and for the conversion of "bourgeois democratic" institutions to "socialism" everywhere. His assertion that this end might be accomplished "legally" and "peacefully" lacked credibility, in view of the vagaries of Krem-

---

[2] See, for example, Khrushchev's speech to the Indian parliament, published in *Pravda*, November 22, 1955.

lin semantics; at the same congress Mikoyan asserted that communists had seized power in Czechoslovakia, Bulgaria, Hungary, Rumania, and Poland by "peaceful" means.[3]

Soviet propaganda in the underdeveloped countries appeals particularly to the radical anti-Western nationalism which has developed in recent years. Khrushchev in his Twentieth Congress speech hailed "the intensification of the national liberation movement in Brazil, Chile, and other countries of Latin America," and he asserted that the Soviet Union could assist "former colonies" in achieving "economic independence," in training a technical intelligentsia, and in restoring and further developing their "ancient national cultures." In an apparent effort to arouse anti-Western racial feeling he contrasted the contemporary significance of Asia with that of an earlier period in which, he emphasized, international relations had been shaped "primarily by people of the white race." In a section of this speech, entitled "The Collapse of the Colonial System of Imperialism," Khrushchev appealed to assorted sentiments through extended tributes hailing the "rebirth" of India, the Arab East, and Southeast Asia and the "awakening" of the peoples of Africa. This change in strategic orientation was, of course, accompanied by a turn toward courtesy and correctness in relations with bourgeois governments headed by such men as Prime Minister Nehru of India, President Sukarno of Indonesia, and President Nasser of the United Arab Republic.

As if to reassure communists that he was not deviating from Marxist-Leninist fundamentalism, Khrushchev bluntly reiterated his belief in the necessity of revolutionary violence. He reminded his audience of Lenin's teaching that established authority does not voluntarily renounce power. To be sure, he added, it might be possible in some countries to elect socialist governments in accordance with constitutional procedures, but once in power the "working class" could convert parliaments "from organs of bourgeois democracy into real instruments of popular will." Khrushchev's speech was followed by many authoritative speeches and articles by Soviet theoreticians and party leaders which provided a framework for understanding the Kremlin's cultural policy in

[3] *XX Sezd kommunisticheskoi partii sovetskogo soyuza*, Moscow, 1956, Vol. 1, p. 317.

the underdeveloped countries. For a significant eight-page piece, the leading Soviet expert on the Far East, E. Zhukov, borrowed Khrushchev's title, "The Collapse of the Colonial System of Imperialism."[4] Zhukov suggested that in the present stage of world history Moscow could make good use of Asian, African, and Latin American nationalism and anticolonialism. The "national liberation movement," he stated, was weakening the world capitalist system. The major task of communist parties in countries such as India and Indonesia was to support measures to strengthen the "economic independence" and the "national sovereignty" of their countries. In contrast to past directives urging openly revolutionary tactics, communist parties were advised to collaborate "with all progressive social forces" and to display tact and good manners toward representatives of "bourgeois nationalist" movements. In this connection Zhukov praised Prime Minister Nehru, but he took pains to stress an earlier statement made by Mr. Khrushchev during the latter's visit to India, making it clear that Nehru's proposed "socialist path" for India must not be identified with the Soviet conception of socialism. Perhaps his most significant statement was a confident assertion that ". . . the active role of the working class and of its militant advance guard, the communist party, is increasing everywhere; it is natural, therefore, to expect that in the future the working class will achieve universal predominance in this struggle. This, however, is a long and complicated process."

In the last chapter we had something to say about the post-Stalin revival of Oriental studies in the Soviet Union. This revival brought to the surface significant indications of the motives of Soviet cultural policy. For example, B. G. Gafurov asserted, in a report which he delivered in June 1957 at an All-Union Conference of Orientalists, at Tashkent, that Soviet scholars should express their sympathy and understanding for the "anti-imperialist struggle of the workers," which would be headed "at a certain stage" by the "national bourgeoisie."[5] He directed Soviet scholars to explode bourgeois theories, based allegedly upon a belief in the

[4] E. Zhukov, "Raspad kolonialnoi sistemy imperializma," in *Partiinaya Zhizn*, No. 16, August 1956, pp. 41-48.

[5] B. G. Gafurov, "O perspektivakh razvitiya sovetskogo vostokovedeniya," in *Sovetskoe Vostokovedenie*, No. 3, 1957, pp. 10-17.

"organic backwardness of the peoples of the East." Soviet scholars were to demonstrate how the "republics of the Soviet East" had, with the active help of the great Russian people, overcome their former backwardness in the shortest possible time and had become "the lighthouse of communism in the East."

Spurred by such pressures, Soviet diplomats, scholars, artists, scientists, athletes, and engineers set out to smile their way into the hearts of Asians and Africans. Two major techniques played a particularly prominent role in this many-sided effort. One of these was to utilize exchange visits as occasions for publicizing these Soviet achievements most calculated to convince Asians, Africans, and Latin Americans of Soviet solicitude and respect for them. The other and closely related technique consisted in the careful cultivation of the predispositions and susceptibilities of peoples whose traditions, aspirations, and grievances had been carefully studied.

An attempt was even made to efface the unfavorable impression made on Asian and African peoples, particularly Moslems, by traditional Soviet antireligious propaganda. Much publicity was given to such events as the 1954 visit of a group of Indonesian women to a Moslem seminary in Soviet Central Asia or the pilgrimage in 1957 of "Soviet Moslems" to Mecca, Medina, and Cairo.[6] Another typical gesture to religious sentiments was the interview with the Imam of the Moscow mosque, Kamarattin Salikhov, broadcast by Radio Moscow on its Near Eastern Service in Turkish on May 24, 1958. The Imam criticized Western denials that there was freedom of religion in the U.S.S.R. All religions, he declared, including the Moslem faith, were separate from the state. This meant, he argued, that the state did not interfere in religious matters.

And yet, in 1954, as it was about to launch its campaign to woo non-Soviet Asians, the Kremlin also intensified its domestic drive against religion. An article in the leading Soviet philosophical journal attacked Buddhism, Islam, and Christianity as instruments of

[6] See *Pravda*, August 13, 1954, and *Izvestiya*, July 2, 1957. For a discussion of Soviet treatment of Moslems within the U.S.S.R., see Richard E. Pipes, "The Soviet Impact on Central Asia," in *Problems of Communism*, Vol. VI, No. 2, March-April 1957.

social oppression and political reaction.[7] In a lecture broadcast over the Home Service of Radio Moscow not long after President Nasser of the United Arab Republic had completed his first 1958 trip to the Soviet Union, Professor L. I. Klimovich asserted that Islam, like any other religion, was a remnant of a society which the Soviet people had left far behind.[8]

Numerous reports were published in the Soviet press on "scientific-atheistic parties" in "houses of culture." Also, antireligious museums were being reopened during these years. In 1956 I visited the Leningrad antireligious museum, housed in the former Kazan Cathedral, and saw many exhibits and texts vilifying the Moslem and other religions.

A technique, which might be characterized as "collective flattery," by which Moscow attempts to cultivate particular ethnic, religious, political, or other groups, is also applied on a national level in efforts to win the good will of entire peoples. The mass deportation of the Moslem Chechens and other small peoples during World War II for alleged collaboration with the Germans, the subjugation of the Baltic peoples in 1940, and the more recent crushing of the Hungarians in 1956 serve as reminders of the gap between profession and practice in Soviet nationality policy. Nevertheless, a skilled application of the Stalin formula referred to in Chapter 1 to peoples who have had little opportunity for first-hand experience of Soviet reality can, at least in the short run, pay propaganda dividends.

The expression of appreciation for Asian, African, and Latin American cultural traditions has both a positive and negative aspect; while striving to win friends for the Soviet Union it seeks also to alienate the peoples of these areas from the West, particularly the United States. The communists charge that United States "imperialism" and "cosmopolitanism" threaten to destroy native cultures and to substitute for cherished folk values "the decadence of Hollywood."

A good example of this dual approach was an article by the well-

[7] "Nauchnoe i religioznoe mirovozzrenie," unsigned article in *Voprosy Filosofii*, No. 5, 1954.

[8] Selections from statements referred to above can be found in *Problems of Communism*, Vol. VII, No. 4, July-August 1958, p. 46.

known Soviet writer Ilya Ehrenburg which appeared in a Soviet literary magazine in the summer of 1956. After a month of travel in India, Ehrenburg published a detailed and highly appreciative discussion of Indian culture aimed, obviously, at pleasing Indian intellectuals. At the same time he accused the British and the Americans of seeking to spread the view that Indians were opposed to technical progress, that they were quaint but hopelessly backward. Ehrenburg of course attributed the poverty of India to decades of British "exploitation." Pointing out that contemporary India seeks and is achieving material progress, he went on to stress that Indians, unlike Western Europeans, and in special contrast to Americans, would never be satisfied with mere physical comfort. Indians, he declared, felt that material progress was not sufficient, but must be accompanied by the advancement of human welfare and general spiritual development. In short, Ehrenburg made a calculated effort to interlard just praise for India's achievements and aspirations with half truths or outright misrepresentation of Western attitudes, counting on the receptivity of his audience to the former to make the latter believable.[9]

Ehrenburg, who has often been sent on important foreign cultural missions, was also the star performer in connection with the award of a Stalin Peace Prize to the Chilean poet Pablo Neruda in August 1954. On this occasion he couched an appeal to various shades of liberal and radical sentiment in terms calculated to stir antagonism to the United States; the due tribute he paid to Chile's national heroes, cultural heritage, and economic achievements was capped with the message that a people which, like all others in Latin America, had "defended" its national culture and its national independence against "heavy odds" was a great people.[10]

In a similar vein *Pravda* for August 15, 1954, described the grandeurs of the pyramids of Egypt and praised the "work-loving" Egyptian people who had created them, but at the same time expressed indignation at the poverty to which "foreign exploitation" allegedly had subjected them.

A corollary and implicit aim of such statements is to convince

[9] I. Ehrenburg, "Indiiskie Vpechatleniya," in *Inostrannaya Literatura*, Moscow, June 1956, pp. 196-222.
[10] *Pravda*, August 13, 1954; Ehrenburg's address and Neruda's reply dominate the front page of this issue.

foreign peoples that only in socialist countries are their national cultural traditions sincerely appreciated. Toward this end, other devices, mentioned earlier in this book, are used by Moscow, such as exhibitions in honor of classical—or less frequently contemporary "progressive"—writers and artists, and public commemorative ceremonies in which prominent Soviet political leaders play a major role. These devices are often combined, as on the occasion of a public ceremony in Moscow in November 1956 honoring the Indian national poet Kalidas.

In keeping with the duality of Moscow's policy toward underdeveloped countries, one might expect that visitors to Russia from these lands would be shown only those aspects of Soviet life which would make a favorable impression upon them and that they would not be taken to see things which would give offense. In this connection, it is interesting that while many Asian and African delegations have been taken to Uzbekistan, the showplace of Soviet Central Asia, relatively few have been allowed to visit Kazakhstan and Kirghiziya, where there has been such a flood of Russian and Ukrainian immigrants in recent years that Kazakhstan, in particular, is rapidly losing its "native" character.[11] The Kremlin apparently was concerned, in the case of Mr. Nasser, lest he see something of the seamier side of Soviet policy toward Moslems. Commenting on this matter, the *Economist* for May 17, 1958, observed: "A dash into Moslem Asia was kept as short and as innocuous as possible. In a two-day visit to Uzbekistan and Azerbaidzhan little was said on the Russian side, and nothing at all by the Egyptians, about the position of Moslems in the Russian empire."

A somewhat more detailed examination of the Soviet cultural offensive in a few key countries may give added meaning to the foregoing observations. With the exception of communist China, India has now for several years been the main target of Soviet cultural penetration. The drive in India actually began on a considerable scale several years before the death of Stalin. As long ago as March 1952, Howland H. Sargeant, then Assistant Sec-

[11] The Uzbek Russian-language newspaper, *Pravda Vostoka*, is one of the best sources of information on the procession of Asian and African visitors to Uzbekistan. For interesting comment on the policy of selective display in Soviet Central Asia, see *Central Asian Review*, Vol. v, No. 3, 1957, p. 233.

retary of State for Public Affairs, called attention to a burgeoning Soviet effort to plant "the idea of Soviet interest in the arts" in India.[12] One could, of course, trace the Soviet campaign in India much farther back than the 1951-1952 years. As far back as 1948, for example, VOKS organized an "evening devoted to acquainting leaders of Soviet culture with Indian art," which was attended by such Soviet notables as the movie producer Vladimir Pudovkin and the composer Yuri Shaporin, as well as by the Indian ambassador, Madame Lakshmi Pandit.[13]

However, Soviet policy before 1950 or 1951 was not only hostile to the Nehru government but was openly encouraging communist violence in India. With the temporary abandonment of revolutionary subversion by the Indian communists it became easier for Moscow to push its coexistence line in India. In 1951 the Indo-Soviet Cultural Society was formed, shortly after the return of a group of pro-Soviet Indian intellectuals to their native land from a visit to the Soviet Union. This society began to organize exhibits on such subjects as "Stalingrad today," "Moscow University," and "A happy childhood." Festivals of Soviet films were held in India in 1951 and in 1952. The Soviet water colorist Klimshin spent two months in India in 1951, and in the following year two other Soviet artists traveled in that country.[14]

Even before the death of Stalin, the head of the Indian communist party was allowed to travel to the Soviet Union, and several prominent noncommunists attended the East Berlin meeting of the World Peace Council in 1952. Various pro-Soviet organizations were permitted to carry on their work unhampered. Apart from a ban introduced in 1952 on the display of Moscow publications in railway book stalls, the Indian communists have been free, even during the insurrectionary phase of their activity, to disseminate in India both locally produced and imported literature.

[12] See United States Department of State *Bulletin*, Vol. xxvi, No. 667, April 7, 1952, pp. 535-540. For an even earlier warning on the same subject see the article by Edward W. Barrett, Sargeant's predecessor as Assistant Secretary of State for Public Affairs, entitled "The Kremlin's Intensified Campaign in the Field of Cultural Affairs," *ibid.*, Vol. xxv, No. 649, December 3, 1951, pp. 903-907.

[13] *Pravda*, July 9, 1948.

[14] For these and additional details on the late-Stalin era, see L. S. Gamayunov, *Iz istorii razvitiya kulturnykh svyazei nashei strany s indiei*, Moscow, 1955, pp. 30-38.

But, according to one Indian writer, it was not until 1953 that the Soviet propaganda drive in India, which up to that year had remained an essentially partisan manifestation, gained appeal outside of Indian communist and procommunist circles. The Indian government, according to this writer, readily accepted the new Soviet professions of respect and friendship offered by the successors of Stalin. It was no longer necessary for Moscow to entice noncommunists to visit Russia by free trips and other inducements. The Indian government itself began to sponsor a host of good-will delegations. From this point on, "visitors from Russia, to whom the locally suspect Indo-Soviet Friendship Society used to play the host, were now welcomed with open arms by the government."[15] Moscow made good use of its new opportunities. Soviet cultural propaganda in India developed in 1954 into a drive which had national appeal. It was, perhaps, more successful in India than in any other noncommunist country. The above-cited Indian author believes that there were two reasons for this success: Soviet economic aid, which was carried on in a manner calculated to avoid giving offense to the Indians and to win their gratitude, and, secondly, Indian opposition to military alliances such as the Baghdad Pact, sponsored by the West. During the B and K tour, millions of Indians were taught by their political leaders to chant the slogan "Indians and Russians are brothers."

A number of Indian writers have called attention to some of the social-cultural roots of Soviet influence in India. As a perceptive Indian editor has written, "in a society where the artist or writer finds it difficult to live, even the smallest support or patronage assumes importance. In the last four years communist patronage of the arts has become a strong factor. Indian fiction is being translated and published in East European languages. Indian music put down in staff notation is being sent to Moscow and other communist capitals. The Communist Party of India which arranges for such patronage to the artist is, thereby, able to win their allegiance."[16] It has also been asserted that "passionately aspiring to rapid industrialization Indian economists and intellectuals have turned to the Russian example."[17]

Soviet awareness of Indian susceptibility to apparent concern for Indian industrialization is indicated by such press items as the story in *Komsomolskaya Pravda* for August 15, 1958, entitled "Is There Oil in India: The Americans Said No! The Russians Say Yes!" According to this account, English and American "imperialists" refused to admit that there could be oil in India, because they wanted to continue to profit by sale of petroleum products to India. However, Soviet engineers and specialists were now helping and teaching Indians how to drill for oil. The article quoted a very friendly statement by Prime Minister Nehru thanking Soviet specialists for helping to train "cadres of young Indian specialists," and expressing satisfaction regarding harmonious Soviet-Indian collaboration for the welfare of India. In 1959 there was further development of Soviet-Indian collaboration in the development of the Indian petroleum industry.

The Soviet cultural- and technical-exchange effort was accompanied by an information program designed to furnish appropriate guidance to the Soviet cadres entrusted with its execution. Archives, historical works, and anthropological studies were combed for evidence of previous friendly relations between Russia and India. Research turned up such odd bits of information as the fact that Karl Marx had once praised the work of the Russian scholar Kovalevski on the social structure of India under the British occupation.[18] Frequent favorable references began to appear to the trips made to Russia by the Indian poet Rabindranath Tagore and by Mr. Nehru, who made his first trip in 1927. Other familiar techniques, such as exhibitions of Indian art, large-scale translations of Indian books into Russian, and display of Indian films in Soviet cinemas were employed. Expensively bound and printed books by Soviet artists, such as the distinguished Soviet Uzbek musician and composer Mukhtar Ashrafi, member of a Soviet cultural delegation which visited India in 1955, and attractive postcards with reproductions of sketches and paintings made in India by such painters as Gerasimov, Efanov, and Chuikov appeared in Soviet

[17] Ramani, *op.cit.*, p. 40.   [18] Gamayunov, *op.cit.*, p. 20.

bookstores.[19] A leading American educator of my acquaintance who met Mukhtar Ashrafi in Tashkent in 1958 found him very affable and apparently eager to make a trip to the United States. Ashrafi and the American drank a toast to the further development of cultural relations. Such episodes are interesting and encouraging, for they indicate that behind the façade of official anti-Americanism there may be, among Soviet intellectuals who participate most actively in Soviet-Asian exchanges, attitudes which, if they are someday allowed to be more fully expressed, may lead to better mutual understanding among all peoples.

In 1953 the daughter of Prime Minister Nehru visited the U.S.S.R. The Indian Minister of Health also visited Russia in 1953 and there were a number of visits by Indian delegations, including artists, an Indian soccer team, and a trade-union group. In 1954 the Soviet Academy of Sciences played host to Indian scientists. An Indian peace delegation was received by Prime Minister Malenkov. The big event of the year was a triumphal tour by a large group of Indian artists in August, September, and October. The Indians performed in the famous Bolshoi Theater in Moscow and in other leading theaters in many cities of the Soviet Union. They received rave reviews. In the same year an Indian surgeon, Sahib sing Sokhi, was awarded a Stalin Peace Prize. In 1955 Nehru made his visit to Russia. Also, the leading Indian scientist Babha as well as a delegation of Indian physicians, a soccer team, a group of "industrial observers," atomic-energy specialists, and a group of officers of the Indian Air Force visited the Soviet Union. In September 1955 an agreement on commercial cooperation was signed between the Soviet Civil Airfleet and the Indian State Airlines, during the visit of a group of Air India executives to Moscow.

Since Mr. Nehru's visit to Russia was the big event in Indo-Soviet relations, not only of 1955 but perhaps of any year, a few words should be said about it, and at the same time it would be appropriate to describe other important visits by Asian statesmen to the U.S.S.R. Catherine the Great's adviser, Prince Potemkin, might well have envied the skill displayed by proletarian rulers

---

[19] The "Soviet Artist" publishing house put out one of the above selections of postals by leading Soviet artists in 1955. Ashrafi's *Indian Diary* was published in Tashkent in 1956.

in welcoming Nehru, Sukarno, U Nu, the Shah of Iran, the Crown Prince of Yemen, and the President of the United Arab Republic in the Russia of Khrushchev. In planning their reception for Mr. Nehru, Soviet authorities apparently overlooked no detail which might contribute to the desired atmosphere. For example, in the presence of the Soviet Minister of Culture, a monument was unveiled to the fifteenth-century Russian traveler to India, Afanasi Nikitin. The press emphasized that Nikitin was the first European to visit India "with a friendly purpose." During the visit a very favorable review of Nehru's book *The Discovery of India* was published in *Kommunist*, the main theoretical journal of the Soviet communist party.

An equally elaborate reception was accorded Sukarno, with the usual receptions by the highest officials, presentation of flowers by children, vast crowds in streets and stadia, and the like. On the evening of August 28, 1956, at a general meeting of the Department of Economic, Philosophical, and Legal Sciences of the U.S.S.R. Academy of Sciences it was unanimously resolved to grant Sukarno the degree of Doctor of Juridical Sciences. An expanded session of the Learned Council of Moscow State University unanimously elected Sukarno an honorary professor of the university.[20] First-class motion-picture and television films were made in connection with these visits and the movies were shown widely in India and in Indonesia. According to one American correspondent, the master stroke of Soviet handling of the Sukarno visit was the assignment of Mr. Rashidov, a Soviet Uzbek official, as official representative to him of Soviet titular chief of state, Klimenti Voroshilov.[21]

The Crown Prince of the feudal Arabian kingdom of Yemen was shown around Moscow State University by its rector, Academician I. G. Petrovski, and by the chairman of the presidium of the Supreme Soviet of the Azerbaidzhan Soviet Republic, M. A. Ibragimov. The prince apparently displayed keen interest in the opportunities available for foreign students in the university. He was quoted as saying that the excellent conditions for scientific research which he had seen in the university constituted a guarantee

[20] *Pravda*, August 29, 1956.
[21] William J. Jorden, in the *New York Times*, October 2, 1956.

of progress, the necessary condition for the welfare of peoples, and the establishment of mutual understanding.[22] From the Kremlin's point of view, the visit was a big success.

By August 1958, incidentally, Soviet influence in Yemen had apparently grown so great that U.A.R. President Nasser was reported to be disturbed by it. There were said to be more than two hundred Soviet technicians in Yemen, and Nasser was thought to be particularly concerned about construction by Soviet engineers of coastal fortifications in Yemenese territory which commanded a strait through which all traffic to and from the Suez Canal passed.[23]

Beginning in 1956, many Indian engineers and industrial experts began to go to the Soviet Union to receive assistance and instruction in connection with implementation of technical-assistance and economic-aid agreements made in 1955 or 1956. A very important event, which led to closer Indian-Soviet technical contacts, was the signature in April 1956 of an agreement under which the Soviet government undertook to construct a large steel mill at Bhilai in India. In May 1956 a Soviet-Indian agreement was signed providing for regular steamship service between Bombay and Odessa. In March 1957 it was announced that India had sent ninety-one metallurgists to the Soviet Union to complete their technical training.[24] During the academic year 1956-1957 about a dozen Indian students selected by the Indian Ministry of Education were studying in Moscow. Most of them were doing work in the Russian language. About 450 Indian youths took part in the 1957 Youth Festival in Moscow.[25] In connection with Indian participation in the Youth Festival it is interesting that George Abrams reported that, while American and British guests of the festival were quartered five to a room, Indians, Arabs, and Africans were put up in rooms with two or three people. Instead of cafeteria-type meals, the Soviets gave the delegates of "uncommitted" countries their own dining halls, with waiters and candlelight service. Display windows of large Soviet stores showed mixed white and Negro

[22] *Moskovski Universitet*, June 19, 1956, front page.

[23] *New York Times*, August 31, 1958.

[24] *Pravda*, March 21, 1957. See also *Times of India* for same date, stating that, in addition, eighty metallurgists were to be sent to West Germany but that there were no plans to send any to other Western countries.

[25] *Komsomolskaya Pravda*, August 5, 1957.

dummies and the dummies of black-skinned children were used to display the best of Soviet wearing apparel. While, according to Abrams, most of the Indian delegates "saw through this preferential treatment," it seems to have made an impression on the Syrian and Egyptian delegations.[26] Visitors to the U.S.S.R. in 1956, while I was there, noticed that luxury foods, such as oranges, were placed on the tables of Asian delegations, but not on those of European groups.

Literaturnaya Gazeta for February 12, 1957, carried a very friendly article on four Indian oil engineers who already at that time had been working for several months in laboratories and research institutes in Baku. During the years after 1955 Indian singers and dancers continued to receive a cordial reception and an excellent press in the Soviet Union. Evidence that the popularity of Indian culture in Russia was reaching out to the masses was furnished by such events as an "evening of Indian culture" held in the Hammer and Sickle Factory in Moscow.[27] Presumably such reports made good reading in India.

In addition to Indian scientists, engineers, and technicians invited to Russia under the terms of bilateral exchange agreements, others, of course, visited the Soviet Union in connection with various multilateral arrangements. For example, in 1956, by an agreement between the Soviet Ministry of Agriculture and the Food and Agriculture Organization of the United Nations, a "large group of specialists of hydrography" from India, Sudan, Ceylon, Syria, Tunis, Pakistan, and other countries attended lectures given in Moscow by Soviet scientists and then toured Uzbekistan.[28] In the same year forestry specialists from India, Iran, Tunis, Sudan, Pakistan, Israel, Peru, and Chile as well as other countries took a two-week course in Kiev in connection with the "international seminar for problems of forest economy."[29]

In terms of stature and influence within their own society, Soviet political and cultural emissaries to India matched Indian guests to Russia. We shall comment in a moment on the well-known speech-making tour by B and K in November and December 1955. The two top Soviet leaders took with them on this expedition the

[26] Abrams, *op.cit.*, pp. 15-16.   [27] *Pravda*, February 28, 1957.
[28] *Pravda Vostoka*, August 18, 1956.   [29] *Pravda Ukrainy*, September 8, 1956.

Minister of Culture of the U.S.S.R., N. A. Mikhailov; the president of the presidium of the Uzbek Soviet Socialist Republic, S. R. Rashidov; the head of the Soviet secret police, Army General I. A. Serov; and five other high-ranking officials. Presidium member Mikoyan received a warm welcome during his visit in March 1956 and so did Marshal Zhukov in January 1957. So many Soviet visitors came to India in 1956, 1957, and 1958 that a major effort would be required even to list them. As *U.S. News and World Report* for June 22, 1956, stated: "Engineers, athletes, musicians, teachers, writers, trade unionists, journalists and others from Soviet Russia and the Red satellites are all over the place. At times there are so many groups from Eastern Europe visiting New Delhi on one mission or another that you hear as much slavic conversation in the hotel lobbies as you do English."

Of course, Americans, Englishmen, and even West Germans were also "all over the place." While on a lecture assignment in a midwestern American university in 1958 I had the opportunity to discuss with an Indian veterinarian some aspects of Soviet-American cultural competition in India. The Indian assured me that his people were much less mistrustful of the "thousands of American specialists" in his country than of the Russians. He contrasted the easygoing manner of former American Ambassador Bowles with Soviet secretiveness, and pointed out that even Mikhail Menshikov, while serving as Soviet ambassador in India, traveled in a bullet-proof car. On the other hand, like many other Asians with whom we have talked, the veterinarian said that the American exchange program suffered from a number of defects, such as unwillingness of Americans to learn local languages and failure of many Americans to associate on friendly and intimate terms with the local population. Also—and again his views here coincided with those expressed by other Indians and Southeast Asians interviewed —this man felt that the whole Soviet effort benefited from the fact that, in Soviet foreign economic policy, loans at low rates of interest were employed to finance development projects, as contrasted with, on the one hand, grants or, on the other, high-interest loans, which was the usual policy of Western countries.

Another advantage of Soviet-bloc aid projects, from a public relations point of view at least, consisted in the fact that communist countries did not invest capital in local industrial enterprises and therefore escaped some of the criticism leveled at Western private firms, which could be accused of seeking to gain control of Asian industries. The Soviets and their communist partners also were able, according to many reports, to foster the appearance of nonintervention in the economic life of developing countries by requiring their technical personnel employed in those countries to live modestly and to limit their social contacts with the local population. In contrast, the very high—by local criteria—standard of living of Americans, and at times their obtrusive display of wealth, have reportedly aroused resentment.

While 1958 saw no spectacular developments in Indo-Soviet cultural relations, it was marked by a steady growth of important kinds of contacts. For example, in January a Soviet women's delegation, headed by Madame Zueva of the Ministry of Culture, toured India. According to the *Times of India* for January 4, 1958, the Soviet women, at a visit to an Indian textile mill, declared that its equipment compared favorably with Soviet machinery. Taya Zinkin in the *Manchester Guardian* for February 15 reported that 136 engineers and 150 operatives of the Bhilai steel mill had gone to the U.S.S.R. for study under a U.N. technical-assistance arrangement. Indians were reported as saying that in Russia they learned more than in the West, though they had less fun! Miss Zinkin also wrote that at Bhilai Soviet personnel conducted classes in the Russian language every day after lunch. Her story was one more of many bits of evidence of the tie-up in Soviet policy between economic assistance and cultural penetration, and on the energetic effort being made to extract the maximum propaganda value out of the Bhilai steel plant, in particular, and yet at the same time to avoid giving the impression that any strings were attached to Soviet aid.[30]

A number of bilateral or multilateral cultural collaboration projects were reported, such as training of Soviet and Bulgarian bal-

[30] On the strategy of Soviet economic policy in the developing countries see, for example, Ernest Bock, "Soviet Economic Expansionism," in *Problems of Communism*, Vol. VII, No. 4, July-August 1958, pp. 31-39. As Mr. Bock observes, while Moscow does not attach political conditions to its aid grants, "the grants themselves are carefully conceived and channeled to produce economic consequences favorable to the achievement of Soviet political objectives."

lerinas at the School of Indian Classical Dance, in Madras, under the sponsorship of the Soviet Ministry of Culture, or joint Indian-Soviet production of a film on the life of Afanasi Nikitin.[31] In July an Indian youth delegation in the U.S.S.R. was received by Mr. Khrushchev. One member of the Indian group reportedly excused himself for taking so much of the busy leader's time, to which Khrushchev replied with praise for the "great and noble" Indian people and assured his guests that he was prepared to continue the conversation. Much of it apparently was given over to attacks on the United States and Pakistan and expressions of hope that Kashmir would be united with India.[32]

Early in 1959 the Bhilai plant was already producing some steel and, according to an article by W. Averell Harriman in the *New York Times* for March 18 of that year, it was expected that by 1961 it would have a capacity of a million tons, or one sixth of India's total. Mr. Harriman reported that he heard that the U.S.S.R. was negotiating to build plants to make heavy machinery, optical glass, and pharmaceuticals in different parts of India. The Russians, he noted, had made a decision to "participate in India's development in a spectacular way." This emphasis on the spectacular was doubtless a factor in attracting attention to Soviet projects, including Bhilai, which in reality apparently, in terms of progress completion on schedule, lagged behind the steel mill being built by the West Germans.

Ruth Widmayer, teaching as a Fulbright fellow in a Calcutta university, pointed to the close coordination between Soviet cultural policy and the activities of the communist party of India, in an article in the *Progressive* for May 1959. One of the sources of funds of the CPI, she reported, was "the sale of thousands of books in all the Indian languages, printed in Russia, for every age group and on many subjects," at prices equivalent to less than ten cents. The Soviet books, printed on excellent paper, and "immensely popular" included Indian and Russian classics, as well as Western fairy tales, Shakespeare, et cetera.

At the invitation of the Indian government a Soviet governmental delegation made a "state visit" to India in February and

[31] *Ogonek*, January 3, 1958; *Komsomolskaya Pravda*, May 18, 1958.
[32] *Komsomolskaya Pravda*, July 8, 1958, front page.

March 1959. Headed by the veteran party leader A. A. Andreev, this delegation also included N. A. Mukhitdinov, in his capacity as chairman of the Commission on Foreign Affairs of the U.S.S.R. Supreme Soviet; M. I. Kuchava, Minister of Foreign Affairs of the Georgian Republic; Sergei Kaftanov, a leading figure in Soviet cultural exports to the East; and one of the deputies of Minister of Culture Mikhailov. As reported in Soviet newspapers, the theme of the visit was the U.S.S.R.'s actual and potential contributions to the economic and cultural development of India. During a visit to the Central Planning Commission in Delhi the Soviet leaders dwelt on the prospects for assistance to the countries of Asia and Africa opened up by the new Soviet Seven Year Plan. Mukhitdinov, who as an Asian probably could make a deeper impression on Indians than his Russian colleagues, assured his audience at the Indian Council on Foreign Relations that Afro-Asian peoples could safely rely on disinterested help from Russia in building their economy and culture. One of the high lights of the trip, as described in *Pravda* for March 2, was a visit to a model farm equipped with Soviet agricultural machinery which had been given to India following B and K's visit in 1955 and where a "Soviet consultant" served as adviser. Mukhitdinov there paid emotional tribute to the "remarkable people" of India, thanking the workers of the model farm, in particular, for their warm and friendly words about the U.S.S.R., which he promised to transmit to "comrade Khrushchev."

In reply, the former Indian ambassador to the Soviet Union, K. P. Menon, not only thanked the Soviets for their gift but stated that he regarded the U.S.S.R. as his "second homeland."

Perhaps it should be added that during this journey the Soviet representatives not only praised Indians but also bitterly attacked the Western "colonizers," whom they accused of acts of aggression and of seeking to prevent Afro-Asian industrialization.

The nature of Soviet exchanges with India and of Soviet reporting of them indicates that in addition to winning good will they had at least two other important purposes. One of these seems to have been demonstration to Indian intellectuals that the artistic and spiritual culture of Soviet Russia were on a high level. The other was to convince Indians that it was safe, and profitable, for India to accept Soviet assistance in many fields. There was always the implication, usually kept tactfully in the background, that ultimately any society which expected to become fully "progressive" would have to adopt the Soviet brand of socialism. One wonders also if Soviet solicitude about India, and other Afro-Asian lands too, was not to some degree inspired by considerations connected with the appeal that Peiping, as a non-European center of communism, could have for discontented Asians.

The first point may be illustrated by the sending to India in January and February 1954 of a group of artists of the Bolshoi Theater Ballet, including the outstanding ballerina Maya Plisetskaya. The Soviet artists performed in New Delhi and in four other principal Indian cities. The proceeds of the performance were turned over to the Prime Minister's Relief Fund. The leftist newspaper *Blitz* for January 23 reported that Bombay had "extended an affectionate reception" to the Russian performers. *Blitz* said that the tour refuted the assertion of "enemies of the Soviet Union" that Soviet art was "all propaganda and no art." *Blitz* waxed sarcastic regarding the behavior of an American who refused to stand when the Soviet national anthem was played in the Bombay theater and commended him to Senator McCarthy.

In contrast, some Indian bourgeois newspapers expressed disappointment with what they regarded as the banality of the Soviet performance. One Indian newspaper expressed the opinion that in view of what the Russians had sent to India the Indians ought to send a troupe of snake charmers to Russia. Even unfriendly Indian critics, however, were impressed by the vigor of the Russian folk dancers, and it was noted that the Azerbaidzhanian singer, Beibutov, stole the heart of his audience when he sang a number by the poet Iqbal in Urdu. Apparently Indians who were favorably disposed to the Soviet Union for ideological and political reasons, as well as those whose taste was not very sophisticated, were more impressed by Soviet artists than were the highbrow critics of the leading English-language newspapers.[33] Even among the more

[33] For some interesting observations, see *New York Times* for February 5, 1954.

sophisticated, however, there were probably many who were flattered that members of the famous Bolshoi troupe had been sent to India.[34]

The message of Soviet scientific and technical leadership has been presented to the Indians in many ways, some highly dramatic and others on the no-less-effective level of day-to-day cooperation in solving tasks important to the Indian economy. In 1956 the Indian Minister of Industry stated in the Indian parliament that arrangements had been made to accept Soviet assistance in the establishment of a pharmaceutical industry in India, and at the same time Soviet physicians helped their Indian colleagues to establish what the Tass correspondent in India reported was the first children's hospital of a new type in India.[35] In March 1957 the Indian Ministry for Production adopted a plan prepared by a group of Soviet specialists for the building of a factory in India to manufacture optical glass with the purpose of "freeing India from the necessity of importing semi-finished optical glass." These examples could be multiplied.

It is true, of course, that there is still much mistrust of Soviet intentions in conservative and nonsocialist circles in India, and in 1958 and 1959 Prime Minister Nehru on numerous occasions was publicly critical of communist ideology in general and of some aspects of Soviet and Chinese communist policy. However, there have also been significant indications in the last two or three years that admiration for and confidence in the Russians has been growing in India. One indication of this fact is increasingly close Indian-Soviet collaboration in such vital fields as international air transport. Moscow has made good use of its new jet passenger aircraft, such as the TU-104, in displaying Soviet technology to the Indians and to other Eastern—and, for that matter, Western—peoples. By September 1957 the TU-104 had landed in airfields in Delhi, Rangoon, and Jakarta as well as in London, Paris, and other points in Europe and the United States. Gifts of Soviet jet aircraft had been made to Prime Minister Nehru, the Shah of Iran, and Mr. Sukarno, among others.

[34] This impression is based in part upon a reference to the above event in a letter received from a member of the staff of the Indian embassy in Washington in 1956.
[35] *Pravda*, March 19, 1956.

Even before the dazzling 1957 Soviet triumphs in launching two artificial earth satellites within a matter of weeks, many people throughout the world, particularly in such countries as India or Afghanistan, had probably come to regard the modern Russians as workers of miracles. In the spring of 1957 an American magazine editor who had traveled widely in India told me that Indian engineers with whom he had talked, and who had been in the Soviet Union in the summer of 1956, had come back "in awe." This report was all the more impressive in view of the fact that the Indian engineers in question had been trained in the West. In view of all this, it is not surprising that while in most countries polls taken following launching of Sputnik I indicated continued belief in United States technological supremacy, in India the majority polled expressed the opinion that the Soviet Union would make the next great scientific-technological advance. Another poll showed that a considerable number of Indians "now think their biggest benefactor is the Soviet Union." Whatever its ultimate reasons, the impact of the Soviet exchange program upon Indian opinion has been considerable. It should be kept in mind, in appraising it, however, that Indian-United States student and technical exchanges, even in 1956-1959, were on a far larger scale than those between India and the Soviet Union. According to an official Indian government source, there were already about 2,400 Indian students in the United States in September 1956.[36]

It should also be noted that Moscow was able to retain and even increase its prestige in India despite the crude tactics employed by Bulganin and Khrushchev during their 1955 junket and despite the Hungarian situation. While much that was said by Bulganin and Khrushchev in India—in particular their abusive attacks on Britain and the United States—was embarrassing to the Indian government, their protestations of friendship and admiration for India and their convincing accounts of Soviet industrial, agricultural, and cultural progress since the bolshevik revolution undoubtedly impressed many Indians. Another theme which was probably very pleasing to Indians was B and K's advice that India should develop her own national industry and their assurances that she would become a great world power if she did not permit for-

[36] Letter from Education Department, Embassy of India, September 26, 1956.

eigners to interfere in her economic development. Perhaps most important of all, before, during, and after the B and K trip the Soviet government adroitly exploited Indian resentment against American support of Portugal on the Goa issue and of Pakistan's position in the Kashmir question, as well as Indian resentment at the attack by Israel, Britain, and France on Egypt. Similarly, Russian propaganda played on East Asian resentment at American and British troops' landing in Lebanon and Jordan in 1958.

In 1959 there was probably some shifting of Indian attitudes toward the Soviet and democratic power blocs. Friction with China over Tibet and other issues caused Indians to reexamine their attitudes toward all communist countries. According to all reports, President Eisenhower's trip to India—and other countries—aroused even more enthusiasm than had B and K's tour four years earlier. Only time would tell whether these events presaged a fundamental reorientation or merely marked a temporary change of mood.

In other disturbed lands, many of which share India's vague preference for socialism over capitalism and resent various aspects of American, British, or French foreign policy, Moscow has energetically applied its combination of appreciation of native folk culture with display of the Soviet model for rapid modernization. The impression is given to impoverished intellectuals and idealistic youths that in a socialist society there is no conflict between modernization and defense of traditional values against Western pressures, and that imperialism, on the other hand, simultaneously destroys local cultures and throttles national economic development.

Egypt, of course, offers a striking example of the eagerness and ability of the Kremlin to pour cultural resources into areas where poverty, economic underdevelopment, and anti-Western feeling could, partly because of Western tactlessness and arrogance, be exploited to Soviet political advantage. As far back as 1947 the Kremlin began a play for Egyptian sympathy by support in the U.N. Security Council for Egypt's demand that Britain withdraw its troops from the Nile Valley.[37] Soviet exploitation of Israeli-Arab differences since 1948 is too well known to require discussion. The overthrow of the corrupt monarchy of King Farouk in Egypt and the efflorescence of Egyptian nationalism which fol-

[37] *Newsweek*, October 6, 1947.

lowed offered a fertile field for Soviet cultural penetration. The campaign began modestly, with favorable articles on Egyptian history and culture, the publication of scholarly works, and the holding of exhibitions. Typical of this phase was the article by V. Maevski, entitled "In Egypt," in *Pravda* for August 15, 1954, to which we have already referred. Maevski combined classical archaeology with Marxist social analysis. Egyptians, he said, were beginning to get acquainted with their "polite Russian friends." The terrible human conditions in the midst of potentially rich natural resources, the contrasts between peasant huts and the palatial villas of wealthy businessmen, most of them allegedly connected with foreign capital, as well as symbols of the "American way of life," with its gangster films and comics and the ubiquitous Coca Cola sign, furnished him with his texts. Moscow stepped up its program during crucial 1955, the year of the Soviet-inspired Egyptian-Czechoslovak arms deal. This was an important part of the strategy which enabled Russia to outflank the "northern tier" by which Anglo-American diplomacy had sought to deny her a major role in Middle Eastern affairs. Egypt accepted communist assistance for several reasons, among which some of the most important were resentment caused by Anglo-American partiality to Israel, Russian willingness to buy large quantities of her economically vital cotton, and a general feeling of animosity toward Western "imperialism." In 1956, of course, anti-Western sentiment was intensified by a number of well-known factors, of which American tactlessness in withdrawing an offer of aid in building the Aswan Dam and military aggression by Israel, Britain, and France were the most obviously significant. Soviet cultural policy was carefully calculated to play upon Egyptian grievances against the West and Israel, as well as upon Egyptian national pride and President Nasser's personal ambitions.

In September 1955 occurred the gala opening in Cairo of a "permanent" VOKS exposition. This event was attended by the cream of the Egyptian elite. One of the most important Soviet figures present was the VOKS "plenipotentiary" for Egypt.[38] In the same year a group of Soviet Moslems returning from Mecca held a press conference in Cairo, and they also visited the famous

[38] *Pravda*, September 4, 1955; *Sovetskaya Kultura*, September 8, 1955.

Moslem university Al Azhar. Marshal Voroshilov, president of the presidium of the Supreme Soviet, sent tactful greetings on the occasion of the Moslem New Year to President Nasser.

A key event in the stepped-up cultural campaign in Egypt was the visit to Cairo of the then Soviet Minister of Foreign Affairs, Dimitri T. Shepilov, in June 1956. Shepilov made his trip on the occasion of Egyptian Independence Day, June 18. Reports on Shepilov's expedition were featured in the Soviet press for June 17-21. On June 18 Shepilov made a long and eloquent speech. He expressed solidarity with the principles proclaimed at the Bandung Conference in Indonesia in 1955. Shepilov assured the Egyptians that the U.S.S.R. had no selfish ambitions in the East. He quoted Lenin on the coming "renaissance" of Eastern peoples and asserted that the predictions of that "great friend of the peoples of the East" were about to come to pass. He promised the Arab peoples that in the peoples of the Soviet Union they would find "good neighbors and companions" who could, on the basis of their own experience in overcoming past economic backwardness, help the Arabs to solve the problems of building up their political institutions, developing their national economy, and reviving their national culture with its "thousands of years of tradition."

Shepilov's visit was followed by a flood of Soviet delegations to Egypt. By September 1956 Egyptian Army officers were reportedly fraternizing with "the 2,000 Soviet officers, technicians and economists" in Egypt, and there had been thirty Soviet-bloc cultural and technical missions in Egypt in the spring of 1956 alone.[39] Nevertheless, Nasser had reservations about Soviet objectives, and in 1957 there were indications that he might return to his previous position of real neutrality. However, he allowed the Soviets, at the Cairo Conference on Asian and African Solidarity in December 1957, to conduct inflammatory anti-Western propaganda, featuring, for example, demands for nationalization of foreign-held resources. In the meantime, the flow of Egyptian stutents to Russia was increasing, although it was still on a modest scale, even in 1958, and Egyptians and Syrians were among the most enthusiastic participants in the Sixth World Festival of Youth and Students in 1957.

[39] *Reporter*, September 20, 1956.

As in Egypt, so also in Syria, Moscow intensified its cultural-exchange program as Syrian-Western tension mounted. Perhaps even more interesting was the increasingly close cultural contact in 1955, 1956, and 1957 between the Soviet Union and Lebanon. In this connection it is interesting to note that the Russian Palestine Society, affiliated with the Academy of Sciences of the U.S.S.R., was reactivated in 1954. This society engages in studies of archaeology, anthropology, historical geography, and ethnography of the peoples of the Middle East.[40] Recognition by Syrian scholars of the work of Soviet Arabists was indicated by the election, in March 1955, of the Soviet scholar Bertels as a corresponding member of the Arabian Academy in Damascus.[41] In March 1956 the head of the Syrian National Committee of Partisans of Peace was awarded a Stalin Peace Prize. The ceremony of presentation in Damascus was attended, according to *Pravda* for March 20, by "representatives of the Movement of Partisans of Peace of Lebanon, Jordan and Iraq." The presentation was made by the well-known Soviet writer Nikolai Tikhonov, and other Soviet notables attended. Among them was the deputy chairman of the Spiritual Administration of the Moslems of Central Asia and Kazakhstan. Beginning in 1955 large groups of top-flight Soviet folk dancers and other artists made very successful tours in Syria and Lebanon. In 1956 S. Kaftanov headed a mission to Syria, Lebanon, and Egypt. One result of the mission was the signing of an agreement between Syria and the Soviet Union providing for "exchange of experience and achievements" in science, literature, art, higher education, and secondary education, and in physical culture and sports. Agreement was also reached regarding exchange of information and of material regarding "problems of culture," the organization of exhibitions, tours of artists, and exchanges of films and radio programs.

Kaftanov was apparently so pleased with the results of the mission that he concluded an article with the statement that "in the near future close cultural relations between the Soviet Union and Egypt, Syria and Lebanon, as well as with other states, will play an ever growing role."[42] Soviet influence did not grow so rapidly in Lebanon as it did in Syria. American ties with Lebanon, seat

[40] *Izvestiya*, June 5, 1955.
[41] *Pravda*, March 19, 1955.
[42] *Sovetskaya Kultura*, October 25, 1956.

of the influential American University of Beirut, remained strong and close. However, Moscow was subjecting Lebanon to intense and astute pressure, directed especially at students and teachers, and at doctors, lawyers, journalists, writers, and artists.

The Soviet press expressed approval of the formation of the United Arab Republic in February 1958, as might have been expected, but its relative lack of enthusiasm lent credence to reports that Nasser actually had been motivated, in part, in his incorporation of Syria into the new republic, by concern at the growing influence of Syrian communists. In May, on his Soviet trip, Nasser received standard "red carpet" treatment, was photographed with Soviet school children, pelted with flowers, played up in *Pravda*, et cetera. Perhaps in preparation for Nasser's trip, the Soviet Society for Friendship and Cultural Relations with the Countries of the Arab East, to which we referred in Chapter VI, was established. Prime Minister Khrushchev at a state dinner assured Mr. Nasser that "the whole socialist world" was behind Nasser in his struggle for the independence "of all the Arabs."[43]

At a reception at Moscow University the rector of that institution stressed Soviet reverence for "the ancient culture of the Arab peoples," and, incidentally, noted that ninety-five Arabs were enrolled as students at the university.[44] Nasser also visited Tashkent, Baku, Sukhumi, Kiev, Leningrad, et cetera, and, according to the Soviet press, received a tumultuous welcome everywhere.

And yet this trip does not seem to have been completely successful, from the Kremlin's point of view. An irritable article by I. Ivanov in *Trud*, the leading Soviet trade-union newspaper, for June 8, 1958, entitled "Voices of Friends and the Scream of an Ill-Wisher," attacked the Egyptian newspaper publisher Mustafa Amin, one of the Egyptian newspaper notables who had accompanied Nasser on his May trip, for writing allegedly trivial pieces of "boulevard" journalism about his observations in Russia and for "slanders against the Soviet state system." Ivanov called Amin a "dollar worshipper" and castigated him for quoting John Gunther's book *Inside Russia*, which, said Ivanov, was "recommended by Washington to its propaganda service."

[43] *Pravda*, May 1, 1958.
[44] *Ibid.*, May 4, 1958.

There were, in fact, many indications in 1958 and 1959 that Nasser, as the *Economist* for April 26, 1958, put it, wanted "to be in the happy position of playing one rich suitor against another." This was difficult, thought the *Economist*, as long as the Russians continued to "choose their words more tactfully than the Americans." But in August 1958, as *Newsweek* chortled, perhaps too soon, the "sudden get-together of Arab arch-rivals" at the U.N. General Assembly session on the Middle East crisis "yanked the rug from under" the Soviets.[45] Nevertheless, Soviet cultural and political penetration, if temporarily checked, was already considerable and the groundwork for further solid advances had been laid. As of the summer of 1958, for example, more Syrian students were apparently enrolled in Soviet-bloc universities than in free-world institutions. According to the newspaper of the Soviet Ministry of Education, *Uchitelskaya Gazeta*, for July 9, 1956, study of the Russian language was to begin in both secondary schools and higher educational institutions of the U.A.R. in 1958-1959. On June 7 the same newspaper reported that beginning in the fall of 1958 the U.A.R. would send three hundred students annually to study in the Soviet Union. There was a possibility that the technical intelligentsia of some Middle Eastern countries, if not the whole intellectual elite of these countries, would in a decade or two be predominantly Moscow-oriented. At least a temporary setback of Soviet cultural penetration in the U.A.R. was reported by Jay Walz in a *New York Times* dispatch for October 11, 1959, containing, among much startling information, news that withdrawal of approximately 650 Egyptian and Syrian students from the Soviet Union and East Europe had been completed by October 1, and also reporting that in Cairo interest in Soviet films and publications had diminished "in recent months."

In attempting to account for the Soviet-Arab cultural *rapprochement* that followed the political "breakthrough" of 1955, Walter Z. Laqueur has pointed to what he regards as certain affinities between "Soviet civilization," with its foundation in socialism, and the "aspirations of the intelligentsia in backward countries." Even if one does not fully share Mr. Laqueur's pessimistic, almost fatalistic outlook on the future of relationships between the East and Russia,

[45] *Newsweek*, September 1, 1958, p. 23.

it is difficult to refute his view that Soviet culture has more appeal in the East than in the West. As he points out: " 'Socialist realism' may not be taken seriously in the West, but it did make more sense than *l'art pour l'art* in countries like Egypt, Syria, or Iraq. The neo-classicism of Soviet painting and music was . . . easier to understand and master than Western modernism."[46]

Laqueur, like other students of Asia, Africa, and Latin America, points also to the impoverishment of the "new intellectuals" as a factor predisposing them to rejection of the West and attracting them toward Soviet culture.

By 1957 there were many indications of an energetic Soviet effort to establish cultural relations with Liberia, the Sudan, Ethiopia, and other African lands. For example, Ethiopian librarians, trade unionists from "Black Africa," Liberian agricultural officials, and "Sudanese peasants" were received by high Soviet officials in September 1957.[47] In January 1958 a troupe of Soviet artists performed in Ethiopia, and in April several Soviet films were shown in Addis Ababa. In March 1958 Soviet artists toured Eritrea, and gave eighteen concerts in Tripoli and Bengazi, Libya. In comparison with American and British information and cultural saturation of these countries, particularly in the film field, the Soviet showing was small, but it was growing. It gave evidence of Moscow's determination to knock on all doors in the non-Soviet world, while keeping those of the communist world closed, at least in such fields as the cinema, where American films had not, as of late 1958, secured any access at all. By the summer of 1958 Soviet contact with Ethiopia had become close enough for Emperor Haile Selassie to visit Russia, where he was lionized and was presented with a jet airplane, among other gifts.

The Soviet cultural campaign was extended in 1956 and 1957 even to such hostile countries as Turkey and Pakistan. Athletes, especially wrestlers and soccer players, bulked large in Soviet-Turkish exchanges. Soviet artists who performed in Turkey included the pianist P. Serebryakov, on tour there in May 1958.

[46] Walter Z. Laqueur, *The Soviet Union and the Middle East*, New York, 1959, p. 292. Part two, chapter six, presents a good brief survey of "Soviet Cultural Policy and the Intellectual Climate in the Arab World."

[47] *Pravda*, September 5, 1957; *Pravda Vostoka*, September 29, 1957; *Sovetskaya Kultura*, September 10, 1957.

There was a Soviet pavilion at the Turkish Trade Fair at Izmir in 1957. During the 1956-1959 period Russia dangled before both Turkey and Pakistan tempting offers of trade and technical assistance and Soviet trade with both countries increased substantially. The Russians began construction of a number of industrial enterprises in Turkey in 1957 and 1958. Their cultural strategy supported a design to detach these crucially important countries from the Anglo-American bloc. In this drive every effort was made to exploit the difficult economic situation of both countries.

Moscow in 1957 and 1958 developed still further its already strong position in Indonesia. The well-known Uzbek dancer, Tamara Khanum, and her ensemble enjoyed a great success there in December 1957, according to *Sovetskaya Kultura*.[48] Khanum was followed by another Uzbek troupe, which on a two-month tour gave twenty-six performances and was received by President Sukarno.[49]

That Soviet sources were not idly boasting in claiming successes in Indonesia for Russian cultural efforts was indicated by the warmth with which at least one Indonesian newspaper, *Times of Indonesia*, reported Marshal Voroshilov's visit, in May 1958. This paper in its May 6 issue called Voroshilov's visit a "great honor," for Voroshilov was a "representative of a truly great world power" and the first titular head of state to accept the general invitation to foreign leaders to visit Indonesia, extended by Mr. Sukarno during his 1956 trips.

Also to be expected was Moscow's expression of sympathy for Algeria in the years after the anti-French insurrection began there in 1954. In Russia meetings and demonstrations and collections for food gifts and other help were reminiscent of manifestations in favor of Spain in 1936-1938 and similar to those for Egypt in 1956. Algerian students who attended the 1957 Moscow Youth Festival were lionized.

1956-1958 saw a brisk flow of Soviet-Ceylonese cultural exchanges. In November and December 1957 Soviet artists gave seventeen concerts in Ceylon. In January 1958, as noted earlier, the Soviet-Ceylonese cultural agreement was signed. *Sovetskaya Kul-*

[48] *Sovetskaya Kultura*, December 19, 1957.
[49] *Ibid.*, January 28, 1958.

tura for January 23, 1958, took satisfaction in quoting a Ceylonese newspaper, *Pinamina*, to the effect that the agreement was a "step forward in the development of the culture of Ceylon." According to the same Soviet paper, for February 4, 1958, when the Soviet writer Sabit Mukhanov, from Kazakhstan, arrived in Colombo, he was greeted by friendly shouts of "Russian-sputnik."

A Soviet Armenian artist in an article in *Sovetskaya Kultura* for March 18 stated that the Soviet artists, on their Ceylonese trip a few months before, had been greeted with shouts of "peace, friendship," in Russian, by Ceylonese who had taken part in the Youth Festival.

In May 1958 the newly formed successor society to VOKS sponsored an exhibition devoted to contemporary Ceylonese opera. There were other Soviet exhibitions in 1958 on Ceylonese themes, and Soviet cinematographers also did a documentary on that picturesque and exotic country.

Soviet interest in the East, at least in the case of many Soviet citizens, is, of course, not merely political. Many Soviet intellectuals are genuinely fascinated by the music, dances, and costumes of countries like Ceylon, India, and Indonesia, which have traditionally held for educated Russians much the same attraction as for Englishmen and Americans. Also it is possible that Russians find it easier to establish rapport with Asians than do Americans or Western Europeans. Not much scholarly research has been done on such matters, but what little is available tends to confirm this supposition. For example, an American anthropologist reported, on the basis of his military service in Korea, that while both Russians and Americans displayed amusement at Korean culture, the Russians treated Koreans, as individuals, with more respect than did the Americans and, in contrast to the Americans, displayed no racial prejudice.[50]

In Japan, where many students and intellectuals were predisposed to look with favor upon Soviet socialism, the Soviet cultural effort was already on a large scale in the period 1955-1957. In fact, as early as 1952 Mr. Howland Sargeant, in a speech referred to earlier in this chapter, had called attention to Soviet flooding

[50] David L. Olmsted, "Two Korean Villages," in *Human Organization*, Vol. 10, No. 3, fall, 1951, pp. 33-36.

of Japan with a great variety of scientific and other books. Some of the best Soviet artists, such as the violinist David Oistrakh, who was in Japan in 1955, have made other successful tours in that country in later years. Soviet reporting of Japanese-Soviet cultural relations placed heavy emphasis upon the sufferings experienced by the Japanese as a result of the American use of atomic bombs in World War II. In November 1957 the distinguished Russian pianist Emil Gilels played in Japan. His tour was followed in December by that of the Soviet singer Alla Golenkova. In April 1958 the Japanese puppet theater Avadzi flew to the U.S.S.R., where its performances received rave reviews. This was the first trip, according to Soviet sources, that the troupe had ever made beyond Japan's borders.[51] Also in 1958 the Leningrad Symphony Orchestra, a Soviet circus troupe, the cellist M. Rostropovich, and numerous other Soviet artists, as well as scientists and scholars, visited Japan, while on the Japanese side the puppeteers were followed to Russia by, among others, a trio of Japanese writers, who were invited by the Union of Soviet Writers, and a delegation of Japanese publishers.

The Soviet cultural-exchange program in Latin America is normally on a small scale, but is perhaps larger than one might expect, in view of the remoteness of the area. Exchanges with Latin American countries in the four years 1953-1957 accounted for less than ten per cent of all reported exchanges between the Soviet Union and noncommunist countries. Certainly Soviet cultural influence in Latin America was far smaller in scale than American influence in Western Europe—which Moscow regards as more in its sphere of influence than it is willing to admit Latin America is in that of the United States—or than United States or Western European influence in Latin America. Nevertheless, Soviet influence in Latin America was growing in the post-Stalin years, and had behind it a record of assiduous effort and solid achievement which North Americans could ill afford to ignore.

In recent years the people of the United States have been reminded by a number of alarming events of the importance of Latin America to their security and of the belief of some Latin Americans that their northern neighbors were taking them too

[51] See, for example, *Sovetskaya Kultura*, April 15, 18, and May 10, 1958.

much for granted. On the other hand, much good will was built up by the activities of some private United States firms, such as the United Fruit Company.[52]

We are, in 1960, too close in time to the explosions in Guatemala in 1954 and in Cuba in 1959 to feel that even strategic Central America or the Caribbean are safe from communist pressures. The Guatemala episode was a dramatic warning that Central America could be a susceptible target for Soviet effort. Tons of excellently prepared cultural and propaganda material printed in Prague in Spanish was discovered, incidentally, in Guatemala after the fall of the pro-Soviet regime.[53]

When, in talking to *Pravda* editors in 1956, I cited Guatemala as evidence of unwarranted Soviet interest in the internal affairs of foreign countries, my hosts reacted angrily. They took the counteroffensive and accused America of seeking to crush the "workers and peasants" of Guatemala, as part of a general United States program of interference in "liberation" movements. While in America in 1959, Mr. Khrushchev made similar use of the Guatemalan case to distract attention from Soviet behavior in Hungary.

As early as 1954, twenty-six delegations from the Latin American republics visited the Soviet Union and six Soviet delegations went to Latin American countries.[54] In 1955 the Soviet press reported official functions in Moscow honoring "the noted Argentinian physician, Jose Maria Penn," an "evening of Argentinian cinema," a visit by the Brazilian architect Oscar Niemeyer, and numerous other signs of keen interest in Soviet-Latin cultural exchange. Articles were published expressing admiration for Mexican film art and sympathy for Mexican film workers in their struggle against the "cruel competition of Hollywood."[55]

As far as Mexico was concerned, post-Stalin interest represented

---

[52] See, for example, front-page comment in *Barron's Weekly* for August 4, 1958, on the record of United Fruit and a book about United Fruit by a former president of Ecuador, Galo Plaza, and an American economist, Stacy May. According to *Barron's*, United Fruit, "in fostering economic progress in the less developed countries, puts to shame all the creaking apparatus of foreign aid."

[53] Keith Monroe, "Guatemala: What the Reds Left Behind," in *Harper's Magazine*, CCI, July 1955, p. 58.

[54] Bowen Evans, *Worldwide Communist Propaganda Activities*, pp. 95-100.

[55] *Pravda*, March 13, March 16 and April 28, 1955; *Sovetskaya Kultura*, April 28, 1955.

an effort at a continuation of the exceptionally successful achievements of Soviet Ambassador Konstantin Umanski during World War II in launching an attractive cultural program.[56] Among the landmarks in this history was the organization in 1944 of the Instituto de Intercambio Cultural Mexicano-Ruso, which still publishes an impressive literary-scientific magazine, *Intercambio Cultural*.

In 1956 the famous, politically controversial Mexican muralist Diego Rivera spent several months in the Soviet Union undergoing treatment for skin cancer, from which he was pronounced cured. (He died, however, not long afterwards.) The cordiality displayed toward Rivera by his Soviet hosts, and the length and purpose of his visit illustrated the Soviet effort to win, or perhaps to regain, the favor of Latin American intellectuals. This effort was set back temporarily by Soviet suppression of the Hungarian revolution. In the first half of 1957 Soviet-Latin American exchanges fell off considerably from the 1956 level. As is indicated by names such as Neruda, mentioned toward the beginning of this chapter, and Rivera, it seems likely that communists and fellow-travelers played a more important part in Latin American exchanges with Russia than was the case in most parts of the world in the post-Stalin era. According to press reports which cannot be verified, Neruda broke with communism, at least for a time, as a result of the Pasternak affair. Careful attention to political attitudes and considerable bias in reporting marked Soviet press accounts of interviews with Latin American artists who performed in recent years in Russia.

For example, *Sovetskaya Kultura* for September 24, 1955, in an interview with the Argentine dancer Maria Fuchs, who had been invited by the Ministry of Culture of the Soviet Union to perform in the U.S.S.R., quoted her to the effect that she was hardly able to live in the United States on the scholarship which had been granted to her. Fuchs also said that she created dance numbers such as "Street Girls" after her experience in New York. She waxed ecstatic about artistic life in the Soviet Union.

In 1957 the Soviets sent some of their best artists and composers to Mexico, Argentina, Uruguay, and other Latin American coun-

[56] See, for example, *New York Times*, January 27, 1945; McMurry and Lee, *The Cultural Approach*, pp. 120-124.

tries. Among them was Aram Khachaturyan, the outstanding Soviet Armenian composer. Soviet basketball players, chess masters, and other exponents of Soviet culture also displayed their talents south of the Rio Grande. In December 1957 a Soviet cultural delegation, of which two prominent members were Konstantin Simonov and Ilya Ehrenburg, visited Uruguay. It was clear that a dogged effort would be made to overcome the geographical, religious, and cultural barriers to successful penetration of an area potentially highly vulnerable to various kinds of revolutionary propaganda and susceptible to the calculated flattery of which the Russians are past masters.

A report in the Mexican newspaper *El Universal* for February 3, 1957, that the Soviet government was planning to invite Latin American students and professors to the U.S.S.R. for study and research in the field of nuclear energy perhaps indicated that Moscow was planning to extend to Latin America the role which it was claiming in Asia and Africa as teacher of the higher technical arts to the less-industrialized peoples of the whole world. Spanish was one of the six official languages of the 1957 Youth Festival. Statements by Brazilian, Uruguayan, Bolivian, Venezuelan, and other Latin American delegates at the festival, as reported in the Soviet press, indicated that the Latin Americans had found conditions in the Soviet Union better than they had expected.

In 1958 the Soviet cultural press published enthusiastic reviews of the performances in Russia of the Cuban ballerina Alicia Alonso and the Argentine pianist Antonio de Raquo. The usual exhibitions devoted to Latin American graphic arts and the like were held. An informative article in *Sovetskaya Kultura* for May 27, 1958, highly praised the work of the Argentina-U.S.S.R. Society in the development of exchanges of persons and publications. In the same month the distinguished Russian violinist Leonid Kogan was on concert tour in Uruguay. A few months earlier two young Soviet pianists, Sergei Dorenski and Mikhail Voskresenski, had added to the fame of Soviet music by winning prizes at the international piano contest in Rio de Janeiro.

Throughout the whole period Soviet comment on all types of exchanges stressed appreciation for the distinctive character of Latin American culture and tried to create the impression that

that culture was threatened with extinction by influences emanating from the north. Stalin Peace Prizes were awarded to Pablo Neruda, to former Mexican President Cardenas, and to the Colombian man of letters Sanin Cano. Clearly Moscow was determined not to make the mistake, sometimes made by Washington, of underestimating the importance to Latin America of the arts and letters, or of failing to take due and well-publicized note of the richness and vitality of Latin American culture.

The Soviet effort surveyed in this chapter is impressive. It would be a mistake to consider that it can be all-powerful or that it will necessarily prove detrimental in the long run to the interests and values of the Western democracies. For the longer term the very zeal with which this offensive is being conducted may have beneficial effects outweighing its subversive aims. Certainly the increase in intercountry exchanges and contacts offers a welcome contrast to the extreme Iron Curtain isolationism of the past and, attempts at camouflage notwithstanding, gives more people more opportunity to see for themselves what are the myths and what are the realities of other societies and systems. If such contacts continue to grow, cultural exchange may come increasingly to serve its proper aim—not the promotion of Soviet interests, but the encouragement of genuine international cooperation, along with growing respect for diverse cultures *and* for cultural diversity.

It is even possible that, if carried very far, contacts between Soviet Asians, for example, and their cultural kinsmen beyond the borders might prove a centrifugal force, tending to weaken rather than strengthen the Soviet regime. There is much evidence that Moscow has usually feared more than it has favored such movements as Pan-Turanianism and Pan-Arabism, although in respect to these forces the economically powerful U.S.S.R. of the late 1950's is in a far-more-favorable position than the weak Soviet regime of the 1920's and 1930's. The experience of Turkey, which in the 1920's and 1930's accepted extensive economic assistance from Moscow, suggests that it may be possible for a developing country to be on relatively friendly terms with the Russian bear without being swallowed by him. As Ivar Spector has noted, "The history of the U.S.S.R. to date does not indicate that any Muslim regime has toppled like a house of cards due to Soviet radio or press propaganda, unless as in Iran (in the case of Azerbaidzhan, in 1945-1946) that propaganda has been accompanied by military intimidation and outright invasion."[57]

An increasingly active phase of Soviet policy toward the underdeveloped countries, which, in a sense, forms a part both of foreign economic policy and of cultural diplomacy, is medical and public health assistance. By 1959, according to State Department unclassified Intelligence Information Brief Number 104, dated March 16, the U.S.S.R. was operating hospitals in Addis Ababa, Tehran, New Delhi, and Phnom Penh, Cambodia, and was negotiating with Libya, Nepal, and Yemen regarding construction of Soviet gift hospitals in those countries.

The U.S.S.R. had announced establishment of medical scholarship programs for Asian, African, and Latin American countries suffering from a shortage of trained medical personnel. In the fall of 1958 the U.S.S.R. held a special seminar for medical specialists and public health experts from the Near East, Southeast Asia, North Africa, and Latin America.

The future of the developing countries will, of course, be made, not in Moscow, Peiping, or Washington, but in and by those countries themselves. Nevertheless, Western policy can help the underdeveloped countries to choose freely between the Soviet totalitarian and Western democratic paths to modernization. Economic aid, technical assistance of medical and other sorts, and exchanges of persons are among the most important instruments for achieving these ends. Oscar Gass has expressed the hope that, "in the measure in which the underdeveloped countries come to share our adherence to political democracy and a humane culture, they will not choose to associate themselves with world communism."[58]

To achieve the maximum possible success in communicating with and gaining the good will of Asians and Africans, and Latin Americans too, Westerners will have to make a greater effort than they have so far, not only to counter the Soviet technical-assistance program but also to study and understand the languages and cultures of underdeveloped countries. There is certainly no excuse for the

[57] Ivar Spector, *The Soviet Union and the Muslim World 1917-1956*, University of Washington Press, 1956, p. 140.
[58] Oscar Gass, "The United States and the Poorest Peoples," in *Commentary*, February 1958, pp. 93-104. See p. 103.

wealthy United States, in particular, to lag behind the Soviet Union in the technical-organizational aspects of the cultural competition. Still less is there any excuse for Western arrogance and complacency. As Edwin Reischauer has observed, in a book crammed with useful information and wise suggestions, Americans in their dealings with Asians have too often "approximated the arrogant dictation" of the communists, and have "ignored the basic democratic ideals of a free exchange of ideas and a reciprocity of influences."[59]

It is not inevitable that we must help the Kremlin to persuade the peoples of the East that they can derive more "democracy" or even more "socialism"—in the original Marxian sense of a movement away from privilege and inequality toward classlessness —from Soviet totalitarianism than from American "people's capitalism."

In the period since the bulk of this chapter was written Soviet policy in the underdeveloped world has had its ups and downs but its vigor and determination have remained impressive. Perhaps the most conspicuous recent manifestation of these qualities was announcement during Khrushchev's Indonesia sojourn in 1960 that the U.S.S.R. had decided to establish a "University of Friendship of the Peoples" for Asians, Africans, and Latin Americans. *Sovetskaya Kultura* for February 25, 1960 stated that the new institution would train engineers, agricultural experts, physicians, teachers, and so on. It would open with five hundred students and would eventually have three to four thousand. The impact of this bold move is difficult to appraise. Perhaps those who study there will be so clearly identified as Soviet-oriented that the venture will be self-defeating. Certainly future development of such Soviet programs as this one bears the most careful watching. On a more scholarly level, a major event of 1960 was the holding in Moscow from August 9 through 16 of the xxvth International Congress of Orientalists, with B. G. Gafurov presiding.

[59] Edwin O. Reischauer, *Wanted: An Asian Policy*, New York, 1955, p. 232.

CHAPTER VIII

SOVIET CULTURE AND WESTERN EUROPE

WESTERN Europe's unique role in world affairs impels both Moscow and Washington to accord to it attention out of proportion to population or area. Every index available shows that Western Europe is the principal target of Soviet cultural diplomacy. Moreover, the Soviet cultural offensive first assumed prominence in Western Europe —in 1951, well before the Kremlin had begun to "normalize" cultural relations with Asia, Africa, or the Americas. Despite increased Soviet activity in recent years in such countries as India, Egypt, Indonesia, or Japan, the number of persons involved in official cultural exchanges between Western Europe and Russia has consistently exceeded that between Russia and all the rest of the noncommunist world combined—and by a wide margin. This fact has been abundantly documented in valuable compilations by Bowen Evans and Evron Kirkpatrick, but perhaps some figures should be presented by way of illustration. In 1955 there were 363 recorded visits by Western European delegations to the Soviet Union, a figure comprising well over half of the total of 577 delegations from the noncommunist world, excluding North America, which visited Russia in that year. The predominance of Western Europe as the destination of Soviet travelers was even more pronounced. Of a total of 412 delegations from Russia to noncommunist countries in 1955, 337 went to Western Europe. Moscow continued to regard Western Europe as the prime target of its persuasions in 1957, 1958, and 1959.[1] Since 1952 there has usually been a considerably greater volume of exchanges between, for example, the Soviet Union and Sweden, with its population of seven million, than between the Soviet Union and Japan, with one hundred million. During the years 1953-1956 Soviet cultural pol-

---

[1] Kirkpatrick, *op.cit.*, p. 101. For the same general pattern as of 1954 see Evans, *Worldwide Communist Propaganda Activities*, pp. 92-100. For 1956 see figures in Kirkpatrick's *Year of Crisis*, the 1957 version of his series on Soviet international propaganda; it presents a pattern similar to that of earlier years, and the same trend is recorded also in the unclassified Department of State Intelligence Report, Number 7546, entitled "The Soviet Bloc Exchange Program January-June 1957," Washington, D.C., 1957, pp. 18-22.

icy-makers considered it desirable to devote vastly greater resources, in proportion to the population involved, to tiny Iceland than to vast and teeming Indonesia. After Hungary, Soviet-Icelandic exchanges dropped sharply, but Moscow displayed impressive propaganda skill in rebuilding its influence to a new peak in the strategic island country in 1958.[2] As of the academic year 1958-1959, at least one Icelandic student was enrolled for advanced study in the U.S.S.R., and, according to one official American report, twenty Icelandic medical students were enrolled in Soviet medical schools.

Another country of Western Europe which usually receives Soviet attention far out of proportion to its population is Finland. For example, for the first half of 1957, Finnish-Soviet exchanges were on a bigger scale than those between the Soviet Union and France, England, Italy, Japan, India, or Egypt. In fact, a kind of "saturation" technique was applied to Finland, where, among other things, Soviet television programs played an important part in the cultural effort. So close are Soviet-Finnish tourist contacts, for example, that in recent years even Americans in Leningrad have frequently been asked, by the ubiquitous black marketeers of that city, if they were Finns with suits or shoes to sell. Finland, nevertheless, has preserved a firmly Western cultural orientation.

The predominance of Europe in Soviet cultural policy is reflected in indices other than those so far mentioned. Despite exceptions, such as the celebrated visit of B and K to India, Burma, and Afghanistan, the post-Stalin leaders have spent more time in Western Europe than in Asia and the disproportionate attention received by Western Europe in the post-Stalin era thus far would undoubtedly have bulked even more prominent if the events in Hungary had not, temporarily, diminished the attractiveness of Soviet culture. In 1956 G. M. Malenkov, for example, made a rather successful trip to England. His deportment differed so favorably from the expectations inherent in the British stereotype of a Russian bolshevik that he succeeded very well in his mission of paving the way for the visit by Bulganin and Khrushchev which

---

[2] For an illuminating account of the earlier phases of the Kremlin's economic and cultural campaign in Iceland, see Porter McKeever, "How to Throw Away an Airbase," in *Harper's Magazine*, October 1956, pp. 40-44. See also Mary S. Olmsted, "Communism in Iceland," in *Foreign Affairs*, Vol. 36, No. 2, January 1958, pp. 340-347.

followed, though the atmosphere was clouded by the indignation aroused in many British circles by the visit, a few weeks later, of Soviet secret police chief Serov, to prepare security arrangements for the protection of his superiors. Of course, prior to all of these visits, the atmosphere of Soviet-West European relations had already been sweetened considerably by the summit conference of July 1955. B and K, on their British trip, found that the charm which had worked so well in India had less effect on the more sophisticated British, however.

During the first half of 1956 the heads of government of France, Sweden, and Denmark, among others, visited Russia. Scheduled return visits did not take place, nor did British Prime Minister Eden make the visit apparently planned to return that of Bulganin and Khrushchev to England. Throughout the post-Stalin period there were frequent contacts between high-ranking leaders of Western European political parties and Soviet leaders. For example, in 1954 former Prime Minister Attlee visited Russia and in 1957 and again in 1959 Aneurin Bevan was in the Soviet Union. Both Bevan and Attlee, incidentally, also visited the United States in the post-Stalin years. Many French statesmen, including in 1958, Pierre Mendès-France, visited Russia and other communist countries. In 1955 the "grand old man" of the French Radical Socialists, the late Edouard Herriot, even presided over the World Peace Assembly at Helsinki, which immediately preceded the summit conference at Geneva. These examples illustrate Soviet efforts to break out of the political isolation of the late-Stalin era. Cultural, athletic, and scientific exchanges helped pave the way for "normalization" on the diplomatic level, but the latter also facilitated the Soviet cultural campaign.

Soviet exchanges with Western Europe are certainly on an impressive scale in comparison with the pattern of the Stalin era. Where previously there were a few score delegations every year, consisting mostly of communists and open fellow-travelers, today hundreds of delegations and thousands of persons cross frontiers in both directions. By 1956 travel by Western Europeans in Russia and, to a somewhat lesser degree, travel by Soviet citizens in Western Europe, had lost much of the exotic or sensational character which it still possessed in 1953 or even 1954. However, there was no such steady growth over the post-Stalin years of relatively intimate contacts between Western Europe and Russia as between Russia and countries like India, Ceylon, and other underindustrialized lands. Opinion in noncommunist Europe was more sensitive than in Asia or Africa to sudden shifts on the international political arena. Among the most striking examples of international events which suddenly altered the developing image of Soviet respectability were Hungary and Suez in 1956 and the Middle East and Far East crises of 1958. An interesting example of the interaction between international politics and cultural relations was the cancellation, under government pressure, of Soviet ballet performances in Paris as French forces succumbed to attack by Indo-Chinese communists at Dienbienphu in 1954. The French government explained that the step was taken because of fear of anti-Soviet demonstrations. The Soviet press, in contrast, stressed the avid interest displayed by Parisians in the Soviet ballet, even giving picturesque details regarding profits made by speculators in tickets for its scheduled performances. Soviet newspapers asserted that French artists and their visiting Soviet colleagues spoke a "common language." But the main emphasis in the Soviet press was on criticism of the French government for its alleged desire to nullify the favorable impact which performances by the greatest Soviet artists could have upon French public opinion.[3]

Probably the careful cultivation of Europe reflected not only its crucial geopolitical and technological significance but also Kremlin realization that, with the possible exception of North Americans, Western Europeans, or at least a noncommunist majority among them, constituted an exceptionally critical, skeptical, and at times even hostile audience so far as Soviet propaganda was concerned. This was, then, a garden which would have to be cultivated with skill and persistence and it was clear throughout the period that despite strong "sales resistance" and numerous temporary reverses Moscow was determined to continue its program of demonstration and blandishment.

Like the United States, Canada, Australia, New Zealand, and a few other non-European countries, many of the countries of

---

[3] See, for example, article by People's Artist of the U.S.S.R., Dudinskaya, in *Pravda*, July 25, 1954, occupying one third of p. 4.

Western Europe enjoy advantages over the U.S.S.R., in terms of standards of living and cultural prestige, which make their cultures interesting and attractive to ordinary Soviet citizens, and especially perhaps to the Soviet scientific and artistic communities. A measure of prophylactic caution was hence indicated in cultural relations with Western Europe, although not quite to the extreme degree which Moscow considers necessary in dealing with the rich and seductive United States. Soviet strategy in dealing with noncommunist Western Europeans has been to place on display, so to speak, expert and skilled practitioners of various kinds, carefully selected and provided with appropriate settings.

The strategy has been one of displaying tangible evidence in support of propaganda themes set forth by the top leadership and disseminated by propaganda media. Intimacy of contact has, however, been discouraged. There is evidence of fear in Soviet official circles that too much knowledge of life in noncommunist Europe might upset the mental equilibrium of Soviet citizens. It was reported, for example, that when the French socialist André Philip, in a conversation with Khrushchev, proposed exchanges of French and Soviet workers, the Kremlin boss accused Philip of "slyness" and said that Philip wished to embarrass him, since he knew well that the standard of living in France was infinitely higher than in the Soviet Union.[4] There were many other indications of ambivalence in the Kremlin's attitude toward exposure of Soviet citizens to Western European cultural influences.

Soviet press accounts of performances by noncommunist Europeans or United States artists in Russia, and also articles on Western cultural figures, are usually written in a more restrained tone than those concerned with Asians, living or dead. Quite correctly, the Soviet press can emphasize the "folk" character of much Indonesian or Burmese music and dancing. In the contemporary East the Soviets can successfully operate as exponents of "modern" European artistic and literary forms, and as accomplished per-

[4] C. L. Sulzberger, *New York Times*, September 5, 1956. On Soviet sensitivity to the comparison between French and Soviet standards of living see also *Franc-Tireur* for May 24, 1956, reporting that Vinogradov, Soviet ambassador to France, had told French journalists and French Foreign Minister Pineau that French workers lived better than Russian workers but that someday, it was hoped, the Russians would achieve a higher standard of living than the French.

formers of the vital and lively elements of Slavic, Transcaucasian, and Central Asian art forms which they have carefully preserved within the framework of the celebrated Soviet nationality policy, which professes to clothe a "socialist content" in appropriate "national" forms. The astuteness of Soviet cultural policy in Asia and Africa consists in large measure of the tact and modesty with which these claims are advanced. Feeling secure in their mastery of scientific, artistic, and industrial skills capable of impressing peoples in an early stage of modernization, the Russians can afford to display magnanimous appreciation of the accomplishments of peoples whom they regard, in terms of their own technological-materialistic criteria, as less advanced than themselves. But in Western Europe Soviet Russians still feel that they have to prove themselves, in terms of techniques, media, forms, and skills which originated in Italy, France, Germany, and other lands with long traditions of creative originality and distinguished performance.

Soviet Russians, of course, display tact also in dealing with Europeans. In this respect some Americans might do well to follow their example. However, the Soviet political leadership fears European influence. Perhaps in part because, to a certain extent, the European leadership classes are regarded as agents of the United States, and also because the mingled pride and inferiority complex of the Russians do not permit them to be as generous in praise of European as of Afro-Asian achievements, adjectival sobriety is displayed in Soviet comment on cultural contacts with Western Europe. These differences between Europe and Asia should not be exaggerated. They pertain primarily to types of activities and to contexts in which there is a strong political element. Probably one of the strengths of Soviet cultural policy, particularly since the death of Stalin, has been its willingness to give full credit to excellence of performance regardless of the nationality or the ideological affiliation of the performer. American violinists, French or English dramatic actors, and German string quartets receive the same warm appreciation for virtuosity. However, this appreciation of individual or group performance is supplemented, if the particular master belongs to a favored political group or nation, by references to the "greatness," "ancientness," and "folk" character of his nation's culture and, if the group in question adheres to the policy of the "socialist camp," to the "progressive" and "democratic" character of its ideology. The Kremlin sees no inconsistency in blasting Turkish, West German, or American foreign policy and at the same time expressing the warmest appreciation for Turkish musicians and admiration for Turkish wrestlers, for American weight lifters, and for West German soccer players. The Soviet communists regard bourgeois artists, scientists, and other members of the intelligentsia as servants, but not members, of the capitalist "ruling class," and as at least potential recruits for service in the socialist intelligentsia which their doctrine assures them will come into existence everywhere as the Soviet system inevitably extends its sway.

The Russians have apparently done remarkably little boasting about their long string of victories over Western Europeans in basketball, soccer, rowing, track, and many other sports, all of which originated outside of Russia. These same observations apply, though with some qualifications, to the sputniks and other scientific marvels that have astounded the world. These have, however, been publicized with a tongue-in-cheek astuteness that has suggested their originality and military potential and concealed all evidence of possible failures encountered in development and testing.

If the Soviet attitude toward Western European culture and its exponents is more reserved than the corresponding attitude toward the underdeveloped countries, it is, of course, considerably more favorable than that displayed toward American culture. In fact, cultural and ideological anti-Americanism is a major ingredient in the Soviet approach toward European intellectuals. Exploiting real and contrived affinities and certain fears and resentments, Moscow has attempted to establish a common "European" front with Western European intellectuals against Washington. This policy, of course, does not prevent the Russians from simultaneously stressing Russian-American ties. The Kremlin, usually correctly, calculates that each of its audiences is sufficiently preoccupied with its own relationship to Moscow to pay relatively little attention to what it says to the others. This is not always true, of course. At times, Soviet preferential treatment of Europeans as against North Americans can be elephantine and ineffective. For example, at the Tenth International Congress of Historical Sciences in Rome, in September 1955, a leading American historian, on behalf of the American group, proposed to the head of the Soviet delegation that the two groups hold a joint discussion session. The proposal was pointedly ignored, but the Soviet delegation ostentatiously invited their British colleagues to a meeting. The British historians, who were amused by the transparency of the Soviet maneuver, agreed to meet with their Russian counterparts and took the opportunity to put blunt questions on such down-to-earth matters as the failure of Soviet historians to answer letters addressed to them by British scholars. In 1956 both the French and British ambassadors in Moscow delivered television addresses, but no invitation was issued to the American ambassador, who finally succeeded, however, as noted earlier, in making brief TV appearances in 1958 and 1959. Student exchanges, and other types of relatively intimate exchange between the Soviet Union and Western Europe have been more restricted than with Asian and African countries. It has been easier for Western Europeans to get relatively long-term visas for sojourns in Russia than for Americans, though by 1959 some easing of policy in this matter toward both Western Europeans and Americans was discernible.

The post-Stalin "cultural line" toward Western Europe was set forth authoritatively by Ilya Ehrenburg, a frequent Kremlin spokesman on cultural matters, in a *Pravda* article published on March 25, 1954, entitled "The Fate of Europe." Ehrenburg began with a quotation from the classic Larousse French dictionary, which included in its definition of Europe such Russian areas as the Ural Mountains, Transcaucasia, and the Caspian Sea, as well as the more familiar Western European areas bounded by the Mediterranean Sea and the Atlantic and Arctic Oceans. If there were a few French politicians who did not know where Europe began and ended, Ehrenburg complained, American "fantasies" were more to blame for this situation than French secondary schools. The concept of Europe, continued Ehrenburg, could not be restricted to the countries of the EDC. It would be a strange Europe indeed without London and without Moscow, without Berlin and without Warsaw, without Prague and without Stockholm. Despite all of its variety and differences, Europe represented a cultural unity, with common sources of civilization and common achievements, based upon "the exchange of spiritual and material values." "Our Europe," said Ehrenburg, "is not a desert or a pampas, it is the most thickly populated part of the globe." A threat to any part of Europe was a threat to the whole of Europe, he continued, embellishing the theme of the common vital interests of Europeans with a long list of historical, literary, artistic, and scientific confrontations of Russian, Eastern European, and Western European symbols. The students of Oxford and the Sorbonne, like those of Charles University or Moscow, he observed, were aware of the contributions to science which had been made by Pasteur, Cuvier, Einstein, and Pavlov.

Ehrenburg spoke of Soviet-West European cultural exchanges, some of which had already taken place and others of which were planned for the immediate future. It was good, he felt, that the people of Moscow would soon see the dramatic works of Molière and that Italian films would appear on the screens of Leningrad, Prague, and Budapest, while music lovers in West Germany would have the opportunity to hear a Soviet virtuoso. It should be interesting for Western Europeans to learn of the advances of Soviet medicine, about Soviet books for children, about the construction of "the new Warsaw," and about the progress of Czech printing art.

In conclusion, Ehrenburg declared that it was time that the "philistines of the West" stopped saying that the Soviet people did not understand the European countries. From ancient times Russians had dearly loved "the freedom-loving people of France, and the culture of England, and inspired Italy." Who could forget Herzen's words about "the sacred stones of Europe," or the love of European culture felt by Belinski and Saltykov, Gogol and Turgenev, Chekhov and Gorki, Blok and Mayakovski? The Soviet people, "together with all of the states of Europe," wanted to defend the great monuments of the European past as well as to assure Europe's future.

Two months after publishing the above article, Ehrenburg went to Paris, where he presented a Stalin Peace Prize to the prominent Russophile politician Pierre Cot. He said, among other things: "We are living in great and difficult times. On the mind and heart of every man, on the mind and heart of every people depends the fate of our civilization—the lapidary clusters of this astounding city which surrounds us, and the books of future Balzacs, Dickenses and Tolstois who are now light-heartedly playing in the Luxembourg Gardens, in Hyde Park and on the Pushkin Boulevard. You, Pierre Cot, have always defended the cause of peace, of France and of human dignity, of friendship among peoples, and the right of all the mothers, the builders, the horticulturalists to a life free of enervating anxiety and humiliating fear."

In *Sovetskaya Kultura* for August 9, 1955, Ehrenburg who, together with Boris Polevoi, Mikhail Sholokhov, and a few other intellectuals, has been a frequent spokesman for the Kremlin, recommended that an exhibition of Swedish home furnishings should be opened in Moscow. He suggested that, in return, Soviet children's books be made available in Sweden. Ehrenburg's suggestion—one of many that followed Premier Bulganin's endorsement of expansion of international contacts in his speech at the Supreme Soviet session in July 1955—reflected the growing desire of the Soviet upper-income groups for modern comforts and conveniences. Like such events as the exhibition of Danish home furnishings in 1954 or the sensationally popular British fashion show of 1956 and the perhaps even more successful French show in 1959—neither of which, however, appears to have brought commercial advantage to their sponsors, except, perhaps, in terms of publicity—Ehrenburg's proposal could be regarded as one of many efforts to give an appearance of reality to the hope that Khrushchev has held out to European—and American—businessmen that with improved political relations the Soviet Union would become a profitable market.

Let us now survey briefly Soviet culture contacts with a few major Western European nations. Great Britain is certainly one of the most significant of these, from the Soviet and British as well as from the American point of view. Throughout the period we are studying there seems to have been something of a contest between the Kremlin and the British Foreign Office to guide exchanges through particular channels or to prevent the other side from exercising such guidance. On the British side the emphasis was on an effort to induce the Soviets to loosen controls, both over

Soviet citizens sent to Britain and over British travelers to and in the U.S.S.R. This aspect of the British position was stated by Christopher Mayhew, chairman of the Soviet Relations Committee of the British Council, in a letter which he addressed to the editors of *Pravda* in 1958. He pointed out that Britain was willing to cooperate with Russia in encouraging organized exchanges. However, he emphasized, the long-range British objective was to achieve "the normal free communication we enjoy with other countries of the world," in which "the cultural contacts approach the freedom of those between, say Moscow and Leningrad."[5]

Even a culturally homogeneous and politically sophisticated democracy such as Great Britain works under certain handicaps in cultural exchanges with the centralized Soviet state. As we have suggested, these disadvantages are offset by the vulnerability of citizens of a totalitarian state to external influences, if and when these can be brought to bear. It is understandable that London, like Washington, has pressed for normal and free access by private citizens and institutions to their Russian colleagues and counterparts. It is also understandable that Moscow has encouraged visits to the Soviet Union by members of ideologically oriented organizations such as the British-Soviet Friendship Society, the Scotland-U.S.S.R. Friendship Society, and the Society for Cultural Relations with the U.S.S.R. Also, even in 1955 and 1956, after action had been undertaken by the British Council to sponsor an increasing number of exchanges in competition with those arranged by communist-front organizations in the first year or two after Stalin's death, the B.S.F.S. brought to London the Moscow State Folk Dance Company, the pianist Eugene Malinin, and the violinist Leonid Kogan, and also presented a mixed recital of musicians, dancers, and acrobats. By these actions the B.S.F.S. helped to keep in pro-Soviet hands direction of some attractive and successful exchanges.

Moscow thus continued, at least for a time, to have the best of both worlds. It arranged for sponsorship of Soviet cultural activities in Britain by pro-Soviet organizations and thereby built up their prestige and influence, and at the same time bargained on

[5] *The Times*, London, February 13, 1958.

the government level, where the Soviet Ministry of Culture dealt with the British Foreign Office and with the semiofficial British Council. It is true, of course, that the British government could have refused visas to any Soviet group or individual not approved of by the Foreign Office, but except for a few months after the Hungarian uprising such action would have been poorly received by segments of British public opinion. Establishment of the Soviet Relations Committee followed a year or more of growing dissatisfaction in noncommunist British circles with the unsatisfactory state of Anglo-Russian cultural relations. This dissatisfaction was expressed forcefully in an article in the weekly *Economist* for November 13, 1954, entitled "The Smiling Monolith." The *Economist* called Moscow's policy a "cultural offensive" designed to appeal to "ordinary people over their elected governments' heads."

Calling attention to the bureaucratic and elitist nature of the Russian program, the *Economist* criticized the refusal of the Soviet government to grant a visa to a "simple Briton" who had requested permission, as a fan, to accompany the Arsenal football team on its trip to Moscow. The Soviets were also criticized for stalling about British suggestions for "genuine long-term exchanges between British and Russian universities." Noting that the Soviet ambassador could publicly attack British policy in London, while the British ambassador had no such opportunity in Moscow, the weekly defined the Soviet policy of coexistence as "a period during which they make full use of the propaganda and political facilities accorded them by democratic institutions in other countries, while their own empire remains an inviolate monolith." Determined British pressure for reciprocity in cultural relations was not without some effect, as subsequent developments have indicated.

In February 1956, at the invitation of the S.R.C., Mr. N. A. Mikhailov, the Soviet Minister of Culture, came to London for negotiations looking toward a normalization of professional, educational, artistic, and other exchanges. While in Britain in April, as a member of the Bulganin-Khrushchev party, he continued the negotiations, together with Soviet Ambassador Malik and officials of the British Council. Sharp bargaining on both sides led in 1956 to conclusion of an agreement less formal than those later made between Russia and the United States, France, or some other noncommunist countries, but one regarded by interested English-men interviewed by me as reasonably satisfactory, considering the incompatibility of the ultimate objectives of the two governments.

For a few months in late 1956 and early 1957 most Anglo-Soviet exchanges were suspended and a few were cancelled, but by the summer and fall of 1957 a pattern had been worked out which probably was more satisfactory to both sides than any previous one. Further progress was made in 1958. It is interesting to note that it was the Russians who pleaded for a resumption of contacts after Hungary, with overtures by their London embassy and statements by the head of their State Committee for Cultural Relations, in which the functions of that body were likened to those of the British Council. On the British side, Prime Minister Macmillan, in a letter to Marshal Bulganin, published June 16, 1958, regretted that there still existed barriers on the Soviet side "to the unrestricted exchanges of persons and information which is the necessary basis for mutual understanding."

In this and other ways the British government continued for some time to present with more firmness than that displayed by most other democratic governments the case for completely free communication between East and West. The British-Soviet debate was carried into 1958, mainly by Christopher Mayhew and Georgi Zhukov. Mayhew's letter to *Pravda*, mentioned earlier, was a major British move in the cultural contest.

After complaints by Soviet Ambassador Malik that Soviet-British exchanges were too few, the 1958 debate originated in proposals submitted by the British Committee to Mr. Zhukov early in 1958 for exchanges for that year, and in Zhukov's reply of February 12, proposing an enlarged joint Soviet-British program of sponsored exchanges. As of that date many individual British exchange proposals had been accepted by Moscow, and organized exchanges were proceeding satisfactorily on a modest scale, though the Soviets were still stalling on a British proposal to receive three hundred Soviet students in Britain, a curtailed version of which they finally accepted. In April the Soviet Relations Committee, in replying to Zhukov, associated itself with a note of the British government, dated April 23, which took the line that, while it was desirable to continue to expand organized contacts, an attempt should also be made to remove the obstacles remaining on the Soviet side to free communication between the two countries. Also, on April 27 and May 4, Mr. Mayhew published articles in the London *Observer* advocating unfettered exchanges. He argued that, while organized exchanges could probably be partially credited with the post-Stalin decline in mutual ignorance and prejudice between the Soviet and non-Soviet worlds, three main obstacles to free communication remained.

Mr. Mayhew saw these as: a basic difference of approach to "free contacts," the British interpretation of which Mr. Zhukov had already characterized as an attempt to revive the "cold war"; a Soviet desire to shield the Russian people from dangerous Western political ideas; and, finally, the Soviet government's contacts with communist cultural organizations in the West.

The Soviet government rejected the British position in a note of June 16, and in an article by Zhukov in *Pravda* for June 9, to which reference has been made earlier, attacking Conrad Hilton for his alleged desire to "infect the Russians with capitalism" and including sharp criticism also of Christopher Mayhew. In the meantime a U.S.S.R.-Great Britain Society had been founded in Moscow on April 8, but Soviet jamming of the B.B.C. continued and in June the Soviets even jammed a B.B.C. broadcast of interviews with members of their own Moscow Art Theater, despite twenty-four hours' advance notice of the broadcast given by the B.B.C.

The sharp exchanges of opinions and demands in early 1958 led to British delay, until March 1959, in signing the long-range cultural agreement desired by Moscow; but it did not prevent inauguration, long before signature of the agreement, of important exchanges. In the academic year 1957-1958, British efforts to effect an exchange of university professors were crowned with modest success. Five Soviet scholars, the first to come to Britain for long stays in many years, registered for study at British universities, including Oxford and Cambridge. A summer exchange of students between Oxford and the University of Moscow, cancelled in 1957, took place in 1958 and was followed by another similar exchange in 1959. We will have a word to say about some of these particularly significant exchanges in the survey that follows.

British-Soviet exchanges during the last five or six years have been varied and on a scale extensive enough to require a small book for a full catalogue and description.[6] In each of the three years 1954-1956 a dozen or more artistic and musical groups were exchanged and about the same number of trade-union and co-operative delegations were exchanged. Six Soviet athletic teams visited Britain in 1954, and four in each of the two following years. The category designated as "technical, professional, governmental and scientific" by United States government agencies accounted for thirteen British delegations to Russia in 1954 and an identical number of Soviet delegations to Britain, with twenty-seven in this category going from Britain to the U.S.S.R. in 1955 and eighteen in the opposite direction, and twenty-six from Britain to Russia in 1956 and thirty-one in the other direction.

Heavy emphasis upon technical and scientific exchanges, which continued to increase in 1957, was probably intended, on the Soviet side, not only to acquire useful knowledge of British methods but to give an impression of Soviet power. The latter objective was also served by the visit of the Soviet cruiser *Sverdlov* to Britain in June 1953, by an exchange of fleet visits in 1955, and by many other actions including threatening statements regarding Soviet rockets, some of which were even made by Khrushchev while he was a guest of the British government in April 1956. There was less tourist exchange between Russia and Britain than between the Soviet Union and the United States and some European countries, such as France or Sweden. However, considerable publicity was given by the British press to tourist exchanges, particularly to motor trips by Britons, which began in 1957. Throughout these years the British press gave much more publicity to athletic exchanges than to any other kind. This British press practice was followed also in most continental European countries. For many reasons, including the large spectator participation involved, and the brilliant success of Soviet athletes, sports exchanges undoubtedly played a very important role in the total Soviet effort. All over the world, of course, the Soviet Union gained prestige as a result of

[6] In 1954 thirty-two Soviet delegations visited the United Kingdom. The figures for 1955 and 1956 were, respectively, 36 and 49. Forty-four British delegations visited Russia in 1954, 62 in 1955, and 46 in 1956.

its victory over the United States and other capitalist countries in the 1956 Olympic Games. The performance of Soviet athletes as emissaries of good will, at least in Britain, was marred somewhat by a ludicrous incident in August 1956, when Nina Ponomareva, a Soviet woman discus champion, was arrested on charges of shop-lifting four cheap hats.

Judging from the available evidence, a capable and reasonably representative British delegation attended the 1957 Youth Festival in Moscow. It numbered more than 1,600 and it made a better impression on Soviet youth than did the much smaller American delegation. Many of the British youths who attended the festival were impressed by Russian material progress, energy, and vitality but were also unfavorably affected by totalitarian regimentation. It was apparent even from the Soviet press that some of the British students who came to Moscow at this time were well informed about Soviet institutions and able to give a good account of themselves in specialist discussions. This was indicated, for example, by a guarded but suggestive account in *Komsomolskaya Pravda* for August 11, 1957, of a discussion regarding Soviet practices of compulsory assignment of graduates of educational institutions to governmentally designated employment, in which a British delegate took part.

Also, in the festival's seminar on economics a British delegate had the temerity to speak in defense of the capitalist system and to contrast the degree of freedom in Britain with the lack of freedom in Russia. Like some of their American or continental comrades, some British delegates were accosted and questioned about themselves and life in their home country. Many British delegates were entertained at homes and in restaurants by Soviet acquaintances, but there was some police interference with such contacts, and this, in the opinion of competent British sources, helped the more perceptive English delegates to form an accurate impression of Soviet realities.

Perhaps the reactions of the more discriminating British—and non-British—delegates have been set forth as well as they could be in the following excerpts from two articles by the Reverend Mr. W. F. Laing in the *Scotsman* for August 17 and 26, 1957: "Of those who went sympathetic, some were confirmed but many more were shaken. The crowd violence once or twice, the vast numbers of soldiers standing by on all major occasions, the ugly customers in plain clothes who formed supporting lines behind the soldiers in controlling crowds . . . the removal of Russian students from the rooms of their British friends by police, the complete and unrelenting watch on all movements on every floor of the hostels—all accumulated to leave deep disturbances." He added that "there can be no doubt whatever at the genuine welcome given by the ordinary Russian to the ordinary Westerner. It was more surprising and even more overwhelming for some than the blinding glare of the official show. . . . It was not always easy to find real privacy, but many Russian homes were visited. The housing conditions were often appalling. . . . Their clothes were drab and unattractive." Mr. Laing noted also, however, that the festival undoubtedly succeeded in its main objective, which he took to be that of presenting "an unforgettable impression of the power of the Soviet Government, and of the achievements of the Russian people." And, like perceptive American observers, he emphasized that the festival had a much greater impact on many Asians and Africans than on most European participants—a judgment that is probably applicable also to the 1959 Vienna Festival.

It might, incidentally, be appropriate in connection with this account of the British-Soviet encounter at the 1957 World Youth Festival to mention the fact that the British delegates were required to pay a total of only £47 for their visit—a sum which, though larger than that paid by many other delegates, could barely have covered their travel fares.

The Moscow Youth Festival was, in British press opinion and coverage, by far the most important British-Soviet cultural encounter of 1957. As in other Western countries, it led to spirited discussion of the pros and cons of contacts with communists. The majority British opinion, according to American and British official and press sources available to me, was that such contacts were, on the whole, mutually beneficial. However, as in the United States, disapproval was expressed of the way in which such events as the festival were exploited by their Soviet sponsors, and there was some concern over the risks involved in encounters between slick professional Soviet youth leaders and the politically innocent foreign delegates—a category to which most members, even of the British delegation, probably belonged. While Christopher Mayhew did not hesitate to speak out publicly in criticism of the Soviet machinations which he felt were involved in the festival, British policy toward it was more flexible than that of the American authorities. Partly as a result, the fact that preparatory organizational work in Britain was done by a communist-front group, proscribed both by the labor party and the noncommunist National Union of Students, did not, as might have been the case otherwise, produce a British delegation composed mainly of communists and communist sympathizers. Indeed, as has already been indicated, some members of the British delegation were highly competent spokesmen for democratic ideals, capable both of exerting a salutary influence on Russian youths and of acquiring valuable first-hand knowledge of Russian conditions which could not have been obtained had they not attended the festival.[7]

Perhaps it may now be interesting to take a quick look at a range of representative British-Soviet exchanges in significant fields. Lord Adrian, one of the most distinguished of British scientists and also the master of Trinity College, Cambridge, visited Russia as head of a delegation representing the Royal Society, from May 18 through June 1, 1956. The visit was made in return for one by members of the Soviet Academy of Sciences to Britain in 1955, and was under the auspices of the S.R.C. On his return Lord Adrian told the *Times* that there was far more freedom in Russia in scientific matters than previously and that his delegation had been warmly welcomed everywhere as a means of increasing contacts between scientists of the two countries. Lord Adrian predicted that there would be an increase of such visits. His prediction proved to be correct. One of the most outstanding of the many Soviet scientists who have been in England in recent years was the physicist Igor Kurchatov, who was a member of the Bulganin-Khrushchev party in 1956. At a visit to the British nuclear power station at Harwell, Kurchatov created something of a sensation by his statement about Soviet progress in the development of atomic power.

[7] The *Sunday Dispatch* for July 8, 1957, stated that only one third of the delegates fell into the above categories. Our evaluation is based mainly on material obtained from British and American official and other informed sources.

A considerable number of British scientists have delivered lectures before academic audiences in the Soviet Union since the death of Stalin. Most of them have been noncommunists, but they have included figures like John Bernal, brilliant Marxist physicist, who received a Stalin Peace Prize in September 1954 and has made subsequent enthusiastic visits.

In November and December 1955 the Tennent Theatrical Company, headed by Peter Brooks, enjoyed a successful tour in the U.S.S.R. An Intourist guide told me in Moscow in 1956 that she had enjoyed the Tennent group's production of *Hamlet* more than any other foreign cultural importation that she had yet seen.[8] The London Philharmonic Orchestra was very well received in Russia in September and October 1956. In May 1957 the British conductor Sir Malcolm Sargent was cordially received on a concert tour of the Soviet Union. Like most foreign artists who have toured Russia, he was apparently highly pleased by the enthusiasm of Soviet audiences. Perhaps the main British artistic presentation in the post-Stalin years was at the 1957 Youth Festival, where, among other events, performances of Shakespearian drama and John Osborne's *Look Back in Anger* were put on by the Theater Workshop Repertory Company. In December 1957 Beryl Grey, a member of the Sadler's Wells Ballet, achieved the unique distinction of performing in "Swan Lake" and "Giselle" as a temporary member of the Bolshoi Theater Ballet in Moscow and then went on to a successful tour of other cities.

In 1958 the English pianist Peter Kitin performed in the U.S.S.R. In 1957 and 1958 a number of exhibitions devoted to various aspects of British civilization were held in the Soviet Union and contacts occurred between film and television leaders of the two countries, but most of the flow of artistic exchanges in 1957-1958 was from Russia to Britain. In part, this resulted from a visit to Russia by the Czech-born British impresario Victor Hochhausen in June 1957. Hochhausen signed up a large number of Russian artists for British visits. Some of these occurred in 1957, but most of them took place in 1958, which was a banner year for Soviet artists in England.

[8] For Soviet press reaction see, for example, *Sovetskaya Kultura*, November 3, 1955, and *Pravda*, December 2, 1955.

The Soviet violinist Igor Oistrakh, son of the famous David Oistrakh, the cellist Rostropovich, the pianist Emil Gilels, the Bolshoi Theater Ballet, and the Moscow Art Theater Company were among the many top-flight Soviet artists and companies whose performances in Britain since the death of Stalin have enlivened the cultural scene. They all, apparently, made a good impression, although British critics, in their quiet way, made it clear that they did not regard them as superior to other competent European performers. Perhaps the most successful Soviet artistic performers, in terms of mass appeal, were the clowns, acrobats, and beasts of the Moscow State Circus, which played to capacity houses in London and all of the other main British cities in the summer of 1956. The Moscow circus, incidentally, like several of the Soviet folk-dance groups which have performed in Europe in recent years, got top billing not only in Britain but in many other European countries. In June 1956 I watched a large matinee audience respond with delight to the antics of the Russian circus at the huge Haringay Arena near London. In the summer of 1956 in London and Paris and again in 1957 in London and Brussels I came across conspicuous evidence in the press and on billboards that Russian artists had already established an enviable reputation in the European entertainment world. In July 1957 an impressive Soviet film version of *Othello* played to large audiences in Munich. This film had already been shown in Britain. A Soviet circus again toured Britain and other Western European countries in 1958 and 1959. According to one American diplomatic source, the Soviets facilitated their access to the European entertainment market, especially in Belgium, by offering very favorable business deals to the impresarios who arranged for performances by Soviet artists.

However, Russian success in the world of the arts was based more on quality of performance than on skillful marketing. Of course, it was impossible to predict, on the basis of only a few years of experience, whether the vogue for things Russian would prove long lasting, but as of 1958 European sources reported that the exchange of theaters and ballets was still receiving a degree of attention that one European scholar in a letter to us described as "spectacular."

We have already referred to some of the British-Soviet academic exchanges. The brief Oxford-Moscow University exchange of visits by professors in 1956 resulted in publication of a number of interesting press items in England, among which three articles by the British scholar Dr. Enid Starkie and an article by a Russian colleague, Professor Olga Akhmanova, all published in the *Sunday Times*, are worthy of mention. Professor Akhmanova was sufficiently impressed by the Oxford tutorial system to suggest at least the advisability of reducing obligatory attendance at lectures in comparable Soviet institutions and of increasing the number of "individual consultations." She observed that at Oxford the teacher-student ratio was roughly the same as in Moscow University—that is, one to ten. Both Professor Akhmanova and Dr. Starkie were obviously pleased by their experiences in one another's countries and both wrote gracious and polite accounts thereof. Dr. Starkie concluded her series with the statement: "There is every chance that the seed sown by these visits will bear fruit, and that an interchange of students and teachers will become possible. Such meetings can do nothing but good. They will not prevent war if it is to come, but they may lead to knowledge, understanding and sympathy, and these are precious commodities to share, even in opposing camps."[9]

Professor Akhmanova, incidentally, led a party of Russian teachers of English who took a three-week course at Somerville College, Oxford, in July 1958.

Of considerably greater interest, perhaps, than such formal exchanges as the one just touched upon were some of the encounters between British and Soviet students, particularly those in which the participants on one side or both dispensed at times with the usual perfunctory platitudes so dear to the hearts of Soviet tourist authorities, even if no monopoly of theirs. If British students gave a surprisingly good account of themselves at the Youth Festival in 1957, this was probably due in part to previous explorations of Soviet terrain by a few sharp-witted British youths, and also to the sound and honest guidance of teachers and other interested persons.

As far back as 1953-1954, there had been much negotiation and some student exchange between the two countries. One of the more

[9] *Sunday Times*, September 30, October 7, 14, and 21, 1956. October 21 issue for Dr. Starkie's statement.

interesting of these early ventures was an exchange of student delegations in 1954, arranged between the National Union of Students of England, Wales and Northern Ireland and the Anti-Fascist Committee of Soviet Youth, which later changed its name to the Committee of Youth Organizations of the U.S.S.R. Fred Jarvis, president of the British body, described the three-week Russian trip made by twenty members of his organization in the summer of 1954 in the November-December issue of *Problems of Communism* for that year. His article pointed to interesting confrontations of British images of British life with Soviet stereotypes thereof, and observed that "the more noncommunists that go to the U.S.S.R. and speak the truth, the better."

Judging by the way in which they have been reported in the official Soviet youth press, the Soviet student and youth delegations which have gone to Britain in reciprocation of visits like that described by Fred Jarvis have found confirmation in their observations in Britain for the views regarding life in a capitalist country which they had been taught before seeing it on the spot. However, one wonders if perhaps these emissaries have not been stimulated by their experiences to thoughts that they did not see fit to express. This reflection is based in part on what I was told in Britain in 1957 by a young Soviet refugee scholar who had met some members of Soviet youth delegations.

Some twenty-five British students visited the Soviet Union in September 1956 for a short period on an officially sponsored tour, and a similar visit was made by a group of Soviet students to England. One of the most interesting, even if partly abortive, British-Soviet student exchanges resulted from the trip made to Moscow by a party of five Cambridge University students, at the invitation of Moscow University, in September and October 1956. This objective, thoroughly competent, and well-trained group succeeded unusually well in piercing the Soviet hospitality curtain and seeing Soviet life clearly and whole. A brief report of their trip by Rex Brown, one of their number, appeared in the *Manchester Guardian* for October 25, 1956. This was followed by a franker, more critical account in *Everybody's* magazine, after it became clear that the planned return visit by a similar, small Soviet student group to Cambridge was not going to be made. As is so often the case, the Soviet students and authorities offered no explanation of the cancellation. British-Soviet student exchanges expanded considerably in 1957-1958 and apparently still further in 1959. Fairly large-scale officially sponsored summer student exchanges occurred in 1957, and during the academic year 1957-1958 a small number of longer-term exchanges of advanced scholars took place. British efforts to apply in these exchanges the practices normally followed in British international student exchanges with Western countries—with full access on both sides to information on the prospective candidates and the possibility, for example, of placing notices in Soviet newspapers of anticipated opportunities to study in Britain—met with rebuffs from the Soviet side, but these obstacles did not prevent some progress from being made.

A somewhat-superficial but nevertheless-useful glimpse of one facet of a Russo-British scholarly exchange was given by an article in the London *News Chronicle* for February 24, 1958, entitled "Quiet Studies the Don." The article was based in part on an interview by the columnist "John London" with Victor Ivanovich Israelyan, a Soviet scholar doing research at Cambridge on Anglo-Soviet relations during World War II. Also present at the interview was Mrs. Irina Kudryasheva, a Soviet teacher of English who was studying instruction methods at Cambridge. Mr. Israelyan's cautious, negative views on British education for historical research and his enthusiastic appreciation of his opportunity to pursue research in England were reported. Perhaps the most interesting information conveyed was the statement that "every evening he dines at High Table alongside Professor Butterfield, the Master of Peterhouse, and Professor Denis Brogan." Israelyan was, at the time, one of the five post-graduate students, reportedly all members of the teaching staff of the Moscow Institute of International Relations, placed at the end of October 1957 at Oxford, Cambridge, and London Universities.

In the summer of 1956, V. Gerashchenko, First Deputy Chairman of the State Bank of the U.S.S.R., took part in a summer banking school at Oxford. And, while we are on the subject of bankers, it is interesting to note that in June 1958 two officials of the Bank of England paid a visit to Russia and established contact with the Soviet State Bank, the first since the early 1930's.

The *Manchester Guardian* for January 16, 1958, reported arrival in the U.S.S.R. of the first British Council delegation ever to visit Russia, "to further the teaching of English in Russian schools." The group made arrangements for thirty Russian teachers of English to visit Russia in the summer of 1958.

Dozens of other interesting British-Soviet exchanges, such as the visit by British steel manufacturers, reported in the *Economist* for April 27, 1957, might be mentioned. There is little doubt that all of this was at least doing a good deal to strip away the veil of misinformation between the two countries, though, as Gerard Fay noted in the *Manchester Guardian* for June 19, 1958, "to find out real figures and to be convinced that they are real is not easy for the foreigner in Russia." He added that "there is a blandness about the way false information is proffered which makes belief come hard."

The 1959 Anglo-Soviet agreement on cultural exchanges, already mentioned, was followed by negotiations in Moscow between the Soviet Relations Committee of the British Council and the Soviet State Committee for Cultural Relations with Foreign Countries, in which agreement was reached on specific exchanges during 1959 and the first quarter of 1960 "in the fields of culture, education, science, technology, industry and agriculture." The program agreed upon provided for an extension of exchanges of students and teachers, and of specialists in the fields listed above, as well as for further development of exchanges in the arts and for festivals of British and Soviet films and exhibitions of books.

Both sides expressed the hope that their exchange of views on problems of cultural cooperation would help to "develop normal contacts between citizens and institutions of the two countries." It was agreed that the next meeting of the two sides would take place in London in 1959 to agree upon a program of exchanges in 1960-1961.

Most of the exchanges provided for in the rather substantial first-year program were for short periods. However, a section of its educational part stipulated that there should be an exchange of "20 postgraduate students from each side (10 in language and 10 in other subjects)." As in the U.S.-Soviet graduate-student exchange, each host country undertook to pay a stipend, covering board, lodging, and other expenses, to the incoming students. Another significant feature of the program was its inclusion of provision for exchange, between the Royal Society and Soviet Academy of Sciences, of two research workers from each side to work in scientific institutions for a period of up to ten months.

It appeared in the autumn of 1959 that conscientious fulfillment of the foregoing might be useful to both sides. The agreement represented a compromise, one surmised, between British desire for unfettered exchange and Soviet desire for the respectability conferred on Moscow by formal agreement. The Russians won prestige but the British succeeded in including, for example, exchanges of students at teacher-training colleges and of special courses for language teachers, and in getting agreement on exchange of "an increased number of students and young people for short visits," in accordance with suggestions made by the National Union of Students, the Scottish Union of Students, and other organizations. The latter type of exchange was, apparently, one which responsible British circles regarded as capable of achieving an especially desirable impact.

Franco-Soviet cultural exchanges, in terms of numbers of delegations, have been on approximately the same scale, since the death of Stalin, as British-Soviet exchanges. Because of internal divisions in France, the French government and interested noncommunist circles in France perhaps found it more difficult than the British to develop a clear-cut and balanced national policy for intercultural exchanges. Opinion in France regarding this, like other international problems, was more highly polarized than in Britain or America. During most of the period under examination there were probably far more Frenchmen than Englishmen who uncritically accepted the official Soviet image of the motivations of Soviet foreign cultural policy. It should also be noted that, for various reasons—among which fear of Germany, as well as anti-Americanism, probably bulked large—many bourgeois French politicians were persuaded to undertake actions and to make statements which facilitated some of the objectives of Soviet "peace" policy. On the other hand, many conservative Frenchmen, like their counterparts in Italy and West Germany, were more likely than were British conservatives blindly to fear and suspect Soviet policies. But perhaps the most important difference between British and French political attitudes toward contacts with the Russians consisted in the fact that most of the leaders of the French socialist party were considerably more critical of Russia than were the leaders of the British labor party or of most other European socialist groups.

The Kremlin apparently classifies France, in socio-political terms, as an "underdeveloped" country but one with exceptionally attractive and interesting artistic and literary traditions. The Soviets have often acted as if they did not take France very seriously as a military or industrial power. Perhaps partly for this reason, they are somewhat more willing to "trust" the French than the British. Perhaps one evidence of a growing, but still severely limited, Soviet confidence in the capacity of Soviet intellectuals to exert influence on French colleagues was the small but slowly expanding exchange of students between French and Soviet universities in the post-Stalin years, to which we shall presently turn. Lectures by French scholars in Moscow—some of them, to be sure, by French communists[10]—and reviews of French scholarly works in Soviet publications became fairly frequent in the post-Stalin years.[11]

Another indication of a relatively high degree of intimacy in Franco-Soviet cultural relations was the fact that there was considerably more exchange of tourists between France and Russia than between Russia and the United Kingdom. In 1957 Mr. Vladimir Ankudinov, head of Intourist, stated that about ten times as many French tourists had visited the Soviet Union in 1956 as had Britons.[12] On the other hand, there was no visit to France by Khrushchev until 1960 and, in general, fewer high Soviet officials visited France than England. Also, it proved even more difficult for the French than for the British government to formalize exchanges on a mutually satisfactory basis. According to a French official with whom I talked in the summer of 1957, the Soviets were at that time reluctant to conclude a formal cultural agreement of the kind desired by the French, apparently because

[10] Garaudy was one of these, and another was Georges Sadoul, whose successful defense of his dissertation was reported in *Pravda* for September 29, 1956. In 1956 the strongly anti-communist French socialist, André Philip, delivered a lecture to an academic audience in Moscow.

[11] See, for example, review of a book entitled *La Liberté*, by Roger Garaudy, in *Kommunist*, No. 17, 1955.

[12] *The Times*, March 8, 1957.

they found it more advantageous to deal directly with interested French organizations and individuals. However, in the area of university-student exchange, a Franco-Soviet arrangement, administered on the French side by a semiofficial selection and screening committee of scholars, came into force in 1955. And in October 1957, following negotiations between a Soviet delegation headed by the chairman of the State Committee for Cultural Relations with Foreign Countries, G. A. Zhukov, and the chief of the Cultural-Technical Section of the French Ministry of Foreign Affairs, Roger Seydoux, agreement was arrived at on Franco-Soviet exchanges in 1958 in the fields of "education, science and culture" and a permanent Franco-Soviet commission was established. The commission was to review periodically problems involved in cultural exchanges between the two countries.[13]

The Franco-Soviet agreement constituted a compromise, in which the French had to postpone, for a time at least, their plan to open several French reading rooms under French supervision in the Soviet Union, as well as to give ground once again on their demand that Soviet publishing houses respect the proprietary rights of French authors and publishers. Even in early 1960 Paris found Moscow remaining insistent that it was still in no position to accede to these requests.

The French found, moreover, as the Americans did in the Soviet-American cultural negotiations which opened in Washington a few weeks later, that the Soviets were still far from ready to move toward Western conceptions of freedom of exchange in the radio and television fields. The French Foreign Ministry, unlike the State Department, preferred to leave these matters open, rather than to accept an agreement "in principle." The Soviet-French agreement did, however, include a section on film exchanges.

Its most important sections, from the French point of view, were those providing for continuation and expansion of academic exchanges, including, for the first time, systematic exchanges of secondary school students and teachers. It also provided for a number of exchanges in the field of the arts, several of which, especially the one involving the Bolshoi Theater Ballet and the French Grand Opera Ballet, in May and June 1958, received

[13] *Pravda*, October 10, 1957; *Le Monde*, October 1, 10, 11, 1957.

extensive publicity in the French and Soviet press. Of interest, perhaps, in this connection was the statement by François Reiss in a review of the Bolshoi's performance in the magazine *Education Nationale* for June 12, 1958, that the meeting of Soviet and Western art could result in a happy synthesis in which each side took the best from the other.

Along slightly different lines, Alfred Fabre-Luce, after a trip to Russia, wrote in *Le Monde* for July 7, 1958, that the French should show the Soviet people the differences between the conceptions of French culture represented by Balzac and Aragon, by de Maupassant and Stil. Fabre-Luce urged that Soviet citizens be offered free trips to France and that the offers be widely publicized. He expressed confidence that "we shall profit by exchanges for we need to be simplified by them, and they need to be made more complicated by us."

Fabre-Luce's reaction to what he saw of Soviet culture was somewhat similar to the cool reception given by some French critics to the Bolshoi Ballet. The critic of the communist newspaper *L'Humanité* greeted its opening performance with ecstasy, but some of the noncommunist critics called the performance "dowdy," "old-fashioned," and "too long." Apparently a Soviet Georgian dance ensemble, in France in December 1957 and January 1958, received a better reception. Perhaps it fitted well the stereotype of exoticism in terms of which many Frenchmen, one gathers, still tend to view things Soviet. Many other important Franco-Soviet artistic events occurred in 1958, including a tour of France by the famous Moscow Art Theater. In May 1958 the Soviet composer Dimitri Shostakovich became, apparently, the first foreigner to be awarded the French Order of Art and Literature.[14] In the same month the Soviet cartoonists' team "Kukryniksy" took part, in Paris, in the founding of the International Association of Caricaturists.

It was the opinion of the well-informed noncommunist French officials, scholars, and intellectuals with whom I talked and corresponded in 1956, 1957, and 1958 that Franco-Soviet exchanges, particularly among students and professors, benefited both sides. The French sources queried apparently felt that, so far as the

---

[14] *Sovetskaya Kultura*, May 23, 1958.

impact of Russian ideas on France was concerned, it would be moderated if French intellectuals, including communists, could get a good first-hand look at Soviet culture and life. Certainly the sophisticated and critical reactions to the Soviet scene of most members of the French socialist delegation that visited Russia in May 1956 indicated that, while Russian material power could impress intelligent Frenchmen, the latter entertained the deepest reservations about many features of the new Soviet civilization.

Like many other Western European and North American visitors, including businessmen, whom I interviewed, the French socialists were shocked by the lack of adequate safety regulations in Soviet factories. Many other indications of the exceptionally severe exploitation of labor under Soviet socialism disturbed them. They also found Soviet life less exotic and more grim than they had expected. Besides being a failure from the point of view of the Soviet attempt to revive a socialist-communist "united front" in France and other Western European countries, the visit by the French socialists probably resulted in injuring the vanity of the Soviet leaders. They were obviously annoyed by the irreverent attitude of the French, reflected, for example, in the mischievous glee with which Henri Dusart reported in *Populaire* for May 25 that he had noticed oil dripping on the biscuits in a bakery which his party visited. In August 1956 the Soviet press came out with acrid criticism of the leaders and many of the members of the French socialist delegation. They were accused, among other things, of propagating falsehoods and of violating their promise to report objectively.[15]

After Stalin's death there began a very small-scale Soviet-French educational exchange program, which has been such a significant aspect of Franco-Soviet cultural relations that it deserves description in some detail. By the summer of 1958 perhaps ten Soviet youths, who identified themselves as students of French language and literature, had already studied in Paris; and a considerably larger number of French students, mostly in the field of language and literature, had studied at the University of Moscow. French

[15] *Izvestiya*, June 30, 1956; *New York Times*, August 5, 1956; *Le Populaire*, May 22-June 6, 1956. See also *Franc-Tireur* for May and June 1956, particularly the illuminating series by Georges Altman, beginning May 22.

students in Russia were mentioned in occasional cautious Soviet press items.[16]

According to my sources, French and American, most of the French university students who studied in the Soviet Union during the first year or two of this exchange were communists or fellow-travelers. Nevertheless, almost all of them reportedly moved toward the political "right" after their experience in Soviet Russia. According to one account by an American who had considerable contact with French students, the only member of one group of French students who still considered himself a communist after his experience in Russia in 1955-1956 stated that, while he himself was still a communist, he did not think that there were any real communists at all in the Soviet Union. Another trustworthy American told me of a conversation in Moscow with a French student who had found Soviet fellow-students in the musical field to be completely indifferent to official political doctrine. French and other foreign students performed many useful services as channels of information.

In the period prior to the academic year 1957-1958 French students in the U.S.S.R. were supported by stipends, much larger than those normally awarded to Soviet students, granted by the Soviet government. However, beginning in the academic year 1958-1959 the French government took over the financing of French students. Apparently, concurrent with this change of arrangement, the political complexion of the French students sent to Russia became more conservative. However, according to a reliable French informant, the conditions under which French students lived and worked in Russia also became more restrictive than they had been in the years 1954-1957. As of January 1958, according to an American official source, eleven French students were enrolled in Soviet educational institutions, including two at the Soviet center for atomic research at Dubna, near Moscow. This may have been a slightly smaller number than in preceding years, for *Le Monde* of October 1, 1957, stated that twelve French students had studied at Moscow University "last year." Seven French students were

[16] See, for example, "French Students in Moscow," in the April 1956 issue of *Vsemirnye studencheskie novosti*, and mention of speech by French graduate student at an evening "devoted to French culture," organized by VOKS, and reported in *Sovetskaya Kultura* for December 20, 1955.

admitted for the whole 1958-1959 academic year at the University of Moscow alone. Of these, four were linguists, one each was an economist, an historian, and a mathematician. This pattern of distribution by disciplines was similar to that which had prevailed previously, as throughout the whole period most of the French students in Russia were specialists in linguistics, apparently partly because the Soviet side displayed coolness toward the acceptance of students in other, more ideologically sensitive fields. The French pressed steadily for inclusion in their contingent of at least a few first-rate students of law and social science and achieved a measure of success in this effort. Also, they sought, with increasing but not complete success, to persuade the Russians to admit to Soviet universities the full quota of French students, set at fifteen as early as 1954. Apparently their success in this effort reached its highest point thus far in the negotiations for the 1959-1960 exchange.

A gradual growth of Franco-Soviet academic exchanges occurred throughout the 1954-1960 period, with the over-all volume of exchanges larger than ever before in 1959-1960. New categories were added to the French-Russian exchange pattern in 1957-1958 and 1958-1959. In 1956-1957 there occurred the first exchange of secondary school students between France and Russia.

These began with a precedent-making visit to the U.S.S.R. by Jean Triomphe, a teacher at the Paris Lycée Pasteur, and Leon Robel, of the Lycée St. Charles, Marseille. Triomphe and Robel took with them five students from Pasteur and three from St. Charles. The pupils had studied Russian a minimum of two years. Contact was established in Moscow with Deputy Minister of Education of the R.S.F.S.R. Zimin, and with the administration of School Number Two, one of the Soviet secondary schools in which instruction in French begins in the second grade. It was from this school that the Soviet school pupils who made a vacation trip to France in 1957 were selected.

Messrs. Triomphe and Robel considered their visit very useful and successful. Their group, they reported, had seen much of a "tourist" character, but also much that was "original." On the whole, the Soviet hosts had been most friendly and the French children left Russia loaded with Russian books, photographs, and souvenirs. The teachers expressed regret, however, that no actual classroom life had been observed and that so much time had been spent on trains. They were particularly pleased with the excellent practice their charges had enjoyed in speaking Russian.[17]

As a follow-up to the Triomphe-Robel trip, Soviet schoolboys from Moscow School Number Two spent a month in France, and ten pupils of the Lycée Pasteur spent a month in the U.S.S.R. in the summer of 1957. These two visits were described and appraised objectively in two articles in the French academic publication *Les Langues Modernes* for November-December, 1957.[18]

Georges Davydov, the leader of the 1957 French group, felt that despite numerous difficulties and a degree of confusion that he and his charges found trying, the experience in Russia had been a rich and useful one. Like most other intelligent travelers to Russia, Davydov thought that one of the great values of the trip was the opportunity it afforded for casual conversations with ordinary Russians, which, he said, had "helped us to better understand a people, so different from ours in appearance, but so much like us in its deep humanity." Most important of all, of course, was the beneficial effect of the trip from the linguistic point of view.

Although written in tones of polite restraint, Davydov's article conveyed a sense of the wonderment of a cultivated Western European regarding some of the outlandish features of Soviet life and the mystery of Soviet administrative procedure. His party did not receive their Soviet visas until the day of their departure. The "sports camp" where his youngsters spent most of their time was located in an isolated spot. The tent in which they slept was flooded more than once by rain. The heavy Russian food apparently taxed the capacities of French digestive tracts. But all this was worth enduring in the interests of education, and particularly for the contribution such field experience could make toward correcting a situation in which most French teachers of Russian had had no chance to talk to Russians in their native land. After all, as Davydov pointed out, the Russian language students of today would be among the researchers, army officers, and diplomats of tomorrow. Despite the tact displayed by M. Davydov in reporting to his

---

[17] *L'Education Nationale*, Vol. 13, No. 4, January 24, 1957, pp. 5-6.
[18] The French visit to Russia was dealt with by Georges Davydov on pp. 571-577; the Russian visit to France by Jean Triomphe on pp. 578-579.

French colleagues on his trip to Russia, he was, I learned in Paris in December 1958, refused a visa to make another visit. Perhaps one reason for the visa refusal was the fact that his fluent Russian and his Russian-emigrant background aroused Soviet suspicion, but, as is usual in such cases, one can only guess the basis for Soviet action.

In the same issue of *Les Langues Modernes*, Jean Triomphe summed up the results of the visit, by nine Soviet schoolboys and two teachers, to France, which matched the French trip just described, and which resulted from Triomphe's own Russian visit in 1956. The Soviet youths, according to M. Triomphe, spoke very good French. The group began and ended their visit in Paris, but spent most of their time at the Pyrenees vacation center of Bagresis-de-Bigarre. Judging from M. Triomphe's account, the visit was a success from the point of view of visitors and hosts alike. This was indicated, among other ways, by the enthusiastic appraisal of its results made by Madame Ludmilla Dubrovina, First Deputy Minister of Education of the R.S.F.S.R., in a conversation with M. Triomphe in September 1957.

To be sure, Triomphe did note that "unforeseen" delay in the arrival of their Soviet guests disturbed somewhat the meticulously planned schedule arranged for them by top-ranking French educational and cultural figures. He also observed that the Museum of Modern Art in Paris "alarmed" the Soviet youngsters. However, he stressed that, with the help of the Director General of Tourism, the Didier and Larousse publishing houses, the cultural center of the France-U.S.S.R. Society, and several other named institutions, the Russians returned home with a fine collection of books, phonograph records, and documents of all sorts on France. Besides being an interesting, representative episode, the one described by Triomphe was a pioneer venture for, together with a vacation trip led by him to Russia in the summer of 1956, it helped to inaugurate the whole program of Franco-Russian exchanges on the secondary school level.

In 1958 there was another Franco-Soviet exchange of schoolboys, twenty-five French teachers of Russian went to the U.S.S.R., ten French students received three-month scholarships in Russia, and, finally, three French professors of Russian literature were given permission by the Soviet government to go to the U.S.S.R. for scholarly research. While apparently reasonably well-satisfied with this program on the whole, the French authorities concerned with it did regret, according to one private report to me, that the Russians were pressing the French, in negotiations for the expansion of the program in the future, to send specialists on French, rather than Russian, language and literature to the U.S.S.R.[19]

According to reports in Paris newspapers, such as *Figaro*, a UNESCO-sponsored exchange of schoolboys between France and the U.S.S.R. took place in July and August 1958. On each side ten boys took part. The French boys, selected from the Lycées of Nanterre and Enghien, were accompanied by five teachers, while the ten Soviet boys came to France in the company of two of their teachers.

The by-that-time apparently regular sending of French students to the U.S.S.R. for university study continued in 1958-1959, although no numerical data on this matter came to our attention. Also, in the summer of 1958, according to French sources, twenty-five French secondary school teachers of the Russian language spent almost a month in the Soviet Union.

Franco-Soviet exchange traffic remained brisk in 1959; for example, the Moscow Tretyakov Gallery, the Leningrad Museum of Russian Art, and Ilya Ehrenburg, in his capacity as private collector—an interesting touch!—loaned some Marc Chagall canvases to the Musée des Arts Décoratifs for its June show, and in the same month the Pushkin Theater of Leningrad played for five nights at the Sarah Bernhardt International Theater Festival. According to "Genet," writing from Paris in the *New Yorker* for July 11, these "Russian manifestations," during the futile Geneva Conference, "produced an inevitable civilized feeling of optimism, especially among certain French intellectuals and the simple French people, whose interpretations, and consequent trusts, often seem identical."

---

[19] Numerous brief items in Soviet newspapers in 1958 reported on aspects of Franco-Soviet educational exchanges. For example, *Komsomolskaya Pravda* for April 11, 1958, reported attendance by B. M. Firsov, of the U.S.S.R. Committee of Youth Organizations, at the annual conference of the National Union of Students of France, and the same paper for July 22 carried an item on the presence in Moscow of French school children, invited by the R.S.F.S.R. Ministry of Education and the Moscow Department of Education.

Tribulations, but also achievements in many ways similar to those of the French in their effort to "normalize" cultural relations, usually culminating in some sort of formal governmental agreement, were experienced by a number of other Western European nations. Norway and Belgium are interesting examples. Until 1954 and 1955 cultural contacts between Norway and the Soviet Union were sporadic. Most of them were channeled through the Norwegian-Soviet Friendship Association. However, following a visit of the Prime Minister of Norway to the Soviet Union in November 1955, responsible and representative cultural interchanges increased and the role therein of the Norwegian-Soviet Friendship Association diminished. On October 12, 1956, Norway and the Soviet Union signed a cultural agreement, which went into effect in 1957.

As early as March 1953 Soviet women skaters and a Soviet ice hockey team performed in Norway. The Soviet hockey team defeated its Oslo hosts in two games, by scores of 10 to 2 and 8 to 0.[20] In November 1955 a Soviet soccer team defeated a Norwegian team in Oslo by a score of 8 to 0.[21] In February 1956 a Soviet team won the men's World Skating Championship at Oslo.[22] These athletic accomplishments, which were fairly typical, probably gained admiration and even good will for the Soviet sportsmen, particularly in Britain, West Germany, and Scandinavia. Of course, the Soviets did not always win. For example, a Soviet hockey team was defeated by a Swedish team in February 1955 in Stockholm.[23]

A substantial number of exchanges took place between Norway and the Soviet Union in 1956 in most major fields. A Soviet professor of geography delivered some lectures at Oslo University and three Soviet nuclear-energy experts visited Norway in February. In May there was an exchange of actors and theater directors in connection with the Ibsen Theater Festival. The peripatetic Soviet violinist David Oistrakh gave concerts in Bergen and Oslo in May. A Soviet agricultural delegation visited Norway in August 1956. A similar Norwegian delegation was in the Soviet Union in 1955. There were a number of other technical exchanges in

[20] *Pravda*, March 21 and 23, 1953.
[21] *Ibid.*, November 4, 1955.
[22] *Ibid.*, February 13, 1956.
[23] *Ibid.*, February 18, 1955.

keeping with the evident determination of Stalin's successors to avail themselves of the best in Western technology.

There was a very small exchange of students between Norway and the Soviet Union in 1955 and 1956. It was disrupted by the Hungarian events, but was resumed, still on a small scale, in 1958-1959. From data obtained by correspondence with one of the two Norwegian students who were in Russia in 1956, I have the impression that the Norwegians, neither of whom appears to have been a communist sympathizer, were allowed an exceptional degree of freedom of travel, by Soviet standards, and were in every way treated with great cordiality. As of November 1956 two Soviet students had studied in Norway. Like the two Norwegians, they went abroad on fellowships from the host country.

A number of tourist groups were exchanged between the two countries in 1956. These tours were organized by Intourist in cooperation with Norwegian travel agencies, and it was estimated that about 150 persons took part on each side.

A delegation from the Soviet Communist Party Press which was visiting Norway in the early part of November 1956 returned home ahead of schedule at the request of its hosts, following the events in Hungary. Indignation about Hungary was exceptionally keen in the Scandinavian countries, particularly in trade-union circles. Norway, like Switzerland, Holland, and Spain, withdrew from the 1956 Olympic Games. Scheduled ratification of the Norwegian-Soviet cultural agreement did not occur in the Norwegian Parliament. The Danish Parliament also failed to ratify a cultural agreement concluded in 1956.

However, by the fall of 1957 the Soviet press was again able to report a considerable number of athletic and other exchanges with Scandinavian countries. For example, *Pravda Vostoka* for October 13, 1957, reported prominently a visit to Uzbekistan by a delegation of Danish women, headed by a member of the staff of the Danish Ministry of Social Welfare. The Danish women were introduced to, among other persons, members of the "spiritual administration of the Moslems of Central Asia and Kazakhstan." They reportedly expressed satisfaction with the progress made by Uzbek women under the Soviet regime.

Even during the first half of 1957, seven delegations were exchanged between Norway and the Soviet Union, and fourteen between Sweden and the Soviet Union, as well as ten between Denmark and the Soviet Union. These events were among many in Europe and America demonstrating that the conclusion, drawn by the *New Statesman and Nation* of London, on December 15, 1956, that Soviet actions in Hungary had "united the whole world, socialists and anti-socialists" against the Soviet Union had been premature. However, Soviet sources offered considerably less evidence of exchange activity with the Scandinavian countries in 1957 and 1958 than in 1955 and 1956. A Soviet circus troupe did tour Sweden in May 1958, and in the same year a number of scientific and educational exchanges took place. During the 1958-1959 academic year two Norwegian students apparently studied in Russia. No data were available on student exchanges with other Scandinavian countries for that year.

In Belgium, and to a lesser degree in Holland, Soviet folk dancers and other entertainers seem to have enjoyed exceptional success. Belgian-Soviet exchanges of delegations increased from eleven in 1954 to thirty-eight in 1956, but fell to only five in the first half of 1957. The signing of a Soviet-Belgian "agreement on cultural cooperation" was the feature news in *Pravda* for October 26, 1956. Because of events in Hungary, however, this agreement was denounced by the Belgian Parliament.[24]

Until the signing of a Soviet-German Federal Republic cultural accord on May 30, 1959, neither the West German nor the Italian governments had made cultural agreements with the Soviet Union. There was a considerable amount of cultural, scientific, and athletic exchange between these countries and Russia, however. In addition, a considerable number of important international scientific and academic conferences, in which the Soviet Union participated, were held in these two countries. For example, as we noted in Chapter v, some thirty Soviet scholars attended the Tenth International Congress of Historians at Rome in September 1955. Nineteen Soviet specialists took part in the XXIV International Congress of Orientalists in Munich from August 28 to September 4, 1957. While the Soviet historians made a poor impression in Rome, Soviet Orientalists made a good impression in Munich by

---

[24] *Lettre de Belgique*, No. 44, 1956, p. 43; No. 45, 1956, p. 11.

presenting scholarly papers of high quality and, on the whole, refraining from making propagandistic statements.[25] Although the Soviet exchange traffic with Italy was quite heavy, and in the first half of 1957 actually topped that with Great Britain, it was viewed with mistrust by noncommunist Italian circles and received extremely scant reporting in the conservative Italian newspapers, such as *Corriere della Sera* of Milan. This attitude resulted in part from the tendency of the Soviet embassy in Italy and the Italian Association for Cultural Relations with the U.S.S.R. to exploit cultural exchanges for one-sidely political and even, apparently, for intelligence purposes.[26] As we have already noted, Soviet "tourists" who visited Italy and Germany made an energetic and probably at least partly successful effort to demonstrate expert knowledge and deep appreciation for the classical art, music, and literature of these two countries. Beginning in 1958 the Soviet tour ship plying between Leningrad and Odessa crossed Italian ports off its route, after tourist visas had been refused by Italy, apparently because of Italian fear of possible Soviet influence on the spring 1958 elections.

Perhaps the most spectacular event thus far in Soviet-West German cultural relations was the game in Moscow in August 1955 between a picked national Soviet team and the world champion soccer team. Eighty thousand fans packed the Dynamo Stadium to watch the Russians win by a score of 3 to 2 and hundreds of Western German fans who had come to see the game received a friendly welcome. There were many other popular and successful athletic contests between the two countries, among them the 10 to 10 tie in a match between Soviet and West German boxing teams at Hamburg in March 1957. Athletic competition with the Russians had become so popular in West Germany by 1957 that Chancellor Adenauer considered it desirable, during the election campaign, to rescind a ban which had been imposed on visas for Soviet soccer teams.

In the years after the establishment of diplomatic relations be-

[25] On this Munich conference see, for example, *Sueddeutsche Zeitung*, August 31, September 1, 1957, and the excellent article by Nicholas Poppe in the October 1957 *Bulletin of the Institute for the Study of the USSR*.

[26] For some interesting detail on the situation in Italy, see Evans, *Worldwide Communist Propaganda Activities*, pp. 140-141.

tween West Germany and the Soviet Union in 1955, normal cultural contacts, which had previously been almost nonexistent, developed fairly rapidly but they remained subject to the vicissitudes of the tense and mistrustful political situation in which the Soviet Union, West Germany, and other Soviet orbit states, and the United States found themselves with regard to such problems as German rearmament and reunification. Moscow, by sending highly competent and tactful specialists and intellectuals to West Germany, and by cordial hospitality toward and appreciation of the talents and persons of West German visitors to Russia, probably succeeded in breaking down some of the anti-Russian prejudices so deeply ingrained in the minds of most West Germans. On the other side, some West German officials and experts, particularly specialists on the Soviet Union, became convinced that much was to be gained for West German interests by a quiet and careful expansion of contacts between West German and Soviet artists, scholars, and scientists. This point of view found public expression in a series of articles published by the best-known German expert on Russia, Klaus Mehnert, in the influential Stuttgart weekly *Christ und Welt*, after his return from a long journey in Russia and China. In 1958 a delegation of high-ranking Soviet youth leaders toured West German universities and reported their very negative impressions in several issues of *Komsomolskaya Pravda* in April. A German student group visited Russia in June. During 1958 Soviet soccer and other athletic teams played German teams both in Russia and in Germany.

The cultural "accord" signed in Bonn in May 1959 between the German Federal Republic and the U.S.S.R. was based on agreement expressed in a communiqué of April 28, 1958, looking toward a cultural pact. Somewhat more detailed than the Anglo-Soviet agreement mentioned earlier, it closely resembled the British agreement, although it provided for initial exchange of ten, rather than twenty, graduate students, for example, on both sides, and, unlike the Soviet-British agreement, included athletic exchanges. Interesting features of the accord were its provisions for exchanges of exhibitions of scientific books, for the sending of a German modern architecture exhibit to Russia in return for a Soviet show on applied Russian folk art, and for exchanges of elementary and secondary school textbooks, syllabi, et cetera. Implementation of the program, which covered the years 1959 and 1960, was left to the Soviet State Committee for Cultural Relations and the Bonn Central Exchange Office.

The accord envisaged, certainly, a considerable expansion of Soviet-German cultural trafficking. In student exchange, for example, even the modest ten-ten trade planned for the first year compared very favorably with the 1958-1959 figure, based on United States official sources, of three West German students in Russia and, so far as was known, no Russians in the Federal Republic. Also, like the Anglo-Soviet agreement, the accord regularized exchange and thus, as the West German publication *Diplomatische Korrespondenz* put it, provided for a precisely defined, limited program, which would assure a "balancing" in the interests of both parties. *Diplomatische Korrespondenz*, quoted in the official Bonn press bulletin, also noted that the accord could not, in the nature of things, be of the "classic" type such as can be made between two partners with a common mentality, where it is possible to draw a clear line between "culture" and "political influence."[27]

Heightened international tension after 1956 and the manifestations of unrest among segments of Soviet youth led to some tightening of surveillance over the less formal kinds of contacts between Soviet citizens and Western European visitors, but in terms of numbers of contacts, exchanges continued to expand in 1958 and 1959. While there were more Asian students in Moscow than ever before in the fall of 1957, there were fewer from Western Europe than in 1956. This contraction did not last long and, as we have pointed out, in connection, for example, with British-Soviet relations, a very promising start was made toward development of types of exchange relationships which could bring substantial benefits to all of the interested parties. On the other hand, the promises of intimacy and spontaneity, held out by certain trends in the period before Hungary and the campaign against "revisionism" which followed, faded after 1956. A rise in the level of international tensions was the most obvious reason for the return to

[27] The text of the accord, as well as the material cited from *Diplomatische Korrespondenz*, is contained in *Bulletin des Presse und Informationsamtes der Bundesregierung*, No. 96/S.933, Bonn, June 2, 1959.

rigidity, but other factors could be discerned. It had become apparent to the Soviet leaders that when relations between Soviet students and, for example, French exchangees were allowed to move toward informality, all sorts of difficulties could arise. Even a moderate relaxation of controls permitted a few intellectually curious Western European students—and also a handful of Russian-speaking diplomats—to obtain and disseminate information regarding social and political attitudes of Soviet youths which the Kremlin regarded as embarrassing. Then too, the aftermath of Hungary, and the results of the bold experiment of exposing thousands of young Russians to contacts with Westerners at the 1957 Youth Festival apparently stirred some uneasiness about the ability of Soviet youth to resist the appeals of "decadent, bourgeois culture." Perhaps also, the Kremlin found itself losing some of its initial advantages of greater previous experience and tighter organization for the political exploitation of culture contacts, and Western Europeans, contrariwise, became less fearful of contacts and more confident that despite ideological cleavages within their countries their way of life had many attractions for the heavily indoctrinated but impressionable Russians. By 1958 Russians no longer seemed quite so exotic to Europeans as they had in 1953 or 1954. The vigorous performances of Soviet dancers, athletes, and scientists still commanded attention and respect, however, and Soviet military power probably seemed as awesome as ever. But Western Europeans felt, if one may judge by correspondence and conversations with some of them, that the West had nothing to fear from full familiarity and mutual disclosure of ideas and conditions. The real problem, as our informants saw it, was one of persuading Moscow that progress toward informal, unpublicized, and effective working arrangements among, for example, scientists or educational administrators or legal scholars in the West and their colleagues in the U.S.S.R. could be beneficial to both sides. The experience was too short, probably, and the evidence too inconclusive, to draw firm conclusions about the results or probable future trends of Soviet-West European exchanges in the 1953-1959 period, but the record on the whole seemed rather encouraging. Some progress had been made toward establishing a more normal pattern of relationships among the various competent, interested, and responsible elements concerned than had existed in the Stalin era. European governments, professional groups, and individual intellectuals and scholars were taking a practical and sensible view of the future prospects and potential results of exchanges. They appeared to feel that good progress was being made, but that future achievements would be difficult and slow. Many were pleased that some useful exchanges of a largely technical and functional nature, yielding on both sides useful information and, incidentally, reducing mutual ignorance and prejudices had occurred. There was hope that as a by-product of such exchanges there would come a gradual growth of mutual understanding and perhaps even of good will.

Of course, the Kremlin also gained, from its point of view, from the "normalization" of Russian-Western European cultural relations. The new pattern, perhaps, facilitated Soviet information-gathering. The opportunity to display the best features of Soviet culture under favorable circumstances, and the tendency of people in nontotalitarian societies to associate even a limited increase in face-to-face contacts with friendly personal contacts tended to reinforce Soviet "peace" propaganda. However, Kremlin reluctance to plunge very deeply into the sea of intimacy, and the considered judgment of sophisticated Europeans that the open society stood to gain from relaxation of international communications barriers indicated that old Europe had little need to fear, and, indeed, might benefit by increasingly close acquaintance with the new, still somewhat inchoate civilization taking shape in Soviet Russia, provided that care be taken to prevent exchanges from becoming merely instruments of Soviet propaganda. Terms of the cultural accords concluded in 1959 and 1960 between Western European nations and Russia indicated continued development of the pattern herein described. Such nervous Soviet actions as removal from a British book exhibition in Moscow late in 1959 of numerous books, including works on Hitler by leading historians, clearly indicated how far Russia still had to go before she could feel secure in a free exchange of ideas.

CHAPTER IX

PATTERNS OF SOVIET-AMERICAN
EXCHANGE

T HE pattern of Russian-American cultural interchanges and indeed the total pattern of communications between the two superpowers is a complex and, in only too many ways, an obscure and contradictory one. It reflects the mingled sentiments of hostility, hope, and missionary zeal which inspire the interacting official policies of Moscow and Washington. It also mirrors the differences of tradition, organization, and approach between the monolithic, hierarchical Soviet state, with its enforced homogeneity of ideas, and the loosely organized and, to Soviet eyes, almost chaotic pattern of American democracy. The governments of the two countries share a desire to utilize cultural exchanges to exert influence on the "ruling circles" and the "people" of the "other side" in the world-wide power struggle. Each, in some degree perhaps, entertains hopes of modifying the internal political regime of the other and each, to a probably controlling degree, is aware that the two systems must, willy-nilly, look forward to an indefinite period of competitive coexistence.

Because they fear uncontrolled, spontaneous, people-to-people communication, particularly when it involves contact with a rich, free society like that of the United States, the Russian leaders have devoted impressive effort and skill to outwitting their American opponents in the battle of wits involved in cultural exchanges between two mutually mistrustful but eagerly curious peoples. To their task the Russian rulers bring a rich experience in political stagecraft. Moreover, Moscow can with little difficulty send the best Russian dancers, the ablest scientists, or the finest Soviet athletes to America and it can usually rest assured that these cadres will carry out, with a fairly high degree of discipline, whatever mission is assigned to them, whether it be one of ingratiation, vilification, or simple observation. Similarly, the Kremlin can see to it that hospitality is lavished upon visiting American Congressmen, businessmen, or scientists, and, to a considerable degree, it can control even the physical environment in which the occasionally vodka-happy but more often merely uninformed visitors pass their travel time. Surveying the illusions sometimes created by the systematic planning of persuasion, noncommunist students may be driven to ask themselves in irritation and even in indignation whether confused amateurs can learn to cope with disciplined professionals.

This is not to suggest that the Kremlin hopes in the foreseeable future to convert more than a handful of Americans to its brand of socialism. Its propaganda objectives vis-à-vis Americans lie predominantly in the areas of ingratiation and "anaesthetization," as well as in those of distraction, disorientation, confusion, and concealment. These tactics are, in turn, subordinated to the grand design of morally and physically disarming the United States. Touchy issues are usually avoided by Soviet representatives in official conversations with Americans. The blurring rather than the sharpening of issues is indeed the Soviet objective in many of these encounters. At the same time, the Kremlin seeks, wherever possible, to sap the faith of Americans in the foreign policy of the American government and in all American political parties except the communist. To this end unwary Americans are inveigled, if possible, into endorsements of Soviet views on such subjects as "peace" or "disarmament" or "cultural exchange." In connection with this last term, it is a regrettable fact that by constant reiteration of their devotion to it the Soviets have succeeded in persuading many persons, inside and outside of Russia, that the United States obstructs cultural exchanges. The Kremlin's skittishness about such matters as allowing Soviet students, particularly if not drawn from the upper ranks of the official youth leadership, to come to America, is carefully covered up. Khrushchev's warnings, reiterated even after his return to Russia from America—via China—in October 1959, that the U.S.S.R. cannot allow Soviet people's minds to be "poisoned" by unrestricted admission of American books, films, et cetera are, of course, played down in Soviet statements for American audiences.

In general, efforts are made to convince Americans that they have nothing to fear and much to gain by accepting Soviet views on international issues. Bland assurances that simple good will can settle all international problems have bulked large in statements made by Soviet officials in recent years to visiting American delegations. Even when such declarations, presented at length and often widely publicized, have little impact on those to whom they are immediately addressed, they can consume much of the time that might be devoted to gathering objective information about Soviet realities. Moreover, travelers whose heads are crammed with Soviet slogans, the demagogy of which they are unaware, may, upon their return home, act as unconscious carriers of Soviet propaganda.

It is partly for such reasons that one is inclined to attribute less significance to the assurances frequently made by Soviet scholars and men of letters to their American colleagues that the first step toward better international relations is mutual "understanding." This is the sort of statement which, if made by a polite and charming guest—or host—after a good dinner, can work wonders on some Americans; one cannot be so sure of effects of such blandness on Russians. Probably it has little effect, but we cannot be sure.

There is not as yet, and cannot, so long as the United States remains a free society, be on the American side of Soviet-American exchanges such uniformity of strategy and coordination of execution as is practiced by the Kremlin and its agents.

There have often been differences between stated American official policy regarding contacts with communist countries and the opinions thereon of important segments of public opinion. Prominent labor leaders, including, for example, George Meany and to a lesser degree Walter Reuther, have tended to take the position that Soviet-American exchanges are both detrimental to American national interests and morally reprehensible. Groups holding to this view, which is strongly supported by some religious circles, and by many organizations of anticommunist political refugees, argue that contacts with communists lull Americans into complacency about Soviet objectives, facilitate Soviet espionage, and discourage anticommunists behind the Iron Curtain.

By contrast, some businessmen, many Protestant clergymen, and probably most American educators and natural scientists believe that individual Americans, and also American national interests, can benefit by first-hand contacts between qualified Americans and Soviet colleagues in their various fields of endeavor. A strong statement in support of this position was made some time ago to me by a scientist friend, who asserted that cultural exchange is the only alternative to mutual annihilation. Not only do Americans differ, sometimes with their government and often with one another, regarding the desirability of cultural exchange, but they obviously differ widely regarding its consequences and potentialities. And, outside of the State Department, very few Americans have devoted any systematic thought to the strategy and tactics of cultural diplomacy.

Even within the executive branch of the government, serious differences of opinion regarding cultural policy have been reported from time to time in the daily press. It is clear that throughout the post-Stalin period President Eisenhower and the East-West Contacts Staff of the Department of State have favored a vigorous program of cultural exchanges with Russia, while other elements of government, including a few militant members of Congress and of security units within and outside of the State Department, have at times sought to restrict the program to a bare minimum or even to achieve total closure. The fragmentation and relative lack of coordination characteristic of American administrative methods can sometimes result in puzzlingly inconsistent behavior. For example, within less than one month, in 1957, we learned of the use by American authorities, in one case, of surveillance methods over Soviet visitors reminiscent of the most obnoxious Stalinist techniques, but, in another case, a Soviet scientist had traveled apparently unaccompanied by either Soviet or American officials to a leading American university where he enjoyed a perfectly normal visit with a number of colleagues in his special field. There is, at times, some inconsistency in American official public statements regarding cultural relations with communist states. President Eisenhower's warm interest in doing everything possible to develop such relations has been referred to. One is interested, therefore, to note that Christian Herter, at the time Undersecretary of State, in a speech in San Francisco on November 6, 1957, threw cold water on the possibility of developing cultural understanding "between people who deify science and those whose lives are attuned to religious principles."[1]

[1] Department of State *Bulletin*, Vol. XXXVII, No. 961, November 25, 1957, p. 832.

As we have tried to make clear, and as we hope will be confirmed more fully in this chapter than in preceding ones, the advantages enjoyed by the communist rulers over the American government, the numerous private American education and other competent organizations concerned, and the people of the United States in the cultural-exchange field are in many ways more apparent than real and perhaps more transient than durable. To the extent that Americans live up to the values inherent in their own democratic traditions, they enjoy the precious advantages of freedom of personal judgment, freedom of movement, and, above all, freedom of expression, which of course astonishes and impresses many Soviet citizens. It is the universal human desire for at least some degree of freedom, thwarted but not destroyed in a regimented society, which can, at least in the absence of brute countervailing force, upset all the calculations of the Soviet master manipulators, as the events in Hungary and Poland in 1956 and their echoes ever since among Soviet students once again reminded both the Kremlin and the world.

By hard work and careful planning the Soviet leaders can contrive to offset and even counterbalance the potential advantages of their democratic opponents. By shielding all but a selected, indoctrinated handful of their subjects from the contagious influence of personal freedom, by implanting in their minds negative stereotypes about "Wall Street," unemployment, lynchings of Negroes, American "intervention" in the internal affairs of foreign countries, and the like, and by presenting to American visitors to Russia an attractive picture of Soviet life, the communists hope to win the battle of ideas. If Americans believe that the progress, welfare, and safety of mankind depend upon freedom of communication and assurances to people everywhere of access to information about the forces that shape their lives, they cannot be satisfied with their present inability to communicate effectively with the peoples of the U.S.S.R.

Our ultimate objective should be equal freedom for Russians and Americans to know, to understand, and to judge one another's culture, system of government, and way of life. Until this goal is attained, even the most intelligent and well-meaning people in both countries, and especially in the Soviet Union, will remain victims of propaganda myths and misconceptions. But of course we must realize that, as long as the Soviet rulers feel that their security and survival depend upon continued existence of an elaborate system of controls over information, they will continue to be willing to devote, as they have now for several years, greater resources to such activities as jamming American radio broadcasts than the United States does to sending out its own radio broadcasts. It is possible that insulation of the Soviet public from uncensored, unprocessed information about life in the non-Soviet world is more important to the Kremlin even than maintaining its grip on, for example, East Germany. Certainly the controls will not be abandoned quickly. However, it is likely that the rather zigzag tendency to relax them will continue as Soviet Russia becomes a stronger, more advanced, and more stable state.

Because it considers that the stakes are high, the Kremlin plays the international public-relations game with suave but deadly seriousness. Some Americans, serene in their belief that democracy is an infinitely better system of life than communism, are prone to forget that the advantages of freedom can mean little to those who are denied knowledge of them. There is, in the American-Soviet confrontation of casualness with grim purposefulness, a threat that the well-meaning but relatively uncommitted competitor may lose the contest by default. In the pages that follow we shall see, together with evidence of a salutary American impact on some Russians in some Soviet-American exchanges of persons, evidence, in other cases, of unfortunate failure by Americans effectively to meet the challenge posed by the Soviet version of cultural diplomacy.

In other instances, happily, we find evidence of a mutual desire, particularly in meetings of American and Soviet physicians, engineers, and natural scientists, to maximize the benefits which can accrue to both sides in honest exchange of expert knowledge and skills. Unfortunately, while mutuality of interests is a major factor in Soviet-American exchanges and one that will grow in importance if contacts continue to develop, the Soviet political leaders, by whose conceptions the total Soviet program is guided, have displayed little evidence that they have moved, since the death of Stalin or even since Khrushchev's American visit, toward a philosophy of "live and let live." In such a pattern hospitality becomes a political technique, violinists are soldiers, and acts of communication are moves in a war of nerves.

Many examples could be cited of what seems like communist unfairness, by American standards, but probably appears to the Kremlin as the legitimate enhancement of state interests. It is no secret, to touch again on the problems involved in Soviet and American distribution in the United States and the U.S.S.R. of official magazines in one another's language, that *Amerika* is more popular in Russia than *USSR* is in this country. Despite its restrained tone and style, *Amerika* enjoys among ordinary Russians something of the same fascination as Sears Roebuck catalogues have long held for goods-starved Soviet citizens. But, judging from numerous conversations we have had with recent visitors to the U.S.S.R. and with other informed sources, it would be an understatement to report that Soyuzpechat, the official Soviet distribution agency, has not displayed enthusiasm for the dissemination of *Amerika* to the interested Soviet public.

It is apparently accessible to far fewer Russians than its regular printing of 50,000 copies and its evident popularity would suggest might be the case. In contrast, *USSR* stands in big, conspicuous piles on every major newsstand in New Haven, for example.

Irked by slow sales of *USSR*, at least in the first months of its United States debut, the Soviet authorities created numerous obstacles to the availability of *Amerika* to Soviet citizens. In several instances reported to me by recent travelers to Russia, copies of *Amerika* have been put on display in places where they could be seen easily by parties of American visitors, only to disappear immediately after the departure of the foreigners for whose benefit they were apparently displayed. In respect to this segment of the Soviet-American exchange picture, however, as in the whole process, one should restrain the temptation to generalize. Together with obstructionism, there has been on the part of the Soviet authorities a considerable measure of correctness in carrying on the distribution of *Amerika*. On our visits to Russia in November 1958 and July and August 1959 we again observed evidence of this mixture of motives and policies in respect to *Amerika*.

Somewhat similar problems exist in the area of exchange of

motion pictures. Moscow has usually produced more talk than action about this matter. While the difficulties inherent in dealings between a government monopoly on the one side and a number of competing private firms on the other have played their inevitable part, the main difficulty seems to have been Kremlin sensitivity regarding the eagerness of Soviet citizens to see Hollywood films and the more modest attraction of Soviet films for American audiences. Nevertheless, even in this difficult field there has lately been some evidence of progress toward a mutually satisfactory bargain.

In view of the foregoing, one approaches the problems and potentialities of Soviet-American exchanges with a mixture of faith, hope, and patience.

Our position is one which is not likely to meet with the approval either of the timidly suspicious or of the naïvely optimistic. It is based upon faith in man's intelligence and good will, if given access to adequate knowledge, to solve international problems, but it also recognizes the obstacles to international understanding which arise from conflicts of national interest, as well as from ignorance, prejudice, and ideological and cultural differences. This outlook, which is fortunately shared by many Americans inside and outside of government, as well as by many educated Soviet citizens, recognizes that the beneficial consequences of communication, if undertaken in good faith, may be more important than the immediate and obvious negative consequences. It does not regard exchanges as a panacea but it rejects the "hard-boiled" view that they are of no value.

Soviet-American exchanges can be divided into two broad major categories: technical and political. Of course, the technical and the political ingredients are closely intermingled, perhaps in the majority of cases. The Soviet leadership probably considered that the mission of, for example, the agricultural delegation which it sent to the United States in 1955 was one both of technological reconnaissance and of indirect ideological persuasion and suggestion. In many Soviet-American exchanges, however, either the political or the technical element has been clearly dominant.

Examples of preponderantly political exchanges of persons are the visit of seven Soviet journalists to the United States in 1955 or, on the other side, the visits to the Soviet Union in 1955 and 1957 of William Randolph Hearst, Jr. Exchanges, the purpose of which is observation of political institutions, such as the exchange of election observers in 1956 and 1958, upon which we have already commented, can be classified as either technical or political, or both, depending on the aspects thereof in which one is interested.

One could assign to the political-ideological category all exchanges of clergymen between the two countries, although some American clergymen who have taken part in such activities could legitimately point out that, as far as they were concerned, the purpose was the promotion of peace, good will, and other mutually beneficial objectives. While this position toward their visits is taken by most prominent private American citizens who travel to the U.S.S.R., there can be little doubt that the Soviet authorities regard such visits as highly political in nature.

Of course, the Soviet authorities try, as a rule, to extract the maximum political advantage out of all acts of visitation, whatever their special field, personnel, or direction may be, or at least to minimize any negative political consequences that may result. When, in August and September 1958, and again in June and July 1959, Yale University students and recent Yale graduates astonished and delighted Soviet citizens in Moscow, Leningrad, Odessa, and other cities by their fine singing of Russian folk songs—obviously political "Soviet" songs were avoided—the Soviet authorities were confronted by a problem that may have baffled them a bit. The "Yale minstrels" attracted so much attention and succeeded, sometimes by evading the ministrations of Intourist, in spreading so much exuberant good will and so many novel notions that, on occasion, they caused some perturbation among Soviet authorities. In addition to a largely unsuccessful attempt, exercised, however, with more tact and finesse than is usually displayed by the Soviet security authorities, to confine the Yale tourists—most of whom, especially in the second year's group, spoke Russian well—within "guided tour" channels, the principal tactic adopted to deal with them by the Soviet authorities was that of attempting to convince them, and as many Soviet citizens as possible, that the relatively high degree of freedom of action allowed them was proof that freedom in general prevailed in the U.S.S.R., and was evidence of communist devotion to peace and the cause of cultural exchange.

This Soviet tactic of "rolling with the punch" was probably less successful in the case of the somewhat brash but bright and remarkably well-prepared Yale students than it usually is. A member of the group told me that the freedom permitted them, for ulterior purposes, he felt, by the Soviet authorities was a façade. In support of this interpretation he cited much evidence, including the fact that Intourist discouraged all efforts to get in touch with university students or faculties, except in so far as this occurred either in street meetings or by unauthorized, but in a number of instances highly rewarding, entry into the buildings of educational institutions, when some fascinating conversations occurred with Soviet students and educators. One of these semiclandestine visits involved a conversation between American students and a self-styled "Chekist"—a traditional Soviet term for a secret police officer—who finally betrayed his amazement at the boldness of American behavior by asking, "Is it really true that in America you don't have to carry documents?" The fact that the Yale singers were granted visas again in 1959, though after a long delay, may have indicated Kremlin confidence—or a desire not to do anything to spoil the atmosphere which the Soviet authorities were trying to build up in connection with the Soviet-American exchange of exhibitions in 1959—and an effort to distract attention from their threats to Berlin. Perhaps such trips can occur annually.

The "Yale minstrels," at least in 1958, were invited into many Soviet homes and they established intimate contacts with a number of Soviet musicians. Scores of Soviet citizens asked members of the group to correspond with them. However, there were also indications, of the kind familiar to previous travelers, that some Soviet citizens who met them had, or were caused to have, second thoughts about pursuing the acquaintance, however brief and casual. One heard in interviews with the Yale boys the old story of broken appointments and even of denial of previously established identity, or, sad to relate, of disappearance of Soviet citizens with whom contacts had been made. Discovery of these seamier sides of Soviet reality was, perhaps, one of the useful aspects of this illuminating experience.

Another aspect of the Yale singers' experience that was, in its way, salutary was their discovery that, while many of the Soviet students they met voiced grievances, particularly regarding irritations in conveniences and limitations in Soviet life, almost all of them seemed to support quite solidly the official Soviet condemnation of United States foreign policy. The young Americans learned from arguments about Lebanon and Formosa, and, to a lesser degree, Little Rock, modern art, and a host of other topics, some of the difficulties of communicating with the representatives of a closed system. Even in the area of international politics, however, there was some "give" in the position of some Soviet youths, at least a few of whom admitted that Soviet conduct in Hungary had been shameful.

To be sure, such admissions did not come from the lips of "activists," sprinklings of whom were normally present or appeared among the eager, curious crowds who were everywhere attracted by the singing tourists. Sometimes the minority of political "activists" in crowds were shouted down by their fellow-citizens, who wanted to hear what the Americans had to say. Usually they did not stay to the end of the six- or eight-hour conversations that followed the informal street concerts given by the "minstrels."

Among the interesting conversations reported by this unusually perceptive group was one with an Intourist guide who told them that they were the first group of Americans with whom the guide felt it was possible "to talk." This episode reflected the good impression that can be made by visitors equipped not only with command of Russian but also with a knowledge of Russian history, art, literature, and even of the specific historical monuments of Moscow and Leningrad, which was, in some cases, better than that of their Intourist guides.

In 1959 the Yale group numbered thirty, instead of only eighteen, and included two Negroes. The latter, who were talented jazz musicians, apparently scored a sensational hit with an impromptu concert which they gave for students of the Chaikovski Conservatory in Moscow. From what we learned of the preparations, linguistic and otherwise, made by the Yale boys for their second trip and judging by press accounts of its progress, they acquitted themselves even better in 1959 than in 1958. While the relative official leniency and public cordiality displayed toward the Yale singers was encouraging, it also served once again to highlight the difference, in Kremlin eyes, between tourists and those who wish to take a longer, deeper look at Soviet reality.

Moreover, there was evidence that, as might have been expected, police agents were assigned to "tail" the singers on their second tour, and apparently they were also subjected to a somewhat greater amount of organized heckling than in 1958.

The behavior of the official Soviet youth delegation, already mentioned briefly in an earlier chapter, that visited America in July and August 1958—in exchange, be it noted, not with the Yale tourists but with a broadly representative American delegation, organized under the auspices of the Council on Student Travel and led by Professor Ralph T. Fisher, Jr., of the University of Illinois—was in stark contrast to the breezy informality of the Yale and other American students in Russia.

Perhaps one motive for the sometimes-insulting behavior of some leaders of this group was fear of giving the Kremlin even the slightest reason to doubt their complete devotion to Soviet doctrine. Some competent Americans who came in frequent contact with the professional youth leaders included in this delegation interpreted their actions as an attempt to build a record which could, if the Kremlin so desired, be used to justify discontinuance of further youth exchanges. Their behavior probably can best be accounted for as an exemplification of the kind of offensive-defensive pattern to which Soviet communists commonly resort in what, for motives often puzzling to noncommunists, they regard as conflict situations. It should be pointed out that not all members of the group shared their leaders' militancy, but those members of the Soviet delegation whose outlook was that of genuine students, rather than of student bureaucrats, apparently played a subordinate part in the activities of this expedition which included such oddities, according to first-hand reports, as pejorative remarks by at least one of its members about the quality of the meat served to him and his colleagues at meals.

The belligerency and even the bad manners occasionally displayed by some of Mr. Khrushchev's emissaries reflected an aspect of basic Soviet behavior to which, in this book, we have not had occasion to pay very much attention. While for most of the purposes of cultural diplomacy, in a period of coexistence, the tactics of dissimulation are more appropriate than those of bluster and intimidation, it must be remembered that, to a disturbing degree, the underlying attitude of the bolshevik professional revolutionary still remains that of the militant propagator of the "truth," whose mission, in international relations, is not one of studying and understanding "alien" culture, but of discrediting "bourgeois" culture as part of the task of paving the way for the "re-education" of the still un-Sovietized majority of mankind.

The other side of this particular coin is that some features, apparently, of the program arranged in this country for the 1958 Soviet youth delegation left something to be desired from the point of view of tact and appropriateness. It was, for example, a dubious decision to bring Soviet visitors into somewhat provocative contact with Russian political emigrants. Also, as has been true in other cases, this major Soviet youth group was, perhaps, not given so much free time or opportunity to meet American students casually as would have been desirable, although the complaints to this effect made by its leaders were of an exaggerated and unfair character. Moreover, it seems likely that the attitude of some American journalists who came in contact with the Soviet youth and student delegation was not calculated to put the visitors at their ease. Planning was better for the 1959 exchange.

Many important, mutually profitable American-Soviet technical exchanges occurred in the post-Stalin years, particularly as the East-West Contacts Staff of the State Department stepped up its activities in 1956 and 1957. The flow of such exchanges became so rapid after the conclusion of the January 1958 exchange agreement that only a small fraction of them can be even mentioned in this chapter.[2]

Among the outstanding Soviet-American technical exchanges the most widely publicized of all, perhaps, was that of Soviet and American agricultural specialists and, on the Soviet side particularly,

---

[2] Technical and other types of exchanges, not only between the U.S. and Russia, but also with other communist countries, are listed in the unclassified "Report on the East-West Exchange Program," released by the East-West Contacts Staff in September 1958, and covering, mainly, the period February 15-July 1, 1958.

of agricultural administrators in 1955. Because of its significance as a pioneer venture and the propaganda aura in which it was enveloped, we shall presently deal in some detail with various aspects of this exchange of "farmers." The very important exchange of automation engineers in 1955 and 1956, and the exchanges of steel executives and experts in 1958, as well as the visit to Russia by the United States Electric Power Group in August 1958 were among other high lights of the technical-exchange program. The American Steel and Iron Ore Mining Delegation to the Soviet Union was headed by Mr. Edward L. Ryerson, director and former chairman of the board of the Inland Steel Company, and included high-ranking executives of United States Steel, Bethlehem Steel, and other major steel concerns, as well as such nonindustry experts as Professor M. Gardner Clark, of Cornell University.[3]

The American Electric Power Group was headed by Mr. Walker L. Cisler, president of the Detroit Edison Company, and included other electric utility executives, as well as Philip D. Reed, chairman of the finance committee of the General Electric Company, and Gwilym A. Price, chairman of the board of the Westinghouse Electric Corporation. It must have been arresting, and probably it was salutary, for Soviet electric power leaders to be told by a businessman of Mr. Reed's stature that, contrary to the Soviet propaganda stereotype, large American corporations made much smaller profits on military contracts than on normal civilian business, and much preferred the latter.

Names like those of Philip Reed and Gwilym Price, as well as those of other prominent industrialists whom we shall have occasion to mention, as well as those of hundreds that cannot be mentioned for want of space, suggest that the top leaders in Soviet and American industry have, once again, but to a greater degree than in the period prior to World War II, acquired at least a formal personal acquaintance with one another. The same can be said of leading personnel on both sides in most major fields, and perhaps particularly in the natural sciences, especially those relating to medicine.

[3] A general report by the American steel delegation, with a foreword by Benjamin F. Fairless, entitled "Steel in the Soviet Union," was published by the American Iron and Steel Institute in 1958.

As early as June 1957 the East-West Contacts Staff of the Department of State had organized thirteen scientific, technical, and cultural exchanges between the Soviet Union and America, in which seventy-three American and fifty-seven Soviet representatives had taken part. From mid-1957 on, organized exchanges became such a common feature of Soviet-American relations that they ceased to attract much attention or to be regarded as novel or strange experiences, though, of course, the pattern of communication that they represented remained a peculiar one, by American standards. In the period February 15-July 1, 1958, to cite one on which fairly complete official American data are available, some twenty major scientific and technical exchanges, or one-way visits, usually involving reciprocity, took place between the two countries, and in some of these, especially on the American side, fairly large delegations were involved. During the first half of 1958, according to United States government sources, about four hundred Soviet scientists, experts, and other nonofficial personnel visited this country, a figure more than six times as large as that for the same period of 1957.

We have interviewed and corresponded with participants in dozens of Soviet-American technical and scientific exchanges and they have, with a near unanimity that is impressive, reported that, although political attitudes and security regulations on both sides often exert an inhibiting effect, the exchanges, on the whole, have been of a genuinely professional, scientific character and have been not only mutually useful but cordial and pleasant. As a rule, both the Soviet and the American press report the primarily scientific and technical exchanges less conspicuously and more objectively than they report the more political exchanges. Some very important exchanges of this character are not reported at all by the press in one country or the other or are reported so inconspicuously that they pass virtually unnoticed. It is clear that both governments very wisely have attempted to carry on these mutually useful exchanges with a minimum of publicity. Naturally, of course, this policy increases the difficulties of the researcher.

In 1957, and to a conspicuously greater degree in 1958 and 1959, Soviet-American exchange travel by educators and educational administrators, especially by American pilgrims to sputnik-land, bulked increasingly large in the total pattern. These visits by educational professionals, of course, overlapped to some degree with those made by scholars in the arts and sciences concerned less with pedagogy and more with disciplinary content. The ice was broken in September 1957 when Professors Gerald Read, of Kent State College, Ohio, and William W. Brickman, of the School of Education of New York University, visited the U.S.S.R. to make advance arrangements for a visit in 1958 by several score members of the Comparative Education Society which took place, as planned, in September and October 1958.

In October 1957 Kenneth Holland, president of the Institute of International Education, went to Moscow to discuss possibilities for Soviet-American exchange of students, a matter regarding which a number of American scholars had already talked to Soviet officials and in which the fall of 1958 was to see encouraging progress. Mr. Holland also delivered a lecture to a group of members of the Academy of Sciences of the U.S.S.R., which was briefly noted in *Pravda* for October 12, 1957. He thus joined a small but growing band of American scholars and opinion leaders who have addressed this august body in recent years.[4]

The trickle of Soviet-American educational exchanges became a small torrent in 1958 and 1959. Besides the trip by members of the Comparative Education Society, in which a prominent role was played by such leading American specialists on Soviet education as Dr. George Z. F. Bereday, of Teachers College, Columbia University, and William H. E. Johnson, of the University of Pittsburgh, other American missions deserve mention which in terms of the status of their members were highly significant.

In May and June 1958, United States Commissioner of Education Lawrence G. Derthick led a large delegation to the U.S.S.R., a report on which, in a public speech by Dr. Derthick, was one of the main news items in the *New York Times* for June 14. In September 1959 the United States Office of Education issued a long official report based on a second Derthick-led survey. In June and July 1958 Dr. Edward H. Litchfield, chancellor of the University of Pittsburgh, led a group of seven college presidents on a

---

[4] Dr. Holland contributed an article describing his Soviet trip to the *News Bulletin* of the Institute of International Education for November 1957.

two-week trip. Chancellor Litchfield's group issued a thirty-two-page report on their experiences in the fall of 1958. In November 1959, under the auspices of the Institute of International Education, scores of American educators who had traveled to the U.S.S.R. gathered in New York to compare notes on their experiences.

American educators who have been in Russia recently have reported, for the most part, that they were impressed by the scope and driving force of the Soviet educational system, but that its ideological regimentation and over-specialization made it unsuitable for American needs, even if worthy of careful scrutiny. As the Litchfield group concluded, "The Soviets profit from specificity of object . . . but, by the same token, they may well suffer from the counterpart dangers of overdirection, lack of breadth and lack of creative individuality." A few American educators have reacted uncritically to their Soviet travels, at least if one may judge by press reports attributing to them statements accepting at face value Soviet claims regarding, for example, the "autonomy" of the educational authorities in the various non-Russian republics of the U.S.S.R. On the other hand, in the opinion of *Uchitelskaya Gazeta* and other Soviet educational periodicals, some of the American educator-visitors of 1958 expressed themselves in a tendentious manner in reporting their Russian experiences.

The flow of ranking personages of the Soviet educational world to America was much thinner than that in the opposite direction, but some important educational administrators, such as Madame Ludmilla Dubrovina, a deputy minister of education of the Russian Federated Soviet Republic, have visited this country.

In addition to exchanges of persons, 1957 and 1958 saw important radio exchanges between Soviet and American educators, educational administrators, and scientists. In the period shortly after the launching of the first Soviet artificial earth satellite a number of distinguished American scientists interviewed Soviet colleagues on a radio program originating in New York. Also related to exchanges of information among educators was the C.B.S. "Youth Wants to Know" series in September-October 1958, in which American students in Moscow interviewed, among other persons, Mr. V. P. Elyutin, the U.S.S.R. Minister of Higher Education. Mr. Elyutin, one gathers, has found American visitors something of a problem in the post-Stalin years, but, like many of his colleagues, he has displayed remarkable energy and good humor in dealing with their requests and questions—as we can testify on the basis of personal experience in 1956.

All of this activity reflected the mutual interest of teachers and students in both countries in one another's work, thoughts, and problems. In this connection it may be of interest to note that some of my colleagues who have negotiated with Soviet educational administrators in recent years regarding, for example, Soviet-American student exchange have reported that their Soviet partners in the negotiations have seemed enthusiastic about establishing exchanges, but have been under constraint, because of attitudes prevalent in other, more powerful segments of the Soviet bureaucracy.

On the less positive side of this picture, it should also be noted that certainly one Soviet motive in cultivating American educators is exploitation, for propaganda purposes, of the interest and sympathy aroused abroad in Soviet education, not only by Soviet industrial and scientific achievement, but also by the widespread view that in the new Russia scholars are rich and honored men—a view contradicted by the low pay and status of most Soviet schoolteachers, university instructors, and "scientific workers," but not entirely incorrect if placed in a perspective which recognizes the vast gulf between chauffeur-driven members of scientific, pedagogical, and medical academies and their less-successful colleagues and competitors.

In terms of mutuality of interests and values and relative objectivity of reporting, artistic exchanges, of which the trip by the "Yale minstrels" might be considered an informal example, fall into much the same category as educational, scientific, and technical ones. The same characterization applies, to a considerable degree, to athletic exchanges and would be wholly accurate if the desire of the athletes were the only factor involved. Prior to the 1958 agreement, athletic exchanges between Russia and America had been restricted to the 1952 and 1956 Olympic Games and to a few other contests, such as that between American and Russian weight lifters which took place in the Soviet Union. But in 1958 the pace quickened, with, for example, visits by American men's and women's basketball teams and a large American track team to Russia and a triumphal tour of America by Soviet wrestlers. The year 1959, of course, saw the gala, gigantic Soviet-American track meet at Philadelphia. Soviet-American chess matches have been reported fully and objectively on both sides. If it is true that one reason for Western difficulty in dealing with the Russians has long been a touchy Russian inferiority complex, then perhaps Americans should welcome the opportunity which Soviet-American chess competition, for example, regularly gives to the Russians to salve their tender egos.

One other significant type of exchange, to which we shall devote some special attention in this chapter, consists of the visits made by American academic specialists on Russia to the U.S.S.R. By the end of 1958 approximately three hundred "area specialists" had visited Russia and, of course, many others had gone to Poland, Czechoslovakia, or other communist countries. Since these travelers went as private individuals, and on the whole no Soviet counterpart visits took place, there was in their activities no element of formal, organized exchange, although some of the American professors who visited the U.S.S.R. discussed with their Soviet colleagues, and with the appropriate Soviet officials, the possibility of future exchanges of graduate students or scholars, particularly in such fields as history, language, and literature. A major 1958 event, at which sixteen American Soviet area scholars—the most distinguished of whom was the noted philologist, Professor Roman Jakobson of Harvard University—presented papers, was the Fourth International Congress of Slavicists held in August in Moscow. The congress received a considerable amount of publicity in Soviet mass media, designed, in the words of an unfriendly American student who was not a participant but was in Russia then, to prove that "all brains meet in Moscow." Professor Jakobson had already, after an absence of some thirty years from his native Russia, been cordially received on a visit in 1955, when he was greeted at Moscow Airport by some thirty Soviet officials and scholars! Equal cordiality was displayed toward him in Czechoslovakia in 1957, but in 1958 the Czechoslovak press published attacks on him, including insinuations regarding the allegedly sinister motive of his visit to Prague.

In a good concise account of the Moscow congress in the December 1958 issue of the *ACLS Newsletter*, Professor William B. Edgerton, a participant, asserted that the "fruitful contacts" made at it clearly outweighed its negative features. Among the latter he mentioned sharp attacks on American scholarship planned in advance by "a group of academic party faithfuls." According to Professor Edgerton, Professor Leon Stilman, of Columbia University, had the sympathy of the overflow audience to which he delivered, in Russian, an eloquent reply to the attacks.

Technically, of course, most of the Russian-speaking—or at least Russian-reading—American historians, economists, and political and social scientists who have been in the U.S.S.R. in recent years traveled as tourists and, as far as ordinary Soviet citizens were concerned, they were droplets in the stream of thousands of American visitors to the U.S.S.R. between the death of Stalin and the end of 1958. Their impact, both in the Soviet Union and at home, may have been considerably greater than that of most other kinds of travelers. For one thing, most of the academic travelers, after their return home, wrote articles or gave lectures, often illustrated by colored slides or motion pictures, describing their Russian experiences.

Somewhat similar activities were often engaged in by many non-academic travelers. For example, the visit of Mr. C. S. Allyn, president of the National Cash Register Company, in 1956 was reported in an interesting and elaborate colored issue of *N.C.R. Factory News* for September 1956. Such travel books as Supreme Court Justice William O. Douglas' *Russian Journey*, Marshall MacDuffie's *The Red Carpet*, or John Gunther's *Inside Russia Today* are among the best-known products of post-Stalin American travel to Soviet Russia, which also produced countless illustrated lectures to luncheon clubs throughout the land.

The Soviet-American exchange of agricultural delegations in 1955, which was, incidentally, followed by a number of less-formal visits by "farmer" groups, as well as by further exchanges of experts, is among the individual exchanges which are particularly worthy of extended treatment. The exchange consisted of travel by twelve high-ranking Soviet officials in the United States from August 16, 1955, through August 24, and of reciprocal travel by seven American farmers, three agricultural experts, one journalist, and one businessman in the Soviet Union from July 12 through August 18. Arrangements for the assistance and accommodation of the Soviet visitors were made under the general direction of the Department of State and the Department of Agriculture, but most of the details of hospitality and display of farms, agricultural experiment stations, and laboratories and the arranging of contacts were handled, on the American side, by local authorities and private groups and individuals. The Soviet delegation was headed by Vladimir Matskevich, a Deputy Minister of Agriculture, who later, in October 1955, was promoted to the position of Minister of Agriculture. Most of his fellow-delegates were also primarily bureaucrats, but they were clearly dominated by the outwardly genial but tough and wily Matskevich, who, according to one American who traveled with the Russians, was "hated" by his colleagues. Americans who came in contact with the Soviet delegation were impressed, incidentally, by the fact that the majority of the Soviet agricultural officials who constituted it were trained in science as well as in administration. William Lambert, dean of the College of Agriculture of the University of Nebraska, headed the American agricultural delegation to the U.S.S.R. in 1955. Travel and other arrangements for the American farmers were made by the Soviet Ministry of Agriculture.

This exchange, and the extensive and unusually favorable publicity which it received, particularly on the American side, can be attributed partly to the brief *détente* in American-Soviet relations which occurred in 1955. If one were to attempt to identify the individual who played the largest personal role in bringing it about, however, the name of Lauren K. Soth, editor of the *Des Moines Register*, would come to mind. Mr. Soth's newspaper proposed the exchange in an editorial of February 10, 1955, commenting on a speech in which Mr. Khrushchev, in January of that year, had recommended that the Soviet Union introduce the American type of corn-hog agriculture. Probably because of the favorable attitude of President Eisenhower, the State and Justice Departments waived the then-obligatory fingerprinting requirement, strict enforcement of which might have made the exchange impossible, in view of the earlier refusal by the Soviet government to permit eleven Soviet student editors to come to the United States in the spring of 1955. In their rather different ways, the leading American and Soviet newspapers, such as *Pravda* and the *New York Times*, gave the exchange their blessing.

Secretary of State Dulles voiced a somewhat reluctant approval. American public opinion regarding the agricultural exchange of 1955 was very favorable, but the Soviet visit was marred somewhat by demonstrations by anti-Soviet refugee groups, consisting, in large part, of Ukrainians. The most important incident of this nature occurred in Minneapolis. Similar demonstrations were directed against the Soviet delegation of journalists later in the year, especially in Cleveland. Needless to say, episodes of this character which have occurred sporadically throughout the years since 1955, particularly in connection with Anastas Mikoyan's American "vacation" in 1959, furnished much ammunition for the Soviet press, and they probably did a good deal to offset the generally favorable impressions derived from the experiences and observations of Soviet delegations in the United States. We shall not discuss the visit of the Soviet agricultural delegation to Canada, which began on August 25, except to say that it was probably a failure, in large part, because in Canada there were even more violent demonstrations by Ukrainian refugees than those which occurred during the United States visit.

Resembling somewhat in their motivation the Russians who traveled abroad in the time of Peter the Great, the copious note-takers of 1955 and subsequent years "pumped" their hosts indefatigably, even unmercifully. There was much less of this deadly seriousness on the American side. Judging from all the available sources, including full coverage in the *New York Times*, the Americans found much less to learn, at least about agricultural techniques, in the Ukraine and Kuban and in the stark virgin lands of Kazakhstan than did the Soviets amid the tall corn of Iowa and Nebraska, or in Texas and California.[5] While the Americans were impressed by much that they saw, particularly in the areas of child care and education, they were shocked by the many evidences of poverty and hardship which came to their attention even during

[5] The American delegation traveled 10,000 miles, according to the *New York Times* for August 21, 1955. The Soviet delegation traveled 12,000 miles and saw twelve states, according to Harrison Salisbury in the same paper for August 23.

what was, on the whole, a carefully guided tour. The Americans were also irked by the elaborateness of Soviet hospitality.[6]

After returning to the United States, a member of the American delegation complained that his group had been tied to a schedule that "did not give us much freedom" and that they had visited only one collective farm that they had selected themselves.[7] However, some members of the American delegation, in particular Professor D. Gale Johnson of the University of Chicago, made many valuable observations. The observations made by the Americans were, nevertheless, in comparison with those made by the Soviets, of a limited and particular character. The Soviets were able to obtain a broad view of the American agricultural pattern, which was undoubtedly of great value to the Soviet government in changing and improving national policy in the field of agriculture.[8]

What were the results of this exchange? It probably was one of numerous events in 1955 that contributed to relaxation of tension. There were also more tangible results, particularly in terms of partial achievement of some Soviet objectives. Let us examine both main kinds of result. The American farmers in Russia and the Soviet agricultural bureaucrats in America received overwhelmingly friendly receptions. Latent sentiments of friendliness on both sides were activated. The Russians were welcomed by cheering crowds in Des Moines and in Omaha. The crowds in Des Moines carried welcome signs, some of them in Russian.[9] Matskevich's jovial manner, tact, and skillful public-relations techniques played a large part in the success of the Soviet delegation. The Soviets submitted cheerfully to photography and interviewing, and, in spite of their determination to acquire as much information as possible during their trip, they did a good deal of sight-seeing. They gave the im-

[6] See, for example, the *New York Times* for July 31 and August 3, 1955.

[7] *Ibid.*, August 21, 1955.

[8] The value of the trip to the Russians was indicated in many Soviet publications, among which the following are especially interesting: "otchet o poezdke v Ameriku," in *Partiinaya Zhizn*, No. 3, 1956, pp. 69-76, and a book by Matskevich, *Chto my vide li v SSHA i Kanade*, Moscow, 1956. It is interesting to read in Matskevich's book criticisms of John Strohm, an American agricultural expert selected by the Agriculture and State Departments to act as chief guide for the Soviet delegation, on the ground that Strohm would not let the Russians see things which had not been planned in advance. Matskevich also poked fun at Strohm's Russian.

[9] *New York Times*, July 17, 1955.

pression that they were trying to act as American as possible. They went to fairs, visited private homes, and even attended church services. The friendly attitude of many American newspapers, particularly in Iowa, also undoubtedly contributed to the cordial reception given by Americans to the visiting Russians. It should also be noted that most of the American officials who were in any way involved with the Russian visit displayed a friendly attitude. For example, Mayor Wagner of New York, Secretary of Agriculture Benson, and dozens of other American officials held receptions or arranged luncheons or dinners for the Soviet delegation. Perhaps the high point of the Soviet visit, from the point of view of creating good will toward the Soviet Union in the United States, was Matskevich's brilliant performance at a National Press Club luncheon in Washington. On the other hand, the state governors assembled at a Governors' Conference in Chicago seemed uneasy and embarrassed by Matskevich's invitation to them to visit the Soviet Union. However, in 1959 a delegation of American state governors did tour Russia. In return, Soviet party and government officials, led by Dmitri S. Polyanski, were in the U.S. early in 1960 under the auspices of the Institute of International Education.

In their own very different way, the American farmers in 1955 proved to be as talented emissaries of good will for America as Matskevich and his colleagues were for the Soviet Union. They received a hero's welcome in Kharkov, were wildly cheered in Novorossiisk, and caused a near riot in Dnepropetrovsk.[10] The Americans gained much good will by wearing Russian and Ukrainian shirts, by giving out badges, of which Russian children, especially, are very fond, by making favorable statements in guest books, and by a ready willingness to sing American folksongs.

While in the United States, the Soviet delegation arranged for the purchase of sixty Santa Gertrudis cattle and invited Mr. Roswell Garst, president of a large American firm specializing in hybrid seed corn, to visit the Soviet Union. Mr. Garst made the visit and, in return, in the fall of 1955, a group of Soviet seed experts visited the United States. It is interesting, incidentally, that Khrushchev in 1959 included a rather spectacular visit to Mr.

---

[10] *Ibid.*, July 19, 22, and 29, 1955.

Garst in the crowded schedule of his American tour. The Soviet Union ordered $1,500,000 dollars worth of farm machinery and equipment, including tractors, planters, plows, cultivators, hay balers, and garden tractors, and $1,700,000 dollars worth of hybrid seed corn, early in 1956.[11] In August 1956, in an interview with Senator Ellender of Louisiana, who found the Soviet scene so interesting that he made three visits in all to Russia, Mr. Khrushchev reportedly said that the Soviet Union had benefited greatly from what the Soviet delegation learned in the United States.[12]

By 1957, despite a worsening of Soviet-American diplomatic relations connected with crises in Eastern Europe and the Middle East, and despite an increasing Soviet tendency to claim that the Soviet Union was now ahead of the United States and England in scientific development, the communist party had officially adopted the slogan "In the next few years catch up to the United States of America in the production of meat, milk and butter per head of population."[13] One of Adlai Stevenson's most vivid impressions of his 1958 Russian trip was the omnipresence of exhortations to the Soviet population to "catch up" and surpass America in agriculture and, indeed, in all fields of endeavor. A major Soviet documentary film, "Wide Is My Native Land," shown, among other places, at the Soviet exhibition in New York, made much of the slogan "Corn is the queen of the fields," but failed to indicate the American background of Khrushchevian "corn-hog" agriculture.

Subsequent to the spectacular 1955 "farmer" exchanges, agricultural exchanges between Russia and America became more serious in character, and also more routinized. Very interesting material on the further development and results of these exchanges was contained in the Department of Agriculture magazine, *Agricultural Research*, for January 1, 1959.

If the 1955 agricultural exchange was primarily a technical one, but with many political-ideological overtones, the exchange of automation specialists in the same year was perhaps as purely a technical-professional affair as possible. The automation exchange

[11] *Ibid.*, February 22, 1956.
[12] *Ibid.*, August 7, 1956.
[13] This slogan was included in the "appeals" issued by the Central Committee of the communist party of the Soviet Union in 1957 in connection with the celebration of the fortieth anniversary of the bolshevik October revolution.

was a highly significant one in several respects. It was conducted in a quiet, businesslike fashion. It involved, on both sides, high-level, competent personnel. And, fortunately, it set an example for this type of exchange which was followed in others in subsequent years. Together with other 1955 exchanges, this one put Soviet specialists on the road toward acquiring the knowledge of American precision techniques which the Russians still needed if they were to "overtake" America. Such exchanges may not have brought as much tangible professional benefit to the Americans as to the Soviets, but they have yielded a knowledge of Soviet achievements and a consciousness of the challenge which they pose to American industrial leadership that could not have been obtained any other way.

During the summer of 1955 representatives of the Soviet Union approached American officials with a proposal for a limited exchange of automation engineering personnel. The Soviets asked permission for Russian engineers to visit plants in the United States and they proposed, in return, to allow an equal number of American engineers to visit Russian industrial facilities. The Russians selected three engineers to attend the Chicago Machine Tool Show and to visit several American industrial plants during the fall of 1955. In turn, the American government arranged for three engineers selected by the American Society of Mechanical Engineers to make a similar study of twelve Soviet industrial plants and technical institutes in December. The Americans were Nevin L. Bean, technical assistant to the general manager of the Automatic Transmission Division of the Ford Motor Company; Dr. Weldon Brandt, engineering manager of Director Systems for Westinghouse Electric Company; and Dr. A. C. Hall, general manager of research division, Bendix Aviation Corporation. In his careful thirty-nine-page report on the trip, Mr. Bean presented a wealth of material regarding machinery, research, and education and production methods. He noted that the Russians appreciated accurate and factual criticism of their plants and processes and he was impressed by their "aggressiveness in attacking problems involved in bringing their industry abreast with manufacturing conditions in other countries."[14] Mr. Bean concluded his report with the ob-

[14] Bean, *op.cit.*, p. 39.

servation that since the Soviets were graduating more engineers and technicians than the United States, and were able to put them to work solving the riddles of industrial expansion, it was entirely possible that they could rather quickly narrow the gap between their productive capacity and ours.

Let us turn now to the activities in the United States of a suave, smooth, and thoroughly political delegation—namely, that composed of the seven Soviet journalists who arrived in New York on October 17, 1955, and left America on November 18. The delegation of Soviet journalists was headed by Boris Nikolaevich Kanpov-Polevoi, well-known *Pravda* war correspondent, war novelist, and secretary of the governing board of the Union of Soviet Writers. It is, incidentally, interesting that Polevoi returned to America briefly in 1958 to attend a "reunion" of Soviet and American war veterans.[15] Another member of the group who had achieved distinction not only as journalist and editor, but as one of the most highly paid of Soviet poets, was Anatoli Vladimirovich Sofronov. At a luncheon given for the delegation at the Men's Faculty Club of Columbia University on October 18, 1955, which we attended, Mr. Sofronov told one of the Americans present that his cash income usually ranged between 20,000 and 30,000 rubles a month. In view of the fact that the maximum rate of income tax in the Soviet Union is thirteen per cent, this represents a very substantial net income. The Soviet journalists were well dressed and prepossessing. They were affable and some of them had a sense of humor. They seemed self-confident and well-poised, but, as a rule, their behavior was noticeably circumspect. Like the agriculturalists, they declared that their purpose was to see "the best" that America had to offer, a gambit which would lend credence to whatever criticisms they chose later to make. They also asserted that they had come to promote the "spirit of Geneva." The fact that this "spirit" was being curdled at the Geneva Conference of Foreign Ministers which ended in failure just before the Soviet journalists departed perhaps helps to explain the contrast between the journalists' affability in conversations with their American

[15] *New York Herald Tribune* for October 19, 1955, published a photograph of the members of the Soviet journalistic delegation interviewing Keith Funston, president of the New York Stock Exchange, and listed their names.

hosts and the acerbity of the reports that they published after their return home. Perhaps the most important member of this delegation was Aleksei Adzhubei, then editor of *Komsomolskaya Pravda*, and now of *Izvestiya*. Mr. Adzhubei, son-in-law of Khrushchev, returned to America with Khrushchev's party in 1959. The journalists, like the agriculturalists, operated as a disciplined unit. According to an unfriendly article by Frank Kluckhohn, a Washington public-relations expert who accompanied the group throughout most of its itinerary, the Soviet journalists were sensitive to the presence of Washington-based Tass correspondents, who also accompanied the party and who reported directly to Moscow on the journalists' activities in the United States.[16] It seems probable that in all of these Soviet-American encounters, on both sides, whatever published reports result tend to be influenced by a mixture of stereotypes, of which the bearers are largely unconscious, and of more-or-less conscious manipulation.

I believe, however, that unconscious stereotyping, as well as conscious distortion, assume somewhat different forms on the two sides. The types of Soviet citizens who represent their government in international exchanges bring to their task a highly structured pattern of opinions combined with exceptional skills in the manipulation of words. As representatives of a system with an official orthodoxy, which is, however, subject to interpretation by an all-powerful center, they tend to assume that the United States also is under the control of a monolithic authority which pursues relatively stable long-range goals by a variety of flexible but coordinated maneuvers.

Americans, even assuming that they support whatever line of policy their government has succeeded in articulating, tend to project to foreigners their own relatively trusting attitudes and optimistic assumptions. Of course, Americans also, with their rather benevolent, even if often irritating, kind of ethnocentrism, also tend to extend to other countries institutional and cultural pat-

[16] Frank Kluckhohn, "Around the U.S. with Seven Reds," in *Reader's Digest*, May 1956, pp. 37-61. Kluckhohn's observations regarding the exercise of control over the delegation from outside its membership correspond, essentially, to comments by Tania Long in the *New York Times* for September 11, 1955, according to which the Soviet agricultural delegation, at least during the Canadian part of its trip, was never quite free of control by the Soviet embassy.

terns to which they are accustomed. These observations, in so far as they are pertinent to Soviet behavior, seem particularly appropriate to a Soviet delegation of the kind represented by the seven journalists, although they probably apply to a considerable degree to most Soviet delegations, and even, to a certain extent, to Soviet scientists and technical men.

Probably the most valuable information regarding the experiences of the seven journalists is in Polevoi's "American Diaries" which occupied 180 big pages in the Soviet literary monthly *Oktyabr* for February, March, and April 1956.[17] We shall focus mainly on Polevoi's "diaries," but it should be noted that the remaining printed output of this influential delegation was enormous.[18] The degree of uniformity of subject matter and opinions expressed in all of the articles written by the seven Soviet journalists during and after their trip was somewhat staggering. They all agreed that Cyrus Eaton, who entertained them hospitably at his home in Cleveland—he had also been visited by the Soviet agricultural group—was as sensible and fine a person as a millionaire could be. There was also an impressive consensus regarding the high merits of Howard Fast and Lion Feuchtwanger. Frank Kluckhohn and Edmund Glen, State Department representatives attached to the tour, came in for a great deal of not-too-gentle ribbing. Alleged restrictions and surveillance—the group, although it visited New York, San Francisco, and most of the major cities in between, was not allowed to go to Detroit—were the subjects of many indignant observations. One other interesting and curious note, among many, was the veneration displayed by all of these writers for the American nonogenarian writer Ethel Voynich, whom the delegation visited in her apartment in New York. Mrs. Voynich is the author of *The Gadfly*, a novel about an Englishman who joined up with Italian patriots in their struggle against Austrian and papal power in the 1840's. This novel has always been popular in Russia, both before and after the bolshevik revolution, but it experienced a special vogue after the

[17] B. Polevoi, "Amerikanskie dnevniki," *Oktyabr*, 1956, No. 2, pp. 93-143; No. 3, pp. 88-153; No. 4, pp. 86-151.
[18] For example, A. Adzhubei contributed eleven long articles to his newspaper, *Komsomolskaya Pravda*, and N. Gribachev contributed thirteen equally voluminous pieces to *Literaturnaya Gazeta*.

death of Stalin. At the time of writing, *The Gadfly* and Mitchell Wilson's *My Brother My Enemy* were perhaps the two novels by living Americans which were most popular among Soviet readers.[19]

Polevoi began his account with an explanatory note to his readers stating that "a precise itinerary" for the Soviet journalists' trip had been prescribed by the State Department. The Soviet delegation did not object to this stipulation, he asserted, because they were determined to look for the "best" in America, and who could be better informed on "the best" in America than "the owners of the house"? The Soviet delegation did not wish to accept the State Department's offer to provide two interpreters, because two members of the group spoke fluent English.[20]

According to Polevoi, the presence of these interpreters, who were, he claimed, attached to the party against its wishes, narrowed its horizons, but in spite of this, he assured his readers, the trip was "interesting."

Polevoi, perhaps to guard against any possible suspicion of a lack of political sophistication on his part, pointed out that although he had returned to the U.S.S.R. tired, from a trip to Scotland, where he attended a literary festival in honor of the poet Robert Burns, he felt a high sense of duty in accepting his government's suggestion that he head a delegation to the United States. The rather peculiar tone of Polevoi's diary is suggested by his statement that the invitation to go to America was "like a telegram at the front." Although sharper in tone, Polevoi's report followed the same general lines as Ilya Ilf's and Evgeni Petrov's already-mentioned book, *One Story America.* Unfortunately, Polevoi, although a very astute man, lacked the genius of his predecessors. He tried hard, however, to achieve the same standards and in general applied similar criteria in his judgments of American life. Like them, he expressed admiration for the "simple people" and the "toilers of America," whose "golden hands" had created everything of which America was proud. He castigated "powerful forces"

[19] Harvey Breit published a brief history of the Voynich novel since its publication in 1897 in the *New York Times Book Review* for March 31, 1957.

[20] One of these was Vladimir Berezhkov, with whom we talked during the trip, at Columbia University, and whom we visited in the editorial office of *New Times,* the weekly of which Berezhkov was, and still is at the time of writing, deputy editor, in Moscow.

who did not like the "Geneva spirit." He professed inability to understand a "freedom" under which Soviet journalists had to travel about the United States accompanied by "hordes of detectives" and molested by "crowds of drunken hooligans" who were permitted to insult foreign guests. Polevoi concluded his account by saying that the more he and his colleagues had traveled in the capitalist countries, the more they loved their Soviet motherland, where "the state takes care of us."[21] The benevolent but somewhat patronizing attitude displayed in Polevoi's diaries toward "ordinary" Americans perhaps reflects the mixture of democracy and condescension toward their own masses felt by members of the Soviet elite.

Perhaps one part of Polevoi's task was to demonstrate to the Soviet public that even the "simple people" of America had by now become so thoroughly corrupted by the influence of Hollywood movies, television, and advertising that they had lost some of the admirable qualities observed earlier by Ilf and Petrov. Polevoi suggests this interpretation in the symbolism of his search for John Smith, a "real American" whom he had met at the meeting of Soviet and American forces at Torgau, Germany, in May 1945, but whom he was unable to find in 1955. In reporting his conversation with Lion Feuchtwanger, Polevoi rather subtly suggested the identity of attitudes of Russians and "other Europeans" toward American culture. This theme was touched upon many times, among others at the beginning of the diaries, where Polevoi described how Gertrud Haym, an "anti-fascist" German, who had lived in the United States, had had some nice words to say about the American people but had noted that "new Europeans" do not know how American big business through its "cultural mass production" had made such a shambles of American culture that a European was inclined to doubt if American culture existed at all. Despite clichés, barbs, and precautions, however, Polevoi's travel report, like those of his colleagues, presented a more attractive and believable image of American life than any which had been available to Soviet readers during the late-Stalin era.

The seven journalists' accounts suggested to Soviet readers something of the teeming activity, material prosperity, and glittering

---

[21] Polevoi summed up his impressions in *Oktyabr*, No. 4, 1956, pp. 148-151.

gadgetry of America. They also let enough facts about American life and customs filter through to fascinate many a Soviet reader. For example, Polevoi wrote an amazed description of a football game between Leland Stanford University and San Jose State College, which provided Soviet readers with a piquant, and perhaps new, anthropological tidbit. I would venture to suggest that America as seen by these seven members of the new, tough Soviet ruling class presented a far more attractive picture than the America perceived by many continental European left-wing intellectuals.

Vladimir Berezhkov, who as deputy editor of *New Times* was a member of the journalists' mission to the United States, told an American in Moscow in June 1956 that he and his colleagues felt that their trip marked a kind of "rediscovery of America." Berezhkov pointed out, for example, that one result of the articles written by his party was that the Soviet people knew for the first time about the fifty-five million automobiles owned by Americans. During this conversation Berezhkov said that he was scheduled to give a lecture on the trip at a Moscow hospital that very evening, and he cited this as one of many indications of the very wide publicity given to it. An attempt to wangle an invitation to attend the lecture, however, was met with the statement that this would be very difficult, since "special arrangements" would have to be made.

Naturally, in a situation such as this a foreign visitor wonders if he is being shielded from the possible embarrassment of hearing an overtly friendly Soviet citizen criticize the United States. In face-to-face encounters, at least, even the Soviet journalists or professors whose writings are most vitriolically anti-American make an effort to be pleasant to their foreign hosts or guests. Whether this represents hospitality or dissimulation is often difficult to guess. Berezhkov not only agreed that ideology was not the main factor in international disagreements—he could easily do this within the framework of the Soviet coexistence line—but when it was pointed out to him that the United States had no monopoly on juvenile delinquency and crime, he replied that there was plenty of crime in the Soviet Union too, and, in apparent pride, said that the Soviet press was devoting more space than it used to to crime reporting. But when does prevarication cease to be politeness, or universally acceptable "realism" and become a crime against the human personality?

My confidence even in the elementary area of factual detail was somewhat shaken, as far as Polevoi's diaries are concerned, by comparison of his recollections of the luncheon which he, together with members of the Columbia University faculty and the Soviet journalists, attended on October 18, 1955, with Polevoi's description. Among other things, the names of the three individual Americans mentioned by Polevoi were hopelessly garbled. These details would not seem so important if Howard Fast, in his recent book *The Naked God*, had not reported that Polevoi, in the presence of several witnesses, had assured him that the Soviet Jewish writer Kvitko was alive, and in fact was living in the same apartment house as he was, when, in fact, as a Polish communist newspaper later revealed, Kvitko had been dead for years.[22]

Probably one of the Soviet objectives in cultural exchanges with America is strengthening of the impact of Soviet domestic propaganda by giving it the support of eyewitness accounts. This purpose can be even better served, however, by selective reports of interviews with visiting foreigners. An example of this technique is the article published by *Izvestiya* for October 19, 1955, in which alleged statements by some of the thirteen members of the House of Representatives who had visited the Soviet Union during the summer of 1955 were used to create the impression that the Congressmen were impressed by the friendliness and peaceful intentions of the Soviet people and by Soviet economic strength and progress, as well as by the value of the exchange of delegations in the strengthening of peace and the relaxation of tensions.

The *Izvestiya* article concluded with a statement attributed to Senator George M. Malone, of Nevada, to the effect that the United States should concentrate on making its own system work and stop interfering in other people's business.[23] It seems to be true that many of the American politicians and businessmen who have visited Russia since the death of Stalin were bemused by

[22] Howard Fast, *The Naked God*, New York, 1957, pp. 133-134.

[23] In 1955 nine United States Senators and eighteen members of the House of Representatives visited Russia. Subsequently, many Senators and Representatives made individual trips, and some of them, such as Senators Russell B. Long and Allen D. Ellender, of Louisiana, published lengthy accounts of their experiences.

much of what they saw. Curiously enough, there is much evidence that the more conservative these visitors are in their economic and political philosophy, the more favorably they are likely to be impressed by the Soviet Union. Liberals, or at least some of them, such as former Senator Benton of Connecticut, who went to the Soviet Union in 1955, accompanied by a very competent Russian-speaking American expert on the Soviet Union, or Mrs. Franklin D. Roosevelt, who, after cancelling a trip in 1955 because she was refused permission to take an American interpreter, made the trip in 1957 with her own interpreter and returned for another brief trip in 1958, and also Adlai E. Stevenson have been impressed by massive Soviet progress in education, for example, but have also emphasized the high cost in human values paid by the Soviet people for rapid industrialization. As a rule, Soviet leaders and Soviet communications media replied vigorously, and sometimes furiously, to criticism by American visitors. Supreme Court Justice William O. Douglas, for example, was blasted for his criticism of Soviet "colonialism" in Central Asia.[24] Among other things, Justice Douglas was accused of having said nice things about the Soviet Union to his hosts but of contradicting himself in the articles he published after his return to the United States.[25]

On the whole, the ten to twelve thousand Americans who had visited the Soviet Union by the end of 1958 were persons of high status. The costliness of travel to and in Russia was perhaps a sufficient reason. It would have been beyond the means of most academicians, had it not been for the wise policy of a number of foundations and other private foundations which financed the travel of many scholars and scientists. Such physicians as Dr. Paul Dudley White, or public figures like Mr. Ellsworth Bunker, at the time of his visit to the U.S.S.R. head of the American Red Cross and later named ambassador to India, were among the Americans whose visits to the Soviet Union disproved Soviet statements that Americans were "afraid" to visit communist Russia.[26]

[24] See, for example, the article by V. Borovski in *Pravda* for July 30, 1955.

[25] See, for example, L. Sedin, "Douglas versus Douglas," *New Times*, No. 52, December 1955, p. 23.

[26] When I was asked in the summer of 1956 by a group of Soviet economists at a meeting arranged by VOKS why Americans were "afraid" to visit Russia, I replied, "I am here," and went on to explain that the high cost of travel and the

Some of the highest-ranking American military officials, headed by Air Force General Twining, attended the Soviet air show in June 1956. Irritation was aroused on the Soviet side by the failure of the United States government to invite a corresponding Soviet delegation to this country, apparently somewhat in contradiction to American assurances made in connection with General Twining's trip. Many leading American writers, artists and art critics, and scientists have visited Russia. Among the American artists Isaac Stern, Jan Peerce, Van Cliburn, and Leonard Bernstein, to name a few, made an especially favorable impression. Marvin Kalb, a talented young observer of the Soviet scene who was on the staff of the American embassy while Isaac Stern toured Russia, expressed the opinion in his book *Eastern Exposure* that this tour did more to improve Russian-American relations than fifty diplomatic conferences.

As for Mr. Cliburn, it is probably safe to say that no living American is held in such affection by Russians, particularly by ladies, as he is. Americans were reminded of this fact by display at the 1959 Soviet Exhibition in New York of boxes of candy bearing his photograph, and travelers to the U.S.S.R. who have talked to Soviet young people have received confirmation of Cliburn's popularity in numerous conversations. Russians, of course, are pleased to think that they "discovered" Mr. Cliburn's talent, a view that made some American embassy officials think that it would be salutary to send other talented young American pianists on Soviet tours to demonstrate the abundance of musical accomplishment available in this country.

The post-Stalin era saw a parade of leading American journalists to the U.S.S.R. Among them, to name a few, were Joseph Alsop, James Reston, John Gunther, Louis Fischer, Dorothy Thompson, Marguerite Higgins, Maurice Hindus, and John Scott. Among the books which have resulted from these journalists' visits, perhaps the most perceptive are Fischer's *Russia Revisited*, which appeared in 1957, and Gunther's book, already mentioned, which came out in 1958. Among other recent books which resulted

---

artificial exchange rate were much more potent obstacles than alleged fear. Only a feeble effort was made by the Soviet hosts to pursue the theme further.

from travel to Russia one might mention Sally Belfrage's *A Room in Moscow*, Santha Rama Rau's *My Russian Journey*, and, on a different level, Adlai E. Stevenson's *Friends and Enemies*. The somewhat freer conditions of journalistic work in Moscow after Stalin's death led to an increase in the number of journalists on regular assignments in the Soviet capital. New elements also entered the world communication picture, including regular radio broadcasts by, for example, C.B.S. and N.B.C. Moscow radio correspondents.

In 1954 Soviet scientists and technologists began once again to attend international conferences in considerable numbers and to shed the hostile and churlish manner which they had been made to assume in the period from 1947 until the death of Stalin. By December of 1957 they had relaxed to such an extent that Robert Wallace, in a survey of Soviet science published in *Life* magazine, wrote that "in certain fields, at least, their freedom of communication seems greater than that permitted their counterparts in the U.S.—a situation which troubles many American scientists greatly." Wallace quoted the distinguished biologist Detlev W. Bronk, president of the National Academy of Science—who, incidentally, together with the chemist Linus W. Pauling, was elected in 1958 to honorary membership in the Academy of Sciences of the U.S.S.R. —on the desperate necessity for Americans to learn from Russian scientists. He also observed that when Russian scientists meet their American colleagues "they usually speak with candor."[27] Mr. Wallace's observations serve as a useful reminder that not all obstacles to Soviet-American scientific exchange have been on the Soviet side.

Some of the American scientists whom I queried have expressed opinions similar to Wallace's, but others have asserted that the Russians "were not as communicative as they could have been," as one scientist reported regarding the International Conference on Neutron Interactions with Nuclei, which five members of the Academy of Sciences of the U.S.S.R. attended. The conference was held at Columbia University from September 9-13, 1957. According to this source, the Soviet participants did not present anything that had not already been printed in one or another of the

[27] "First Hand Facts on All Russian Sciences," *Life*, December 16, 1957, pp. 108-122. Quotations on p. 109.

scientific journals published in the U.S.S.R., and at times it was obvious that they had done further experiments that they hid behind the language barrier, or said that they did not remember particular figures. Another scientist who had been co-author of a rather critical article on the behavior of Soviet scientists at the Geneva Conference on Peaceful Uses of Atomic Energy in 1955 stated in a letter to me that in his opinion most Soviet scientists, like most scientists of all countries, would be as communicative as scientists are in general if they were not operating under directives for withholding information. He added that, if one discussed with Russian scientists problems which had no political implications, there was no apparent hesitation on their part to give their views, and cited in this connection the behavior of a Russian mathematician at a scientific conference in Canada. He concluded, however, with the observation that apparently there were directives which prevented Soviet scientists from freely discussing many points that Americans would not consider as classified. Probably individual scientists, especially on the American side, tend to form their opinions regarding such matters on the basis of their own personal experience. This experience is likely to vary, depending upon the particular field, the changing policies of governments, the personalities of individual scientists, and even the whims of Soviet or American bureaucrats.

A Soviet scientist who attended a conference of biologists in New York in November 1957 told scientists at Yale University, while he was in New Haven, that, because of unnecessary delay in the handling of his visa by the American embassy at Moscow, his permitted time in this country was so short as to be almost useless. This matter, however, was straightened out. This Soviet scientist also expressed the opinion that the British method of "balancing" exchanges on an annual basis was superior to the American practice of demanding a *quid pro quo* in each individual case. Apparently he seemed to feel that the American government had been somewhat reluctant to issue a visa to him. Two American scientists with whom I have corresponded have indicated that even in 1957 it was still difficult to persuade the State Department to make necessary arrangements for participation by Soviet scientists in conferences held in this country. Scientific contacts, though increasing rapidly, are still by no means a routine matter. Most of the American scientists who attended the Conference on Neutron Interaction, for example, had never spoken to a Soviet scientist before. Still, the situation differs enormously from that which prevailed before the death of Stalin. Indeed, had one predicted to even sophisticated Americans in 1952 that by 1960 Soviet scientists would enjoy their present degree of freedom and security, or their present prestige, incredulity or derision would have undoubtedly been the response.

During the last few years a fairly steady stream of Soviet natural scientists, as well as a few leaders in non-science fields, have visited such major centers of scientific research as the Massachusetts Institute of Technology and in smaller numbers have come to universities such as Harvard, Yale, and Columbia. Yale, for example, was visited by four Soviet microbiologists in January 1956, and in August 1956 by four Soviet combustion experts, all of whom were members of the U.S.S.R. Academy of Sciences, as well as by a Soviet expert on antibiotics in November 1957.

In October 1958 a distinguished Soviet legal scholar, traveling alone—something unimaginable in the late-Stalin era—paid a visit to Yale, after having already visited George Washington University and Harvard. I had the pleasure of sitting next to the Soviet scholar at dinner and perhaps the best and most significant thing that I can say about the experience is that, while it yielded nothing very novel in the way of information, it seemed outwardly like a perfectly normal one, which the participants on both sides enjoyed and also found interesting and profitable. However, in this case, as in so many other Soviet-American contacts, correspondence preceding, as well as following the visit, revealed the continued extreme difficulty of communication. Letters were left unanswered on the Soviet side, and it was not even known whether they were delivered. This visit was made, in part, as one phase of an effort by legal scholars and law schools of the two countries to bring about a regular exchange of students and scholars in the field of law. With the exception of this seasoned lawyer-diplomat, and a Soviet historian, the only other Soviet visitors to Yale in 1956-1958 not in the field of natural science were the dignitaries of the Russian Orthodox Church, headed by Metropolitan Nikolai, who spent a few hours on the campus in June 1956. Professor William B. Edgerton accompanied them as an interpreter and guide. Yale was also the first American university visited in January 1959 by a five-man delegation of Soviet engineer-educators returning a visit made by Americans in the same field in November 1958. A Soviet antibiotics expert came in 1959.

By one of those coincidences which would have been impossible a few years ago, the New Haven visit of the Soviet law professor to whom we referred above was preceded, by one day, by that of a distinguished Soviet historian, in the U.S. in connection with planning for the next international congress of historians. According to a Yale faculty member who met both the legal scholar and the historian, the latter was considerably more self-assured in manner than the former. The Soviet historian, who had, a few weeks before, been in England for an Anglo-Russian historical conference, displayed evidence that he did not lack a sly wit. Shown works of Lenin, Stalin, and Trotski in the Yale University Library, he remarked that Yale had "a well-balanced collection."

Among the most immediately useful and cordial American-Soviet exchanges, with the possible exception of the artistic ones, are those in the medical field. Participants in these and related encounters have involved some very distinguished persons, including, on the American side, Drs. Paul Dudley White and Howard Rusk, who in August 1956 visited the U.S.S.R. for the purpose, among others, of placing the already-considerable two-way medical traffic on a more regular and frequent basis, and, on the Soviet side, former Minister of Health Miterev and the present Soviet Deputy Minister of Health Zhdanov.

Tentative first steps toward inaugurating such exchanges had been taken as long ago as 1955, when Major Paul W. Schafer of the United States Medical Corps ended the most extensive survey of Soviet medicine by an American since 1945 with the conclusion that Soviet authorities were ready for regular exchanges of medical delegations, resident physicians, and postgraduate students.[28] At least the first part of Major Schafer's prediction was verified by the increasing number of exchanges of medical and pharmaceutical delegations which occurred in 1956, 1957, and 1958.

[28] *New York Times*, August 28, 1955.

While these exchanges were valuable and promised much for a mutually beneficial American-Russian "longevity race," to borrow an expression coined by Mr. John T. Connor, president of Merck and Company, they were perhaps less useful than had been expected because of Soviet unwillingness, or inability, to supply to foreign physicians disease rates and other vital statistics, readily available in most countries. Also, in evaluating the encouraging progress made so far in this crucial field, it should not be forgotten that the current exchanges represent not so much an innovation as, in some degree at least, a resumption of exchanges of persons, information, and publications broken off by Moscow in 1946-1948.[29] However, it appears that the extensive program of American-Soviet medical research collaboration announced in October 1959 may add new and fruitful dimensions to previous cooperation.

One of the first and most important serious exchanges in the field of medical science was the first exchange of microbiologists, in January and February 1956. The Soviet delegation consisted of three men and one woman; their visit, and their itinerary, were planned under the auspices of the United States Public Health Service, although a prominent role in bringing about this exchange was played by Dr. John R. Paul of Yale Medical School, and Yale was one of the universities visited by the Soviet group. In connection with Dr. Paul's visit to Russia it may be worth noting that in addition to him a considerable number of Yale scientists, including Dr. Henry Margenau, of the Department of Physics; Dr. Dirck Brower, an astronomer; Dr. Aine Hille, a mathematician; and several others have made one or more visits to that country in recent years. Dr. Paul and Dr. Michael Shimkin, of the Public Health Service, who spoke Russian fluently, were members of the five-man American group that returned the Soviet doctors' visit. The available information indicates that this exchange was highly satisfactory to both sides. There were a few lively political arguments, in which one or more members of each group defended, respectively, the Soviet and the American position, without in either case convincing their opponents, so far as could be judged. But for the most part this exchange was distinguished—

---

[29] On this subject see, for example, *New York Times*, November 19, 1948.

and in this it was probably typical of recent Soviet-American scientific exchanges—by a relatively free, frank exchange of scientific opinions and facts and by much fruitful, keen observation, not all confined to professional matters.

With the exception of one young man who seemed to be the "political" member of the group, the microbiologists behaved in New Haven like simple, sincere, and friendly individuals. They were not so well dressed as the Soviet journalists whom we had met a few months before, and they were far less smooth and controlled in their behavior. As a matter of fact, while they said nothing that their government could object to, they were quite jovial. At the same time, they gave evidence of taking an extremely serious attitude toward their work. It was interesting that they, like many other Soviet scientists about whom we have reports, stated that they received all of the relevant American scientific journals. They all spoke some English, but they seemed to be very pleased that there were Russian-speaking Americans present and also pleased to learn that Americans were studying the Russian language and Russian literature. However, the young man whom we took to be the "political" member of the group seemed scornful of what he took to be excessive interest among American students of Russia in classical authors such as Dostoevski. He said that the Soviet writers were the ones whose works Americans should be studying. When I told one member of the group that while I worked in the American embassy in Moscow I used to go sometimes to Soviet restaurants, he smiled slyly and said that he was not in the habit of going to restaurants, implying, apparently, that there was something disreputable about being seen in such places—an attitude we had earlier encountered in Russia. This was one of the details which confirmed the impression that these were probably people who lived mainly for their work.

Dr. Howard A. Rusk has been perhaps most prominent among American physicians in pointing out that, while medicine seems to be one of the fields in which the Soviets still lag far behind the United States, we could learn a good deal from Soviet practice in certain areas, such as rehabilitation. Doctor Rusk has also been sharply critical of what he has regarded as the failure of the United

States government to support with adequate enthusiasm and money the activities of the World Health Organization.[30]

In September 1956 a Soviet Red Cross delegation consisting of four persons, headed by Professor G. A. Miterev, formerly Minister of Health of the U.S.S.R., visited the United States. The trip lasted for three weeks and the group went to New York, Chicago, St. Louis, Nashville, Washington, D.C., and other cities. Hotel accommodations and other details were arranged by the American National Red Cross. The delegation was accompanied by two American interpreters. A competent American who traveled with the delegation considered that the trip had a very good effect on the Soviet visitors. One of them, in a private conversation, admitted that as a result of his trip he was "confused," having found that conditions in the United States were different than he had been led to expect. The Soviet delegation seemed to be deeply impressed by what they had seen of the American standard of living. They were apparently amazed to see well-dressed Negroes, for example, riding in new automobiles. They asked many questions about prices, including the price of houses. Even one of the worst slums of Chicago did not impress them as being very bad.

On the other hand, this group found it very difficult to understand American conceptions of freedom of the press. When a member of the delegation, in an interview in Washington, stated that there was a connection between smoking and lung cancer, this made newspaper headlines. Actually, this was a minor part of his speech, since he had devoted most of it to peace. The Soviet delegation was quite disturbed by the incident, and they found it difficult to understand that American journalists used their own discretion in deciding what the "news" was. Similarly, when the delegation heard of a mistake involving a photograph of President Eisenhower, one of them asked anxiously, "What will happen to the editor?" They could not understand that the editor would not be punished, since, as they put it, this was a "political" matter. The interest taken by the members of the Soviet Red Cross delegation in such matters as the price of houses and automobiles, as well as air-conditioning, ice water, and other conveniences, is apparently

[30] On the latter point see his article in the *New York Times* for April 7, 1957.

typical of even high-ranking Soviet visitors. One American scientist described to me how, when he showed a Soviet professor through his home in 1957, the Russian displayed keen interest in appliances such as the electric refrigerator, but said, "We have these now too in the Soviet Union." Interest in American comforts and luxuries should not, however, be interpreted as indication of a lack of pride and patriotism on the part of Soviet people. They are determined to have these luxuries themselves, and some of them may share the Kremlin's professed confidence that before many decades have passed the Soviet Union will actually outproduce even the United States, at first in heavy industry and possibly, eventually, in the field of consumers' goods. They have been receiving a stream of assurances on this score since the death of Stalin. With such tangible evidences of progress in Moscow, for example, as the many department stores that have been opened since the end of World War II, the thirty-three-story skyscraper university on the Lenin Hills, and the veritable forest of cranes working on huge new housing developments, they are probably more confident than they used to be that their government's promises of future prosperity have a firm foundation in fact. Exchanges of scientific delegations, in particular, may help feed Soviet national pride and confidence, for one of their results has been to elicit from American and other Western scientists expressions of admiration for Soviet scientific progress and, sometimes, of envy at the quality and quantity of equipment available to their Soviet colleagues. We have been told by reliable sources in contact with eminent American scientists, including members of the faculty of M.I.T., that at least some of them have reported finding in laboratories in remote Siberia better equipment than they had in their own university laboratories.

Delegations of experts, such as the Soviet Red Cross group, have refrained, usually sedulously, from overt propaganda statements. The Soviet Red Cross group confined its propaganda role mainly to attempting to create the impression that there was no difference between the Soviet Red Cross and the American Red Cross. Only once during the trip did this particular delegation attempt to "pull a fast one." One of its members, in a press conference, said that, since the American and Soviet Red Cross organizations both shared common humanitarian aims, they were both in favor of prohibition of use of atomic weapons. The representative of the American Red Cross who was present immediately pointed out that since this was a political question he was not empowered to join the Soviet group in taking a position with regard to it.

Three Soviet experts, together with two Czechs, two Poles, and two Rumanians, attended the Symposium on Venereal Diseases in Washington, D.C., in May and June 1956, and five Soviet medical scientists attended the Hematology and Blood Transfusion Congress at Boston in August and September 1956, to mention two important instances of highly successful visits to this country by medical personnel of communist-ruled countries. In October 1957 six Soviet women medical scientists toured the United States.[31] The Russian women doctors traveled in the United States under the auspices of the National Academy of Science. They were, unfortunately, refused permission to accept invitations to visit homes in Brooklyn, New York, and New Canaan, Connecticut, because of State Department restrictions which forbid Soviet nationals entering certain parts of the United States.[32] The visit by Soviet women physicians was returned by a similar American party in 1958. Dr. Leona Baumgartner, New York City Health Commissioner, perhaps the most prominent member of this delegation, described its observations in widely publicized press and radio reports. Dr. Baumgartner was favorably impressed by much that she saw. She appeared, however, to have been disappointed at Soviet unwillingness to disclose data regarding disease rates and other matters.

In September and October 1957 a group of American physicians, headed by Dr. Thomas Parran, director of the University of Pittsburgh School of Public Health, visited, among other Soviet cities, Alma-Ata, Frunze, Stalinabad, and Tashkent. A member of this group told me that the trip had "overcome much of his skepticism" regarding Soviet medicine, although he found that on the whole the Russians were some thirty years behind the United States in most aspects of medical practice. While I was on the campus of the

[31] *Pravda Vostoka*, September 3, 1957; *New York Times*, October 31, 1957.
[32] Letter by Henrietta O. Rogers to the *New York Times*, November 9, 1957, criticizing restrictions imposed on the Russian women doctors.

University of Pittsburgh in June 1958 I was introduced to an official of the Soviet Ministry of Health who was, while in Pittsburgh, the guest of Dr. Parran. The perfectly normal pattern of professional relations between guest and host was one more of hundreds of bits of evidence known to us which indicate the salutary change in Russian-American cultural-scientific relations since the death of Stalin. Perhaps in this connection it is appropriate to refer to a letter sent to me from a distinguished American woman physician who wrote, "I should certainly like to add my voice to those recommending extension and intensification of East-West exchanges." Like other American physicians and scientists who have become acquainted in recent years with Soviet colleagues, this physician expressed the opinion that the barriers between the scientific community of the two countries were very slight and that it was "the Russian political leaders" who caused "most of the difficulty."

Another interesting medical exchange was that of pharmaceutical delegations in January and February 1958. The American delegation arrived in the U.S.S.R. in January for a two-week tour and their Soviet counterparts came here in February. The United States group consisted largely of executives of the Smith, Kline, and French Laboratories of Philadelphia, but it also included Dr. W. Horsely Gannt, director of the Pavlov Laboratory at Johns Hopkins University. The existence of this laboratory, and of the American Pavlov Society, flattering to Soviet scientific pride, was reported in a Soviet press item in 1955, which stated that Dr. Gannt "was, in the past, a pupil of the great Russian scientist."[33]

In November 1956 an American anthropologist, Professor Laurence Krader, then of American University, spent a month in the Soviet Union talking to Soviet anthropologists and traveling widely in Central Asia. He was able to obtain much interesting information regarding the impact of Russian culture on the native

[33] *Literaturnaya Gazeta*, August 20, 1955. Three Soviet scientists attended the sixth annual conference on High Energy Nuclear Physics in Rochester in April. Five Soviet scholars and one Czech scientist attended the Second International Acoustics Congress at Cambridge, Massachusetts, in June 1956. In July 1956 two Soviet representatives attended the International Congress on Biology at Providence, and in August four Soviet specialists attended the Sixth International Symposium on Combustion at Cambridge. Also, in the same month three Soviets attended the International Congress on Anthropological and Ethnological Sciences at Philadelphia.

peoples of Central Asia and even to do a certain amount (

In 1957 a highly successful exchange occurred betw
and American specialists in the fields, respectively,
anthropology and Sumerology. Professor Samuel No;
of the University of Pennsylvania, spent two months
archeological collections in the custody of the Institute
Studies of the Soviet Academy of Sciences, while an (
was spent at the University Museum, in Philadelphia,
Georgi F. Debets. According to a letter by Professo
the *New York Times* for December 29, 1957, the p(
cession of A. N. Nesmeyanov, the head of the Aca
ences, was required to cut red tape which threate
issuance of a visa to him, but once in Russia he was
the utmost cordiality and given every possible consi
"Debets-Kramer trade" was the first of its kind, b
exchanges did not multiply rapidly, other encoura;
of scientific collaboration, such as a six-month peri(
by a Soviet microbiologist at the Selman Waksm;
Rutgers University, arranged by Dr. Waksman, ;
in certain nonpolitical fields, the prospects for fruit
might be good if scientists had their way.

Three Soviet scientists attended the Informatio
posium at Cambridge, Massachusetts, in September
ber 1956 three Soviet scientists attended the Conf
Aids to Navigation at Indianapolis, and in Nove1
experts attended the International North Pacific
mittee meeting at Seattle. In January 1957 five
attended the meeting of the World Meteorolog;
at Washington, D.C. Eleven Soviet scientists att
Congress of the International Commission on Irri
age at San Francisco in May 1957. These typical
the range and significance of scientific contacts,
summer and fall of 1957, increased steadily, an
even more numerous. Moreover, plans for 19;
in 1958, envisaged a further increase. A sign;
direction was the rather loosely drafted but on t'
ing agreement on scientific exchange reached
Academy of Sciences and its American counter

313

the latter's president, Dr. Detlev W. Bronk, in Moscow in
November 1958. This agreement acquired increased precision
through further negotiation and was signed in June, 1959.

Thus the way was paved for a new phase of scientific exchange,
at a higher level than ever, which even by 1958 was on a scale
so vast that mere listing of participants would require hundreds of
pages. Already by 1959 a handful of more or less "operational"
scientific exchanges had occurred. American scientists, such as Dr.
James W. Guy of Purdue University, had attempted to do research in Russia. The results of these earliest efforts indicated that
much remained to be accomplished if fruitful scientific collaboration
was to replace tourism by scientists.

The 1958 visit to the U.S.S.R. by American psychologists, referred to in Chapter v, was the first opportunity enjoyed by competent Americans since the early 1930's to make a comprehensive
survey of work in progress in psychology and related fields. Some
distinguished Soviet psychologists, including Professor A. A. Smir-
nov, director of the main Soviet center of psychological research,
the Scientific Research Institute of Psychology of the Academy of
Pedagogical Sciences, were in the United States in November and
December 1958, as members of a major delegation of educators,
which visited America in return for the tour led in June of that
year by Lawrence G. Derthick. From all reports the Soviet psychologists, who received the same kind of cordial reception here
as their American counterparts experienced in Russia, thoroughly
enjoyed their trip. A psychologist was among the 1959-60 American graduate students in Russia.

In the arts, as in the sciences, exchanges in 1957, 1958, and
1959 were so numerous and in some cases at least attained such
scope and complexity that it is impossible to offer more than the
briefest of surveys. Blanche Thebom, Metropolitan Opera soprano,
enjoyed a brilliantly successful tour of the Soviet Union in December 1957. Her radio and television statements about this tour
indicated that she was deeply moved by the enthusiasm of Soviet
audiences. Her tour, very favorably commented on in *Pravda*,
Sovetskaya Kultura, and other papers, was arranged by the well-
known impresario Sol Hurok, through the Soviet Ministry of Culture, as part of a program of artistic exchanges. These exchanges

included a second, 1958, appearance by the outstanding Soviet pianist Emil Gilels, who had been here in 1955, and tours in this country by the violinist Leonid Kogan, by the one-hundred-member Moiseev Dance Ensemble, and by the conductor Kiril Kondrashin, who appeared on programs with the young pianist Van Cliburn.

During the spring and summer of 1958 by far the greatest array of American artistic talent yet seen and heard by the Soviet public basked in the same kind of warm, enthusiastic reception as their Soviet counterparts were enjoying in America. The Philadelphia Orchestra's 1958 tour, in May and June, in Kiev, Moscow, and Leningrad, was much longer and offered far more performances than had the Boston Symphony Orchestra on its brief trip in 1956. Leopold Stokowski made a triumphal tour, also in May and June, conducting Soviet orchestras in several major cities. In a sense Stokowski's tour was a counterpart to Kiril Kondrashin's. The American baritone Leonard Warren also performed in Russia in 1958. Many American music and art critics, including Howard Taubman, Faubion Bowers, and his well-known journalist wife Santha Rama Rau, also journeyed to the U.S.S.R. to report on this burst of artistic exchanges, and both Mr. Bowers and his spouse published books based, in whole or in part, on their trips.

Perhaps the biggest sensation of 1958 was the victory by Van Cliburn in Moscow, in April, in the Chaikovski piano competition. Cliburn's success in Russia was matched only by that of the brilliant Moiseev troupe in America. Judging from all reports, on both sides these ventures were highly successful.

Typical of Soviet press comment on the American artists' performances was the assessment of Leonard Warren as an "excellent artist" and a "singer of great culture" by the Soviet singer A. Ivanov in *Sovetskaya Kultura* for May 20, 1958. The triumphal achievements of Van Cliburn and of the Moiseev troupe are too well known to need recounting, though perhaps it is worth recalling that almost the whole hour of Ed Sullivan's television show on June 29, 1958, was given over to the Moiseev group, and that their first four final performances at Madison Square Garden brought the biggest mail-order response in the history of the Garden. The Berezka troupe, composed exclusively of women, which arrived in this country in November 1958, was very well received.

Even greater acclaim greeted the performances of the famous Bolshoi Ballet, which danced before elite American audiences in 1959, and Americans in concert halls and as members of TV audiences enjoyed the performances of the giant troupe, selected from the Bolshoi Ballet and other companies, which followed the Bolshoi. Of course there were, in connection with these artistic exchanges, a few "pinpricks," as Howard Taubman put it, involving, on the American side, refusal to allow Soviet jet planes to land the Moiseev dancers at the New York International Airport, some unfortunate demonstrations by anti-Soviet refugees, and a few hostile letters to the press, and, on the Soviet side, unexplained delays in granting permission to travel to particular cities and churlish press complaints about alleged failure of the United States government to show "friendship" for the Moiseev dancers—although such reports preceded the friendly gesture made by the late Secretary of State Dulles in visiting with the Moiseev troupe at their Washington performance on June 17. According to American press reports in 1959, Igor Moiseev, the leader of the troupe bearing his name, reported so enthusiastically to a Soviet lecture audience on his impressions of America that he was instructed by the Minister of Culture, Nikolai Mikhailov, to express himself on this subject with more restraint in the future.

The Soviet tours of the Ed Sullivan variety show, discussed in Chapter iii, and of the New York Philharmonic Orchestra, both in the summer of 1959, brought to five the number of large American artistic contingents which had, by the end of 1959, performed in the U.S.S.R. Despite the difficulties arising from the incompatibilities between Soviet bureaucracy and American show business, the 1955-1959 artistic exchanges went off with sufficient smoothness to give some hope for expecting a further expansion of this important kind of contact in the future.

On the negative side of the artistic exchange equation, it should be noted that, as the Soviet authorities gradually expanded the range of American literature and drama available to Soviet audiences, indignation mounted among American writers whose works were presented to Russians without financial compensation to or even permission of their authors. So seriously was this matter regarded by Americans concerned with artistic exchange that Robert C.

Schnitzer—general manager of the International Cultural Exchange Service, administered for the Department of State by a private organization, the American National Theater and Academy —informed officials of the Soviet Ministry of Culture, while he was in Moscow in September 1959, that continuance of unauthorized production by Soviet theaters of American dramatic work would be detrimental to the exchange program.

It should be noted that less than half of the American artists or art groups that performed in the Soviet Union after 1954 were financed directly or indirectly by the United States government. The Ed Sullivan show and Holiday on Ice, for example, were purely private ventures, from the financial point of view, although the negotiations for these and other ventures, of course, involved official Soviet-American dealings. The same pattern, incidentally, prevailed in respect to such American sports groups as the Harlem Globe-Trotters basketball team, which played in Moscow and Leningrad in 1959, or to major Soviet attractions in America, including the Sol Hurok-sponsored Bolshoi Ballet, the Moiseev dancers, and others. Opinion is divided in competent American circles as to whether or not the role of government, on our side, should be greater, in exchanges of these types, than it usually has been, or whether, in fact, a free-enterprise system in cultural and entertainment fields is compatible with a decisive government role in policy for exchanges. But there is wide agreement that this country could better utilize the opportunities presented by American-Soviet exchanges in movies, drama, and the like if more government money were available. Larger funds might facilitate selection and availability of the best talent at the right time.

As we have noted elsewhere, it is even more difficult in the case of artistic exchanges than in other areas to find immediate and specific political relevance, and one is inclined to agree with the numerous artists, journalists, and critics, Soviet and American, who saw in the success of the Soviet-American artistic exchanges of recent years an influence for good will, or at least a means of providing millions of Russians and Americans with some happy hours conducive to friendly memories.

It may be interesting to learn the reactions of one of our friends to the final, triumphal performance at which the Moiseev dancers won the hearts of their audience by doing a spirited Virginia Reel. This source, impressed by the fine rapport between dancers and audience, experienced a sense of shame at being surprised that Russians are human beings too!

Toward the beginning of this chapter we had a few words to say about the large Soviet youth group that visited the United States in July and August of 1958 and about the corresponding American group which was in the U.S.S.R. at the same time, under the general leadership of Professor Ralph T. Fisher, Jr. With the possible exception of travel by American "Russian experts" and, we would emphasize, with the very definite exception of long-term exchanges of graduate students and professors, this is the type of exchange which is probably the most significant for the future of Soviet-United States relations.

It should be noted that the exchange between this group, which, including leaders, numbered forty-one, divided among subgroups selected by four major private organizations—namely, the Lisle Fellowship, the Experiment in International Living, the Union of Student Christian Councils, and the Y.M.C.A.-Y.W.C.A.—and the Soviet group, selected by the Komsomol-affiliated Committee of Youth Organizations of the U.S.S.R., was not the only officially sponsored or semiofficial youth exchange of 1958. In addition to numerous aggregations of tourists, and the rather special "Yale minstrels" group already discussed, other noteworthy visits were made, in both directions. These included, for example, a visit in April and May by six carefully selected American student editors chosen, according to a *New York Times* report for April 20, 1958, from more than a hundred applicants on the basis of experience in student publications, campus activities, academic achievement, and knowledge of contemporary social and political affairs. This visit was reciprocated by that of a corresponding group of Soviet student editors. While the American student editors were the third such group to visit the U.S.S.R. since the death of Stalin, their Soviet colleagues were the first such group to succeed in complying with the requirements of Soviet foreign policy and United States visa regulations. There was also, in August and September 1958, a visit to this country by three young Russians, in their twenties or early thirties, under the auspices of the Young Friends Committee of North America, a Quaker organization. One of the Soviet youths, Vladimir Yarovik, had made the acquaintance of one of his Quaker hosts, Mr. Robert J. Osborn, while Mr. Osborn was an observer at the 1957 Youth Festival in Moscow.[34]

In general, such groups, on both sides, consist of able, well-trained young people, with at least a sprinkling of members fluent in the language of the host country. Mrs. John S. Davison, for example, a member of the American student editors group mentioned above, reportedly spoke Russian well and, judging by articles she contributed to the *Wall Street Journal* after her return, was an alert observer. We cannot discuss here, and in fact only in the future will it be possible to appraise, the potential of these pioneer visits for improved public understanding in each country of the aspirations and way of life of the other.

Let us say only that we feel that this positive potential is far greater than appears from the limited press coverage given in both countries to all or most of these visits. On the whole, the most useful visits have been the least publicized.

This statement applies, perhaps especially, to the group led by Professor Fisher. Brief, factual articles concerning its sojourn in Russia appeared in various Soviet newspapers and magazines, such as *Komsomolskaya Pravda* and *Ogonek*. Some of the *Komsomolskaya Pravda* stories on the "representatives of American youth" had a human-interest flavor, and some of them, perhaps, were slanted to bring out propaganda points. But it must be emphasized that, in view of Kremlin denunciation of American policy at the time in Lebanon, the Soviet press coverage of the American youth group's activities, though somewhat reserved, was surprisingly friendly. Soviet press handling of the corresponding Soviet youth group in the United States was considerably briefer, more cautious, and more official-sounding than the semi-informal Soviet reporting on the American guests.

The American press took a somewhat similar attitude. The arrival and first few days in New York of the Soviet youth delegation was front-page news. The *New York Times*, for example, carried large photographs featuring the attractive female members of the group. Subsequent reports were brief, not very informative,

[34] *New York Times*, August 12, 1958.

and in a slightly needling tone. A brief *New York Times* story on August 15, based on an Associated Press dispatch from Moscow, quoted Mr. Fisher to the effect that the itinerary arranged by the Soviet youth authorities had been too crowded and formal to permit adequate time for personal contacts with Soviet young people and that the delegation had been exposed to "numerous toasts and hard liquor." Perhaps these observations may have been, in part, in the nature of a reply to tendentious and sometimes sarcastic statements by Mr. Bugrov and other leaders of the Soviet group that they had been denied opportunities to meet "young workers," to observe trade-union activities, et cetera. Unfortunately, in this instance, even the usually scrupulous *New York Times*, by slanted selection from Mr. Fisher's remarks, created an unintendedly critical impression of his reactions to his experiences in Russia.

Some of the articles published by members of the Fisher-led group after their return to the United States verged on the sensational in their tone. One of the weaker aspects of the American approach toward Soviet-American relations has always been the tendency of individuals in our competitive economy to capitalize on their Russian experiences in a fashion which has contributed little to depth of understanding at home and has furnished evidence to bolster frequent Soviet charges regarding the lack of "seriousness" of American students, journalists, and scholars. It should be emphasized here that Professor Fisher and, in general, all of his colleagues in selecting and leading his group behaved with highly commendable tact.

A sympathetic, somewhat unsophisticated treatment of the U.S.-U.S.S.R. 1958 summer student exchange appeared in a special November 1958 issue of the Y.M.C.A. magazine, the *Intercollegian*. This issue contained answers by Soviet and American participants to questions about impressions formed and misconceptions encountered during their visits to one another's countries, as well as thoughtful comments by such authorities as Paul B. Anderson, of the International Committee, Y.M.C.A., and Professor William B. Edgerton.

The statements by Soviet and American participants in this pioneer venture indicate that it was a particularly interesting confrontation of Soviet collectivism and American individualism. Doubtless both groups better understood their own society, as well as one another's, as a result of the experience. If the experiment had had no other result, it would have been useful. There seems no reason to doubt—and our interviews with several of the American participants strengthen the impression—that Paul Anderson was correct in asserting that all who took part in the delegation or in meeting with them had their lives enriched.

At the same time, however, one is inclined to share Professor Edgerton's view that "thirty days are just enough to turn tourists into self-confident, ignorant experts on the country they have visited. Six months or a year in the country would diminish both their self-confidence and their ignorance." I would add that from what I have learned of the participants on both sides of the exchange—especially the Soviet one—whatever inner change might occur would not be likely to be reflected in overt statements, which on the Soviet side, at least, seem to have been strained through a fine-meshed ideological sieve. Nonetheless, the sincere appreciation for hospitality and the obviously genuine pleasure resulting from rewarding personal experiences on both sides probably transcended, to some degree, differences of ideology, customs, and institutions.

Certain aspects of this exchange and some characteristics of its participants deserve special mention. Permission, by the Soviet authorities in charge, to the Americans to split up into four groups and spend about a week in excellently equipped youth camps represented an unusual privilege. The stays at camps offered opportunities for lively discussions. At the camp near Kiev, according to one of the Americans, Soviet engineering students minced no words in denouncing American "aggression" in Lebanon. On the other hand, some of them, after initial incomprehension and mistrust, became fascinated by the examples of modern art shown to them by Americans.

With few exceptions, the American group appears to have been an understanding, sympathetic one, eager to go more than halfway in the search for mutual understanding, although there were some complaints on the Soviet side, especially by overzealous "activists," that the Americans were excessively concerned with observing and photographing the seamier sides of Soviet life. Perhaps this feeling was in its way an equivalent to irritation among some who met the Soviet delegation in America because of its efforts to make propaganda. In part such misunderstandings reflect the clash of Soviet "purposiveness," which regards exchanges as opportunities which must be fully exploited to disseminate regime-approved images of the Soviet system, and American individual curiosity and desire to "see for oneself." A few of the members of the American delegation may have been guilty, at times, of that lack of sensitivity which is, in a way, the American equivalent to the dogmatism displayed by Soviet representatives when cornered or under pressure from their superiors to engage in aggressive propaganda or to be purposely obnoxious. One major weakness of this large and, in most ways, excellently prepared group was that only a handful had sufficient fluency in Russian to carry on the more demanding types of conversations. Only two or three members of the group could converse effectively in Russian over the telephone. Like the French groups mentioned in the last chapter, the Council on Student Travel party found that one valuable result of their trip was the fillip it gave to their interest in the Russian language. Also, like the French, the Americans, at least in some instances, found life in Russia strenuous. They were inclined to be rather startled by Soviet indifference to some matters of high priority in bathroom-conscious America.

Professor Fisher's group was not so well trained in the Russian language as were the Yale student group of 1958 and 1959, nor did it have the advantage of as much music and talent as the all-Yale tourists. It did, however, have some good singers and dancers, and they proved to be great assets on many occasions. Comparisons are invidious and not really intended here, but it is possible that in the long run the quieter, more conventional—in terms of proceeding through "channels," both American and Soviet—pattern of the Council on Student Travel-sponsored visit may for some time prove more useful than the free-wheeling style chosen by the "Yale minstrels." Probably it would be highly desirable if both types of visits could in the future increase in numbers. However, this will be true, in all probability, only if sufficient numbers of American youths of balanced judgment, fine character, and fluency in Russian are available. Progress in this direction is being made.

While acrimonious arguments should be avoided in such exchanges, the calm and candid discussions and, above all, the opportunities afforded by them to gather facts and impressions unobtainable in pallid print are of inestimable value. Young people, preferably those in the early stages of graduate study, or the equivalent, are particularly suitable as emissaries of good will, for they possess not only the vitality and generosity of spirit, but also the relative freedom from prejudice essential if ideological differences are to be transcended and the peoples of East and West are to meet one day in closer harmony than prevails in our era.

After hard bargaining in Moscow in February 1959, agreement was reached to repeat in that year the Council on Student Travel-Committee of Youth Organizations Exchange. The American students were in Russia in July and August, this time without an over-all tour leader, and divided into smaller groups, so that they had better opportunities than in 1958 to stay at youth camps and mingle with Soviet youths. The Soviet side chose to come to the United States after the beginning of the American academic year, presumably in the expectation of better opportunities, at that time of year, to present the communist point of view to American students. The 1959 Soviet delegation consisted of able debaters.

Travel by American Protestant clergymen to Soviet Russia has been on a fairly large scale since the death of Stalin. In 1956 precedents were made when two groups of rabbis—probably the first groups of American Jewish religious leaders to visit the U.S.S.R. since the establishment of the Soviet regime—traveled extensively in that country. No further travel by rabbis, apparently, was made from 1956 to 1959. No American Roman Catholic priests have made private trips to the Soviet Union since the death of Stalin. There were newspaper reports in 1956 that Father Walter Jaskiewicz, head of the Fordham University Department of Russian Studies, was planning to make such a journey, but it did not take place. Perhaps the most interesting recent American religious mission to Russia was that of six American Quakers, who traveled twelve thousand miles in the Soviet Union in 1955 and published an extremely interesting report entitled "Meeting the Russians."[35] One member of the group, Professor William B. Edgerton, a

[35] American Friends Service Committee, Philadelphia, 1956.

specialist on Russian literature, was granted permission by the Soviet government to stay for a month after the departure of his colleagues, to do research on Nikolai Leskov, an outstanding nineteenth-century Russian novelist. In 1957 Jerome Davis led an "American-European Seminar on the U.S.S.R.," consisting largely of clergymen, the members of which received an interview with Nikita Khrushchev on July 24.[36] Mr. Davis led another tour in 1959, which also included East Germany in its itinerary. His 1957 party seems to have included several members inclined to listen sympathetically to Soviet "peace" assurances.

Visits by American academic specialists on the Soviet Union to the country of their interest have, since the death of Stalin, constituted perhaps one of the most significant developments in the whole area of Soviet-American contacts. As in other fields, they began on a small, cautious, experimental scale. A handful of mature American scholars visited the Soviet Union in 1955. Among them were Professors Harold Berman and Richard Frye of Harvard and William B. Edgerton, then at Pennsylvania State University. In 1956, 1957, and 1958 more than two hundred American "Russian experts," many of them fluent in the Russian language, visited the Soviet Union and talked to Soviet scholars. Some of them, such as Professor Edgerton and Professor Richard Pipes of Harvard, were very successful in establishing useful contacts with professional colleagues. Such contacts became increasingly fruitful in 1959-60.

We have participated in conferences with, interviewed, or corresponded with almost all of the American-area specialists who have visited Russia in the last three years. In many cases we had several conversations and extensive correspondence with particular individuals. On the basis of these studies, certain observations may be offered regarding the nature and results of recent travel in Russia by American experts.[37] Most of these travelers were in the Soviet Union for thirty days or less, but in a number of cases fifteen- or thirty-day extensions of visas were granted. Intourist took responsibility for the care and guidance of these travelers, but in a few

[36] A twenty-three-page pamphlet compiled by this group was distributed in November 1957 by "Promoting Enduring Peace, Inc.," located at 489 Ocean Avenue, West Haven, Connecticut.

[37] I described my own 1956 trip in the April 1957 issue of the *American Slavic Review*.

cases—such as the visit by Professor Roman Jakobson of Harvard University in May 1955—other organizations, such as the Soviet Academy of Sciences, took a hand. The vast majority of the visiting experts visited only cities where there were Intourist hotels, but again there were a small number of exceptions. A surprising number of Americans were invited to visit Soviet citizens in their homes. Most found travel conditions somewhat freer than they had expected, especially in the crowded, sometimes chaotic conditions of 1958 and 1959. It is our impression, on the basis of a comparison between the 1956 and 1957 experience, that surveillance over the activities of the academic tourists was more carefully organized in the latter than in the former year. However, it was still possible even in 1957, by exercising a little ingenuity, to enjoy a good many hours unaccompanied by a guide. Certainly the pattern was that of the "guided tour," but one that was sufficiently modified to contrast sharply with the "gumshoe" method applied to the few foreigners who succeeded in visiting Russia in the late-Stalin years. In 1959 surveillance had again slackened and in a surprising number of cases did not occur at all in any systematic fashion, although of course the authorities had sufficient knowledge of tourists' activities to prevent their doing anything that they considered harmful to Kremlin security.

Most of the visiting academics were neither surprised nor shocked by what they saw, since their studies had provided them with a framework in which to fit the facts. As far as can be determined, none were in any way seduced, although some of them modified certain previous views formed on the basis of "book learning" alone, and, on the whole, these corrections in the light of experience were useful. Their reactions and observations displayed few of the gyrations evident in the behavior of some of the less-sophisticated American businessmen and politicians who entered Russia for the first time during this period. It is our impression that most of the academics who were making their first trip to the Soviet Union were somewhat more favorably impressed than they had expected to be by material and organizational aspects of Soviet civilization. On the other hand, some of them were rather taken aback by the drabness of clothing and other aspects of the standard of living and by the effects of regimentation upon thought and behavior. A young professor remarked to me in 1956 that Leningrad looked "like the Bowery."

As for the American response to Soviet mass culture, a good example of a sophisticated reaction was contained in the perceptive article by Kathryn Feuer entitled "Russia's Young Intellectuals," in *Encounter* for February 1957. Mrs. Feuer observed that in the U.S.S.R. "for over twenty-five years, there has been a total effort to create a completely false culture." One traveler whose journey took place in 1957 was appalled by the "passivity" of the Soviet people. On the whole, however, most travelers reported a high level of curiosity about the United States and other foreign countries, combined with dismal ignorance, except in the fields of specialization in which Soviet people were working. It was clear that Soviet citizens, except for selected and qualified specialists, did not have access to American publications, outside of those connected with scientific and technical fields. Many of the travelers reported that Intourist guides and other Soviet citizens had accepted gifts of books and a considerable number had asked that books be sent from America. In some cases guides told scholars in 1957 to thank tourists who had been in Russia in 1956 and had sent them books, receipt of which they did not feel free to acknowledge by correspondence. Some specialists, however, had all the latest Western material.

A number of the American travelers obtained access in Soviet libraries to important literary and historical sources, the existence of which Americans had hitherto been ignorant.

Almost to a man, the American academic visitors reported that most of the Soviet people with whom they were able to snatch moments of more-or-less relaxed conversation displayed a high degree of political apathy. Americans also found Soviet citizens extremely ignorant about their own political system—a characteristic shared, unfortunately, by all too many Americans. Most Soviet citizens, they reported, did not appear to be able to conceptualize an alternative to the "planned economy" and one-party state. However, evidence of "ferment" was found, particularly among student youth in Moscow, Leningrad, Odessa, and other large cities. Irritation and embarrassment regarding lack of access to information about the outside world was reported by some of the more perceptive American travelers. Americans of this category who were in Russia after the Hungarian uprising found that many Soviet students were at least skeptical regarding the position of their own government. One gets the impression from talking to these visitors that they exerted considerably more influence on the Russians than the Russians did on them.

However, there was a certain mutual interaction. For example, most of the Americans apparently came back convinced that, at least as far as the "man in the street" was concerned, the Soviet desire for peace was genuine. Some of the Americans were able at least partly to convince some of the Russians with whom they talked that the United States also desired peace. Most of the Americans were almost always treated in a friendly manner by the Russians. There were a fair number of instances, however, in which Russians displayed irritatingly or even threateningly bureaucratic attitudes.

While on the whole the evidence that they brought back regarding Soviet political attitudes was, from the point of view of American concepts of constitutional government, somewhat sobering, there were, even in this sphere, a few rays of hope for the future. I had the impression that at least some of the party members with whom I had arguments—on the whole friendly ones—in 1956 and again in 1958 were less intolerant and dogmatic in their approach to ideological differences between East and West than they felt they could afford to admit. Professor Merle Fainsod concluded an article describing his 1956 trip with a quotation from Alexander Herzen: "At a certain moment the human intellect comes of age; and when it does, it can no longer be kept in bondage, not in the chains of censorship nor in the leading-strings of prudence." One of the most perceptive 1957 visitors told us that he found an awareness, already present in some people and emerging in others, of the superior intellectual freedom enjoyed by Americans as compared with the Soviet people. Like some other recent travelers, he was impressed by the "defenselessness" of rank-and-file Soviet people in ideological questions, and he even seemed to think that the free society gave its citizens an almost unfair advantage. As we have indicated elsewhere in this book, the thinness of the veneer of Marxist rationalizations employed by the Soviet leadership to justify its politics was indicated by some of the encounters between Soviet youths and Western—and also Polish—youths at the Sixth World Festival of Youth and Students in Moscow in 1957. In examining travel reports and interviewing travelers, I have come to the conclusion that it was not necessary to change the opinion, formed during my four years of service with the American embassy in Moscow, that, while the Soviet system of political indoctrination is formidable, it is by no means invincible. If the controls were relaxed long enough and to a sufficient degree, considerable changes in Soviet attitudes might take place rather rapidly.

Perhaps Soviet Russians are only superficial Marxists, but they seem to be fervent patriots. Many of the American scholars who have been in the U.S.S.R. in recent years have reported evidence of strong nationalist sentiments. They found a curious mixture of inferiority and superiority feelings. Here is a people dedicated with deadly seriousness to "culture," science, and technology and determined to realize its destiny of greatness. It was good that several hundred American scholars, many of them young men and women with long years of teaching and research ahead of them, had the opportunity to meet Soviet people and thus to some degree to temper theory with reality.

The most important, probably, of all Soviet-American exchanges we have left, for emphasis, to near the end of this chapter because it is to be hoped that it is but the beginning of a series of steps which if continued may help to bring closer the day when Soviets and Americans shall know one another as colleagues and individuals and not merely as guests and hosts. The *New York Times* for October 5, 1958, was able to report the presence in the U.S.S.R. of twenty-two American graduate students, two of them accompanied by their wives. These students had been selected from about a hundred applicants by a committee of distinguished scholars organized by the Inter-University Committee on Travel Grants. Six of the Americans enrolled at Leningrad University, the others at the University of Moscow. They included specialists in economics, political science, and law, as well as in history, languages, and literature, drawn from major centers of Soviet "area studies," after careful examination of their academic records, language examinations, and personal interviews.

In return, the Ministry of Higher Education sent seventeen students to five American universities, with by far the largest contingent—eight—going to the University of California at Berkeley. Most of the Soviet students were specialists in natural sciences or engineering, although they included, for example, an expert on Jack London who, appropriately enough, enrolled at Berkeley and two other American literature men at Harvard. Others chose the University of Washington, the University of Chicago, and Columbia University.

We had an opportunity in November 1958 to talk at length with most of the American students in Moscow and Leningrad, and we have received much information regarding the Soviet students from some of their American teachers. While, as one would expect, many complexities surrounded this first real, long-term university exchange between the two countries, we believe that it was extraordinarily useful to both sides. Even if, in some ways, the American students in Russia were treated more as tourists and less like students than they would have wished, they had opportunities for experiencing Soviet reality such as have normally been unavailable to diplomats, correspondents, or, for that matter, anyone else. Access to Soviet homes, although not so easy as might have been desired, was considerable.

Most important of all, of course, was the opportunity to add to professional training the unique dimension of graduate study in the Soviet university setting, under the supervision, in some instances, of very distinguished Soviet scholars. Such an experience, to be sure, is not without its difficulties for the American graduate student. He needs to exercise a nice blend of resolute determination, discretion, and tact in order to derive maximum benefit from exposure to the extremely regimented Soviet educational system and to avoid, on the one hand, surrendering something of his scholarly integrity or, on the other, needlessly complicating his relations with academic advisers and fellow-students who can scarcely be expected to understand Western concepts of scholarly freedom. American students and scholars cannot expect, in the foreseeable future, to study sensitive subjects in, for example, the social sciences or to interview public figures, officials, or, in any systematic fashion, ordinary citizens. Moreover, they must be prepared to live under conditions more rigorous than those to which most of them have become accustomed and to cope with a great deal of red tape. Patience, emotional stability, and good health, as well as academic qualifications, are prerequisites for fullest success in this fascinating intellectual adventure which, by unanimous agreement of the American participants in the now-completed first year, was an extraordinarily rewarding experience, despite all its irritations, frustrations, and minor hardships.

As far as the Soviet students in America were concerned, both the 1958-59 and the 1959-60 groups were, according to all reports, received in the friendliest fashion and showered with invitations to visit homes of fellow-students and others. Although both Soviet and American students faced the same basic problem of adjustment to novel patterns, the form assumed by the problem had contradictory aspects for the two groups. The carefully conditioned Soviets were faced, perhaps, with the temptations of relaxation—one might almost say of "de-compression"—while the Americans had to adjust to a maze of regulations and restrictions. Certain kinds of restrictions, of course, such as those on travel, were roughly equivalent for both groups. Naturally too, the language problem on both sides was free of ideological complications. Common to both groups also was the excitement of new sights and new acquaintances. Both groups, moreover, had to deal with such questions as press, radio, and television interviews. The Americans apparently handled these publicity matters with caution and the Soviets with hypercaution, combined with sloganeering. According to one account, one of the Soviet students, asked by an American journalist what he liked best in America, replied, "The Bolshoi Ballet and the Soviet Exhibition." The 1959-60 Soviet group were equally well trained.

There is no doubt that the restrictive atmosphere to which the American students were subjected in Moscow and Leningrad left most of them irritated, to say the least, but at the same time more convinced than ever of the values of freedom and the usefulness of a Soviet sojourn to quicken one's sense of those values, if only by contrast.

However, Soviet restrictions, against a background of provision on the American side of the most favorable possible conditions for Soviet students in this country, gave rise to grave doubts in some quarters about the advisability of continuation of the exchange program unless remedial action were taken by Soviet authorities. The *New York Times* for September 9, 1959, reported that David C. Munford, chairman of the Inter-University Committee on Travel Grants, had written to Soviet Deputy Minister of Higher Education M. A. Prokofiev to the effect that if treatment of American students in Russia did not improve, during the academic year about to start, the program would be terminated. In the meantime, plans had been made, for the 1959-1960 academic year, for 32 Soviet students, mostly in the natural sciences and engineering, to study at Harvard, Yale, Massachusetts Institute of Technology, and other institutions, and for 27 Americans, including, for the first time, several natural scientists, to study in the U.S.S.R.

Also, on November 8, 1959, Columbia University announced that it had concluded an agreement for an exchange of professors with Moscow University. The report on this important development in the *New York Times* for November 9 noted that Harvard University had hoped, after the Harvard-Leningrad exploratory exchange in the spring of 1959, to have the arrangement in operation by September, but that Professor Merle Fainsod, who had been conducting the negotiations for Harvard, was doubtful whether the program could be in effect by February 1960. These negotiations, while they reflected the difficulties remaining to be overcome in the normalization of American-Soviet scholarly exchange, also reflected at least the promise of further gradual progress in this direction.

On November 21, 1959, negotiations begun in August for a two-year extension of the 1958-1959 Soviet-American agreement for educational, cultural, technical, scientific, and sports exchanges were successfully completed, although some parts of the new accord—which, like the one preceding it, was not a formal treaty—would become operational only if further successful negotiation followed.

The main terms of the new agreement indicated that American-Soviet exchanges in 1960-1961 and 1961-1962 would expand at a modest rate, that some significant new elements would enter into the program, but that the over-all pattern would not differ essentially from the one already described in this book. It appeared that the pattern of culture contact would remain a strictly guided one, with the Soviet side continuing to exercise sharp vigilance to prevent exposure of Soviet citizens to ideas, art forms, and influences that Soviet authorities might regard as "alien," "corrupt," or in any way "harmful."

Thus little progress was made, according to Max Frankel in the *New York Times* of November 22, toward the establishment of permanent reading rooms in Moscow and New York. Another disappointment from the American point of view was apparently failure of the Soviets to give any convincing indication that they would permit substantially greater numbers of Soviet tourists to visit America in 1960-1962 than the less than 400 who came in 1958-1960. With regard to exchange of "noncontroversial" radio and television broadcasts—a feature of the original accord which was largely unfulfilled—both sides agreed to make a new try.

Despite these and other limitations, each side gained by the new agreement, or so it appeared in the days after its signature in Moscow by Ambassador Thompson and Mr. Georgi Zhukov. The Americans were able to increase the numbers of graduate students to be exchanged to 35 in 1960-1961 and 50 in 1961-1962, to secure agreement for exchange of 20 to 35 language students each summer, and to elicit agreement regarding living quarters for wives of American graduate students, contacts for the students with research institutions, hospitalization in event of illness, and many related objectives. Moreover, agreement was reached in principle for exchanges of professors between Harvard and Leningrad, Yale and Kiev, Columbia and Moscow, and Indiana and Tashkent Universities.

The Soviets got American agreement for an increase in the number of industrial and technical delegations to be exchanged. They also made it plain that the Kremlin would always insist on control over selection of performers exchanged and screening of ideas contained in such publications as might be exchanged. Some specific exchanges in the arts were agreed upon, including a trip by "My Fair Lady" to Russia and a tour of America by the Moscow Art Theatre. But on other matters, such as a tour of the U.S.S.R. by an American jazz orchestra, Moscow proved "sticky." The United States, for its part, balked at Soviet proposals for exchanges of large numbers of big artistic troupes, apparently because of the financial difficulties involved.

The results of these negotiations, as well as of actual exchanges in the closing months of 1959, indicated that both sides were at least prepared to continue the experiment begun in 1958, but that neither regarded it as a panacea. Above all, each side still realistically viewed cultural diplomacy as a battle of wits. There was a new international "thaw," to be sure, but its duration appeared to depend more on the outcome of future summit diplomacy than on people-to-people contacts. In the meantime, N. S. Khrushchev, in speeches in Vladivostok, Krasnoyarsk, and Novosibirsk after his return from the United States, continued to press for peaceful coexistence, which, he said in Novosibirsk, as reported in *Pravda* for October 14, represented the continuation of the struggle between two social systems on the economic, political, and ideological level. The Soviet leaders, whose visit here in 1960 returned the 1959 trip by American governors, acted as if they took this message to heart.

In the matter of exchanges of graduate students, and of mature scholars also, some progress, or the appearance thereof, was being made. This was indicated by the inclusion in the extension, signed in November 1959, of the U.S.–Soviet cultural agreement, of provision for exchanges of young scholars between several American universities and the universities of Moscow, Leningrad, Kiev, and Tashkent. It still was problematical, however, whether the Soviet Union was as yet capable or willing to provide conditions of working and living which would justify a competent scientist's or a mature scholar's spending six months or a year there. There was also the possibility that if Americans concerned with exchanges did not set up an organizational apparatus with the requisite power and flexibility to assure reasonable equality of bargaining in scientific exchanges, the Kremlin would gain much in this area and give little in return. The Soviets might, for example, cease to provide for American social science students even the somewhat-circumscribed opportunities available to them during the "20-20" exchange, if they could obtain free access for their natural scientists to American laboratories without a *quid pro quo* in either the natural or social science areas.

333

So far as we have been able to learn from members of the Harvard and Columbia delegations which visited Leningrad and Moscow universities in 1959, the great hope of future mutual benefit from academic exchange was still hedged about with uncertainty. It even appeared that Soviet university teachers were more nervous about discussing all but the most innocuous matters than they had been two or three years before. Some of them hinted that there was real concern in communist leadership circles lest Soviet students be led astray by contacts with Americans.

On the other hand, Soviet scholars with well-established positions in research institutes appeared to be freer than ever before to make use of Western source materials in pursuing their research. One hopeful aspect of the Harvard-Leningrad university exchange was the fact, reported by American participants therein and by American students at Leningrad University, that upon its return home the Leningrad delegation, which was headed by Professor Efimov, reputed to be the communist party leader in the university, made a public, objective, and favorable report on its experiences in Cambridge.

In the autumn of 1959 Soviet-American cultural relations presented a paradoxical picture. In the shadow of the Berlin crisis, cultural exchanges, as Christopher Emmett noted in the *New Leader*, had achieved an unprecedented volume—a fact reflected, for example, in the entertainment section of the *New York Times* for June 28, which devoted "three full pages to reviews of Soviet companies of performing artists who were in this country, had just visited, or were about to visit it." Although we do not share fully the alarm expressed by Mr. Emmett about the results of these exchanges, it must be admitted that lavishly publicized visits such as that of Frol Kozlov, probably tended to distract the attention of Americans from the threat to Berlin. Certainly the gullibility of some superficial travelogues which have resulted from recent American travel to Russia, as well as the effusiveness of much of the welcoming publicity accorded visiting Soviet politicians tended to justify Mr. Emmett's misgivings.

As he pointed out, "the impact of America on Soviet visitors, or of American visitors to the Soviet Union, *cannot lead to any action by Soviet citizens to change Soviet foreign policy* except possibly in the long-term future. On the other hand, in America every citizen who is converted to a friendlier and more trusting attitude toward the Soviet Government and its policies can make his voice heard in his community and in Washington itself."[38]

Suggestions made by Emmett and others to turn exchanges to the advantage of democracy rather than totalitarianism, such as insistence on a prominent role for long-term student sojourns, inclusion of American Russian-speaking interpreters in American delegations to the U.S.S.R., and provision of voluntary "briefing" of Americans either going to Russia or dealing with Russian delegations in this country are useful. As we have indicated elsewhere in this book, progress has already been made along such lines, but much remains to be done if dangers are to be minimized and benefits maximized in the cultural encounter. Fears expressed regarding Kozlov's visit could be justified on a magnified scale regarding that of Khrushchev, who certainly impressed many Americans, deceived some, disarmed others, but alerted many to the toughness and cunning of the ideological adversary.

By May 1960 it appeared that American-Soviet exchanges of all kinds, especially in the tourist category, would continue to develop, but for the foreseeable future within the general framework established since 1955. If they were to produce the good effects which their American sponsors hoped they would, the process would more likely be one of gentle persuasion than of hasty conversion. There were hopeful signs, such as Soviet agreement to a small expansion of numbers of graduate student exchanges and the beginning of other types of serious, long-term exchanges. Continued resistance on the Soviet side to access by American scientists to laboratories of the science institute where the bulk of scientific research is done in Russia served as a warning against expecting quick and dramatic results from this kind of contact. The over-all picture remained mixed but still different enough from the Stalinist pattern to justify persistent American efforts to persuade the Russians to dismantle additional barriers to free communication. At the same time, American proponents of international communication would have to continue to fight a battle on the homefront against the native variety of isolationism.

[38] Christopher Emmett's article, "U.S. Soviet Relations," occupied pp. 22-30 of a special section of the *New Leader* for July 20-27, 1959, entitled "At Stake in Geneva," to which U.S. Senator Thomas J. Dodd and Mr. James Bryant Conant also contributed. Italics in original.

CHAPTER X

CONCLUSIONS AND SUGGESTIONS

THE record we have studied shows that even when the U.S.S.R. was poor and weak its rulers made peculiarly effective use of their own version of what some American sociologists call "guided culture contact." The efflorescence of cultural diplomacy under Khrushchev was impressive. However, judged by liberal standards of cultural freedom, the Soviet program continued to seem a perversion of good means for dubious ends. Soviet policy appeared to be as allergic as ever to tolerance of competing ideologies, or to acceptance of the principle that in cultural exchange "whatever is done shall bear some meaningful relation to the cultural values and expectations of both sides."[1]

The predominance of messianism over mutuality in the Soviet approach to contacts and exchanges serves as a warning that the relationships which they foster present to the noncommunist countries risks as well as opportunities. Perhaps the most dangerous of these risks is that of distraction of free-world attention from the frightening realities of Soviet policy. The Bolshoi Ballet could not make a Leninist out of a Rotarian, but it might help him to forget that irreconcilable conflict is basic to the communist creed. Soviet scientific displays could not convert Egyptians to socialism, but they might make it easier for them to forget the price paid by the Soviet people for forced-draft industrialization. The Soviet claim that rent accounts for only five per cent of a Russian family's income might divert the uncritical European or American from the fact that the average family in communist countries lives under what Americans or Englishmen or Danes would regard as aggravated slum conditions. Soviet political advertising, in a word, features attractive packaging but offers no price tag.

Moreover, the overwhelming cordiality of Soviet hospitality, especially in the cases of some egotistical intellectuals or politicians, constitutes a potent form of psychological bribery. The elaborate system of defenses against disclosure of the seamier facts

[1] Clyde Kluckhohn, *Mirror for Man*, New York, 1949, p. 189.

of Soviet life also facilitates the insinuation and preservation of illusions advantageous to the Kremlin. If free men are not to be worsted in the ideological combat they must bear these facts in mind.

Noncommunists should, at the same time, remember that totalitarianism suffers from weaknesses of which the democracies can, in defense against communist compulsiveness, make good use. Despite their considerable skill in public relations, communists fear the give-and-take of free discussion. Spontaneity, informality, and even friendly self-assurance terrify them. They seek to orate but not to converse. Even at their trade and cultural expositions they do not so much explain as proclaim. Intimacy makes them uncomfortable.

The free world need not fear the cultural contest, which in any case, in an increasingly interdependent world, cannot be dodged. As Kluckhohn points out, "contacts between peoples must inevitably increase and mere contact is itself a form of action. A people is altered by the mere knowledge that others are different from themselves."[2] Freedom of communication is of the very essence of civilization. Our basic criticism of totalitarianism, perhaps, is that it limits and distorts communication among human beings. The free nations, especially the richer ones, can deny to Moscow the opportunities, afforded by some forms of exchange, to spread abroad misrepresentation of Soviet life and Kremlin aims, and can at the same time demand that, in return for access to the "know-how" which Moscow desires, their citizens going to Russia be permitted to enjoy a measure of what former Senator Benton has called "know-whom." If we must put up with propaganda junkets by the Mikoyans, the Kozlovs, and the Khrushchevs, let the Kremlin in return give American graduate students and scientists in Russia freedom to travel freely, to do research on topics of their own free choice, and to work in archives and laboratories. In exchange negotiations in which Soviet authorities refuse to pay a reasonable price for the respectability conferred upon their regime and the information made available to their engineers and administrators as a result of the contemplated exchanges, it might

[2] *Ibid.*

337

be best to curtail or suspend the negotiations or exchanges until Moscow becomes more reasonable.

The principle which we advocate for American exchange policy in dealing with the Soviet Union might be described as one of "equivalency." This, it seems to us, is a better term than "reciprocity." The principle of reciprocity, if mechanically adhered to, has certain disadvantages. It may foster Soviet propaganda aims by permitting exchanges which are not really exchanges at all. For example, some problems of semantics and comparative political systems are involved in exchanges of members of Western legislative bodies and members of the Supreme Soviet. Similarly, it would seem that those who fear that misunderstanding may result from the exchange of trade-union delegations between the United States and Russia are not entirely in error. Neither the Soviet "parliament" nor Soviet "labor unions" perform the functions performed in the constitutional democracies by the institutions after which they are named.

Under the principle of "equivalency," it is not necessary always to exchange the same type of personnel, or personnel designated as the same. In some cases, no actual exchanges may be necessary at all. Of course, it may turn out to be difficult to continue indefinitely a pattern in which citizens of country A travel to country B but citizens of country B are not permitted to come to country A. As far as tourist exchange is concerned, this was the pattern from the death of Stalin to the signing of the 1958 Soviet-American agreement. However, this was certainly not the fault of the United States. The Soviet Union has not wished to allow its ordinary citizens to visit capitalist countries. Nor has it yet moved to relax its ban on free access by its people to foreign radio and TV programs. This attitude, we hope, will be gradually modified.

It is, of course, impossible, in the present stage of development of social science, to discuss the results of cultural exchange, even between the United States and noncommunist countries, in terms of simple cause-and-effect relationships. Even under the most favorable conditions research by competent scholars on student exchange and other aspects of international culture contact has not yet led to conclusive results, although findings of researchers to date are suggestive and useful.[3] Very little "scientific" work has been done on international contacts between communist and noncommunist countries.

Some of the reasons for this state of affairs are fairly obvious. Communist governments have not yet begun to welcome systematic interviewing of their citizens by social scientists, nor do they permit their own trained personnel to conduct public-opinion polls among their people, so far as can be known.

The difficulties which confront the researcher because of Soviet attitudes toward international communication may be illustrated in a modest way by the fate, thus far, of an idea which occurred to us in 1955. It seemed to us that it might be useful to conduct a systematic inquiry into the attitudes of Americans toward the Soviet Union before and after they had made trips to that country. This could be done by interviews or by an appropriate mailed questionnaire. Leaving aside the technical problems involved, it soon became apparent that such a project was not yet advisable. It might have seemed to some Americans to represent an inappropriate inquiry into their beliefs regarding controversial matters. The United States government probably could not participate in such an enterprise without difficulty or embarrassment. Finally—and this seemed most important—such a study might lead the Soviet authorities to view with heightened suspicion visits by private American citizens to their country. Even today it seems likely that a higher level of mutual understanding will have to be established between

---

[3] See, for example, Vol. XII, No. 1, 1956, of the *Journal of Social Issues*, edited by M. Brewster Smith, and entitled "Attitudes and Adjustment in Cross-Cultural Contact: Recent Studies of Foreign Students." The research reported in the above publication was pursued under the auspices of the Committee on Cross-Cultural Education of the Social Science Research Council. Dr. Smith presented a briefer account of the results of this research in an article contributed to the May 1954 issue of the *News Bulletin* of the Institute of International Education. Among other outstanding studies in this field, mention should be made of the following: *Colonial Students in Britain*, London, June 1955, published by PEP; *The Western-Educated Man in India*, New York, 1955, by John Useem and Ruth Hill Useem; "America Through Foreign Eyes," edited by Richard D. Lambert, in Vol. 295, September 1954, of the *Annals* of the American Academy of Political and Social Science. Most of the other useful material available is listed in *International Communication and Public Opinion: A Guide to the Literature*, prepared for The RAND Corporation by Bruce Lannes Smith and Chitra M. Smith, Princeton, 1956. See also Francis J. Colligan, "The Government and Cultural Interchange," in the *Review of Politics*, Vol. 20, No. 4, October, 1958, pp. 546-569.

the members of the Soviet leadership class responsible for the conduct of foreign affairs and their Western counterparts than now exists, or may exist for some years, before social scientists desirous of administering structured interviews to Soviet respondents will be welcome in the U.S.S.R. One can easily think of many another American social-science technique that, if it could be applied in the Soviet Union, might yield fascinating results. However, social science is still in its infancy in Russia. Its development must await a growth of freedom which may come, gradually, with an amelioration of poverty and shortages and which may, perhaps, be fostered in some small degree by the tactful display of external example.

If, nevertheless, we are confident that a carefully executed program of exchanges can yield results beneficial to the noncommunist countries, it is because there is evidence that we have already acquired much useful information about Soviet conditions, attitudes, and progress as a result of exchanges of graduate students, scientists, and physicians, for example. It is also because we share Lasswell's opinion, expressed some years ago in his pioneering discussion of the "role of primary contact," that, in face-to-face contacts, "the other person simply does not stay put in the vivid whites or blacks of reaction by category; saints and devils thrive on distance."[4] A Soviet refugee expressed the same belief in somewhat-different terms when he said that the impact of a visit to the United States is especially great on a member of the communist party of the Soviet Union. One never knows what seemingly trivial feature of life in a democracy may make a profound impression on a hard-bitten communist. We were told, for example, by a source we consider authoritative, that the election observers sent to this country by the Soviet government in October-November 1956 were enormously impressed by the fact that the mayor of New York had to stand in line, together with ordinary rank-and-file citizens, before he could cast his ballot.

Of course, Soviet officials and intellectuals who are permitted to meet foreigners are constrained to be cautious in reporting the results of their experiences, particularly if they publish them. Even

[4] Harold D. Lasswell, *World Politics and Personal Insecurity*, New York, 1935, p. 168.

the most opposition-minded Soviet students have sometimes told foreigners, with whom they have on occasion spoken amazingly frankly, that they were well aware of the limits within which they had to operate in order to avoid dismissal from the university, or even more severe punishment, for expressing unorthodox attitudes. On the other hand, there is considerable evidence that information brought back from foreign countries is disseminated more widely than an outsider who credits the Soviet system with complete "monolithism" might suspect. For example, one recent visitor to Russia reported that he was told by a Soviet citizen who had been in America since the death of Stalin that the latter had heard many favorable things about life in America from a member of the Soviet agricultural delegation of 1955. Professor Philip E. Mosely, Director of Studies of the Council of Foreign Relations, wisely counseled Americans, in his report on his 1956 trip to Russia, to take into account the fact that unfriendly public statements sometimes required of Soviet visitors to America after their return do not necessarily furnish a guide to the visitors' real impressions, nor do they constitute a standard by which we can appraise the value of the exchange visit from our point of view. In a word, we must exercise patience and understanding. Professor Mosely himself during that journey set an example of good humor and, one may assume, of persuasiveness of argument that is worthy of mention. Taxed by Soviet officials regarding anti-Soviet demonstrations which had been directed against Soviet visitors to the United States, Mr. Mosely observed that he would have no objection if Soviet citizens were to stage either a "pro- or anti-Mosely" demonstration.

Professor Mosely concluded his report on his 1956 trip with a recommendation, in which we heartily concur, that the West "should be prepared to meet with and cooperate with Soviet intellectuals on their own grounds of professional, scholarly and technical competence, without putting political questions directly in the foreground."[5]

Experience thus far has seemed to indicate that, if political values are to result from cultural exchanges, they will accrue as

[5] Philip E. Mosely, *Foreign Affairs*, October 1956. Quoted material on pp. 81, 83.

extra dividends over and above such immediate gains as enhancement of professional qualifications, exchange of scientific data, and more accurate information, both on the Soviet and non-Soviet sides, regarding rival social systems. There are those, however, who consider that the political potential of exchanges is great. At a conference at Oxford University in June 1957, we listened to a leading British specialist on Eastern Europe urge that the West, by cultural exchanges and radio broadcasts, attempt "before it was too late" to achieve a better basis of understanding than now exists with the Soviet younger generation, which in ten, fifteen, or twenty years will be guiding the destinies of Russia.

Almost alone among those who have discussed this subject, George Kennan has pleaded for a nonutilitarian, one might say a genuinely cultural approach. Mr. Kennan has expressed the view that "continental" countries like Russia and America need and can derive unusual benefit from contacts with contrasting cultures, which can help to overcome the parochialism inherent in isolation.[6] Certainly Russia and America have much to learn from one another and perhaps each can also, from contact with the other, acquire a deeper appreciation of the best in its own civilization.

The individual Americans who participate in Soviet-American exchanges can make a real contribution to the advancement of knowledge, mutual understanding, and perhaps even to world peace. They must be prepared to accord full recognition to Soviet cultural and scientific achievements. They must exercise tact. They must, in much greater numbers than are as yet available, speak Russian correctly and fluently. They would do well to be prepared to give friendly but persuasive and well-informed answers to such Soviet criticisms of American political practices and policies as they feel they can honestly defend.

In this connection we would again stress the power of freedom as a force of persuasion and inspiration to peoples who do not possess it. A salutary impression is often made on Soviet citizens when Americans criticize this or that aspect of their own government's policy—a privilege not at the disposal of Russians. Simi-

[6] For some especially perceptive thoughts on the nonpolitical values of cultural exchange for a "continental" country such as the United States, see George F. Kennan, "International Exchange in the Arts," in *Perspectives USA*, No. 16, 1956, pp. 6-14.

larly, it is useful for Americans to make known, tactfully, as convincingly as possible to their Soviet hosts or guests the fact that Americans can freely study all the aspects of Soviet life on which the Soviet authorities make information available—again a sharp contrast to the situation of the Soviets vis-à-vis America.

Perhaps, in addition to the general suggestions already made for facilitating successful travel in Russia, a few hints of a somewhat more specific nature might be offered, in full recognition, of course, that the objectives and characteristics of travelers vary enormously. It is well to pave the way by formulating one's plans as precisely as possible, and by doing everything feasible to inform the appropriate Soviet personnel and institutions regarding one's plans. Even if, as is likely to be the case—or has in the past— no replies are received to letters, advance notification can often help the responsible Soviet officials to make arrangements which will help the traveler greatly, such as taking preliminary steps in the arranging of appointments and the like. Similarly, since telephone books, including even those several years old, are still not readily available in the Soviet Union, it is well to obtain in advance as many as possible of the telephone numbers and addresses of government agencies, scientific institutions, and other places to be visited. It has often proved useful for foreign travelers to bring with them statistical handbooks, such as the *World Almanac* or the *Statesman's Yearbook* to assist in answering factual questions about wage scales, prices of consumers' goods, and the numerous other economic-social questions in which most Soviet citizens are avidly interested. Whether or not this type of material will be appropriate depends, of course, on the general atmosphere of the ever-shifting and unpredictable international situation. As a rule, it is useful for visiting scholars, scientists, and professionals to have with them, in addition to calling cards, which are now used almost as widely in Russia as in America, university catalogues and other factual, descriptive, nonpolitical material regarding the institutions where they have studied or are employed. Soviet scholars and officials have often been highly pleased to receive copies of scholarly books and reprints of academic publications. Besides being useful to the traveler in identifying himself or his institution, such material can play a useful part in helping to reduce the still-vast ignorance of Soviet intellectuals and officials regarding American—or European—governmental, professional, and academic life.

The resourceful traveler will think of many things not mentioned here. These tips are given mainly to illustrate the fact that, in traveling to the U.S.S.R. even today, one cannot take as much for granted as in travel to other countries. Perhaps, in conclusion, a plea should be made here for more attention on the part of the internationally-minded American public, as well as, of course, the official and private agencies concerned, to the problems for us involved in playing host to Soviet delegations which will probably—we hope—visit America in the future in increasing numbers. We owe these people, at the least, the normal courtesies which good manners require be extended to guests. We cannot require those Americans whose convictions impel them to demonstrate publicly against Soviet visitors not to do so. However, it is well to keep in mind the fact that on our treatment of Soviet visitors will depend, in part, the opportunities that Americans may have to obtain useful information and to achieve, in their relations with all kinds of Soviet citizens, the impact that will be in the best interest of the United States. As we have noted earlier, on the organizational side the centralized Soviet state has some advantages over the United States in providing appropriate hospitality for foreign delegations. Up to the present, at least, the organization and financing of such matters in this country has sometimes left much to be desired. There is no real reason, however, why, if interest is aroused in the matter, the competent American private and official agencies concerned cannot see to it that Soviet visitors to this country are provided with the hotel accommodations, travel facilities, guides and interpreters, and other prerequisites necessary to help them to see and experience this country as fully and fairly as they will and can. As of 1960, it was clear that the East-West Contacts Staff of the State Department, though still somewhat handicapped by lack of funds, had made great progress toward the solution of these important "housekeeping" problems. Also, an increasingly useful role in the exchange process was being played by private organizations, such as the Governmental Affairs Institute, the Institute of International Education, the Council on Student Travel, and many others.

INDEX

Abrams, George, 25, 133, 201-202
Academy of Sciences of the U.S.S.R., 32; 200th anniversary of, 49; 161, 168; 1955 conference on Orient, 181; meetings on Africa, 182; 213, 243; exchange with Royal Society, 250; 303, 325
Adzhubei, Aleksei, 295, 296n
Aeroflot, 71, 78, 199, 208
Afanasenko, E. I., 166, 174
Afghanistan, 80, 209, 227
Africa, object of Soviet cultural diplomacy, 21, 22, 189; compared to Europe in Soviet exchange policy, 76, 77, 188, 226, 233; Soviet study of, 181-83; nationalism in, 190; Soviet cultural activities in, 192-95, 206, 216, 224-25
Agricultural delegations, U.S.A.–U.S.S.R. exchange of, 57, 275, 280-81, 287-92, 341
Algeria, Soviet sympathy for, 217
Allen, George V., 90
Alliance Française, 3
All-Russian Agricultural Exhibition in Moscow, 1923, 45
All-Slav Committee, 162
All-Union Chamber of Commerce, 161
All-Union Society of Africanists, 182
Alt, Herschel and Edith, 110
Alter, Victor, 42
Amalgamated Clothing Workers of America, 54
American National Exhibition in Moscow, 1959, 12, 49, 72, 89, 92-95
American Pavlov Society, 312
American Red Cross, 35; exchange with Soviet Red Cross, 309-311
American Relief Administration, 35
Amerika, 106, 123, 274
Amtorg, 45
Andersen-Nexe, Martin, 39
Anderson, Paul B., 320-21
Ankudinov, Vladimir, 166, 251
Apletin, Michael, 168-69
Arabian Academy in Damascus, 213
Argentina, 73, 91, 221
Argentine-U.S.S.R. Society, 222
Armstrong, John A., 122, 123n
Article 58 Special Section of RSFSR Criminal Code, 101. *See also* Espionage

Ashby, Eric, 49, 175
Asia, object of Soviet cultural diplomacy, 21, 22, 189; compared to Europe in Soviet exchange policy, 76, 77, 188, 226, 227, 233, 265; Soviet study of, 181-83; nationalism in, 190; methods of cultural diplomacy in, 192-95, 206, 224-25
Attlee, Clement, 228

Bandung Conference, 180, 212
Baumgartner, Leona, 311
Bean, Nevin L., 293-94
Becher, Johannes, 39-40
Beibutov, 207
Belgium, 74, 245, 260, 262
Benjamin, Curtis G., 168
Benson, Secretary of Agriculture, 291
Benton, Senator William, 2, 301, 337
Bereday, George Z. F., 283
Berezhkov, Vladimir, 297n, 299
Berman, Harold J., 137, 324
Bernal, John, 244
Bernstein, Leonard, 145, 302
Beryozka troupe, 145, 315
Bevan, Aneurin, 107, 228
Bhilai, 86, 204, 205
Black, Cyril E., 151
Bock, Ernest, 204n
Bolshoi Ballet, 88, 207-208, 245, 252-53, 316, 317, 336
Borders, Karl, 33n, 38
Boston Symphony Orchestra, 145, 315
Botvinnik, 52
Bowles, Chester, 178, 203
Brailsford, H. N., 33n, 36, 37, 38
Brazil, 45, 190, 222
Brickman, William W., 283
Britanski Soyuznik, 123
British Council, 4-6, 160, 236, 237, 238, 249
British-Soviet Friendship Society, 236
Bronk, Detlev W., 303, 314
Brown, Rex, 247
Brownell, Herbert S., 167
Brussels World's Fair, Soviet tourists at, 81; as episode in cultural competition, 87-90, 91
Buddha, Gautama, 2500th anniversary of death of, 185
Bugrov, 320

345

Jews, 82, 136, 140, 162, 323. *See also* Israel
Johnson, William H. E., 38, 283
Johnston, Eric, 53
Jordan, 210, 213
Journalists, foreign, Soviet restrictions on, 103-105; Soviet, on tour of U.S.A. in 1955, 116, 137, 275-76, 289, 294-300

Kabalevski, 145
Kaftanov, S. V., 160, 206, 213
Kalb, Marvin, 302
Kalidas, 195
Kaltenborn, H. V., 47
Kameneva, Anna, 162
Karpov, G. G., 18-19, 165
Kashmir, 205, 210
Kazan Cathedral, 193
Kelly, Sir David, 5
Kemenov, Vladimir, 162, 165, 166
Kennan, George F., 14, 16; on cultural exchange, 342
Kennedy, Senator John F., 89
Khachaturyan, Aram, 222
Khanum, Tamara, 217
Khrushchev, Nikita S., 1; attitudes toward cultural diplomacy, 19, 23, 56, 96, 97, 108, 235, 269; 20, 21, 22, 61, 67, 93, 101; visit to the United States, 95, 104, 105, 123-24, 273, 291-92, 335; 107, 111, 134, 166; visit with Bulganin to India, 189, 197, 202-203, 209-210, 227; on nationalism, 189-90; 205, 214, 220; visit with Bulganin to Great Britain, 227-28, 240, 243; 230, 251, 288, 324, 333, 337
Kirkpatrick, Evron, 226
Kizya, Luka, 162, 163
Kluckhohn, Clyde, 337
Kluckhohn, Frank, 295, 296
Koestler, Arthur, 40-41
Kogan, Leonid, 145, 222, 236
Kondrashin, Kiril, 315
Kovalevski, 198
Kozlov, Frol R., visit to the United States, 78, 92-94, 104, 334, 335; 134, 337
Krader, Laurence, 312-13
Kramer, Samuel Noah, 313
Krylov, B. N., 159
Kuchava, M. I., 206
Kukryniksy, 253

Kurchatov, Igor, 243
Kuznetsov, A. N., 159
Kuznetsov, V. V., 56
Kvitko, 300

Lacey, William B., 7
Laing, W. F., 241-42
Lambert, William, 288
Langer, Paul, 182
Langman, Anne W., 95
Laqueur, Walter Z., 215-16
Lasswell, Harold, 340
Latin America, object of Soviet cultural diplomacy, 21; 83; compared to Europe in Soviet exchange policy, 188; nationalism in, 190; Soviet cultural activities in, 192-93, 216, 219-23, 224-25
Law on Criminal Liability for State Crimes, 124. *See also* Espionage
Lebanon, crisis in, 210, 278, 319, 321; Soviet cultural contacts with, 213-14
Lenin, 18, 28, 30, 32, 171, 172, 190, 212, 306
Lenin Library, 117, 141, 168
Leningrad Museum of Russian Art, 259
Leningrad Symphony Orchestra, 219
Leontiev, Vasili, 184
Lepeshinskaya, Olga, 88
Lerner, Helen, 42
Levine, Irving R., 119
Liberia, 219
Library of Foreign Literature, 117, 118, 186
Libya, 216, 224
Lincoln, Abraham, 185
Lisle Fellowship, 318
Litchfield, Edward H., 283-84
Littlepage, John D., 54
London, Jack, 67, 329
London Philharmonic Orchestra, 244
Long, Senator Russell B., 144, 300n
Long, Tania, 295n
Longfellow, 117
Ludwig, Emil, 41

MacDonald, Dwight, 149
MacDuffie, Marshall, 66
MacMillan, Prime Minister, 69, 74, 106, 107, 238
Maison du Livre Etranger, 55
Malenkov, 166, 199, 227
Malia, Martin, 75
Malik, Jacob, 237, 238

349